# LIVES AND LOVES
## OF THE GODS

Ovid's *Metamorphoses* is a magnificent collection of Greco-Roman myths that has fascinated readers down through the ages. The great English poets—Chaucer, Shakespeare, Spenser—knew him well and were greatly influenced by his abundant vitality and passion and his exquisite poetry.

Unlike the epics of Homer and Virgil, Ovid's poem eschews heroic warfare to focus narrative interest on mythological tales wittily and brilliantly linked by the theme of transformation, through which he explores the limits of human passions and experiences. The treatment is often irreverent, but he added to these human dilemmas the warmth of human understanding. His insight, humor, wit, and sophistication give these stories a lively contemporary flavor.

Horace Gregory's translation of the *Metamorphoses* has been acclaimed by critics as one of the best of modern times. With the fertility of a true poet, he reenters Ovid's world and relates, in modern language, the erotic, tragic, and magical tales of the poem with clarity and brilliance.

---

**Horace Gregory** was born in Milwaukee, Wisconsin, in 1898 and published his first book of poems, *Chelsea Running House*, in 1930. He continued to win prizes and esteem for his poetry while also becoming an acclaimed translator and literary critic. He died in 1982.

**Sara Myers** is Associate Professor of Classics at the University of Virginia. The author of *Ovid's Causes: Cosmogony and Aetiology in the Metamorphoses* and *Ovid Metamorphoses 14*, she has also published numerous articles on Ovid, Statius, Roman elegy, and Roman gardens.

# THE
# METAMORPHOSES

## OVID

*Translated and with an Afterword by*
HORACE GREGORY
*and a New Introduction by*
SARA MYERS

*With Decorations by*
ZHENYA GAY

**SIGNET CLASSICS**

For Bryher

*"Cogitavi dies antiquos et annos aeternos in mente habui."*

SIGNET CLASSICS
Published by New American Library, a division of
Penguin Group (USA) Inc., 375 Hudson Street,
New York, New York 10014, USA
Penguin Group (Canada), 90 Eglinton Avenue East, Suite 700, Toronto,
Ontario M4P 2Y3, Canada (a division of Pearson Penguin Canada Inc.)
Penguin Books Ltd., 80 Strand, London WC2R 0RL, England
Penguin Ireland, 25 St. Stephen's Green, Dublin 2,
Ireland (a division of Penguin Books Ltd.)
Penguin Group (Australia), 250 Camberwell Road, Camberwell, Victoria 3124,
Australia (a division of Pearson Australia Group Pty. Ltd.)
Penguin Books India Pvt. Ltd., 11 Community Centre, Panchsheel Park,
New Delhi - 110 017, India
Penguin Group (NZ), 67 Apollo Drive, Rosedale, North Shore 0632,
New Zealand (a division of Pearson New Zealand Ltd.)
Penguin Books (South Africa) (Pty.) Ltd., 24 Sturdee Avenue,
Rosebank, Johannesburg 2196, South Africa

Penguin Books Ltd., Registered Offices:
80 Strand, London WC2R 0RL, England

Published by Signet Classics, an imprint of New American Library, a division of
Penguin Group (USA) Inc. Previously published in Mentor mass market and
Viking hardcover editions.

First Signet Classics Printing, May 2001
First Signet Classics Printing (Myers Introduction), November 2009
20  19  18  17  16  15  14  13

 REGISTERED TRADEMARK—MARCA REGISTRADA

Printed in the United States of America

# CONTENTS

# INTRODUCTION

For more than two thousand years, Ovid's *Metamorphoses* has continued to engage, fascinate, and inspire readers with its spectacularly entertaining but often disquieting tales of transformation. The poem has been highly influential in Western culture, inspiring such strikingly different artists as Bernini, Rubens, and Picasso; poets (Chaucer, Milton, Ted Hughes), writers (Stendhal, Proust, Kafka); and dramatists (Shakespeare, Mary Zimmerman). Ovid's narrative virtuosity, self-awareness, and ebullient irreverence have assured the epic's enduring popularity.

The poem's fifteen books tell more than 250 astonishingly varied stories of metamorphosis drawn from Greek and Roman mythology, some at great length, others in mere passing. Ovid freely invented new stories and treated familiar tales in new and unexpected ways (many of his reworkings have become canonical, such as in the stories of Echo and Narcissus, and Pyramus and Thisbe). Through a brilliant stroke of genius, Ovid used the unifying theme of transformation to create a world history of Greco-Roman mythology and to explore the tragedies and comedies of human experience, revealing a deep understanding of human psychology. Ovid's world is volatile and often frightening, one in which picking a wrong flower can lead to an unwilling transformation and loss of self. Human bodies, especially female, are subject to external and violating forces, usually represented by the gods, but also by their own strong internal passions, often erotic. Yet Ovid's witty, playful, and ironic voice challenges us to laugh in the face of the vulnerability and frequent absurdity of the human condition, our desires, and our self-deceptions. Above all, Ovid celebrates the art of storytelling and his own consummate ability to hold the reader spellbound with his sheer ingenuity and boundlessly inventive narrative energy.

## OVID'S CAREER

Ovid was born (March 20) in 43 BCE, the year the last army of the Roman Republic was defeated and the future emperor Augustus began his climb to power. Ovid's poetry reflects the experimentation and innovation of the Augustan principate, which transformed the city of Rome and its political, social, and religious institutions during his lifetime, and reveals a deep interest in Augustus' consolidation of his power. Ovid's sophisticated and innovative love poetry had made him Rome's most famous living poet by the beginning of the Common Era, when he signaled a new ambition by beginning both the epic *Metamorphoses* and the *Fasti*, an elegiac poem on the Roman religious calendar. As he was finishing the *Metamorphoses* in 8 CE disaster struck. Ovid's life and poetic career changed forever when the emperor Augustus banished him from Rome to the town of Tomis (modern Constanza in Romania). Ovid gives two reasons for his exile: his poem the *Art of Love,* an entertaining poetic instructional manual for love affairs, and an unspecified "mistake," which remains unknowable. The poem was deemed objectionable for encouraging sexual immortality, specifically adultery. But considering the gap between the publication of the *Art of Love* and his banishment, Ovid's "mistake" must have been the more relevant cause. After Ovid's exile the *Art of Love* was banned from Rome's public libraries. Ovid was forced to remain in Tomis until his death, probably in 17 CE, having failed to convince either Augustus (who died in 14 CE) or, later, Tiberius, to recall him. His fate inevitably has had an impact on the ways in which we interpret Ovid's presentation of the divine power structures in the *Metamorphoses*.

## NARRATIVE DYNAMICS

The *Metamorphoses* is often approached as a compendium of Greco-Roman myth and consequently anthologized and read only in selections. In truth, only a continuous reading can reveal the complexity, inventiveness, and ingenuity of Ovid's thematic and narrative connections. The poem is built for speed and for keeping the reader guessing at what will happen next. Although written in the meter of epic poetry, the hexameter of *The Iliad*, *The Odyssey*, and *The Aeneid*, the great national epic of the legendary origins of Rome, the *Metamorphoses* is unlike any other epic. As part of his universalizing scheme, Ovid incorporates into his hybrid poem almost all ancient genres, including tragedy, comedy, history, philosophy, love poetry, didactic, and pastoral. He challenges the reader to recognize his allusions to a wide range of Greek and Roman literature and to be surprised at his innovations. His distinctive narrative voice draws attention to itself and keeps his authorial manipulation in the foreground through asides, parentheses, puns, and incongruities.

Ovid tells us in his opening lines that his epic's scope will be from the beginning of the world to his own times. This chronological framework takes us from the creation of the world out of chaos to the apotheoses of Rome's first emperors. Yet, throughout most of the poem, any sense of linearity takes second place to patterns of thematic association and contrast. The way Ovid connects sequences of stories by themes, characters, and places tends to overshadow our awareness of a time line. In practice, the poem's many elaborate structures resist the mapping of any orderly architectural scheme, whether narrative or thematic. Three major divisions may be discerned in the poem: the first five books contain mainly Greek myths involving the passions of the gods, books VI through the beginning of XI Greek heroes, and the final five books figures associated with the legends of Troy and Rome. Major themes include the conflict between gods and mortals, the gods' erotic predation on humans, the plight of the artist, and etiology (origins), but Ovid's primary interest was in human passions, especially unusual and extreme passions, and, as throughout his earlier poetic career, love and sexuality.

Ovid's carefully constructed and fluid transitions between stories have long been admired for their skill, subtlety, and ingenuity. In the first tale of book I, Jupiter punishes mankind's impiety with a devastating flood, which leads to the rebirth of humans from stones (Deucalion and Pyrrha), but also the spontaneous creation of a monstrous serpent. Apollo kills the serpent and establishes a festival of commemoration, at which the reward is an oak wreath, because, says Ovid, the laurel was not yet invented. This introduces the tale of Daphne (whose name means "laurel" in Greek), who was transformed into the first laurel tree. After Daphne's transformation, we are told, the local rivers assembled at her father's river, with the exception of Inachus, who did not come because his daughter Io was missing. So, cleverly, follows the long tale of Io, raped by Jupiter and then transformed into a cow to hide her from his jealous wife, Juno. Juno, not fooled of course, places Argus, a hundred-eyed monster, as a guard over Io, but Mercury lulls him to sleep with another rape tale almost identical to that of Apollo and Daphne (Pan and Syrinx) and kills him. Argus' eyes are placed on the peacock's tail (a "just-so" story), Io reverts to her original form (a rare occurrence in the poem), and with the mention of Phaethon, the friend of Io's son, the narrative moves on to the next tale, which, as is typical, continues on into the following book.

Narrative continuity is often achieved through the use of internal narrators, characters within the poem who tell tales for a variety of reasons. These narrative cycles offer Ovid the opportunity to reflect on the act and art of storytelling. Internal narrators are sometimes aware of their earlier literary incarnations; so Mars reminds his father, Jupiter, that in Ennius' early Roman epic he had promised to deify Romulus. Character narrators may offer unusual perspectives; one of Odysseus' men tells what it was like to change into a pig and back into a man (a subjective viewpoint Homer's Odysseus never provides). Many internal narratives reveal the emotional states of their narrators. The recondite and exotic Near Eastern tales chosen by the three Minyades sisters mirror Ovid's own virtuosity in discovering innumerable obscure myths for his poem, while exposing through their common theme of thwarted love the women's own avoidance of the passionate powers of Bacchus, which leads to their transformation into bats.

The identity of the narrator can often change the meaning of a tale when read in context. The story of Pygmalion, for example, the artist whose ivory statue of a beautiful woman (unnamed in Ovid, later known as Galatea) wonderfully comes to life, has typically been read as an uplifting male/artistic fantasy (setting aside our own modern distaste for this literal objectification of the ideal female body). However, we should be aware that the tale occurs within a cycle told by the narrator Orpheus, who has just lost his beloved wife and has forsworn the love of females in favor of males. Both Orpheus and his character Pygmalion have repudiated women and accused them of criminal passions. From their misogynistic perspective, only a purely artificial woman like the statue can escape the vices of females.

Ovid's narrative style is complex, intelligent, and as protean as his theme. He can swiftly shift from the tragic to the comic or from empathy to pathos within the same tale, which creates incongruity and destabilizes the narrative. Ovid's distinctive style often contains more than a hint of irony, inviting the reader to join with him in a knowing enjoyment of his virtuosity. Apollo pursues the reluctant virgin Daphne and suggests that if she slows down, he will too. Humor is often created from literalism and detail. Mercury is so dumbstruck with love that even his little winged boots forget to flap and he begins to fall. Marsyas cries out as his skin is being flayed, "Why do you strip me from myself?" (page 152). Critics such as the seventeenth-century Dryden disapproved of such "untimely wit" at moments of suffering, but Ovid offers a serious way of looking at the world, relentlessly exposing its arbitrariness and cruelty while retaining his humor.

A characteristic feature of Ovidian wit is his exploitation of paradox, a device that functions both at the verbal and figurative level. Narcissus and Echo must each face the paradox that being identical with a loved one actually prevents their union. Myrrha, a girl stricken with sexual passion for her father, expresses the transgressions of incest in paradoxical wordplay: "he's mine, and yet not mine" (page 270). When Myrrha's nurse brings her in the dark to sleep with her unknowing father, she says to him, "take her as she is, / The girl is yours" (page 274).

Ovid both conforms to and subverts epic conventions. The last five books deal with the epic tales of Troy and Rome while almost entirely avoiding the traditional battle scenes. His handling of great mythological heroes such as Hercules, Achilles, or Aeneas skips over their major epic

achievements and focuses instead on marginal tales of trans-
formation. Perseus appears in one of the only two battle
scenes in the poem, in which, through excessive gore and
graphic detail, mixed with comedic touches, Ovid mocks
the pretensions of earlier epic and calls attention to its vio-
lence. In lieu of proper weapons the combatants hurl mix-
ing bowls, chandeliers, table legs, and bars from doorposts,
while the tongue of a chopped-off head continues to swear.
Perseus finally ends the whole debacle by holding up the
Gorgon's head, thus handily petrifying the remaining two
hundred enemies.

## METAMORPHOSIS

Ovid treats the theme of metamorphosis in highly di-
verse ways. People are turned into animals, plants, geo-
graphical features (rivers, rocks, mountains, islands), and
statues. Stones, mushrooms, and dragons' teeth become
humans, women change to men and vice versa, and ships
turn into sea nymphs. We learn that the famous monsters
Medusa and Scylla were once beautiful maidens, until
transformed by angry goddesses. Transformation can come
as punishment, or as rescue from death or rape, although
characters in the poem question whether such a rescue
calls for consolation or congratulation. Metamorphosis is
an ambiguous state, somewhere between life and death,
says Myrrha. The arbitrariness of transformation is high-
lighted in the metamorphoses of many innocents, such as
Callisto, Actaeon, and Dryope, the last punished simply for
picking a lotus flower.

The creation of the universe from Chaos at the begin-
ning of the poem both announces the cosmogonic nature
of the poem's metamorphoses and establishes the "physi-
cal" basis for these transformations in the instability of the
four elements that make up the world: earth, air, fire, and
water. In this world of flux, human bodies are subject to
change and disfigurement from both external (natural and
divine) and internal (emotional) forces. The creation of
mankind from a combination of earth and a divine spark
also establishes and blurs the boundaries dividing humans
from animals and from gods, through which the tales of the

poem will explore what it means to be human. For humans the downward path to animal or even vegetable nature is frighteningly easy, and attempts to equal the gods invariably end in disaster, except for those rare mortals who are deified.

The power of the gods to initiate change is immediately demonstrated in the terrifying first tale, when Jupiter destroys all of mankind in the flood. Jupiter's palace is directly compared to the emperor Augustus' Palatine, which suggests a disquieting parallel between the volatile Olympian power structures and the poet's Rome. Much of the poem explores the conflict between humans and the often arbitrary and absolute power of the gods, which reveals the limitations of human actions, desires, and power. The gods alone remain immutable, but their ability to mutate and mutilate humans is seen everywhere. The different ideological perspectives of gods and mortals are famously represented by the artistic weaving competition between the goddess Minerva and the human Arachne in book VI. Minerva's tapestry depicts the gods in majestic forms dispensing just punishments to presumptuous humans through metamorphosis. Arachne, on the other hand, shows the gods in various deceptive disguises abducting and raping human women, thus unmasking divine cruelty and sexual predation. Finding no artistic flaw in Arachne's tapestry, Minerva, enraged at her insubordination, punishes Arachne by turning her into a spider.

The most common emotions that motivate metamorphosis are sexual desire, anger, and grief. In most cases, metamorphoses are external, imposed by the gods but in other stories the cause is internal; at a moment of crisis the very force of extreme passions can cause a breakdown in the elements and a natural metamorphosis. Their excessive ferocity seems to transform Lycaon and Hecuba into beasts. The Propoetides seem to turn to stone as a natural result of their hardened emotions and denial of love. Several characters, including Cyane, Canens, and Egeria, melt into water or air from extreme grief or unrequited love. Unusual or unnatural sexual desire motivates a number of tales in the poem and affords Ovid the opportunity to explore the pathology of human passions, many of which distort categories of gender, identity, or familial ties. Tereus lusts after his sister-in-law; Medea and Scylla betray their fathers for their lovers; Byblis longs for an incestuous relationship with her brother, and Myrrha with her father. Procne and Althea struggle between their loyalties to their children and to their siblings. Iphis, a woman, loves another woman. More women than men suffer from "unnatural" sexual passion in the poem as in Greek mythology, reflecting an ancient prejudice that the female libido was stronger and less controllable than that of the male.

A great many of the tales in the poem involve sexual violence, attempted rape and rape (rarely explicitly described). The majority of these erotic tales involves divine predation of mortal women, but there are examples of human sexual violence as well (Tereus and Philomena), and even women assaulting men (Salmacis and Hermaphroditus). Ovid usually begins with the point of view of the pursuer, then switches to the perspective of the victim suffering metamorphosis. Daphne is said to look more beautiful to Apollo as she flees; Europa's beauty is increased through her fear. The gods' pursuit of mortal women is sometimes humorously inept, often deceptive through the use of disguises, but almost always destructive. Although Ovid suppresses the physical details of rape, he includes meticulous descriptions of the deformation of metamorphosis, as if in a symbolic representation of the victim's loss of identity and inviolability. Ovid's intense interest in depicting human suffering, whether internal emotional suffering or external physical violence, has generated differing interpretations. Some have argued that he expresses sympathy for the victim, others that he is indulging his own and his readers' voyeuristic pleasure in the depiction of violence. His definite taste for the grotesque (such as Philomena's cutoff tongue creeping across the floor) seems to hint at the notoriously bloody games of the Roman amphitheater.

Ovid shows a great interest in describing the actual physical process of metamorphosis. His strikingly visual concentration on the sequential physical effects of transformation, usually from the victim's point of view, can take on a truly nightmarish quality in its bizarre realism. Scylla steps into a pool and watches with horror as her lower body

turns into a pack of mad dogs and tries in vain to run from
them. Dryope struggles to move and finds her feet literally
rooted to the ground, with the bark creeping up from her
feet; when she tears her hair in grief, she finds only leaves;
her last act is to kiss her baby before her face is covered.
Ovid's descriptions sometimes take on a mock scientific or
naturalistic color. He uses meteorological theory to explain
Lichas' petrifaction: hurled by Hercules over the sea, he
congeals into rock like freezing hail or snow. Blood spurt-
ing out of the wound of Pyramus, who has Romeo-like
killed himself because he thinks his lover, Thisbe, is dead,
is incongruously compared to water bursting out of a lead
pipe.

Metamorphosis may represent the brutal and narrow
reduction of a person to her basest element or emotion
(Hecuba's vengeful rage), or it may only preserve some su-
perficial feature or activity that was prominent in the tale
(Daphne's beauty). Io's temporary transformation into a
"beautiful" cow is just plain funny. Many of Ovid's meta-
morphic tales account for and explain the origins of numer-
ous natural phenomena, such as rocks, plants, and animal
features. Personal histories become natural history. So the
heliotrope flower faces the sun because of Clytie's love for
Sol, bats seek houses and shun the light in imitation of the
Minyades, woodpeckers peck at trees out of Picus' anger
at being transformed, and swans live near water out of the
fear of fire. Some metamorphoses take the form of gro-
tesque punishment, such as Juno's vengeful transformation
of the beautiful Callisto into a bear. Many metamorphoses
involve the loss of the most characteristic feature of hu-
manity, the ability to speak: Io is reduced to mooing, Echo
to repetition. Metamorphosis also operates as actualized
metaphor: Anaxarete is the proverbial hardhearted mis-
tress; impervious to the entreaties of her would-be lover,
she is literally turned to stone.

One of the most frightening aspects of metamorphosis
is the continuation of human consciousness in a new form
and the extreme alienation, fear, and even pain this may
cause. After Actaeon is transformed into a stag he watches
in horror as his own hunting dogs attack him, unable to
call out to them, although Ovid gives us the names of more

than thirty of them. After Daphne is turned into a laurel tree to escape Apollo's pursuit, he feels her heart beating when he embraces the trunk. Though he may interpret the waving of her branches as assent to his possession, Daphne can no longer make her feelings clear—if she still has any.

The instability of the Ovidian world is reaffirmed in book XV by the philosopher Pythagoras, who suggests that Rome itself is subject to the same laws of change. Apotheosis dominates Ovid's Roman tales in the last two books, and is fittingly a final form of metamorphosis. A line of deified Roman rulers is traced from the legendary Aeneas and Romulus to Rome's new emperors, the recently deceased Caesar and his successor, Augustus, reflecting the contemporary development of ruler cult, and Ovid's treatment is characteristically attuned to the political dimensions. In the last lines of the *Metamorphoses*, Ovid boldly claims that he too will become immortal through the eternal fame of his poem. After two millennia, in a changed world that even Ovid could not have imagined, his boast turns out to have been prophetic.

—Sara Myers

# I

# BOOK I

*Swiftly Ovid enters the theme of metamorphoses, the mutability of all things in creation. There is not much doubt that the source of his inspiration is in the first book of Lucretius's* De Rerum Natura *with its statements on the indestructibility of matter. In no sense does Ovid directly imitate Lucretius. The clue of his debt to Lucretius is skilfully concealed: the elder poet began his work with praise to Venus, who is of course among Ovid's favorite goddesses; Lucretius describes the turbulence of nature; he admits the mutability of things, "For whenever a thing changes and quits its proper limits, at once this change of state is the death of that which was before." Ovid's imagination has none of Lucretius's bent toward darkness. He is here to tell us how miraculous changes have taken place, to provide his illustrations of how things change in a number of short, startling incidents, partly of his own invention, partly drawn from his readings in Greco-Roman literature. Others had written of an Age of Gold, but none more memorably than Ovid, and in his retelling of the stories of Deucalion and Pyrrha, of Io and Jove, his good-humoured, half-ironic manner of presenting miracles is irresistible.*

# BOOK I

INVOCATION

Now I shall tell of things that change, new being
Out of old: since you, O Gods, created
Mutable arts and gifts, give me the voice
To tell the shifting story of the world
From its beginning to the present hour.

CHAOS AND CREATION

Before land was and sea—before air and sky
Arched over all, all Nature was all Chaos,
The rounded body of all things in one,
The living elements at war with lifelessness;
No God, no Titan shone from sky or sea,
No Moon, no Phoebe outgrew slanted horns
And walked the night, nor was Earth poised in air.
No wife of Ocean reached her glittering arms
Into the farthest shores of reef and sand.
Earth, Air, Water heaved and turned in darkness,
No living creatures knew that land, that sea
Where heat fell against cold, cold against heat—
Roughness at war with smooth and wet with drought.
Things that gave way entered unyielding masses,
Heaviness fell into things that had no weight.

Then God or Nature calmed the elements:
Land fell away from sky and sea from land,
And aether drew away from cloud and rain.
As God unlocked all elemental things,
Fire climbed celestial vaults, air followed it
To float in heavens below; and earth which carried
All heavier things with it dropped under air;
Water fell farthest, embracing shores and islands.

3

When God, whichever God he was, created
The universe we know, he made of earth
A turning sphere so delicately poised
That water flowed in waves beneath the wind
And Ocean's arms encircled the rough globe:
At God's touch, lakes, springs, dancing waterfalls
Streamed downhill into valleys, waters glancing
Through rocks, grass and wild-flowered meadows;
Some ran their silver courses underground,
Others raced into seas and broader Ocean—
All poured from distant hills to farthest shores.
Then God willed plain, plateau, and fallen sides
Of hills in deep-leaved forests: over them
He willed rock-bodied mountains against sky.
As highest heaven has two zones on the right,
Two on the left, and a fifth zone in flames,
With celestial fires between the four, so
God made zones on earth, the fifth zone naked
With heat where none may live, at each extreme
A land of snow, and, at their sides, two zones
Of temperate winds and sun and shifting cold.

And air arched over all, air heavier than
Fire in the same measure as water carries
Less weight than the entire weight of earth.
Through gathering air God sent storm clouds and
          rain,
Thunder that shakes the heart, ice in the wind
That pierces all with cold—yet the world's master
Did not give all air's space to fighting ground
Of the Four Winds: each had his home and yet
So wildly the Brothers quarrel, even now
The world is almost torn in a war of winds.
Eurus whose winged breath stirs Araby
Went where the hills of Persia glow with dawn;
And where the western shores are lit with fires
There Zephyrus with the setting sun came home;
While ice-tongued Boreas roared in farthest
          north,
Auster, the South Wind, gathered summer storms—
Shining above them floated heavenly aether.

As God divided regions of this world
Into their separate parts, then all the stars
Long lost in ancient dark began to light
Pale fires throughout the sky. And as each part
Of universal being came to life,
Each filled with images of its own kind:
Among the stars gods walked the house of heaven,
And where the sea opened its waves fish spawned;
Earth gathered beasts, and in the trembling air
The flight of birds.

                    Yet world was not complete:
It lacked a creature that had hints of heaven
And hopes to rule the earth. So man was made.
Whether He who made all things aimed at the best,
Creating man from his own living fluid,
Or if earth, lately fallen through heaven's aether,
Took an immortal image from the skies,
Held it in clay which son of Iapetus
Mixed with the spray of brightly running waters—
It had a godlike figure and was man.
While other beasts, heads bent, stared at wild earth,
The new creation gazed into blue sky;
Then careless things took shape, change followed change
And with it unknown species of mankind.

## AGES OF GOLD, SILVER, BRONZE, AND IRON

The first millennium was the age of gold:
Then living creatures trusted one another;
People did well without the thought of ill:
Nothing forbidden in a book of laws,
No fears, no prohibitions read in bronze,
Or in the sculptured face of judge and master.
Even the pine tree stood on its own hills,
Nor did it fall to sail uncharted seas;
All that men knew of earth were shores of home,
No cities climbed behind high walls and bridges;
No brass-lipped trumpets called, nor clanging swords,
Nor helmets marched the streets, country and town
Had never heard of war: and seasons travelled

Through the years of peace. The innocent earth
Learned neither spade nor plough; she gave her
Riches as fruit hangs from the tree: grapes
Dropping from the vine, cherry, strawberry
Ripened in silver shadows of the mountain,
And in the shade of Jove's miraculous tree,
The falling acorn. Springtide the single
Season of the year, and through that hour
The soft breath of the south in flowering leaf,
In white waves of the wheat across the meadows,
Season of milk and wine in amber streams
And honey pouring from the green-lipped oak.

After old Saturn fell to Death's dark country
Straitly Jove ruled the world with silver charm,
Less radiant than gold, less false than brass.
And it was then that Jove split up the year
In shifty Autumn, wild Winter, and short Spring,
Summer that glared with heat: the winter wind
Gleamed white with ice that streamed on field and river;
Then men built walls against both sun and wind—
Their elder shelters had been caves or boughs.
Now grain was planted and the plough pierced earth;
The driven ox whimpered beneath the yoke.

Third came the age of bronze, less soft than silver,
And men in bronze were quick with sword and spear,
Yet all feared Jove. Then came the age of iron
And from it poured the very blood of evil:
Piety, Faith, Love, and Truth changed to Deceit,
Violence, the Tricks of Trade, Usury, Profit;
Ignorant of contrary winds, men sailed the seas:
The mountain oak, the pine were felled and stripped,
Their long beams swaying above uncharted Ocean.
Then land, once like the gift of sunlit air,
Was cut in properties, estates, and holdings:
Not only crops were hoarded; men invaded
Entrails of earth down deeper than the river
Where Death's shades weave in darkness underground;
Where hidden from the sight of men Jove's treasures
Were locked in night. There, in his sacred mines,

All that drives men to avarice and murder
Shone in the dark: the loot was dragged to light
And War, inspired by curse of iron and gold,
Lifted blood-clotted hands and marched the earth.
Men fed on loot and lust; the guest feared host;
Neighbour looked warily with smiles at neighbour;
And fathers had good reasons to distrust
Their eager sons-in-law. If brothers loved
Each other, the sight was rare, and watchful
Husbands prayed for death of wives; stepmothers
Made poison a dessert at dinner—sons
Counted the hours that led to fathers' graves.
Piety was overthrown, and Astraea,
Last-born sister of the skies, left the blood-
Sweating earth to drink its blood, and turning
Lightly swiftly found her place in heaven.

Soon it was rumoured that earth's taste for blood
Was threatening heaven: giants piled hill on
Mountain to make a stair that reached the skies,
To clamber to the throne of Jove, then blinding
Thunder shook Olympus, and Pelion
Thrust down by heaven's bolt crashed over Ossa.
It was reported that when the mountains
With monsters fell from grace, trailing their blood,
Then earth, remembering earlier sons and daughters,
Made human images from blood-wet clay,
The new breed godless, violent in mind;
One saw too clearly they were born of blood.

When Jove from his high seat looked down on earth
He sighed aloud: he thought of Lycaon's altar
Of human flesh, of incident too recent
To be well known. Jove's anger burned his soul,
Was worthy of it: and he named a council
Of lesser gods who sat at his command.
On evenings when deepest heavens are clear
One sees a highroad called The Milky Way
Where gods walk out upon a path of stars
To Jove the Thunderer; on either side
Of palace and high hall, great doors fall open

To the chambered light; guests wandering where
Nobility receives its worshippers.
The lesser deities do not live here;
I choose to call it Palatine of Heaven.

As gods assembled at Jove's throne in state
He stood above them leaning on his sceptre,
Shook heavy locks three times and once again
As land, sea, sky rocked with his weighted gesture;
Then lips grown thick with rage began to speak:
"We live in danger greater than the hour
When lizard-footed giants climbed the hills
And with a hundred hands clawed at the sky.
They were one breed, one will. But now when Ocean
Storms helpless earth, all traces of mankind
Should be destroyed. I swear by all the rivers
Of deepest Hell my best is done to conquer
Human ill; the best is not enough; taint
Must be cut from flesh as with a cleansing
Knife the body cured. I am protector
Of nymphs, fauns, satyrs, and small gods who wander
The village street, down lanes, up shaded hills;
Since we have found no home for them in heaven,
The lands they live in must be cleared of evil,
Where Lycaon, known for his will against me,
Walks like a beast and hides his traps in forests."

All who heard trembled and with anxious lips
Asked who was Lycaon, what breed was he?
And as they spoke the scene was like the day
When hands of madness washed in Caesar's blood
Threatened to blot the very name of Rome,
When all the world stood dazed by thought of ruin.
Even now, Augustus, when your subjects please,
So Jove was pleased by anger of his gods.
He waved for silence with an easy hand;
Their murmuring ceased and he resumed his lecture:
"Lycaon met his fate; here is my story.
I had heard evil rumours of mankind
And with the hope of proving them untrue

I stepped down from Olympus incognito,
No longer Jovian but extremely human,
A traveller walking up and down the world.
It takes too long to list the crimes I saw—
Rumours were less amazing than the truth.
I crossed Maenala where every bush and cave
Was hideously alive with boars, bears, foxes,
Then through Cyllene and the frost-pine forest
Of Lycaeus, and as that twilight dwindled
To ever-increasing dark I stepped across
Rough threshold where Lycaon, bitter tyrant
Of Arcadian wildness, lived. I raised
My hand; peasant and shepherd fell before me
To offer prayers at which insane Lycaon
Looking at them and me began to roar,
'Soon we shall know if this is god or man;
I shall have proof of its divinity.'
The proof was simple. When I had feasted
(So he had planned) and heavily asleep,
Lifted to bed, he hoped to murder me.
Nor was this scheme enough; he took a Northern
Hostage from a cell, slit the poor devilish
Monster's throat and tossed his warm and bleeding
Vitals in a pot; the rest he roasted.
This was the dinner that he put before me.
My thunderbolt struck the king's house to ruins,
And he, wild master, ran like beast to field
Crying his terror which cannot utter words
But howls in fear, his foaming lips and jaws,
Quick with the thought of blood, harry the sheep.
His cloak turned into bristling hair, his arms
Were forelegs of a wolf, yet he resembled
Himself, what he had been—the violent
Grey hair, face, eyes, the ceaseless, restless stare
Of drunken tyranny and hopeless hate.
His house has fallen; others shall follow him;
Far as earth reaches, Furies rule the land;
All men have joined in Hell's conspiracy
Since I have said it: all shall pay the toll
Of early death—and earth an early fall."

THE FLOOD

As Jove concluded, many applauded him,
Some showed approval by a tactful silence;
Both factions gave quick fuel to the stern justice
Of Jove's rage, yet all felt sad, each thinking,
"What would the world be like without mankind?
Who would bring myrrh and sweet herbs to their altars?
Did Jove decide to give the earth to beasts?"
He told them not to fear: they knew the worst,
And he would solve each problem as it came;
He planned a breed of men of heaven's make,
Different in spirit, better than the first.

Then Jove raised thunderbolt against the earth—
And checked the blow. Would heaven break in fire,
And flames pour over earth from pole to pole?
He then remembered that the Fates had scored
A certain distant hour when sea and land,
Earth and the vault of heaven would be consumed
In universal fire. He put aside
The lightning spear Cyclopean hands
Made as his weapon to assert his will:
Another doom for man came to his mind,
A death that stormed beneath the waves, and fell
From air; and then dark rain began to fall.

As straight as rain, quicker than thought Jove locked
The North Wind in the island-drifting cave
Of Aeolus and with him winds that harried
Clouds, but Auster he released, its dark
Wings over earth, the Nubian darkness
Deeper than midnight, beard and long grey hair
In fall of rain, black forehead in wild clouds,
Its great clapping hands thunder in the dare.
And as rain fell Iris, handmaid of Juno,
In rainbow dress drew water from earth's streams
Replenishing the clouds. Nor did rain cease.
Wheat fell before the storm, the uncut harvest
Drifting in rivers as the waters turned;
The farmers' prayer unheard within the tempest,
The heavy labour of long years undone.

Nor was Jove's rage appeased by pouring heavens.
Neptune arrived with armies of the waters,
Rivers assembled at his ocean's floor
To hear his orders: "The hour is all short
For long orations, open your locks and dykes,
Your streaming walls, and springs, unleash the horses
Riding in foam through waterfalls and waves."
At his command the mouths of fountains opened
Racing their mountain waters to the sea.
Under the blow of Neptune's fork earth trembled,
And way was open for a sea of waters:
Where land was the great rivers toppled orchards,
Uncut corn, cottages, sheep, men, and cattle
Into the flood. Even stone shrines and temples
Were washed away, and if farmhouse or barn
Or palace still stood its ground, the waves
Climbed over door and lintel, up roof and tower.
All vanished as though lost in glassy waters,
Road, highway, valley, and hill swept into ocean,
All was a moving sea without a shore.

And in flood's desert one saw a creature,
Perhaps a man, swim toward a vanished hill
That once he knew; another rowed a boat
Over the acres of his plough; another sailed
The fields that were to be his harvest,
Over the roofs of his sea-buried home.
Another caught fish from the floating branches
Of the tallest elms; ships' anchors dropping
In grass-grown meadows and swift keels sped
Over green hill and vineyard. Where yesterday
Thin-legged goats stepped on their way to pasture,
The bearded seal dozed through the deep sea hours,
And mermaids drifting with new-opened eyes
Gazed into cities that were walked by men.
The leaping dolphins dashed through grove and covert
Splashing their sides against oak bough and tree
Till the dim forest swayed beneath the waters;
Over them pursuing wolf swam with the sheep.
The exhausted lion drifting with the tiger,
The plunging thrust of the wild boar, the lightning

Step of the deer perished within the vortex
Of the waters; wing-spent, the circling bird
Wheeled his slow flight into unceasing waves.
Green hills then joined the valleys of the sea
And mountain peaks were islands in strange waters;
And almost every being that breathed on earth
Drowned as it met the flood; those who survived
Died of starvation on the shores of mountains.

## DEUCALION AND PYRRHA

Within the happy fields of fertile valleys,
Before all turned to sea, lay peaceful Phocis
Where the twin-horned Parnassus pierced the clouds.
There, in a little boat young Deucalion
And his bride sailed to the mountaintop that
Now was island and stepped ashore. Their first
Thought was to pray, to praise the Delphic nymphs,
To give their thanks to Pan and most to Themis
Who from her grottoes was the voice of Fate;
She in that day was queen of oracles.
Deucalion had been the best of men;
His wife, his heart devoted to the gods.
When Jove looked down on earth all that he saw
Was a stilled ocean and on a mountain shelf
One man, one woman. Of many thousands sent
To untimely death, only this gentle innocent
And his bride were left to praise the fortunate
Will of God. Jove swept the clouds aside and made
A channel where the North Wind opened heaven:
And earth again looked upward to the sky,
Again the heavens showered earth with light.
Then even the distant reaches of the seas
Fell quiet and to soothe the rocking waters
Neptune let fall his triple-headed spear.
Then ocean's master called to sea-wreathed Triton
Who at echo of Neptune's voice came from the sea
Like a tower of sea-green beard, sea creatures,
Sea shells, grey waters sliding from his green shoulders
To sound his horn, to wind the gliding rivers
Back to their sources, back to rills and streams.

At Neptune's order Triton lifted up
His curved sea shell, a trumpet at his lips
Which in the underworld of deepest seas
Sounds Triton's music to the distant shores
Behind the morning and the evening suns;
And as his voice was heard through land and ocean
The floods and rivers moved at his command.
Over all earth the shores of lakes appeared
Hillsides and river banks, wet fields and meadow,
As floods receded and quays came into view:
A cliff, then a plateau, a hill, a meadow,
As from a tomb a forest rose and then
One saw trees with lean seaweeds tangled
Among their glittering leaves and wave-tossed boughs.
It was a world reborn but Deucalion
Looked out on silent miles of ebbing waters.
He wept, called to his wife, "Dear sister, friend,
O last of women, look at loneliness;
As in our marriage bed our fears, disasters
Are of one being, one kind, one destiny;
We are the multitudes that walk the earth
Between sunrise and sunset of the world,
And we alone inherit wilderness.
The living are lost beneath a dwindling sea.
Even the ledge of mountain where we stand
May drop to darkness; and even the brief shadow
Of clouds that drift and fade is the return
Of midnight to the terror in my heart.
And you, dear soul, what if the Fates had swept
You on these pale rocks alone, to whom would you
Confess your grief, your tears? For if wild sea
Had claimed you then I would have followed after;
O had I Father's gift I would breathe life
Into the lifeless earth, but who are we
To recreate mankind? It is the will
Of heaven to bring us here and we the last
Of human creatures on this earth." They wept,
Yet promised to raise further prayers to God,
To know his will, to hear his oracles.
And hand in hand they came to Cephisus,
Whose waters, scarcely clear, still ran in freshets

Between its grassy sides. They dipped their hands
Into the sacred stream, in priestly fashion
Scattered living waters on bowed head and tunics.
And from the river they walked to Themis' shrine
Whose fires were ashes and where wall and cornice
Still dripped with seaweed and the creeping moss.
Then falling to their knees they kissed the stones
Where sea-washed altar turned their tears to ice
And trembling lips to speech: "O Themis, hear us.
How shall we please the gods? Can piety
In prayer, can goodness still wake pity in
The gods' anger that destroys mankind?
O merciful lady, how can we save
Our brothers, the very race of man from hell,
From eternal nothingness now and forever?"

    Themis was moved and like an oracle
Answered their prayer: "Walk from the temple
With covered head, with girdled tunic open
At breast and shoulder, and as the wind flows
Scatter your mother's bones." Deucalion
Could not believe his ears and silent Pyrrha
Could not obey the voice. Then Pyrrha spoke
Her words in tears: "How can I desecrate
My mother's spirit? O forgive me, Goddess."
"But what did the voice say?" turned in their hearts
And waked their souls until Prometheus' son,
Mild Deucalion, said to the troubled girl
Who stood beside him, "Either I've gone mad
(Yet sacred voices never lead to sin)
Or our Great Mother is the Earth, her bones
Are guiltless stones we throw behind us."

    Though wavering Pyrrha heard her husband's voice,
Both were in doubt, shaken with fear, with hope.
But what harm could be done? They left the temple
With floating robes and veiled heads, then furtively
Dropped pebbles in their trail and as they ran
(Some find this fable more than fabulous,
But we must keep faith with our ancient legends)
Pebbles grew into rocks, rocks into statues

That looked like men; the darker parts still wet
With earth were flesh, dry elements were bones,
And veins began to stir with human blood—
Such were the inclinations of heaven's will.
The stones that Deucalion dropped were men,
And those that fell from his wife's hands were women.
Beyond, behind the years of loss and hardship
We trace a stony heritage of being.

THE NEW WORLD

Within the weed-grown swamps left by the flood
The animal kingdoms of the earth appeared.
The seeds of earth swelled in the heat of noon
As in a mother's womb—as when the seven-lipped
Nile shrinks to its source, so sun's heat wakens
The moss-green river side, and there the peasant
As he turns the soil finds under it a world
Of things that live, half-live, or creep or run
As though one body of earth were alive,
Half dead, so in all things
And in a single body, half motionless,
Inert, yet half alive. As heat and water
Become one body, so life begins; though fire
And water are at war, life's origins
Awake discordant harmonies that move
The entire world. Therefore when fires
Of newly wakened sun turned toward the earth
Where waters still receded from her sides,
All living things in multitudes of being
Became her progeny once more. Some were
Of ancient lineage and colors
And others were mysterious and new.

APOLLO AND DAPHNE

Though earth may not have willed catastrophe
The latest of new creatures was the serpent,
Even you, great Python of hillside and valley
Who haunt the deepest shadows in men's hearts!
Wherever the monster turned, green darkness fell

In winding paths through sacred grove and briar.
Then bright Apollo with his sun-tipped arrows
Whose swiftness stilled the flight of goat and deer
Aimed at the beast with darts that fell in showers.
So Python perished, but not until his wounds
Were black with blood and God Apollo's quiver
Almost spent. That is the reason why
Apollo's games are called the Pythian Feast,
In memory of the serpent's golden death,
In honor of the god's swift victory—
The Feast that brings fleet-footed, swift-riding
Youth garlands of oak leaf as they win the race.
This was before the laurel wreath became
Apollo's gift of grace in shrine and temple
Before he twined the green immortal laurel
Within the sunlight of his golden hair.

Apollo's first love was elusive Daphne,
The child of Peneus, kindly tyrant of the river,
Nor did the god pursue the girl by chance—
The cause was Cupid's anger at Apollo:
Still heated by his conquest of the snake,
Phoebus saw Cupid wind a tight-strung bow,
"Who is this lecherous child," said he, "who plays
With weapons and is not a man? The bow
Was made for me; I am the one who kills
A worthy enemy, wild beasts—and look at
Great Python wallowing in blood; his body
Covers half the countryside. Your business
Is not to play with arrows, but set afire
Your little torch that guides unwary lovers."
The child of Venus glanced at flush Apollo:
"Your arrows may be murder to us all,
But mine shall pierce your veins: as much
As mortals are less than the divine, so
Your poor glory is less than my poor skill."
With that he raised his wings and in quick air
He found a shaded ledge on high Parnassus;
There carefully he made a choice of arrows—
Two darts that were of opposite persuasion,
One, like a golden spear, was sharp as fire,

And is love's fire in the flesh, the other,
Heavy as boredom, dull as lead, he plunged
At a single stroke into white Daphne's breast.
Then Cupid aimed at Phoebus, and love's arrow
With fire of lightning pierced his bones;
Apollo walked as in a tower of flames.
As Phoebus burned with love young Daphne fled
As though she feared love's name, as if she were
The wraith of virgin Phoebe, huntress and child
Who trapped small creatures of the bushband fen,
And ran with floating hair through green-deep forest;
Nor would she hear of lovers or of men,
Nor cared for promise of a wedding day,
Nor Hymen's night of love. Time and again
Old Peneus complained, "Where is my son-in-law,
Daughter, where have you hidden my grandchildren?"
As though the wedding torch were sight of evil
Pale Daphne flushed at every thought of it,
And hid her face against her father's shoulder
And pleading with her arms around his neck
Said, "Father, make me an eternal virgin.
Do what Diana's father did for her."
Peneus agreed, but your enchantments, Daphne,
Had greater powers than a father's will,
Nor could your prayers undo a beauty's charm.
At one look Phoebus loved her; as he gazed,
"Daphne," he thought, "is mine," but did not think
His prophecy might fail him—his hopes, desires
Had outpaced all the Delian oracles;
Then as September fields of wheat and straw
Take fire from a careless traveller's torch
Left smouldering in the wind that wakes the dawn,
So did Apollo's heart break into flames,
The sterile fires that feed on empty hopes.
And while he gazed at Daphne's floating hair
That fell in tendrils at her throat and forehead
He thought, "What if that fair head wore a crown?"
He looked into her eyes and saw the stars
Though staring does not satisfy desire,
His eyes praised all they saw—her lips, her fingers,
Her hands, her naked arms from wrist to shoulder;

And what they did not see they thought the best.
Yet she ran from him swifter than light air
That turns to nothingness as we pursue it,
Nor did she stop to hear Apollo calling:
"O daughter of the deep green-shadowed River,
Who follows you is not your enemy;
The lamb runs from the wolf, the deer from lion,
The trembling-feathered dove flies from the eagle
Whose great wings cross the sky—such is your
          flight
While mine is love's pursuit. Rest where time waits
But where you vanish the way is rough; briar
And thorn and fallen rock make wounds that bleed,
And green pits open where swift unwary fall.
And I who follow am neither pain nor death;
Then walk with me and ask me who I am.
Surely my home is not in mountain passes,
Nor am I shepherd or wild-haired stable boy.
O ignorant, unknowing, thoughtless child
Who runs in darkness—and from whom? from me?
Jove is my father and I am lord of Delphi;
My temples stand at Claros, Patara,
And beyond the cities, glimmering Tenebros,
Enchanted island of the eastern seas.
Where caves and temples speak you hear my voices,
The past, the present, and the yet to come;
My lyre sounds the soul of harmony;
My arrows never fail—and yet one arrow
More certain of its aim than mine wakes fire
Behind the chambers of an indifferent heart.
And if you wait, learn more: I am physician,
The good physician of magic in clever herbs
And artful grasses; yet herbs are feeble cures,
Unhealthy diet for one who falls in love,
Nor can physician cure himself—"

                              As Daphne ran
Phoebus had more to say, and she, distracted,
In flight, in fear, wind flowing through her dress
And her wild hair—she grew more beautiful
The more he followed her and saw wind tear

Her dress and the short tunic that she wore,
The girl a naked wraith in wilderness.
And as they ran young Phoebus saved his breath
For greater speed to close the race, to circle
The spent girl in an open field, to harry
The chase as greyhound races hare,
His teeth, his black jaws glancing at her heels.
The god by grace of hope, the girl, despair,
Still kept their increasing pace until his lips
Breathed at her shoulder; and almost spent,
The girl saw waves of a familiar river,
Her father's home, and in a trembling voice
Called, "Father, if your waters still hold charms
To save your daughter, cover with green earth
This body I wear too well," and as she spoke
A soaring drowsiness possessed her; growing
In earth she stood, white thighs embraced by
        climbing
Bark, her white arms branches, her fair head swaying
In a cloud of leaves; all that was Daphne bowed
In the stirring of the wind, the glittering green
Leaf twined within her hair and she was laurel.

     Even now Phoebus embraced the lovely tree
Whose heart he felt still beating in its side;
He stroked its branches, kissed the sprouting bark,
And as the tree still seemed to sway, to shudder
At his touch, Apollo whispered, "Daphne,
Who cannot be my wife must be the seal,
The sign of all I own, immortal leaf
Twined in my hair as hers, and by this sign
My constant love, my honour shall be shown:
When Roman captains home from victory
Ride with the Legions up Capitoline,
Their heads will shine with laurels and wherever
The Augustus sets his gates, plain or frontier,
Or Roman city wall, the bronze oak leaf
And the green-pointed laurel shall guard the portal
And grace the Roman crown." As Phoebus spoke,
The laurel shook her branches and seemed to bow
A timid blessing on her lover's pleasure.

IO AND JOVE

In Thessaly there is a shaded valley
Called Tempe, with steep groves on every hill;
It is where the river Peneus breaks in foam
At Pindus' foot: and down the mountain's side
The water courses, tossing its spray in clouds
Over tallest trees. Even in distant plains
The roaring echoes of the ceaseless river
Pour from cliffside and cave. Here in the dark
Of hanging rocks, The Father of the Waters,
Old Peneus, sits in court directing colleges
Of greenhaired girls who haunt the forests,
Who lead lost travellers to the banks of rivers
Which he commands. First to his dark throne came
The waters of his land: the poplar-shaded
River Sperchios, Dashing Enipeus,
White-crested Apidanus and the two languid
Streams, Amphrysos and River Aeas;
At last no matter which way they had run
Or leaped or wandered wearily to sea,
All rivers came; they came to celebrate
Or weep the fate of Daphne. Yet Inachus
Deep in his darkest cave did not arrive;
He wept and swelled the waters with his tears,
He wept for Io his lost child, his daughter.
Nor did he know if she still walked the earth,
Or wandered underground among the shades;
Yet gone she was, perhaps dropped into nowhere,
Darker than Hades and less sure than death.

Now it so happened that all-seeing Jove
Saw Io walking by her father's stream
And said, "O lovely child, and you a virgin!
Such beauty merits the rewards of Jove
As well as making mortal husbands happy.
Young lady, take a rest beneath the trees"—
He pointed to a deep grove in the forest—
"The noonday heat destroys a fair complexion.
Why not lie down? And if you fear to walk

Where lions tread, I'll go with you, even in
Dark woods; a god's protection is what you need,
Nor am I of the common race of gods:
I hold a sceptre, it is I who throw
The flashing thunderbolt across the sky—
You must not run away—" But Io ran,
Steering her way across the fields of Lerna,
Until she entered the shady groves of Lyrcea,
And there, cloaked by a sudden thundercloud,
Jove overcame her scruples and her flight.

   As Io fell Juno looked down at Argos
And from clear skies witnessed a single cloud
Bring midnight into noon. Something was wrong;
The cloud was neither fog nor river mist,
But of an origin that could have been divine,
A cause that made her think of Jove, his habits
Of deception, his craftiness, which well
She knew even before this hour. She glanced
Through heaven and he was gone. "Either," she said,
"My mind's at fault, or I'm betrayed," and slipping
Out of aether dropped to earth where she dismissed
The clouds. But thoughtful Jove felt the arrival
Of Juno's spirit in the air, and changed the girl
Into a milk-white cow (even as cow the child
Was beautiful) and Juno gazing at her
Half admitted the creature's charms—then quickly,
As though she questioned nothing else, she asked
The creature's breed, and why it came,
And Jove to close discussion briefly lied:
"This cow is a surprise, a gift of earth—"
Said Juno, "Why not give the gift to me?
It's very pretty." How could he refuse?
And if he did there would be further questions,
More explanations; the cow would then seem
Other than merely cow, more valuable
Perhaps. The ethics of the case, shame, love,
Poor Io's plight—and what did Juno know
Or half suspect?—disturbed him. Jove knew
That she, both wife and sister, knew him well.

Though her unhappy rival was hers to keep
Queen Juno also had a troubled mind:
What would Jove turn to next? Better, she thought,
To give the creature to Arestor's son,
The frightful Argos whose unnatural head
Shone with a hundred eyes, a perfect jailer
For man or beast: the hundred eyes took turns
At staring wide awake in pairs, and two
At falling off to sleep; no matter how or
Where he stood he gazed at Io; even when
His back was turned, he held his prisoner
In sight and in his care. By day the monster
Let her graze, but at each sunset drove her,
Haltered, half starved, weary, to evening diets
Of withered leaves, stale drink—and off to bed
He plunged the creature on sharp stones and clay.
Whenever she tried to stretch her arms toward Argos,
Her arms were forelegs and her weeping voice
Was very like the moaning of a cow
Which frightened her and had no charms for Argos;
At times she wandered where her father's river
Winds through the fields, where once on innocent
Days she walked and played, and now looking
Down as in a mirror she saw great horns
Above her ears and saw a great mouth open
That was her mouth; the apparition ran
And was the shadow beneath her feet, fear
Following fear. Nor did her sisters know
That it was she who walked beside them, nor
Did her father guess that she, the creature
Whom they caressed, was Io, his hand kissed
By her thick tongue. If only she could speak,
Tell him her name, her story—he could save her!
At last with one hoof spelling words in dust,
Her misadventures told, her father threw
His arms around her white neck. "Are you my daughter,
Am I unhappy me? Perhaps it would be better
Not to find you, however lost you were,
I looking for you everywhere on earth.
Must I be doomed to hear the speech of cattle,
And groans and sighs forever from my child,

The bull, her future husband, even my small,
But scarcely loved, by me at least, grandson?
—My house a stable for a herd of cows?
Nor shall death close his doors upon my grief,
Even my disgrace shall seem to be immortal!"
And as they wept aloud, rough, star-eyed Argos
Thrust Io from her father's side and drove
Her to a pasture far from home, where, seated
On a well-worn mountaintop, an easy throne,
He viewed the country with his searchlight eyes.

But now the stern director of heaven's laws
Had seen, had heard enough of Io's tears—
She, after all, was Ocean's fair granddaughter;
He called his son—and Maia's son as well—
And told the boy to see that watchful Argos
Would meet an early unexpected death.
Then Mercury, wing-shod and with a wand
Which as he waved it put his friends to sleep,
Took up his cap and with a step through air
Came down to earth. He dropped his wings, his cap,
But kept his wand, then, as a shepherd straying
A lonely road, he caught a few wild goats,
Kicked them in line, and as he led his flock
Piped an unearthly song. Argos who had
No ear for any kind of music was enchanted;
He called out, "Boy, whoever you may be,
Sit at my side. There is no better grass
That grows than this and the neat shade above it
Is wonderful for shepherds; why not sit down?"

With this as invitation Mercury
Talked like a metronome for hours; he piped,
He hummed, each tune a soporific
For dull ears and yet the hundred eyes,
Heavy or half closed, blinked at him, while some
Seemed blurred, bloodshot in lidless sleep, others
Were wide awake, more truculent than ever.
Argos was sleepy yet extremely curious;
He loved a story. "How was it," Argos asked,
"That reeds like yours, pipe music, were invented?"

THE PIPES OF PAN

    Then Mercury replied, "In Arcady
Among the Hamadryads of the mountains
There was a famous girl of Nonacris
Whose charms attracted many would-be lovers:
She had a birdlike voice; her sisters called
Her Syrinx—twittering and singing, the girl
Was difficult to trap, heard here or there,
She slipped through clutches of most nimble satyrs,
And eluded the pursuit through field and forest
Of rural gods. She envied, imitated
The virgin attitudes of Queen Diana—
Her dress, her manner, all but the goddess'
Golden bow was hers, and some few lovers
Mistook her for Diana; the chase continued.

    "One day as she returned from Lycaeus
God Pan, wreathed with his glittering pine needles,
Said to her, 'Lady—' but before we tell
His speech, there is a story: she did not listen
To him or anything, she ran, ran till
She caught herself up short at Ladon river,
The genial lazy river of sandy beaches;
There, shaken at the sight of Pan behind her,
She begged the sisters of the stream to change
A hamadryad's figure into less
Alluring shape to hasty gods like Pan,
Who as he seized her held a sheaf of reeds,
Which when he breathed his sighs at losing Syrinx
Echoed his loss with melancholy cries,
A tender music of bird-calls that pleased
His ear. 'Lady,' he said, 'this meeting, this
Embrace of wailing reeds and lips is ours.
Pipes are my pleasure; they are mine to keep.'
That's how it is that broken reeds when clipped
With sealing wax make plaintive music—they
Are honored by the name of Pan's fair lady."
Such was the legend that Mercury began
To tell to Argos when the hundred eyes
Swam into sleep; then as the magic wand

Waved them to deeper darkness, Mercury,
Fonder of action than of words, closed in,
His crooked sword hacked the bent neck as nod-
Ding Argos tumbled, crawled, bleeding, the head,
Tossed down the rocks, red cliffside stained with
A darker red. So Argos perished: fires,
All fires that were his glancing sight put out;
A single darkness filled his hundred eyes.

With jeweller's art the raging Juno—she
Was Saturn's daughter in her frenzy—set
The monster's eyes as stars in the tail feathers
Of her pet bird, the peacock, then inflamed
With further rages called the dread Erinyes,
Instructed one of them to haunt poor Io,
Until the creature, fear eating at its heart,
Ran mad by day, by night, throughout the world.
And not until she reached the blessed Nile
Were trials exhausted, and the curse grown weak
Permitted her to fall upon her knees,
To raise her face, her forelegs in the sand,
Until she saw the stars, to moo, to weep,
To moan at Jove and send her hopes to heaven.
Then Jove, his arms encircling Juno's neck,
Grew fond and whispered, "Pity Io, Juno,
That child shall never haunt my mind or bed;
I swear by Death that what I say is true,"
And Stygian waters splashed a benediction!

Then Juno's rage grew calm and Io looked
More human; whitish hair fell from her breasts,
Her sides; her horns receded into forehead;
Her round eyes slanted, and the broad mouth shaped
To lips, the lovely shoulders and fair arms
Returned, hoofs disappeared into shell-colored
Five-toed feet and slender, quickening hands—
No semblance of white heifer left in sight,
Except the very white of Io's body,
Standing erect in whiteness, the girl shaken
By what she might hear if she spoke: the moan,
The fearful lowing of thick-throated cattle;

Yet as she whispered, stammering at each word,
She heard through fears her half-forgotten voice.

IO AS ISIS

Today in Egypt, Io sought and prayed
Has priests in white and white-dressed worshippers;
In time she had a son, and rumour said
The boy Epaphus came from her dark meeting
With virile Jove. And as the story runs,
The boy and mother, both happy and adored,
Receive their homage in the city temples.
Epaphus had a friend named Phaethon,
Child of the Sun, of temper like his own,
Hasty, hot, proud, and both boys loved to talk.
Phaethon said that Phoebus was his father;
The grandson of Inachus, not impressed,
Said, "What a baby, what a crazy fool!
Do you believe all that your mother tells
Or wants to think is true? What fancy dreams
Some people have as fathers!" Phaethon,
Red, angry, and ashamed, ran to Clymene,
Told her of insults, saying, "What was worst,
Mother, I who talk faster, louder than that boy
Had nothing more to say; as you know me,
O Mother, I am always quick of temper
And with answers. If I was born of heaven
Let me know now, give me the right to say
Whose son I am." And by the head of his
Stepfather, Merops, and by his own head,
By torches of his sisters' wedding day,
He begged his mother for a certain sign
That he was Phoebus' son. Then Clymene,
Whether through Phaethon's pleas or by her own
Anger at slighted honour, raised her hands
To tall noon shining in the sky; she stared
Into the whitest fires of the sun: "By that
Great planet whose heat is my delight, who
As I turn to see him look at me, I
Swear my dearest son you are his son, son
Of the life-giving Sun whose light is day—

If I am lying, let darkness overcome me.
Yet where your father lives is not too far;
Go if you wish; the Sun will answer questions."
And as she spoke, the boy rose, almost ran,
For in his mind he walked the highest heavens,
Crossed Ethiopia, his native country,
Then India, which lies beneath the Sun;
With quickened breath he saw his father's palace.

# II

# BOOK II

Phaethon's Ride • Jove and the Arcadian Nymph • The Raven • Ocyrhoe • Mercury and Battus • Mercury and Herse • Jove and Europa

*Starting with the legend of Oedipus, there have been many versions of mother-son relationships, particularly in twentieth-century fiction. Current productions of* Hamlet *tend to stress the scenes between Hamlet and his mother, the guilty queen. There are relatively few memorable stories of father-son relationships, the first of which is the Homeric Ulysses-Telemachus story, so admirably reinterpreted by James Joyce in his* Ulysses. *The Biblical David and Absalom story is still another classic. Ovid's Phoebus Apollo–Phaëton story is of that line, and one of the best in classical literature. Phaëton's doubts as to his paternity, his need to settle them, his bright, impulsive temper, his wilfulness are signs of Ovid's genius in portraying character. No less so are the skills with which he shows a fatherly Phoebus Apollo, his indulgence to his son, and the futility of his warnings, which may be taken as Ovid's warm yet ironic commentary on the helplessness of an elder generation in teaching a younger generation anything. Ovid's Phoebus Apollo, both in his earlier pursuit of Daphne and in his grief over the loss of Phaëton, is less awe-inspiring, less godlike than the god whose arrows fall on Thebes to curse the reign of Oedipus in Sophocles' play. Ovid's Apollo shows something of the great distance between the religious depth of Sophoclean tragedy and the lighter, more domestic temper of Ovidian feeling.*

# BOOK II

The palace of the Sun rose up in columns
Of flaming gold and brass: ivory the ceiling,
And double palace doors were bright as mirrors
In silver light, and yet more valuable
Than gold and silver was the craft that made them.
Across their panels Vulcan carved the waters
That held mid-earth, its continents and islands
And sky above it, and in seas below
The dark gods: song-lipped Triton, ever shifting
Proteus, Aegaeon, his arms tossed round
The backs of two great whales; beside them, Doris
And her daughters, mermaids, some gliding
Through glassy waves, and other girls rock-seated
Sunning green hair while others as though racing
The spray on backs of fishes, each with her own
Gesture and look, were sisterly, of one
Large family of the sea. Then men and cities,
Girls of the forest, nymphs, and all the little
Provincial deities and on each panel
Above them wheeled the blazing sky, six signs
Of Zodiac on right and six on left.

When bright Clymene's son had stepped the stairs
Across the entrance of his father's palace,
The very fatherhood now placed in doubt
He faced his sire, but stepped back from the glare
That dazzled him: Phoebus in purple, glowing
With emeralds, and to his left and right
Stood Day, Month, Year, Century, and all
The Hours at equal distance from each other;
Then early Spring with flowers in his hair,
And naked Summer with a wreath of wheat,

31

Autumn, whose feet were stained with new-pressed wine,
Winter, whose white hair was an icy crown.

The Sun sat in the center of the hall;
His eyes glanced everywhere and fixed the boy
Who stood trembling at the new world he saw,
To whom Sun said, "Why here, Phaethon?
What do you look for in my aethereal chambers?
To meet a father? You, the son no father
Should deny?" The boy said, "O All-Seeing
Light of this great world, O Father Phoebus
(If you will give me right to call you so)
If Clymene does not conceal an error
In sinful dark, in what she hopes is true
O let me clean my spirit of all doubt,
Give me the signature of what I am."
At this the Sun took off his blinding crown,
Called the boy to him, embraced him, said,
"You've every right my son to be my son;
Your birth was of my making and your mother,
The truthful Clymene could not speak wrong;
You need not doubt my lips. Ask any favour
My hand can give—by all the lakes of Hades,
Which I have never seen, yet gods swear by them,
The gift is yours to take." No sooner said,
And the quick boy replied, "Give me your chariot
To drive Sun's wild winged horses through a day."

Then the Sun feared the promise he had made.
Four times he shook his fiery golden hair;
"Your words prove mine have been too quickly said,
I would be happy to unsay them now,
For what you ask is the one gift that I
Would keep beyond your reach; let me attempt
To unpersuade you of your wish, a dangerous one
That asks too much, too far beyond your strength,
Or any boy's. Your destiny is mortal;
What you would do, or ignorantly try
To do, only divine skill, power, art
Can hope to do. Though each god has his charms,
Great Jove who with his right hand hurls dread thunder

Through sky and air can scarcely ride with me—
And who in heaven's more powerful than Jove?
At first the way is steep where even through
Refreshing dawn, horse, rider hardly climb;
Even mid-heaven's road is perilous high
Where one look downward onto earth and sea
Unmans my heart, and as the course declines
A sharp, a precipitous drop, a clifflike fall
Where hand and eye must be both firm and clever:
Tethys, who greets me at the bottom of her waters,
Fears I might tip headfirst into her sea—
This while the firmament circles round forever
And carries with it distant stars and planets
At whirling, blinding speed which mazes all
But me, who with a wary hand drive clean
Through the swift courses of the sky. But you?
Can you ride counter to the whirling axis
Of space, of sky, and yet ride clear? Perhaps
You dream unearthly forests on your path:
Cities of gods, and temples pouring gifts,
Yet all the way is filled with hidden terror,
And if you hold the road, the horned Bull,
The enchanted Archer, the open mouth
Of the wild Lion, Scorpion and Crab
With hairy, knifelike tails, claws reaching
Each against each, to meet, to face the other,
Are in your way. Nor then are horses easy
To control: when they grow hot the fires leap
Within their hearts, stream from their nostrils, lips,
And even I can scarcely hold the reins
To steer the fiery eyes and foaming bit.
Then let me warn you, Phaethon my son:
My yielding to your wish looks like your death—
And there is time for you to change your mind—
Do you need further proof that you are mine?
The true sign is my fear: look in my face;
And if you could, look in my heart, see there
A father's anxious blood and passion.
If you could understand, O son! Turn here,
See all the riches of the world, the light
Of land, sea, sky within your eyes—take all,

Take anything, nothing shall be denied,
Except what you desire, which if you knew
It is a curse, my Phaethon, and not
The honour and the hope within your mind.
What are these arms around my neck, my fool,
My innocent? You must not doubt my word
(Which I have sworn to grant you by Death's waters).
My promise holds—but make a wiser wish!"

His father's sermon closed, yet Phaethon
Rejected all of it and burned to drive
His father's chariot. Then Phoebus took him
To work of art from Vulcan's hands: swift axles
Of gold, of gold the harness, beam, and golden
Tires on silver-spokèd wheels, the cross-piece
Set with topaz, chrysolite, their eyes lit
By the restless, gleaming light of Phoebus' hair.

While eager Phaethon gazed at Vulcan's craft,
Aurora, sleepless in the waking dawn,
Swung wide her purple gates and rose-tipped light
Glowed through her stairs and halls; retreating stars
Were closed in ranks by Lucifer who vanished
Even from his watchtower in the morning sky.

When Titan saw that Lucifer had gone,
The world rose-tinted light, and thin moon's
Crescent fading into sky, he called the speeding
Hours to dress his team, which they, quick goddesses,
Had done at once and led the horses, fed
With ambrosia and breathing fire, from
Their vaulted stalls, and slipped over their heads
The jangling bridles. Then Phoebus stroked
His son's face with a sacred balm, a shield
Against the tearing flames; and as he set
His blazing crown on the boy's head, he sighed
As though his heart held prophecy of sorrow.
"If you cannot construe a parent's warning,
Hear these plain words, my son: forget the whip,
But hold the reins with all your strength; these horses
Race at their will; the difficult art is
To control their speed. Do not take the direct

Road through Five Zones of sky, but cut obliquely
In a wide arc within the Three Zones, skirting
South Heaven and Far North: this is your course;
You'll see trails left by my own chariot wheels.
So that both earth and sky take equal heat,
Ride then the middle of the road, don't sway too far
Toward Writhing Serpent on the right, nor left
Where Altar swings low in the heavens, steer
Clean between the two. Fortuna save you!
May she be at your side to guide you better
Than you lead yourself. Even as I speak
Mist-carrying night falls to the Western Isles.
We wait no longer; we are called to go.
See how Aurora shines and shadows vanish;
Pick up the reins, or if your will has changed,
Take my advice and not my chariot,
Even before you mount, since you are still on earth,
The folly of your desire may be undone,
And you, secure, shall see *me* light the world."

But the mad boy had leaped into the cart;
Cheerful, erect, he held the glowing reins
And thanked his anxious father for the gift.

Meanwhile the Sun's wild horses, Pyrois,
Eous, Aethon, and the fourth, Phlegon,
Filled all the air with fiery whinnying
And with impatient hoofs stormed at the bars
Which Tethys, mindless of her grandson's fate,
Dropped to the ground. The way had opened
Into sky and space: swifter than East Wind
Rising behind their course, the horses flew,
Wing-spread and flying feet through cloud and wind.
Nor could the horses feel the chariot's weight;
Lighter than it had ever been before
It rocked behind them as round-bottomed boats
Unballasted dip to the waves,
Now high, an empty carriage raised in the air.

Weightless the horses flared, flying from their
Accustomed course, their fear-struck driver, shaken
Knew neither how to rein them, nor the road

Beneath their feet (which even had he known
He could not steer the horses in their flight).
Now for the first time since the world began
The circuit of the frozen Northern Bears
Glowed with sun's heat, the creatures almost leaped
(Though they could not) into forbidden seas.
Then the cold Serpent at the ice-bound Pole
Grew mad with fire and it was said that
Boötes, herdsman of the Northern skies,
Slow as he was, and hampered by his cart,
Sweated with heat and fear and ran away.

When the unlucky Phaethon looked down
From the top rim of heaven to small and far
Lands under him, he turned weak, pale, knees shaking,
And, in the blazing light, dark filled his eyes:
He wished he had not known his father's horses,
Nor who his father was, he wished undone
His prayer, his hope—he wished himself to be
The son of Merops. And it was as though
The boy were in a boat, piercing the storm,
As though its futile pilot dropped the rudder
And gave the ship to sail the will of gods.
What could he do? Although much of his way
Unrolled behind him, there were greater reaches
Of sky to go; he tried to measure both,
Forward to West where he was fated never
To arrive, backward to East—mazed, helpless,
He neither held the reins nor let them go,
Nor could he call the horses by their names.
Then in quick terror he saw sky's scattered islands,
Where monsters rise: Scorpion's arms and tail
Opening, closing across two regions of
The Zodiac itself; he saw the creature
Black, shining with poisoned sweat, about to sting
With arched and pointed tail. Then Phaethon,
Numbed, chilled, and broken, dropped the reins.

As the reins fell across their flanks the horses
Broke from their course; riderless charging, wild,
Wherever their desire turned, they followed,

Flaming against the deep-set stars and tossing
Their chariot through wilderness of air.
Up to the top of heaven they blazed, then down
Almost to earth. The Moon in wonder saw
Her brother's chargers race beneath her own,
Break smoking through the clouds, the earth in flames,
Mountains touched first, hills, plateaus, plains,
The dry earth canyon-split, the fields spread white
In ashes; trees, leaves were branches of the flames
While miles of grain were fuel for their own fires—
But these were the lesser losses I regret.
The great walled cities perished; nations fell,
Forests and mountains fed each other's flames:
Athos on fire, Taurus and Tmolus, then Oete,
And famous springs of Ida now burned dry,
And Helicon where Muses danced and sang,
And the pre-Orphic woods of Thessaly,
Aetna a fire of redoubled flames, twin-horned
Parnassus, Eryx, Cynthus, Othrys, and
Rhodope which had lost its snow, Mimas,
Dindyma, Mycale, and sacred Cithaeron—
Nor did its natural cold save Scythia—
Caucasus burned, Ossa and Pindus, and
Taller than both, Olympus, and the sky-riding
Alps and the cloud-carrying Apennines.

Then Phaethon looked down on earth in flames,
Nor could endure them, for the air he breathed
Was like the breath of well-deep furnaces,
His chariot white-hot beneath his feet;
Blinded by flying cinders, ashes, he
Wore a grey pall of smoke and in his darkness
Knew neither his direction nor the will
Of flying feet that drove him anywhere.

And in that hour (so some would think) the creatures
Of Africa turned black, their thick blood drawn
To the surface of the skin. Then Libya
Became a desert where wild flames ate the dew,
Even the rain that swept across her grasses;
Nymphs wept their losses of bright lakes and fountains

Into disheveled hair while Boethia
Wept for Dirce, Argos, Amymone,
And Corinth for her lost Pirenian Spring—
Nor were the broadest rivers left unflamed:
Wide Tanais boiled and steamed, Old Peneus,
Mysian Caicus, rapid Ismenus,
Arcadian Erymanthus, Xanthus—river
That was to burn again when Troy had fallen—
Yellow Lycormas, playful blue Meander,
Thracian Melas and Laconian Eurotas;
And fire tossed on Babylon's Euphrates,
Fire on Orontes and rapid Thermodon
And on the Ganges, Phasis, and the Hister;
Alpheus boiled and banks of Spercheos
Were streamed with fire while the golden sands
Of Tagus melted in flames. And swans
Who swam Arcadian streams in gliding peace
Were singed with fires in the channels of Cayster.
Nile ran in terror to the end of earth
To hide its head which now is still unseen;
Its seven mouths fell open, filled with dust,
The seven beds scorched dry, the same fate falling
On Thracian rivers, Hebrus and Strymon,
And rivers of the West, Rhine, Rhone, and Po—
Tiber, whose promise was to rule the world.
Earth-wide, great canyons opened to the sun,
And to the fears of Pluto and his queen,
The sky shed flares of light throughout their
        kingdom;
The seas shrank into sand and from their waters
The hidden mountains rose and Eastern islands
Came where the waves had vanished. There fish dived
        down
To deepest ocean's floor and dolphins feared
To leap the fiery air. On glowing waves
With bellies to the sky dead sea cows floated;
And it was rumoured Nereus, Doris fled,
Sweltered with all their daughters in a cave;
And three times Neptune tried to raise his arms,
His glorious head above the waves, three times
Fell back, nor could he face the flaming air.

Yet Ancient Earth, child-bearer of all things
Was not subdued, surrounded as she was
By deep and shrinking seas and by her rivers
That sank to darkest wells down to her womb;
Though black with heat and soot she raised her face,
And as she lifted hands to shield her eyes,
She shrank back lower than her usual place
While all things shook as though the world would break.
She cried aloud, "O greatest of the gods!
Is this your will and is this my reward?
Why does your lightning cease? If this
Is death by fire, then let your bolt of fire
Bring death to me so I may suffer you
To cause my death; even now I scarcely speak—"
For flames and smoke had filled her mouth, her throat.
"See my charred hair, ashes are in my eyes,
Across my face; have I earned this for my
Fertility? For me who wear the scars
Of plough and spade? And each year torn and delved
That grass may grow for cattle, grain for men,
And myrrh placed on the altars of the gods?
It may be I deserve an easy death,
But how or why has Sea, your brother, erred?
And why has water, fallen to his share
As third of our estate, dwindled to nothing
And farther from the sky? If you have no
Concern for him nor me, look how your heavens
Blaze from pole to pole—if fire consumes them
The very universe will fall to dust.
In pain, in worry, Atlas almost fails
To balance world's hot axis on his shoulders;
If sea, land, and celestial heavens fall,
The very world we live in falls to dust,
Then we return to Chaos. Save, O Lord,
The charred remains of our poor Universe."

Earth spoke, then stopped, for she no longer
Faced intolerable heat, but crept in
The darkest caverns toward the Underworld.
Then Jove, father of all things, called the gods—
Particularly those who made and guarded

Phoebus' chariot—to be his witness,
To let them see his need to save the world;
He mounted to the highest hill of heaven
From where it was his pleasure to stir lightning
Among great clouds that darken over earth,
But now were empty of all clouds and rain.
Jove's thunder blazed and from his hand a shaft
Poured lightning aimed at Phaethon that burst
Behind his ear and blasted him from sky
And out of cart and out of life as well;
Jove's lightning had quenched fire with greater fire
And Sun's wild team broke harness, bit and rein,
Fragments of chariot falling from the sky,
Axle and torn wheel scattered on hill and plain.

   But Phaethon, fire pouring through fiery hair,
Sailed earthward through clear skies as though he were
A star that does not fall, yet seems to fall
Through long horizons of the quiet air.
Far from his home he fell, across the globe
Where River Eridanus cooled his face.
There Naiads of the West took his charred body
Still hot with smoking flames of the forked bolt
To rest, with these carved words upon his tomb:
HERE PHAETHON LIES WHO DROVE HIS FATHER'S CAR;
THOUGH HE FAILED GREATLY, YET HE VENTURED MORE.

   Then in black grief the Father cloaked his face
And it was said that one day's hours travelled
Without the sun. The burning Earth gave light,
And even in disaster served the world.
When she had said all that grief's lips could say,
Clymene with torn breast walked over earth
Searching the limbs, the bones of Phaethon,
And by a river in a distant land she found them,
Where as she threw herself upon the tomb
She curved her breast against his name in stone
And warmed it with her tears. Then all her daughters
Poured futile tears in memory of their brother,
Beating their naked breasts and calling out

The name of Phaethon by night, by day,
Who cannot hear their cries above his tomb.
Four times the Moon had changed her slender horns
Into a globe of light, yet they rained tears
As though tears were the habit that they wore
And weeping was their only cause to live.
At last the eldest daughter, Phaethusa
Cried, as she walked the grave, her feet grew numb,
And when bright Lampetia came to help her
She too felt rooted into clay. A third sister
Who tore her hair clutched leaves; another found
Her ankles sheathed in wood, another that
Her arms became long branches. As they gazed,
They saw the wooded bark close round their thighs
And creeping up close uterus and belly,
Breast and shoulder, even to fingertips
Of leafy hands; only their lips were free
To call their mother. And what could this
Mad woman do but run to each, to press
Each fading pair of lips against her own?
Or more, if not enough, tear at the bark,
Break twigs where drops of blood streamed from each
              wound,
And each as she was torn cried, "Mother, save
Me, Mother, it is my body that you tear
Within the tree, O Mother, now farewell!"
As bark closed over lips their tears still ran,
Tears that were drops of amber in the sun
Fallen from green sides and branches of young trees,
To flow in clearest waters of the river
And later worn as jewels by Roman brides.

   Cycnus, son of Sthenelus saw these marvels
Of amber tears. Though by his mother's blood
He was a cousin of Phaethon himself
His love for him was deeper than his kinship;
Though he was King of Liguria's province,
Its peoples, its broad lands and great walled cities,
He left his throne to wander, wailing, sighing
Along the Po and through the tear-rained forest

Made darker by the sisters turned to trees.
There as he walked his voice grew thin and shrill,
White feathers sprouted through his hair, his neck
Arched high above his collarbone and webbed
Membrane grew thick between his rose-tipped fingers,
Wings fell across his sides, and where his lips were
Came a blunt beak, and Cycnus was a new
Thing called a swan, a creature who remembered
Jove's burning thunderbolt, unjustly fired
At falling Phaethon. Therefore he feared
The higher heavens and sought out stagnant streams,
Pools, quiet lakes, and, since he hated fire,
He took to shaded waters for his home.

    Meanwhile the father of dead Phaethon
Sat in funereal darkness, dark as when
His face is covered by eclipse; he turned
Hate on himself and on the light of day
And gave his soul to sorrow and grief's anger
And would not, could not stir to light the world.
"I have done enough," he cried. "From the beginning
Of time my fate has been long restlessness;
I tire of labor that shall never end;
Let him who will drive daily teams of light,
And if none cares to, then let Jove take reins,
And put aside the blazing thundershaft
Which robs the father of his son—then he
Shall learn to test the strength, the will,
The temper of my swift fire-footed horses,
Shall learn that he who fails to steer them well
Should never earn death for his punishment."

    As the Sun spoke the gods surrounded him,
Begged, pleaded with him not to blind the world
With an eternal night, and Jove, half stately,
Half apologetic, blamed his intemperate
Lightning shaft and in his kingly manner
Added a threat or two. Then Phoebus harnessed
His wild team whose limbs still shook with fear
And in his grief and fury lashed their sides
Calling hate upon them for his dear son's death.

JOVE AND THE ARCADIAN NYMPH

    Then Jove, omnipotent father, paced his rounds
Testing the firmament where fire had scorched
The ramparts of high heaven; seeing all
Was firm, he looked down at the earth and over
The works of Man. Arcadia had become
His special care: he made her springs, her
Fountains, rivers waken to life again,
Her grass to grow, leaves on her trees to open—
Till forests wore again their usual green.
And as he took his tour of reparation
He saw a girl, Arcadian Callisto,
And at one glance heat flamed within his bones.
No need for her to make herself a garment
Of fine-spun wool or dress her hair as if
She wore a crown, her rough cloak fastened by
A brooch, her long hair looped and held
In a white twist of cloth; her hand grasped either
A strung bow or a burnished spear: she came
As one of Phoebe's girls-at-arms, nor in
That company was any girl more honored.

    Now as the Sun rose to his noonday heat
She sought the darkest grove of an old forest:
She dropped her arrows and unstrung her bow,
Sank to the grass resting her head against
The painted quiver. Jove saw how wearily
She fell and that she was alone. "Surely,"
He murmured, "Wife will never learn of this,
My latest masquerade, and if she does,
The girl is worth the threat of Juno's anger."
As quick as thought he wore Diana's mask,
Her face, her dress, and softly said, "O dearest
Girl of all my company where did *you*
Follow the chase today?" The girl rose, saying
"Hail, goddess whose deep spell on me is greater
Than Jove's himself, I swear, though he may hear."
Jove laughed at being preferred above himself,
And gave the girl, not as a virgin kisses,
But tongue to tongue, a most immoderate kiss;

And as she told him which forest she had travelled
He broke her narrative with an embrace
Which by betraying her revealed himself.
She fought against him with a woman's valour
(O Saturn's daughter, had you seen her, even
You would have been a little sympathetic)
But how could anyone, much less a girl,
Withstand the will of Jove? He had his way
And vanished in the sky while she, because
The forest knew her fall, hated the trees
That were her witnesses and as she walked
Almost forgot her painted sheaf of arrows,
Even the branch where she had hung her bow.

But look! Diana with her troop of girls
Came winding round the sides of Maenalus,
Showing the prizes of the chase. She saw
Our heroine and called aloud; at first
The girl ran from her, fearing Jove Diana
Or Diana Jove, but when her dearest
Friends came near she dropped behind them following
Their trail. How hard it was not to show signs
Of guilt! The girl walked slowly with her eyes
To earth, not as she used to stride, the first
Of girls close to her goddess. Her flushed face
And all she did not say told what she felt—
And if Diana had not been a virgin
She would have seen ten hundred ways the girl
Betrayed herself—in ways, was said, the others
Knew too well. Day passed and the horned moon
Grew to a glowing circle nine times over,
When an hour after the hunt, Diana, languid
With heat of sun, strolled to a brook which poured
Clear waters over sand. In that green shade,
The place delighted her; as she stepped in
She called her girls, "Off with your clothes, my dears.
Since no one's here to see us, we shall bathe."
The Arcadian girl flushed red: as others stripped
She stood aside till they undressed her; even
Then she tried to cover her womb with her

Two hands, and in her terror heard the cry,
"You shall not soil our sacred waters, leave us,"
And with these words the goddess banished her.

Throughout this time the Thunderer's wary wife
Knew the condition of her husband's mistress,
Yet waited for the moment of revenge;
Now it was ripe (and sharp enough to give
A point to Juno's hate); Arcas was born,
The child of Jove's Arcadian adventure.
Therefore she turned a savage eye and mind
Upon the girl and said, "Well, my adulteress,
You did no less than make my injury public;
Here is your son, the very living proof
Of Jove's decline from grace to infamy.
And you shall not go free; that shapely body
That you and Jove loved all too well shall vanish."
With this she seized the girl's forelocks and threw
Her, face to earth; and as the girl raised hands
To plead for mercy, her arms were covered
With bristling black hair, her hands were feet, tipped
By their crooked nails; the lips that Jove once praised
Became a pair of wide, misshapen jaws.
And to prevent her prayers from reaching heaven
Her gift of speech was ripped away and from her throat
Came guttural noises horrible to hear:
Though her emotions were of human kind,
She was a bear, and as she lifted hands
(Paws rather) in grief, in sorrow, though she
Could not say her thoughts, she felt Jove showed her
Lack of gratitude. O there were many times
She feared to sleep in empty wooded coverts;
Restless she walked in sight of her old home,
And paced the meadows that were once her own;
O many days she ran through rocky trails
Pursued by hunters and the call of hounds,
And, though a huntress, fearful of the chase.
Too often she forgot her beastlike being
And trembled as she looked at other bears
That wandered at their will on mountainsides;

Even a wolf would startle all her fears—
And this despite her father, Lycaon,
Who, as a wolf himself, ran with the pack.

Now Lycaon's grandson reached his fifteenth year
And Arcas, ignorant of his mother's fate,
Hunted wild creatures and sought out their lairs;
His nets were woven round Arcadian forests
Where on a day he came upon his mother,
Who looked at him as if she knew him well.
He stepped back from the staring eyes that held him,
Eyes that seemed fixed to pierce his gaze forever,
And with that look a wordless fear possessed him.
He poised a deadly spear aimed at her heart,
But the Omnipotent Father of us all
Held back the thrust, and then, as though his power
Was of the invisible vortex of the wind,
He swept up mother and son into the heavens
And made them neighbouring companies of stars.

When she beheld Jove's mistress in the skies
Glittering against the night, pale Juno's rage
Swelled hot, and like a meteor in flight
She dropped to Tethys and to ancient
Oceanus, two elders of the sea
To whom the gods gave reverence and awe.
They asked her why she came and she replied,
"Why do you question me, the Queen of Heaven,
While still another queen shines in the sky?
Say I am liar, if tonight you do not see
New constellations rising in the dark,
That brilliance which usurps my place in heaven
Of the high north, the farthest, shortest circle
That turns above the pole. With this in sight
Who cares to worship Juno, hold me in awe?
Or who should fear my rage? I seem to glory
Those whom I destroy; what great things rise from
Deeds that I have done. And she I whipped, banned out of
Human shape is now a goddess! Such is
The punishment I give to enemies,
Such the great power for which my name is known.

As in the case of Io, Jove has only
To give the girl freedom from bestial state,
Restore her shapeliness—since I am fallen,
What shall prevent him now from leading her
Into my bed, and Jove himself from being
Her husband and Lycaon's son-in-law?
If this dishonour to your adopted child
Stirs in your hearts, forbid these bearlike
Beings in the stars to wade your waters,
Shut out the creatures who at cost of sin
Shine down from heaven, nor allow that whore
To taint the waters of your sacred streams."

THE RAVEN

The sea gods gave consent to Juno's wish,
And she, great Saturn's daughter, mounted to
Her graceful chariot that veered and floated
Through upper air, drawn by her glittering birds,
Her peacocks, whose tail feathers had been reset
(And not so long ago) with Argos' eyes.
About that time the raven changed his color
From white to black, he who had once been silver-
White as the doves, as geese whose wakeful cries
Were destined to rescue Rome, as white as
River-loving swans. But his tongue doomed him.
The chattering bird was everything not white.

In Thessaly no girl grew half as fair
As pretty young Coronis of Larissa;
As long as she was chaste or thought to be,
O God of Delphi, then the girl was pleasure
In your eyes. But her unfaithfulness
Was closely witnessed by Apollo's bird
Who ran, or rather flew, to tell his master.
The crow came after him on flapping wings
To ask him what was cause of all the hurry,
And when he heard the reason, he replied,
"What futile flight! Do not refuse to hear
My timely warning. Think what I used to be,
Look at me now and find that good intentions

Worked me ill: One day a child was born, his name,
Erichthonius, without a mother.
Pallas concealed him in a box of woven willows
And gave it to three daughters of old Cecrops—
Instructions not to look into her secret!
I hid within the dense yet small-leaved branches
Of a tall elm to see what they would do.
Two girls, Pendrosos and Herse, stood guard
Above the box until Aglauros called
Her sisters timid and ripped off the lid;
They saw a child who seemed to be half dragon!
I told Minerva what the girls had done,
And I, who was still then her favourite bird,
Was sent among the black birds of the night!
Let my disgrace warn creatures of the air
To talk less—if they wish to outwit trouble.
Yet she chose me to be her counselor;
Go, ask Minerva, though she's furious
At me now and very angry, yet she
Will not deny it. My story is well known,
For I was once a princess, daughter of
A famous king, Coroneus of Phocis
(Hear me, nor turn aside); rich noblemen
Had hopes to marry me. But too much beauty
Was the cause of my undoing. One day
I took my lonely walk along the beach,
Pacing the sands; there Neptune looked at me
And was all heat; he begged, he pleaded, then
When smooth words failed, tried force, and I, distracted,
Ran away, the beach behind me, over dune
And hollow until I almost fell from
Weariness into soft sand. I called aloud
On men and gods to save me, and my cries
Reached no mortal ear. Only a virgin
Goddess heard a virgin's prayer; she it was
Who rescued me. And as I lifted up
My arms to heaven I saw them grow like
Shadows of whitest feathers in the air,
And as I turned to toss my stole aside
My feathered shoulders were a pair of wings,
And feathers struck their roots within my flesh,

Nor could I beat my naked breasts with hands,
For both had vanished. As I tried to run,
I floated above sand, above the earth,
And rising lightly flew to higher air,
And at Minerva's side was her chaste friend.
But what is this to me if Nyctimene,
Changed to an owl for her dark sins, has taken
My place of honour at Minerva's court?
You heard what things were said of her at Lesbos—
That Nyctimene shared her father's bed?
And though she is all owl she still remembers
Her guilt, her lust, and in her darkness flies
From sight of men and from the light of day,
Exiled by all who rule the brilliant sky."

The raven answered shortly, "Take your warning,
Its evil and whatever it may mean
Upon yourself; it is an empty omen,"
And went his way to tell his master how
He'd seen Coronis lying in the shade
And with her a young man of Thessaly.
When bright Apollo, god and lover, heard
This news, the laurels melted from his curls,
His face, his color paled, the plectra fluttered
From his hand, and as his heart flamed into
Growing rage, he snatched his usual weapons,
Strung taut his bow, aimed at and pierced the breast
That he so often held against his own.
Then as he drew his arrow from her heart,
And her white belly and thighs ran red with blood,
The girl groaned, "Phoebus, O this deepest thrust
Was well deserved, but first I should have given
The child beneath my heart his light of day,
For now we die as one." And with these words
Her life poured from her veins in blood, body
And limbs grown cold within the cold of death.

Her lover wept too late, too late for tears or
To undo the cruel act done: he hated self,
The self that heard her guilt, the self that fired
With rage, hated the raven who made him hear

The rumours of her sins which caused his anger
And his present grief, hated his bow, hated
His quick arrow and the hand that sped it.
He kissed the fallen girl and tried to force
A victory over fate, but now his arts
Of medicine were useless. When his caresses
Failed, when he at last caught glances of the red,
The glaring pyre that fires white limbs to ashes
(Though faces of the gods cannot shed tears)
His deep heart groaned, groans that the young cow utters
When in her sight the hammer falls—she hears
The blow—aimed at the right ear, through the skull
Of the unweaned calf. Then Phoebus poured sweet-
Smelling ointment on his dead love's breast
And for the last time held her in his arms;
Nor can he let her rest as honoured dead,
Nor bear the thought of his own son consumed
By the same fires that take his mother's body;
He tore the flame-wrapped child out of its womb
And took it to the cave of Centaur Chiron.
The raven, waiting praise for truthfulness,
Stood by, but Phoebus promptly banished him
To night, far from the haven of white birds.

OCYRHOE

Meanwhile Chiron was happily engaged
In rearing a young demigod and proud
Of the prestige that came with it, when look,
His daughter—she, whose hair was reddish gold,
Was also daughter of the nymph, Chariclo,
Whose mother gave the new-born girl to Chiron
Among the grasses near swift-flowing waters,
She who was called thereafter Ocyrhoe—
Arrived in view. And it was not enough
For her to learn her father's gifts of wisdom,
She knew the supernatural prophecies,
Nourished the frenzies that grew hot between
Her breasts and as their godlike fires flamed
She saw the child and spoke: "O blessed boy,
You shall give health and strength to all on earth;

Grow quickly as you can. On many a day
Poor mortal beings shall owe their lives to you,
Even lives among the shades lost underground;
Yet as you raise one figure from the dead,
The gods will learn how you defied their power,
Grandfather Jove will strike, and you, a god,
Shall be a lifeless body, then god again,
Twice-born by fate. And you, O dearest father,
By birth immortal, shall cry in agony
And wish to die, your body in the fires
Of the she-serpent's blood. Then, only then,
Shall the gods let you taste mortality
And the three Fates let fall your mortal thread."
Yet there was more to tell—and she drew breath
As deeply as her heart; she wept: "The Fates
Have silenced me; my speech is failing, and
The gift of prophecy is that much weaker
Than the swift rage of heaven that falls on me.
Even now I seem less human than I was:
The grass tempts me to eat; I see the pasture
Urging me to run; I feel a little like
My father's shape, marelike, four-footed—
But why this change? My father is half human."
Her voice began to murmur and to whine
Until her words were whinnyings and neighs;
Her arms touched earth and moved among the grasses;
Her hands closed into fists and rounded hoofs
Concealed her five-nailed fingers; her broad mouth
Stretched across her face, her neck grew longer;
The cloak that flowed behind her was a tail;
And shadowing the right side of her throat
Her hair was like a red roan's mane. Now she,
Completely changed in voice and figure, was
Another creature, given a new name.

### MERCURY AND BATTUS

    Chiron, the famous son of Philyra, wept
And pleaded through his tears for help from Delphi,
O Lord Apollo! Nor could the god undo
The will of Jove—even if he could, the god

Was out of hearing, and at that moment lived
At Elis, wandering across Massenian plains,
His dress a shepherd's cloak, his stick a sapling
Cut from a tree, his flute a shepherd's pipe
Of seven reeds in his left hand. His thoughts
Were thoughts of love so sweetly played (as it
Was said) his cattle went afield and drifted
Into Pylian meadows where Mercury,
The Atlantic Maia's son, had seen them
As if lost and with his natural cunning
Lured them among the trees and hid them there.
And no one saw the trick except an ancient
Of the fields called Battus, gamekeeper, servant
Of the noble Neleus; the old man guarded
The mares and stallions of his master's herd
And watched them well. Mercury feared his telling
What he saw. He beckoned him as if by
Sleight of hand, led him aside, whispered, "My friend,
Whoever you may be, whoever asks you
About the cattle roaming through these woods
Say nothing. Since politeness should not be
Neglected, take this plump cow for your own."
The old man took the gift quickly and said,
"Dear Stranger, you are safe; even that rock
Will tell a story before I speak a word—"
At which the old man pointed out a stone.
The son of Jove had seemed to disappear,
But actually he changed his voice and features,
And asked a question at the old man's side,
"My friend, have you seen any cattle here?
Now don't deny it, for they are thieves' cattle.
If you speak truth, you'll get a handsome bull
And a new cow." The old man, trapped by sight
Of double gifts, cried, "There they are, you'll see
Them under that tall hill." And there they were.
Mercury laughed, "Old scoundrel, you'd betray
Me to myself before my eyes." Then even
As he spoke the poor frail-hearted servant
Changed to a black flint, "touchstone" now so-called,
And treachery still stains the innocent stone.

MERCURY AND HERSE

As Mercury, gifted by the magic wand,
Rose up on levelled wings, he gazed upon
Munychian hills and plains, the country
Minerva loved, learned Lyceum,
Arboured walks and groves. It was the holiday
That feasted Pallas when her girls walked out
Bearing their secret gifts in flowered caskets,
Head-high, to fill her temple with their treasures;
The winged god saw them winding their way home,
And steered above them, not straight down, but swaying
In an arc, like the quick falcon, when it
Has seen the entrails of a fresh-killed ox
And fears to land because of priests that guard
The sacrifice, yet does not dare to leave;
Flapping his wings he floats above the prey.
That was the way the agile Mercury
Circled Athenian hills and atmosphere.
As Lucifer outshines the brighest stars,
And golden moonlight outshines Lucifer,
So Herse was the loveliest of girls
Set like a jewel within the sacred garland
That worshipped Pallas in their slow procession.
The son of Jove was shattered by her beauty
And in mid-air caught fire as from a shot
From a Balearic sling, white heat increasing
As it flies from earth to cloud. Then Mercury
Shifted his course, fell slightly, landed sheer,
Himself in undisguise—such is the faith
Of those who trust their beauty; yet he dressed
His hair, shaking the gold edge of his cloak
In view, his right hand held at proper stance
His wand which beckoned sleep or banished it,
And his winged sandals shone on slender feet.

Within fair Herse's home were three bed-chambers,
Trimmed rich with ivory and tortoise shell;
Pandrosos had the chamber on the right,
The left Aglauros, Herse's room the center.

Aglauros was the first to see the god;
She asked his name and why he honoured them.
The grandson of Pleione and of Atlas
Replied, "I am Jove's son, the one who carries
His father's messages through air, nor shall
I lie about the nature of my visit;
I want your grace to be my children's aunt
And all your blessings on your little sister;
I come to marry Herse; as her lover
I ask for your permission and good will."
Aglauros glanced at him with the same eyes
That narrowed when she saw Minerva's secret,
Told him that her good wishes had their weight
In gold and she would make him pay her price;
Her bargain struck, she showed him to the door.

At this, war's goddess turned her raging eyes
On Aglauros and breathed so deeply that
The shield across her breast trembled with heat.
She knew the girl had disobeyed her orders,
That she with unclean hands unlocked the secret
Of Lemnian's son, the child born motherless.
It seemed the girl would have her crooked way
With Mercury, friendship with him and bribes
To make her rich, a sister's gratitude.
At once Minerva went to Envy's cave,
A hovel, dark with blood, in a deep valley,
Hidden where no sun ventures, no wind stirs,
And night air falling with continual cold;
No fires were lit to temper rain and fog.
War's virgin stood aside, nor would she enter
That fouled dwelling, but clanged her spear against
Its sagging doors, which, swaying inward, showed
Envy at feast, eating great snakes and vipers,
A perfect diet for increase of venom.
The goddess, sick at the unholy sight,
Turned eyes away, while Envy, leaving scraps
Of half-chewed meats upon the floor, lunged
To her feet and shambled toward Minerva
Who stately stood in armour. Envy moaned,
Changing her face to suit Minerva's sigh,

Grew death-pale, and her body seemed to shrink,
Eyes wild, teeth thick with mold, gall dripping green
To breast, green from her tongue, for Envy never
Smiles unless she sees another's misery;
Envy is sleepless, her heart anxiety,
And at the sight of any man's success
She withers, is bitten, eats herself away.
Although Minerva hated what she saw
In the foul creature's face, she gave instructions,
Clipping her speech: "Make it your duty, woman,
To infect Aglauros, one of Cecrops' daughters,
So that your poison streams within her veins,"
And with this said, she thrust her spear to earth,
And swiftly, lightly vaulted back to heaven.

　　Squint-eyed old Envy saw the goddess vanish,
Nor could she bear to think of so much glory
Without inward whines and tears. She gathered
Up her stick grown thick with thorns, her dark cloak
As cloud on her shoulders, and sped straightly
Her errand. And where she walked all flowers died,
Grass perished, and blight ran over tops of
Highest trees, and as she breathed she tainted
The streets of peopled towns, even in homes.
At last Tritonia's city came to view,
City of art and peace and joy, since Envy
Could not find tears in others' eyes, hardly
Did she hold back her own. But when she came
Into Aglauros' chamber, she set to work
And did Minerva's will: with festered hands
She stroked Aglauros' breast, then placed within
Her heart a nest of thorns, then filled her nostrils,
Until it reached down bone and tissue, with black
Venomous breath. Then to make cause for grief,
Envy placed deep within Aglauros' mind
An image of the marriage yet to come,
As though it shone in magnifying mirrors—
Her sister and the naked god in bed;
At this Aglauros ate at her own heart,
Haggard by day, in misery by night;
As ice is glanced by stray beams of the sun

Slowly she tasted hate to waste away;
As fire smoulders in hidden heat beneath
Dank grasses, creeping to soot-blackened ashes
And self-devouring flames, so when she thought
Of Herse's happy hour, so she was eaten.
Rather than know the measure of Herse's joy,
She longed to die; often she almost told
Her stiff-necked father of Herse's pleasure
In a marriage bed. At last she sat herself
Across the threshold of her sister's room
As if to bar the door against the god.
When he arrived, soft words poured over her,
He begged, he pleaded, yet she answered, "No,
I will sit here until you go away."
"Then we shall keep our pact," said Mercury;
His wand had touched the door which opened wide,
And she who tried to rise felt motionless,
Nor could she stand, a dull weight holding
Her hips and thighs; and coldness like a spell
Came through her limbs that grew as pale as snow.
As cancer winds its roots throughout the body,
From sick vitals to the untouched and pure,
She felt the increasing cold creep to her heart
As if ice stopped her breath, nor could she speak;
Her throat had closed in stone, her face immobile,
And all of her a silent, bloodless image,
Stilled not in white, but rock, her soul stained black.

JOVE AND EUROPA

After the god had punished Cecrops' daughter
For blasphemy in deed and word and soul,
He left Athenian country far below him
And flew to heaven on his outstretched wings.
Where to the highest place his father drew him
In confidence, nor did he speak of love,
But said, "Dear son, the best of messengers,
And loyal to every lively whim of mine,
Slip down to earth at once into that land
Which views your mother's star from its left side;
(It is the place its countrymen call Sidon).

Once there, drive the king's cattle to seashore;
You'll find them grazing near the mountaintop."
No sooner said than done: as Jove commanded,
The cattle marched from mountain to the beach
Where the king's daughter had a common playground
With her Tyrian girls. Royal dignity
And love are seldom known to go to bed
Together—therefore the Father
Of all Gods whose right hand held a three-pronged
Thunderbolt, whose slightest nod was earthquake
Up to heaven, dropped his royal sceptre and
Became a bull. Speaking their tongue, he moved
Among the cows; more beautiful than they
Or other bulls, he strolled spring grasses,
White as the snow untouched by Southern rains
Or footprint on the ground, huge, silky muscles
At his neck and silvered dewlaps hanging,
Small horns as white as if a sculptor's hand
Had cut them out of pearl. And no one feared
His look; forehead and eye were gracefully
Benign. He was so portly, beautiful,
So easy, Agenor's daughter gazed at
Him in wonder. At first she was afraid
(Though he seemed gentle) to touch the creature—
Then she went to him with a gift of daisies
To his snow-white lips. He was all joy, tasting
The future as he kissed her hands, nor could he
Straightly control his love: he danced the grasses
And rolled his whiteness into golden sands.
Then when she came less shy, he gave his breast
To her caressing hands and let her garland
Even his dainty horns with new-plucked flowers.
The princess, innocent on whom she sat,
Climbed to his back; slowly the god stepped out
Into the shallows of the beach and with
False-footed softness took to sea, swimming
Against full tide, the girl his captured prize;
She, fearful, turned to shoreward, set one hand
On his broad back, the other held one horn,
Her dress behind her fluttered in the wind.

# III

# BOOK III

Cadmus • Actaeon • Semele • Tiresias • Echo and Narcissus • Pentheus and Bacchus

*The story of Narcissus and Ovid's recital of the dispute between Jove and Juno over the pleasures of making love have made Book III a famous point of reference in twentieth-century poetry. Paul Valéry's* Cantate du Narcisse *has revived the importance of the Narcissus legend and T. S. Eliot's quotation of the Jove-Juno dispute from Book III in a note to the Tiresias passage in* The Waste Land *has made Ovid's name familiar to nearly every college student in England and the United States. To the educated and sophisticated Roman the argument between Jove and Juno probably recalled gossip of bedroom disputes between Augustus and Livia. It was rumoured that the domineering Livia was frigid; the scene between Jove and Juno, particularly at the moment of her anger, could be read as a high-spirited burlesque, cleverly disguised, of similar scenes in the emperor's household. The plight of Echo, the unfortunate girl who was foolish enough to fall in love with Narcissus, is an Ovidian touch that needs no heavy pointing of a moral.*

# BOOK III

Even now Jove shed the image of a bull,
Confessed himself a god, and stepped ashore
On the beached mountainside of Crete,
This while Europa's father, ignorant
Of what fate fell upon his ravished daughter,
Sent his son Cadmus out to look for her,
Saying if he did not find her, exile
Would be his doom, a warning that was both
Pious and cursed. After Agenor's son
Went up and down the world (who can discover
A secret Jove conceals?) the boy, distraught,
Fearful of Father's anger, strayed from home
To be a stranger everywhere he turned.
Cadmus, a pilgrim, came to Phoebus' shrine
To ask Apollo's spirit where to live,
And Phoebus said, "Go to the countryside,
Where lonely in a field a white ox wanders,
One who has never led the crooked plough
Nor carried the bent yoke across her shoulders.
Go with her till she falls to rest in grass,
And in this place erect your city's walls,
Then to her honour call it Boeotia."
As soon as Cadmus stepped down from Parnassus
He saw the wandering ox who strolled alone
Unmarked by plough or halter. Thoughtfully
He kept in step behind her, singing praise
Beneath his breath to Phoebus who had shown
Him where to go. Meanwhile the beast had led him
Through shoals of Cephisus and past deserted
Plains of Panope, where she stood still and
Lifted her fair head up with wide-spread horns
As though they pierced the very veils of heaven,

61

Then filled the air with her deep cries; she turned
To look behind to see who followed her,
Then kneeled, then sank to rest upon sweet grasses.
Cadmus thanked heaven and bent to kiss the earth,
Such was his praise of unknown fields and mountains.

    With piety in mind Cadmus prepared
Duties to Jove and sent his men to look
For running waters, sacred springs and rills.
The men arrived upon a trackless forest
And deep within it, fast with underbrush,
A cave. There, through a rock-hung arc rushed its
Welled waters; and the place was shared by Mars'
Serpent who wore a golden plume, who as
He rolled his body thick with bile poured fire
From his eyes; flashed from his triple teeth
His three-pronged tongue. When the misfortunate
Tyrians stumbled here, they dipped their pitchers
Into the cave's well; the silence then became
A plangent darkness and a hissing terror
As sea-blue snake's long head rose from the cave
And into outer air. Water jugs and pitchers
Slipped from men's hands and blood ran chill and limbs
Were taken with cold palsy. Then as the serpent
Wheeled in glittering knots, at once he
Had become a great arc, swung more than half
His length in air, as though his eyes looked down
Over the forest. If it were possible
To see him at a glance, he was as high
As long, as sky's snake that shines at night
Between twin bears. Nor did he waste his time,
But fell on the Phoenicians, whether they
Ran or showed fight, stilled or held back by fear.
Some he killed outright with his forked tongue,
And some were crushed within his knotted tail,
Some lost their lives within his tainted breath.

    When sun at noon had narrowed shade on earth,
Cadmus began to miss his men and set out
To find where they had gone, or if they'd strayed:
His shield a lion's carcass, his arms a javelin

And iron-tipped spear—and better yet than these,
A hardy spirit—fit to enter deepest woods,
To see about him the poor bodies of his men,
And above them their victorious enemy,
Gorged with their entrails, eating at their wounds
With blood-wet tongue. Then Cadmus cried aloud,
"O naked dead, all friends grown true to me,
Your vengeance mine, or I shall die with you."
And as he spoke, his body swayed with weight
Of the great stone he hurled with his right hand—
A shot (that would have made thick walls collapse
And towers fall) struck the shrewd serpent, yet
The beast rose unharmed; his scales and dark skin
Were like sheets of iron. But these could not
Endure the javelin-thrust that pierced mid-length
His back, its iron shaft deep-bedded
In his side. The creature, wild with pain, reared
Up his head, saw where he suffered, bit at
The shaft, and, writhing as he eased the folds
Around it, drew it out, yet the sharp spear-
Head held fast within his spine, while greater
Heat waked fires in his rage. His throat grew large
With flooded veins, and white foam gushed and bubbled
At his black jaws. And as his scales scraped earth
A tearing sound grew everywhere, and foul
Dark odours like the breath of Hell through air.
The serpent wheeled in green and yellow rings
As high as trees, then rolling into floods
Like springtide rivers, his heavy breast tore down
The forest as he moved. Cadmus stepped back,
Took up the serpent's rushes at his shield,
The lion's skin, but thrust his spear into
The serpent's mouth; the beast in rage clamped down
The iron bit between his teeth, yet could not
Break it, then his black throat began to bleed
And green grass at his feet grew red with blood.
Because the beast retreated at each spear-
Thrust the wound was shallow, yet hardy Cadmus
Kept the spear forward at the serpent's throat
Until an oak stood at its back; then with
A last lunge Cadmus followed his stroke home

Through beast and oak. The tree swayed double
With the serpent's weight, its great sides moaned
As the spent monster lashed them with his tail.

While Cadmus, victor, stared at his great prize,
The conquered beast, a voice came to his ears,
From where he did not know, but heard it say,
"O son of Agenor, why look at ruins
Of monsters you've destroyed? You too shall be
A serpent in men's eyes!" Cold terror came
At him, he pale and trembling stood with hair
As stiff as frost. But look! His good friend Pallas,
Slipped down beside him from the vault of heaven,
Told him to salt the earth with serpent's teeth
Which were to be the seeds of a new people.
At her command, he steered his deep-forked plough
And sowed the earth with teeth of the dead creature,
The seeds of mortal being. Then (as by magic)
The field began to break and from its furrows
First came a line of lances, then gay plumes,
Fluttering in air, then helmets, iron shoulders,
Breastplates, swords, javelins, shields, till earth
Grew heavy with its crowds of men at arms.
As on a feast day when theatres are thrown open
The curtains part and men rise up from trapdoors
Of the stage—first seen are faces, then slowly
The actors in full dress, their feet in line
Behind the curtain's margin—so was the rise
Of the armed charging army Cadmus saw.

In terror at what seemed new enemies,
Cadmus picked up his javelin and shield;
"Hands up," one of the earth's progeny called out,
"You have no business in our civil war."
With this his broad sword slashed his earth-born brother,
And as he closed with him he fell, struck by
A javelin thrown from another quarter,
And as his slayer turned, he too was killed,
All dying in the same breath and spirit,
The give and take of war, they bent on each.

These brothers of mutual madness and disaster
Died by their common wounds; the young,
Whose lives were all too short, lay groaning
In warm heart's blood on earth which gave them birth—
All except five, and one was Echion,
Who at Minerva's orders dropped his sword
And made a truce with his surviving brothers.
These were the friends that homeless Cadmus had
To build the city of Phoebus' oracle.

Now Thebes arose, and Cadmus, though exiled,
Would've seemed to be the happiest of men,
His wife the child of Venus and of Mars,
His children worthy of their heritage,
O many sons and daughters at his side!
And grandsons grown to men. Yet no man
Is called happy till his death, and all
The taxes at his wake and funeral paid.

ACTAEON

Surrounded by good fortune Cadmus had
A grandson, Actaeon, who was first grief,
Whose forehead wore a most peculiar dress,
A brace of antlers, and whose dogs drank deep
Of his own blood. And these disasters
Were Fortune's errors and not his—for how can
Error without intention be called a crime?

On hillside wet with blood of hunted creatures,
When noon had made all shadows thin, and Sun
Was at midspace between his destinations,
Youthful Actaeon with his fellow sportsmen
Had come upon a place of desolation
And in an easy voice he spoke to them:
"My friends, our traps and spears are stained with blood;
The hunt was good enough; the day was lucky.
When swift Aurora in her golden car
Brings us tomorrow there is more to do;
Phoebus is halfway on his road and rakes

Meadow and plain with his untempered fires.
Call it a day and carry home our traps."
Then men obeyed him and the chase was done.

    Within that region was a shaded valley
Grown dense with prickly pine and cypress leaf,
Its name, Gargaphie, sacred to shelter of
Short-clothed Diana. Hidden within it
Was a cave untouched by art, yet Nature's
Craft had simulated art, had made an arbour
Of moss-grown rock and delicate sandstone,
And from its side bright waters gushed and glimmered
Into a shallow well where grass came round it.
Here when she wearied of the chase the greenwood
Goddess bathed her pure limbs in streams of dew-
Clear waters. As on this day she came
She dropped her javelin, her unstrung bow,
Her quiver to the safe keeping of her
True maid-at-arms; another girl picked up
The cloak that she let fall, two more undid
The sandals from her feet, then Crocale
Of Thebes, more artful than the rest, caught up
Diana's fallen hair in a swift knot,
Leaving her own hair tossing to the wind.
Meanwhile Nephele, Hyale, and Rhanis,
Psecas and Phiale poured silver-quick
Streams of pure waters from enormous urns.
But as Diana bathed—and Fate would have it—
Actaeon, Cadmus' grandson, at his leisure,
Strolling through unknown ways half-stumbled
Into Diana's arbour: as he stepped through
The raining fountain spray that fell around him
Diana's naked girls beat their small breasts
And filled the cave with sharp, falsetto cries,
And tried to shield her with their nakedness.
They gathered round Diana in a circle
Yet the tall goddess stood head-high above them;
Flushed as the clouds at sunset or rose-colored
As the first hour at dawn, Diana seemed
More naked to the view than all the rest.
Then as her girls closed in the ring around her,

She glanced a sidelong look across her shoulder
As though she wished her arrows were at hand,
But failing these, splashed water, sharp as rain,
In Actaeon's face, and through his streaming hair
Foretold his fate: "If you can talk, then speak,
Say that you saw Diana in undress."
And as she spoke his wet hair branched in antlers
Worn by the lively stag; his neck grew long,
Ears pointed, hands were hoofs, arms were thin legs.
And all his body a short-furred, spotted skin.
Diana also placed fear in his heart:
The once heroic son of Autonoe
Ran as he wondered by what miracle
He had become so swift with terror—but when
He saw himself, his face, his branching antlers
In a stream he longed to say, "O miser-
Able me!" but had no words, nothing but
Animal cries while tears ran down his changed,
Bewildered face. Only his mind remained
What it had been: What could he do? Where could
He turn? Go home where a king's palace waited?
Or make his way into a deeper forest?
Shame unmanned one path and his fears the other.

And while he stood in doubt, he saw his dogs,
His hunters, first Melampus, then quick-nosed
Ichnobates crying upon his trail,
The first a Spartan, and the next from Crete,
Then swift as wind the other dogs came after,
Pamphagus, Dorceus, Oribasus
Who came from Arcady, sturdy Nebrophon-
Us, savage Laelaps and Theron, quick-footed
Pterelas, fine-scented Agre, rough Hylaeus
Who had been mauled by a wild hog, the wolfhound
Nape, and Poemenis the faithful sheep dog,
The bitch Harpyia, with her recent puppies,
Thin-flanked Ladon who came from Sicyon,
Dromas, Canace, Sticte, Tigris, Alce,
Snow-haired Leucon, dark-haired Asbolus,
Powerful Lacon and swiftly running Aello,
Thous and fleetest Cyprio, her brother,

Lycisce and the black Harpalos, well known
The white mark on his mid-forehead,
Melaneus and rough-haired Lachne, and
Two dogs named Agriodus and Labros,
Whose father came from Crete, mother from Sparta,
Sharp-voiced Hylactor and the rest, the list
Too long to set it down in print. But all
Were eager for their prey: they leaped high-hanging
Cliffs, crags, rocks, where roads were difficult
Or else no roads at all; they still sped on.
Actaeon flying where he was once pursuer,
Now pursued, outpacing those who once were
His own creatures. If only he could speak:
"Look at your master, I am Actaeon, I—"
But words were lost to him; the air was filled
With barking and dogs' cries. First Melanchaetes
Thrust leaping jaws in Actaeon's back, then
Theridamas and Oresitrophus sank
Iron teeth into his shoulder blade; these two
Had taken a late start, but by a short cut,
Spurting across the mountain, outstepped time;
And while they held their master, the entire
Company gathered for assault, snapping
And tearing at their master's body until
No part of it was clear of wounds. He moaned,
And though his voice was scarcely human,
No voice of living deer made such sad cries,
Sounds echoing through valleys he knew well
And filled the mountain air. As if in prayer
He dropped upon his knees, wordless, to plead
In pantomime, open invisible arms
To those who looked at him. Friends of the hunt,
His friends who had come up with the dogs to
Claim their prey. These, innocent of his fate, cry
The dogs at him for the kill, yet seeking him,
Calling out, at each call louder, "Actaeon!
Actaeon!" as though their friend were far away
(And when he heard his name he tossed his head);
They raised objections to his laziness,
Not being there, with a great prize in view.

Himself might well have longed to be away,
Since he was there, might well have wished to see
Rather than feel the passion of his hounds,
Jaws deep within his flesh and eating him,
Their master, now misfashioned as a deer.
Some say, not till he died of many wounds
Was angry Goddess of the Arrows pleased.

SEMELE

    Ambiguous rumours were: the goddess was
More violent than just; others spoke praise
Of how she stood for chastity and both
Extremes found worthy logic for their cause,
But Jove's wife made no public declaration
Of blame or what she thought, yet secretly
She gloried in the ill fortune that had fallen
Upon the house of Agenor, her hate
Had turned from her known rival, young Europa,
To other members of the Tyrian brood.
Added to this was cause for recent pain,
For Juno learned that willing Semele
Had grown big with the seed of generous Jove.
In injured passion she began to speak:
"What have I gained by all my threats and warnings?
That girl must feel my anger, not my words.
If I'm to keep the name of Empress Juno,
To hold the jewel-wrought sceptre in right hand,
If I am queen of all the world, Jove's sister,
His wife, indeed his sister, I must act.
It seems the girl enjoys adultery,
But this betrayal of my marriage bed
Is of the moment; she conceived, is pregnant
As though to show how big she is, how proud
Of being made a mother by great Jove,
An honour that has scarcely come to me.
The girl is vain of her good looks; I'll make
Her vanity the cause of her disaster.
My name is not Saturnia if she fails
To fall in Hell's dark river by Jove's order."

At this decision, Juno went abroad
Wrapped in a golden cloud to Semele:
Yet she took care (before she showed herself)
To simulate old age, take on grey hair,
A wrinkled skin, bent back, and feebleness
As she stepped to the ground. Then she assumed
The voice of Semele's old nurse, Beroe,
An ancient woman from Laconia.
After much chattering they spoke of Jove;
The ancient sighed, "I hope it's true you were
With Jupiter, but O, I have my doubts;
Many a modest bed has visitors
Who claim that they are gods. To be like Jove
Is not enough. If he is Jove then make him
Prove his love, make him appear before you
In the same fashion as when queen Juno
Takes him in her arms. Tell him to take you
As he is in heaven, dressed in his glory!"

Such was the manner Juno gave advice
To the untutored mind of Cadmus' daughter.
The girl then asked a secret gift from Jove.
"Take what you will," he said. "Nothing's refused;
And what is more, if you have doubts, I swear
By sacred, boiling torrents of the Styx
Of which even the greatest gods show fear,
The wish is yours." Pleased with ill luck, damned by
Her lover's promise, the girl replied, "Take me
The way you take Saturnia in your arms."
She spoke too quickly, for Jove would have stopped
Her lips; he groaned, for she could not unsay
What she desired, nor he his promise. High in
His agony he climbed the hills of heaven,
Folded pale dew around him, fogs and clouds,
Lightnings, storms, thunder, inevitable fire.
He tried to make his strenuous powers lighter,
Nor did he take that heavy, fatal bolt
He had sent down to crush Typhoeus,
The monster of the hundred hands; he took
The lesser bolt, which as the Cyclops made it
Contained less angry vigor and less fire.

The gods called this his "light artillery,"
And bearing it he crossed the threshold into
The House of Agenor, where Cadmus lived,
And Semele's bedroom; nor could her body
Take the full thrust of godly heat and love;
It flamed to ashes in Jove's quick embrace.
The unborn child, ripped from its mother's womb
Was nourished (so some said) until its birth,
Sewn in the hollow of its father's thigh.
Discreetly then Ino, its mother's sister,
Tended the child, and from her girls of Nysa
Took him within a cave and gave him milk.

TIRESIAS

While these events had taken place on earth
By will of Fate and twice-born Bacchus safe
Within his crib, it came about that Jove,
Wine in his veins, grew cheerful and dismissed
Affairs of state to joke awhile with Juno:
"And I insist you women have more joy
In making love than men; we do the work,
While you have all the fun." But she denied it,
So they agreed to settle their dispute
By calling wise Tiresias to court
To be their judge    he who knew well enough
The two extremes of Venus' subtle arts:
One day while walking through a green-grown wood
He thrust his stick between two monstrously
Large and love-joined serpents (and then, O mir-
Acle!) was changed into a woman, and as
A woman lived for seven autumns. Then,
As he came to the eighth autumn he saw
The same two creatures in the act of love,
And stopped to say, "If miracles are done
To those who strike at you and sex is changed,
I strike again—" And so he did; at once
His gender shifted to his sex at birth.
Therefore when asked to settle this light quarrel
Of gods, he took the part of Jove,
And Saturn's daughter (who was offended

More deeply than she had a right to be)
Damned judge Tiresias to eternal blindness;
Then (since no god has power to unmake
What other gods may do) Jove, the kind father
Of them all, gave to Tiresias for loss
Of sight the gift of prophecy, an honour
That made the darkness of his doom much lighter.

## ECHO AND NARCISSUS

Throughout the cities of Boeotia
Tiresias had become a famous man;
Those who came to him for advice could not
Deny the power, his wit, in prophecy;
The first test of his power to tell truth
Came from Liriope, a water-lady
Whom Cephisus raped within a winding brook
And nearly drowned her. Then in her due time
The pretty girl gave birth to a sweet child,
A son so charming even as a baby,
That he inspired girls with thoughts of love—
She called the boy Narcissus. When she asked
Tiresias how long her child would live—
To great old age? the prophet answered, "Only
If never he comes to know himself." Then for
A long time after this his prophecy
Seemed vain, and yet what finally happened
Proved it true: Narcissus' death, the way he died,
And his odd love. For when Narcissus reached
His sixteenth year he seemed to be a boy
As much as man; both boys and girls looked to him
To make love, and yet that slender figure
Of proud Narcissus had little feeling
For either boys or girls. One day when he
Had shied a nervous deer into a net,
A girl with a queer voice stood gazing at him—
Echo, who could not check her tongue while talking,
Nor could she speak till someone spoke to her.

In those days Echo was far more than voice;
She had a body and, though garrulous,

No further gifts of speech than now: in short,
The art of taking, from much said, the last
Few words. Juno had made her so; in time
Gone by when Juno might have startled
Jove in the arms of girls on mountainsides,
Echo kept Juno in long conversations
Until the girls had run away. When Juno
Discovered this, she said, "That tongue which has
Deceived me shall make nothing but the poor
Brief noises of the fewest words." Therefore
It came about that Echo's speech was cut,
Yet she retains the last sounds that she hears,
And says them back again to those around her.
The day she saw the wandering Narcissus
Stroll through the forest, secretly she glided,
Fired with love, to follow him; and as she
Came closer to his side, the very source
Of flames increased her heat; she was as sulphur
At the tip of torches, leaping to fire
When another flame leans toward it. She longed
To lure him with soft words, with girlish prayers.
But being what she was she could not make
Sounds come; she had to wait until she heard
Words said, then follow them in her own voice.
Meanwhile Narcissus, strayed from all his friends,
Began to shout, "Is anybody here?"
"Here," Echo answered, and the wondering boy
Looked far around him and cried louder, "Come."
"Come," she called after him. He glanced behind,
Saw no one there, then shouted, "Why run from me?"
And only heard the same words follow him.
Then he stood still, held by deceptive sounds;
"Here we shall meet," he said, and Echo never
Replied more eagerly—"Here we shall meet."
To make those words come true, she slipped beyond
The shelter of the trees to throw her arms
Around the boy she would embrace. Yet he
Ran from her, crying, "No, you must not touch—
Go, take your hands away, may I be dead
Before you throw your fearful chains around me."
"O fearful chains around me," Echo said,

And then no more. So she was turned away
To hide her face, her lips, her guilt among the trees,
Even their leaves, to haunt caves of the forest,
To feed her love on melancholy sorrow
Which, sleepless, turned her body to a shade,
First pale and wrinkled, then a sheet of air,
Then bones, which some say turned to thin-worn rocks;
And last her voice remained. Vanished in forest,
Far from her usual walks on hills and valleys,
She's heard by all who call; her voice has life.

    The way Narcissus had betrayed frail Echo,
Now swift, now shy, so he had played with all:
Girls of the rivers, women of the mountains,
With boys and men. Until one boy, love-sick
And left behind, raised prayers to highest heaven:
"O may he love himself alone," he cried,
"And yet fail in that great love." The curse was heard
By wakeful Nemesis. Deep in the forest
Was a pool, well-deep and silver-clear, where
Never a shepherd came, nor goats, nor cattle;
Nor leaf, nor beast, nor bird fell to its surface.
Nourished by water, grass grew thick around it.
And over it dark trees had kept the sun
From ever shedding warmth upon the place.
Here spent Narcissus, weary of the hunt
And sick with heat, fell to the grass, charmed by
The bright well and its greenery. He bent
To drink, to dissipate his thirst, yet as he
Drank another thirst rose up: enraptured
Beauty caught his eyes that trapped him;
He loved the image that he thought was shadow,
And looked amazed at what he saw—his face.
Fixed, bending over it, he could not speak,
Himself as though cut from Parian marble.
Flat on the grass he lay to look deep, deeper
Into two stars that were his eyes, at hair
Divine as Bacchus' hair, as bright Apollo's,
At boyish beauty of ivory neck and shoulder,
At face, flushed as red flowers among white,
Enchanted by the charms which were his own.

Himself the worshipped and the worshipper,
He sought himself and was pursued, wooed, fired
By his own heat of love. Again, again
He tried to kiss the image in the well;
Again, again his arms embraced the silver
Elusive waters where his image shone;
And he burned for it while the gliding error
Betrayed his eyes. O foolish innocent!
Why try to grasp at shadows in their flight?
What he had tried to hold resided nowhere,
For had he turned away, it fell to nothing:
His love was cursed. Only the glancing mirror
Of reflections filled his eyes, a body
That had no being of its own, a shade
That came, stayed, left with him—if he could leave it.

Neither desire of food or sleep could lure
Him from the well, but flat upon the grasses
There he lay, fixed by the mirage of his eyes
To look until sight failed. And then, half turning,
Raised arms to dark trees over him and cried,
"O trees, O forest, has anyone been cursed
With love like mine? O you who know the ways
Of many lovers in your shaded groves,
Was there at any time in that long past,
The centuries you knew, one who is spent,
Wasted like this? I am entranced, enchanted
By what I see, yet it eludes me, error
Or hope becomes the thing I love; and now
With every hour increases sorrow; nor sea,
Nor plain, nor city walls, nor mountain ranges
Keeps us apart. Only this veil of water.
So thin the veil we almost touch each other,
Then come to me no matter who you are,
O lovely boy, why do you glide from me,
Where do you vanish when I come to meet you?
My youth, my beauty cannot be denied,
For girls have loved me and your tempting glances
Tell me of friendship in your eyes. Even as
I reach, your arms almost embrace me, and as
I smile, you smile again at me; weeping

I've seen great tears flow down your face; I bend
My head toward you, you nod at me, and I
Believe that from the movement of your lips
(Though nothing's heard) you seem to answer me.
Look! I am he; I've loved within the shadow
Of what I am, and in that love I burn,
I light the flames and feel their fires within;
Then what am I to do? Am I the lover
Or beloved? Then why make love? Since I
Am what I long for, then my riches are
So great they make me poor. O may I fall
Away from my own body—and this is odd
From any lover's lips—I would my love
Would go away from me. And now love drains
My life, look! I am dying at life's prime.
Nor have I fear of death which ends my trials,
Yet wish my lover had a longer life,
If not, we two shall perish in one breath."

   He spoke and half mad faced the self-made image.
Tears stirred the pool to waves, the wavering features
Dimmed in darkest waters. As he saw them flicker
He cried, "Where are you going? Stay with me;
O cruelest lover come, nor leave me here;
It may be fate for me to look at love
And yet not touch it, but in that deep gaze
Increase unhappy love to misery."
Then in his agony he tore his dress
And beat his naked breast with his pale hands.
As apples ripen, some parts white, some red,
As growing grapes take on a purple shade,
Narcissus' breast put on these darkening colours;
And when he saw them—for the pool had cleared—
He could endure no more, but as wax turns
To liquid in mild heat, as autumn frost
Changes to dew at morning, so did Narcissus
Wear away with love, drained, fading in the heat
Of secret fires. No longer were his colours
Gold, white, and red and that vitality
His beauty showed, but something less, scarcely
The boy whom Echo loved too well. Yet when

She saw him, and though still annoyed, resentful,
She felt a touch of pity at the sight,
So when he sighed "Eheu," "Eheu," said she,
And as his hands struck at his breast and shoulders,
So she repeated these weak sounds of grief.
As gazing down the well, his last words were:
"O darling boy whose love was my undoing,"
And all the grove resounded with their saying.
Then with his last "Good-bye," "Good-bye," said Echo.
At this he placed his head deep in cool grasses
While death shut fast the eyes that shone with light
At their own lustre. As he crossed the narrows
Of darkest hell he saw the floating image
Of his lost shade within the Stygian waters.
His sisters of the rivers beat their breasts
And shaved their heads in sorrow for their brother,
Nor were the sisters of the forest silent,
But filled the air with grief which Echo carried.
As they built up his pyre and waved their torches
Across his bier, they searched; his body vanished.
They saw a flower of gold with white-brimmed petals.

### PENTHEUS AND BACCHUS

When Grecian cities heard Narcissus' legend
The seer Tiresias took on greater fame:
Only the son of Echion, Pentheus,
God-mocker, laughed at all his prophecies,
His famous blindness; but the old man shook
His dwindling frosty hairs as if to warn him,
"How lucky you would be if light were dark
So not to see the sacred feast of Bacchus,
For day will come—and I can feel it near—
When, new God Liber, son of Semele,
Shall rule the earth. Unless you honour him
As should be done, you shall be ripped, torn to
A thousand parts, your blood pollute the forest,
Even your mother and your mother's sisters;
So this shall happen, for you will not praise
The coming god, rather your cry will be
That I in blindness see the world too well."

And as he talked, Echion's son, impatient,
Went on his way. Tiresias spoke truth.

    Liber arrived and all the countryside
Was filled with cries and echoes of a feast.
Crowds from the cities whirled into the meadows,
Men, women, even with children at their breasts,
The young, the old, the gentles and the peasants,
All rioted in common celebration.
"Heirs of the serpent's teeth," Pentheus shouted,
"Descendants of old Mars, what brand of madness
Has unwound your brains? Are blaring cymbals,
The noise of horns, magics, and sleight of hand,
Shrieking of women and crazy heat of wine,
As dirty vagrants dance to sound of drums—
Are these your conquerors, O men of war
For whom the naked sword, the roar of trumpets,
And piercing lances held no thought of fear?
Can I respect the elders in this mob
Who sailed horizons of the farthest seas,
Who built up Tyre's walls in wilderness,
Who carried household gods across each threshold—
Are these men fallen without a sign of war?
How can I praise those of my generation
Who once wore battle dress, sword, helmet, shield,
Who now wear vine leaves in dishevelled hair?
Remember your creator was the serpent,
His life your life, how he alone struck down
The many who came at him, how he died
To save his fountain and his glittering well.
How can you go to war with thoughts of glory?
He killed brave men—but are you fit to conquer
The impotent to save your heritage?
It may be Thebes' fate not to live too long;
For my part I would see War and its armies
Destroy her walls, encircle her with flames.
We would be miserable, but honour would be held;
We'd cry aloud our bitterness, our fate.
But now Thebe's taken by a child, a boy
Who does not care to know the arts of war,
Lancers or fighting men, but rather wreaths

Of flowers, perfumed hair, purple and gold-
Stitched dressing gowns. And will you let me pass!
I go this way, for I shall make him tell me
His father has no name, his sacred feast
A cult of lies. Acrisius had the spirit
To close the gates of Argos fast against him—
And now shall Pentheus and entire Thebes
Shake at the thought of this adventurer's
Advance? Go, go at once!" (And this command
Was given to his servants:) "Get the traitor;
Put him in irons and bring him here before me;
I'll have no deadly symptoms of delay."
His staid grandfather warned Pentheus; so
Did Athamas, the king of Thessaly, and all
Advisers, who were urgent, calm, yet futile
To check his will. But these few threats
And warnings stirred his anger; their sharp bridles
Galled him; the more they talked, the more he raged.
So I have seen the rapids of a river
With nothing in their way run like a song
In a mild voice, but dammed by falling trees,
Stones, rocks, they roar and steam in foaming spray,
Their powers increased by all that holds them back.

    Meanwhile Pentheus' servants had returned,
Blood-stained and battered. When he asked them where
Bacchus had gone, they said they had not seen him,
"None but this follower," they said, "one of
His priests—" of dark Etruscan breed,
A devotee of Bacchus, who stood in chains,
Hands trussed behind his back. Pentheus
With eyes of fire glared at him a moment,
Held back by force of will from striking him,
Then spoke: "You who must die to teach the others,
Tell me your name, your parentage, your country—
And why you welcome these new superstitions."
Straightly the man replied, "My name is Acoetes,
My land, Maeonia, my parents poor.
My father left me neither field nor plough,
Nor ox nor sheep nor any other cattle.
He was a fisherman; his only skill

Was of the hook and line, his rod brought fish
Leaping in air to shore; his craftsmanship
Was his one claim to riches, and as he gave
The art to me he said, 'Here's your inheritance,
It's all I own, and you may follow me
To practise it.' At death he left me nothing
But the waters which I have come to call
My heritage. So not to grow pale roots
In native rock, I took to seamanship
To steer the currents with a clever hand,
And learned the guiding courses of the stars:
The raining constellation of the Goat,
To sight Taygete in the Pleiades,
Seven-starred Taurus and the Bears. I know
Home-dwellings of the wind and proper harbours.
It happened that as I set sail for Delos
My ship swayed off into the bay of Chios
And came to land with skilful use of oars.
We tripped to the wet sands and slept the night.
In first grey-red of dawn I waked and ordered
My men to draw fresh water, pointing where
It might be found. As for myself I climbed up
A tallish hill to see which way the wind took,
Then called my shipmates. As we stepped aboard,
Opheltes, who came first, cried out, 'Look at us,
Here we are!' and showed a hostage (or so
He thought) captured upon a lonely patch
Of meadow, a boy, fair as any girl.
He seemed sleepwalking through deep dreams and wine
And barely followed him who caught and led him.
I looked upon his face, his dress, his walk;
The more I saw the more he seemed immortal.
Later I said, 'I do not know what magic
Stirs in that beauty, but I do know this:
It is divine. Whoever you may be
Give us good fortune and forgive these men.'
'No, no, don't pray for us,' cried Dictys, who
Was always swiftly up the topyard and
Steady down ropes, and so cried hearty Lybys,
Then the fair-haired Melanthus who was look-out,
Alcimedon and Epopeus whose great voice

Beat time for oarsmen and revived their spirits,
And all the rest joined in, so hot were they
In their blind hope of ransom for the boy.
'We shall not violate his sacred image,
Not on this ship,' I cried, 'for I am master—'
And when they reached to climb aboard, I fought them.
Then Lycabas, the wildest of the crew,
A murderer, exiled from Tuscany,
Came at me, as I grappled with him, tore
My throat and would have tossed me overboard
If I had not by instinct seized a rope
To hold myself upright. Then as the crew
Cheered Lycabas, young Bacchus (for he was
Bacchus) as if the noise cut through his sleep,
His wine-filled stupor, woke up and said,
'What's this upheaval, cheers? Tell me, O sailors,
How did I come here, and what do you propose
To do to me?' 'Have little fear,' Procrus said,
'Tell me which port you have in mind, we'll take
You to the place where you would go.' 'Then on
To Naxos,' Bacchus said, 'my native land,
Long famous for its hospitality.'
The traitors swore by sea and gods who ruled it
That they would take him there and ordered me
To make sails ready on that painted ship.
Naxos was on the right; I tacked and set
My sails in that direction. Opheltes
Cried out, 'What are you doing, lunatic?
O what insanity'—the others joined him—
'Is in your brain? Turn to the left.' Then most
Of them by signs, by nods, some hissed at my
Right ear their orders till I rose and shouted,
'Let others steer the ship.' I would have nothing
Of their plots, their craftiness; they cursed me,
And whipped up rage in whispers, until one,
Aethalion, spoke up: 'Our safety does not
Rest on your wit alone nor all your skill.'
He manned the rudder at my side and steered
Away from Naxos. Then the god to trick them,
As if he had just learned their falsity,
Looked out to sea from the curved stern and wept:

'O sailors, where is land you promised me?
This is not where I'd go; what have I done?
Where is the honour of this great deceit
Of a small boy and all of you against one?'
I had been weeping and all the wild impious
Crew laughed at my tears. The ship skimmed over waves
With wingèd oars. Then by my God I swear
(And surely he is very near to godhead)
That what I say is true, though it may seem
Beyond good faith—the ship stood motionless
As if she rested for repairs on shore.
The men increased their efforts at the oars,
Spread out full sails to speed their way at double
Power, but vines grew fast around each oar,
And, growing, climbed among the sails and hawsers,
Even decks were overhung with grape and vine,
While Bacchus, crowned with ivy leaf and berry,
Stepped forward with a waving ivy wand,
Bright apparitions of great beasts around him:
Tiger and lynx and teeth-bared spotted panther.
Taken by leaping madness or by fear
The men jumped to the sea. First Medon's body
Changed colour to darkest blue and hunched its back;
Lycabas turned to say, 'What monster are you?'
And as he spoke, his nose became a hook,
His mouth grew wide, skin tough, and scales
Ran down his sides, and Lybys while he struggled
With leaf-grown oars saw his hands diminish
From claws to fins; another clinging fast
To twisted ropes fell backward to the sea,
Arms gone and legless, his tail crook'd and pointed
As a third-quarter moon. The creatures lashed
At the ship's side, plunging through spray, now up,
Now down to the sea's floor, swaying like dancers
At a drunken feast, their bodies flashing,
Lips and nostrils pouring spray, they clipped and spawned.
Of twenty men (the whole ship's company)
I was the last man left, senseless and shaking
With chilled fear. And, as if to steady me,
The god said, 'Now strike swift, set sail for Naxos.'
And when we landed I was priest of Bacchus.'"

Pentheus answered, "We have heard your long
Romance, a story told no doubt to stay
Our passions and to let them cool. Come, slaves,
Take him away; he needs a crucifixion,
And after it eternal Stygian night."
Acoetes, the Tyrrhenian, hauled away,
Was locked in a deep cell, while slaves fetched fire
And irons for his death. His doors swung open;
His weighted chains fell from his legs and arms;
Then he walked free, though no one let him go.

Yet Pentheus stood firm to his intentions,
Nor sent his servants, but himself went out
To holy Cithaeron, loud with the cries
Of Bacchanalian songs; and as a stallion
Whinnies when he has heard brass horns of war
And is all heat to enter in the battle,
So now the air, filled with the songs of Bacchus,
Spurred Pentheus and fired his rage white-hot.

Half up the mountain, edged with a dense forest
Was a plateau, open on every side.
As Pentheus, narrow-eyed, came near the altar,
The first to know him was his mother, first
To clutch at him, to curse him madly, lash
Out at him with an ivy wand and cry,
"Come, sisters, come to see the wild pig plough
Our peaceful meadows! Look at him. I'll tear
Arms, legs, all hanging parts from that rough body."
The riot came from everywhere upon him,
And as he crawled, came after him; in terror
His voice grew soft, admitting faults, mistakes.
Then from his bleeding body Pentheus cried,
"Pity for me, O my aunt, Autonoe!
Remember the poor shade of Actaeon!"
But she had never heard of him; she twisted
Pentheus' right arm from his body, then
Ino, maddened, ripped the left away, nor had
He arms to reach in prayer toward mother, yet he
Showed where they should have been, and dying, cried,
"O Mother, gaze at me!" She screamed at him

And shook her flying hair. Then Agave ripped
His head from fallen shoulders, raised it up
So others saw her prize in blood-red hands;
She cried, "Here is my work, my victory."
Quickly as leaves touched by an autumn's frost
Tremble, half clinging, then are swept away,
Even from the tops of trees, so Pentheus' limbs
Were scattered by mad hands to wind and earth.
Aware of his odd fate, his grave example,
Thebans in crowds came to a new god's altar.

# IV

# BOOK IV

Pyramus and Thisbe • Mars and Venus • The Sun and Leucothoe • Salmacis and Hermaphroditus • Ino and Athamus • Metamorphosis of Cadmus • Perseus

*Ovid's art of interweaving stories is brilliantly displayed in the progress of Book III into Book IV. An excellent variation of the Narcissus legend is shown in the transformations of Salmacis and Hermaphroditus. One can see in Ovid's version of the Bacchus legend the distance between Greek versions of the Thracian legends of Dionysus. The Greeks identified him with the Egyptian god Osiris, the Romans with their wine god Liber. In Athens Dionysus's sanctuary became the site of the Dionysian theatre, and the god became the awe-inspiring source of tragedy. Ovid's Bacchus is not without his own air of mystery, the image of a sleepy, effeminate boy found by sailors, and, as Liber, god of wine, deceptive in his powers. Ovid's retelling of the Bacchus story is one of the more remarkable strokes of his genius.*

# BOOK IV

All welcomed the new god—except the daughter
Of Minyas the rich king, Alchithoe,
Who would not worship at a Bacchanal,
And bravely said he was no son of Jove;
Her sisters joined with her in blasphemy.
Meanwhile a Bacchic priest called out the people
To celebrate a feast, handmaid or slave,
To go on holiday, each girl, like mistress,
Cover her breasts with furs, twist the grape leaf
And myrtle in flying hair, each carry
In her hands the magic vine grown thyrsus.
If disobeyed, he cried, God Bacchus would
Mount up in rage, nor would he show them pity.
Matrons, young wives with babies at their breasts,
Answered his call, left spindle, loom, and basket—
Housework undone. Then lighting at his shrine
Sweet-smelling incense, they began to call
God Bacchus by his many names: Deep-Sounder,
King of All Noises, and the Careless Lord,
Son of the Thunder-Shaft, the Twice-Born Infant
Of Two Mothers, Son of the Orient,
And of the Wild-Haired Mistress of the Skies,
Maker and Husband of the Vine, Lenaeus,
And Nyctelius, the Very God of Night,
And Father Eleleus whose cry is heard
As Hallelujah over all of us,
Iacchus, Euhan—many, many names,
Known over Greece, O Liber, Liberty!
You, the eternal youth that shines in heaven,
And if you come before us without horns,
Your face is like a virgin of the skies.
Even as far as where the distant Ganges

Washes the sun-stained sides of India,
All bow before your Oriental reign:
At your word Pentheus wiped out, Lycurgus
Too, of the double axe, ungodly men!
And both undone—while you, awe-striking Bacchus,
Threw Tuscan sailors into wave-tossed waters.
Even now crowds follow where your chariot
Leads them, the flash, the glitter of the Lynx-
Drawn car—satyrs and women and even
A drunken elder staggering with his stick
Who leans, reeling, against the hollow belly
Of his mule. Wherever you may go, the crowd
Is there, the shrieks of girls, the shouts of boys,
Tympanum roaring and the cry of flutes.

"O gentle Bacchus, be with us forever,"
The Theban women cried; led by the priest,
They worshipped at his shrine. Only the daughters
Of Minyas stayed indoors, guiding their servants
At daily rounds, quick thumbs and weaving fingers
Spinning wool—their absence noted as if they
Had ignored the festival. One sister,
Shuttling the thread with steady thumbs, remarked,
"While others run away from household duties
To waste their time with dubious priests and prayers,
We choose to give our faith to chaste Minerva,
A better goddess than the god they know.
And if the day grows long, we'll spend these hours
While we work at storytelling; let one
Begin and let the others listen." Her sisters
Urged her to be first; at which she wavered,
Silent, for many stories could be told:
She thought of Babylonian Dercetis,
Who (Syrians believed) turned to a fish,
Glittering with scales and diving through clear waters,
Then how her daughter changed to a white dove,
Fated to end her life on high watchtowers;
Then of a nymph, possessed of magic arts,
Who used them wildly, changing boys to fish,
And by her spells and herbs turned her own body
Into a fishlike monster: then she thought

Of how a tree, famous for snow-white berries,
Took on new colours of a blood-red taint.
This last seemed best, nor was it widely known,
And as she went on spinning, she began:

"Pyramus and Thisbe: both the best-looking
Of young people in the East were next-door
Neighbours; they lived within a high-walled, brick-built
City made (so it was said) by Queen Semiramis.
Proximity was the first reason why
They came to know each other; as time passed
Love flourished, and if their parents had
Not come between them, then they would have shared
A happy wedding bed. And yet no parent
Can check the heat of love, therefore, the lovers
Burned with mutual flames. Nor friend nor servant
Spoke for them; their speech was in the gesture
Of a nod, a smile; the more they banked the flames
The more they smouldered with a deeper heat.
There was a fissure in the wall between
Their homes, a small, thin crevice that no one
Had seen. What eyes are sharper than the eyes
Of love? The lovers found the slit and made it
The hidden mouthpiece of their voices where
Love's subtle words in sweetest whispers came
And charmed the ear. And as they took their places,
Thisbe on one side, Pyramus on his,
Both waited, listening for the other's breath.
'O cold and bitter wall,' they said, 'why stand
Between two lovers at your side? Let limbs
And bodies join; at least open your gate
To take our kisses. Yet we do not show
Ingratitude, nor shall we, nor forget
The way through which our words met lovers' ears.'
Divided as they were, each futile day
Was spent in whispers, closing with 'Good night.'
Both pressed their lips against the silent wall.
Next day when dawn outshone the lamps of night
And Sun had dried the dew on frost-white grasses,
The lovers took their places at the wall
And in soft cries complained of heartless fate.

But as they talked they came to a decision:
Under the quiet darkness of the night
To glide from eyes that watched them out of doors,
To leave the town behind them; to prevent
The chance of being led astray they chose
The site of Ninus' tomb to meet each other,
There in the shadow of a famous tree,
The white tall mulberry that waved its branches
Not far from a bright flashing stream of water;
The plot delighted them, but from that moment
The day seemed all too long; the quick Sun lagged,
Then dove into the sea where Night came up.

"No sooner dark than Thisbe, veiled, unseen,
Slipped out of doors, a shade among the shadows,
Ran to the tomb, and took her place beneath
The appointed tree. For love had given her
Audacity. But look! A lioness!
And through the moonlit distance Thisbe saw her
With bloody lamb-fed jaws come up the road
And headed toward well waters for a drink
Where through the moonlit distance Thisbe saw her.
The Babylonian girl, trembling yet swift,
Turned to the recess of a darkening cave,
And as she ran dropped her white cloak behind her.
Meanwhile the beast had had her fill of drinking
And as she wandered back between the trees
She stepped across the cloak that Thisbe wore,
Now empty of its mistress, worried it
Between her teeth and left it stained with blood.
A moment later Pyramus arrived
Who saw the footprints of the beast in dust;
Then turned death-pale, but when he found the torn
Blood-tinted cloak, he said, 'One night shall be
The killing of two lovers. She whom I love
Deserves the longer life; on me all guilt
Should fall, for it was I who sent her out
Through deepest night into this evil place
Where I arrived too late. May all the lions
Who breed beneath this rocky cliff come at me,
Tear at my body and eat its guilt away—

But only cowards merely ask for death.'
At which he gathered up his Thisbe's cloak
And walked within the shadow of the tree,
There where he kissed the cloak and covered it
With tears. 'Now drink my blood,' he said aloud
And thrust the sword he wore into his side
Then in death's frenzy quickly drew it out,
Torn from warm flesh, and straightway fell
Backward to earth. And as a split lead joint
Shoots hissing sprays of water into air,
So his blood streamed above him to the tree,
Staining white fruit to darkest red, colouring
Tree's roots and growing fruit with purple dye.

   "Then Thisbe came from shelter, fearful, shaken,
Thinking perhaps her lover had misplaced her,
Looked for him with her eyes, her soul, her heart,
Trembling to tell him dangers she escaped.
And though she knew the landmarks, the tall tree,
She wondered at the colour of its fruit,
Doubting if it was the same tree she saw,
And while she wavered, glanced where something moved,
Arms, legs it had, stirring on blood-soaked ground,
Then she stepped back; her face had turned as pale
As the green boxwood leaf, her body tremulous
As fair lake waters rippling in the wind.
But when she saw that it was he, her lover,
She tore her hair and clasped her arms with grief,
Then fondled him, tears poured in wounds and blood.
And as she kissed his death-cold lips she cried,
'Pyramus, what misfortune takes you from me?
And O, Pyramus, speak to answer me.
It is your darling Thisbe calling you.
Listen, my dear, raise up your lazy head.'
At Thisbe's name, Pyramus raised an eyelid,
Weighted with death; her face seen in a vision,
And then his eyes had closed forever more.

   "When she discovered her own cloak, the empty
Ivory sheath that held his sword, she said,
'By your own hand even your love has killed you,

Unlucky boy. Like yours my hand has courage,
My heart, love for the last act. I have the strength
To share your death and some shall say I was
The unhappy cause, the partner of your fate;
Only Lord Death had power to take you from me,
Yet even he cannot divorce us now.
O twice unhappy parents, his as mine,
Come, take our prayers, nor think the worse of us
Whom true love and death's hour have made one
And we shall sleep in the same bed, our tomb.
And you, O tree whose branches weave their shadows
Dark over the pitiful body of one lover
Shall soon bear shade for two; O fateful tree
Be the memorial of our twin deaths,
And your dark fruit the colour of our mourning.'
Then Thisbe placed sword's point beneath her breast
The blade still warm with blood from her love's heart,
And leaned upon it till she sank to earth.
Her prayers had reached the gods, had moved both
          parents:
The ripe fruit of the tree turned deep rose colour;
And they who loved sleep in a single urn."

## MARS AND VENUS

     The story ended, but a moment later
Leuconoe began—her sisters silent:
"Even the Sun whose light rules all the stars
Has known love's kingdom; we shall tell of it.
Since he was always first to see what happened
He was the first to find that Mars and Venus
Took pleasure with each other, which was wrong.
Amazed at what he saw, he spoke to Vulcan,
Husband of Venus and great Juno's son,
And told him where he caught them in the act.
Then Vulcan's mind went dark; he dropped his work
And turned at once to subtle craftsmanship,
To make a net so light, so delicate,
So thinly woven of fine-tempered bronze
The casual, glancing eye would never see it—
Less visible than sleekest threads of wool

Or nets that spiders hang from tallest beams.
He made it so it yielded at each touch,
Each trembling gesture or the slightest movement,
Then draped it as a sheet on his wife's bed.
So shrewdly was it made that when the goddess
Took to her bed within her lover's arms,
Both were caught up and held within the net.
Then Vulcan, fisherman, threw wide his doors,
Which shone in burnished shafts of ivory,
And called the other gods to see his catch,
To see how lovers act within their chains.
One god remarked that he half envied Mars,
While Vulcan's bedroom shook with godly laughter:
For many years this tale was told in heaven.

### THE SUN AND LEUCOTHOE

"But Venus Cytherean remembered him
Who had betrayed her, first to tell of her
Adultery, then worked appropriate
Revenge upon him—and the same disastrous
Effect of love: Son of Hyperion,
What matter if you were a shining image,
Your fairest light in streaming golden hair
Pouring its brightness over earth? Even you
Who set the world on fire were caught up
In wild new fires of love. And you whose duty
Had been to see all things on earth, had eyes
Alone to look at Leucothoe.
You came too soon across the Eastern heavens,
And fell too late beneath the Western seas;
And as you turned a hovering deep stare
Over around her you stayed the progress
Of a short winter day. At times your light
That poured from your dark heart turned heat to shade
Putting blind fear into the souls of men,
Nor had Moon slipped between you and the earth,
Rather you had turned thin and pale for love;
You shone for her alone, not for Clymene,
Nor Neptune's daughter who was queen of Rhodes,
Nor fairest of them all, the Lady Persa,

Mother of Circe, nor sweet longing Clytie,
Half dead for love of you, yet put aside.
Leucothoe cast others in the shade,
She who was daughter of Eurynome,
Born in a land where perfume fills the air,
The flowering country of Arabia,
Who when she came of age excelled her mother
As brilliantly as that fine beauty
Outshone the ladies who surrounded her,
Whose father was the king of Persian cities,
Seventh in line of ancient Babylon.

    "Under the Western axis grazed Sun's horses.
Instead of grass they ate ambrosia;
There they took ease after a long day's labour,
Refreshed themselves to ride the skies of dawn,
And while they took their fill of heaven's dinner,
And Night took over rule of earth and sky,
Sun, dressed as though he were Leucothoe's mother,
Entered the young girl's room, she at the center
Of twelve girls, twirling the spindle, threading
The delicate white wool. He stooped to kiss her
As a mother would have kissed her and remarked,
'I come to talk of intimate affairs
To you, my dear, which is a mother's duty,
And all the others have to leave the room.
Get out, you slaves!' And when the last had left,
He turned to her to say, 'I am the one
Who makes all seasons of the year, each day,
Each hour, who sees all things, who opens
The world's eye to all earth's wonders, who looks
At you with infinite delight.' The girl
Went weak with terror; distaff and spindle dropped
From helpless fingers, and the god, revealed,
Showed her his sudden heat, his manliness,
At which she trembled, yet could not resist it;
She welcomed the invasion of the Sun.

    "At this event Clytie grew hot with envy—
Her own love of the Sun ran mad within her—
And quickly told to everyone she saw,

Including the girl's father, how his daughter
Became a whore. The father, truculent,
Ruthless, and cold, refused his daughter's prayers,
Even as she raised her arms up toward the Sun,
Ignored her cry: 'He took me, dazzled me,'
And with brute anger tossed her in a pit
And covered her with sand. Hyperion's son
Pierced the deep grave with light that she might wake,
But all too late, nor could she raise her head,
Even less, her body fast in earth and death.
Nothing more sad since Phaethon's fall in flames
Was this brave sight: he who was charioteer
Of sky's wild horses spending naked heat
To warm the poor remains now cold in death.
Fate willed against him; in reply he scattered
Sweet rain of nectar over the stilled body,
The mound above it, then spoke an elegy
Which closed as follows. 'One day your spirit
Shall be felt in heaven.' At which her limbs,
Moist with celestial dew, melted in air
And fragrance charmed the earth that covered them.
From darkly winding roots far underground
A spray of frankincense broke through the tomb.

    "Though Clytie's gossip and malicious tongue
Could find excuse through unrequited love,
The god of light avoided meeting her,
And thought her less attractive now than ever.
Sorrow had turned her love to deeper madness;
Nor could she look to any friend or sister;
Under broad skies of night and day she sat,
Naked, unwashed, alone; nor ate, nor drank,
And for nine days, weathered by tears and dew,
She languished in the shade. Her face turned only
To look upon the god she loved above her,
To follow his long trail across the sky:
Some said her very limbs grew into earth,
Her colour bloodless as thin grass, yet shaded
Bluish green to red, the likely colours
Of the pale violet; a flower came
Where once herself had been, now fast in earth,

Though less than human, yet her love unchanged,
She turned her face always to meet the sun."

## SALMACIS AND HERMAPHRODITUS

   The story ended, but the strange romance
Had captured every ear. "Impossible,"
Some said; others insisted that the gods
Made all things possible except false Bacchus.
The sisters then called out to Alcithoe
And held their tongues. She ran her shuttle through
The busy loom, then spoke: "I shall not bore you
With telling how young Daphnis of Mount Ida
Was turned to stone: this by a girl who, jealous
Of another, fancied her love betrayed—
Such is the sting that burns rejected lovers.
That story's too well known. Nor shall I tell
How Sithon, turning backside nature's law,
Changed from a man to woman at his will,
Nor how the stones of Celmis were once friends
Of infant Jove, nor how Curetes came
From rain, nor how young Crocus and his loved one
The Twining Smilax changed to little flowers—
I shall enchant your souls with something new.

   "The waters of the fountain Salmacis
Have earned an evil name: the men who take them
Become effeminate or merely zero—
Certainly less than men, which is well known.
The reason why has been a guarded secret.
The infant son of Mercury and Venus
Was nursed by naiads in Mount Ida's caves;
His pretty face showed who his parents were,
Even his name combined their names in Greek.
When he had reached the age of three-times-five
He left the pastures of stepmother Ida
To visit hills and streams of foreign lands;
Boyish delight made rough foot-travel easy
And pleasure came with each strange thing he saw;
He drifted toward the cities of Lycia
Where the Carians settled near their gates,

And there he found a tempting pool of water
So clear that one could read its sandy depth.
No swamps grew there, rank grasses, nor black weeds;
Only the purest water flowed, and round it
Neat turf and dainty ferns as though they were
Eternal greenery. A nymph lived there
Who never stirred abroad, nor followed deer,
Nor entered friendly races with the girls,
Nor took out hunting license with Diana.
Her sisters, it was said, made fun of her,
Or scolded, 'Salmacis, pick up your spear,'
Or, 'Have you lost your pretty painted quiver?'
'Why not take turns at getting exercise;
A life of ease gives pleasure to the chase.'
But Salmacis refused; she took a bath,
Gazed at her lovely arms and legs in water,
And found her private pool a likely mirror
To show her how to rearrange her hair
Even with a boxwood comb. Then, lightly dressed,
She sank upon the turf, or sometimes wandered
To pick a garland of sweet-smelling flowers
Which grew nearby—and that day saw the boy;
O how she yearned to take him in her arms!

    "Yet she held off a while in coming near him;
Stood still a moment till her blood ran cool,
Plucked at her dress and calmly fixed her eyes;
When she was certain that she looked her best,
She chose her words and spoke: 'O lovely boy,
If you are not a god, then you should be one,
Cupid himself—and if your birth was human
How proud, how pleased your parents should have been.
What happy brothers, if you had them, doting
Sisters, and O, the nurse who held you close
To reach her breast. But gladder than all these,
Your lucky bride. If she exists, then let
Our love take shelter in the shade; if not,
Then let us find our wedding bed.' She paused;
The boy flushed red, half innocent of love,
Yet red and white increased his fragile beauty:
As apples ripen in a sun-swept meadow,

Or ivory brushed with paint, or the grey moon,
When brass urns sounding beat for her release
At hour of her eclipse, red under white,
Such were the colours that played across his face.
As the girl asked him for a sister's kiss
And was about to stroke his snow-white neck,
He cried, 'Leave me or I must run away—
Get out of here.' Salmacis, shaken, said,
'This place is yours, but stay, O darling stranger!'
Then turned as if to leave him there alone,
Walked slowly cautiously beyond his view,
Looked back, dropped to her knees behind a hedge.
Meanwhile the boy as though he were unseen
Strolled the green turf and stepping near its waters
Tested the rippling surface with his toes,
Then dipped his feet and, charmed by flowing coolness
Of the stream, stripped off his clothes; and when she saw
Him naked, the girl was dazzled; her eyes shone
With blazing blinding light that Phoebus' face
Poured in a looking-glass, nor could she wait
To hold him naked in her arms. Striking
His arms against his sides, he leaped and dived
Overhand stroke, into the pool; his glittering body
Flashed and turned within clear waters, as if
It were of ivory or of white lilies seen
Through walls of glass. 'I've won, for he is mine,'
She cried, clothes torn away and naked, as she
Leaped to follow him, her arms about him fast,
Where, though he tried to shake her off, she clung,
Fastening his lips to hers, stroking his breast,
Surrounding him with arms, legs, lips, and hands
As though she were a snake caught by an eagle,
Who leaping from his claws wound her tall body
Around his head, and lashed his wings with her
Long tail, as though she were quick ivy tossing
Her vines round the thick body of a tree,
Or as the cuttlefish at deep sea's bottom
Captures its enemy—so she held to him.
The heir of Atlas struggled as he could
Against the pleasure that the girl desired,
But she clung to him as though their flesh were one,

'Dear, naughty boy,' she said, 'to torture me;
But you won't get away. O gods in heaven,
Give me this blessing; clip him within my arms
Like this forever.' At which the gods agreed:
They grew one body, one face, one pair of arms
And legs, as one might graft branches upon
A tree, so two became nor boy nor girl,
Neither yet both within a single body.

"When tamed Hermaphroditus learned his fate,
Knew that his bath had sent him to his doom,
To weakened members and a girlish voice,
He raised his hands and prayed, 'O Father, Mother,
Hear your poor son who carried both your names:
Make all who swim these waters impotent,
Half men, half women.' Which his parents heard
And gave the fountained pool its weird magic."

The story ended, yet King Minyas' daughters
Kept to their work, and by their actions showed
How little they respected great god Bacchus,
Even on his feast day. Then like a blast
The noise of cymbals, trumpets, flutes, rang in
Their ears, and with each breath the air grew thick
With the rich smell of saffron and sweet myrrh;
As if by miracle their thread turned green,
Green shoots among the ivy-growing looms,
Weaving between the clustered grape and vine
That covered purple cloth and deep brocade.
Then twilight came between the dark and light;
Within the evening darkness sunset glimmered
As though red twilight filled the air: house, rafters
Seemed to shake, lamps flamed as if wild fires leaped
From room to room; then apparitions came
Of great beasts roaring through shadow and wall.
Through smoke and fire the sisters groped their way
To escape the flames and, as they floated, tripped,
And almost fell, a delicate membrane spread
Over their legs and feet and thin wings shrouded
Their waving arms. Nor did they know how changed
They were, for darkness covered all. Their wings

Were featherless, yet they sufficed to carry
Small shrunken bodies whose voices grew as frail
As shrill as they. They haunted house and attic,
But not the forest, and hid in eaves and swung
From highest beams, avoiding light of day;
Even their name is of the vesper hour.

## INO AND ATHAMAS

From that time on the godlike power of Bacchus
Was known and welcomed over Thebes. Ino
His aunt told stories everywhere of how
A new god Bacchus worked his miracles;
Unlike her sisters, she alone 'scaped sorrow
Knowing them only through their tears and grief.
She took pride in her husband, Athamas,
And all her children, but beyond these glories
She cherished her adopted son, the god.
Whenever Juno saw her, hate turned to fire
In the queen goddess' eyes. "My rival's son,"
She whispered to herself, "has the rare gift
Of turning sailors into mad sea monsters;
His magic caused a mother to mutilate,
Destroy the body of her son, shrouded
King Minyas' daughters with fantastic wings.
Shall Juno set no answer to that insult
Except poor tears, self-pity and no revenge?
Are these enough for me? Are these the tributes
To my strength, my power? Yet Bacchus teaches me,
For one has much to learn from enemies;
He knew how far the curse of madness reached
When it destroyed Pentheus: why shouldn't Ino,
Fired with her furies, go where her sisters went?"

Dark with funereal yews a road curved down
Through deepening silence to the shores of Hell
Where the dank Styx breathed fog upon the air.
And in that region spirits of the dead,
Fresh from their pyres and tombs, went wandering,
The place a desert, pale and cold and drear,
Where the poor ignorant and newly dead

Had lost the straight way to Death's captive city
In which the palace of dark Dis stood waiting.
The city had a thousand gates and doors
On all sides open to the wind; as Sea
Takes all earth's rivers to its waves, so Death's
Great city welcomed armies of the dead.
Nor did it feel the greatness of a crowd;
Where there was room for all the bloodless shades,
Their earthly habit of living flesh and bone
Dissolved in shadows. While some stormed the squares,
Some strolled the palace of the King of Death,
Some went through motions of their life on earth.
Old Saturn's daughter, Juno, swept her way
Down from her home in heaven to Death's kingdom
(This much she owed to her own rage, her hate)
As she passed through his gates the threshold sighed
Under her sacred bulk; Cerberus lifted
His triune head and howled his triple warning.
Then she turned swiftly to the night-born Furies,
The grave, implacable Three who sat like rocks
In front of Hell's closed doors, their fingers raking
Dark snakes from wild hair. When they saw Juno
Stride through Hell's twilight, these fierce goddesses
Stood at attention, for they ruled the region
Known as the country of the Damned: there Tityos
Gave his liver to the birds as he lay flat across
Nine plots of land; there Tantalus reached lips
Toward water while the tree above him swayed
Fruit beyond his grasp; there Sisyphus heaved
Great rocks uphill or as they plunged down slope
Ran after them; there Ixion revolved
Within his wheel, himself pursuer and
Pursued; and there the daughters of Egyptian
Danaus, who killed their husbands, kept at labour,
Catching quick water into broken urns.

    The sharp-eyed Juno looked at all these creatures,
First, Ixion, then turned to Sisyphus,
And cried, "Why did these brothers earn eternal
Agony and sweat while Athamas lives in
A glorious home—he with his wife who always

Ignore my presence as the queen of heaven?"
Then she explained her hate, told why she made
A trip to Hell; she wished the dynasty
Of Cadmus ruined and Athamas insane.
Threats, warnings, promises came in one breath—
Even the goddesses of Hell must hear her.
When she had finished, grey-haired Tisiphone
Brushed back the snakes that drooped across her
        forehead
And said, "You need to say no more; your will
Be done. Leave our unsmiling quarters;
Go back to heavenly skies where you belong."
The happy goddess sailed away to heaven
Where Iris scattered sacred dew upon her,
Those waters which dissolved all evil taint.

    At once the fatal Tisiphone snatched up
A blood-soaked torch, and drew her cloak, still wet,
Dyed with red murder, over head and shoulder,
Then took a living snake and knotted it
Smartly around her waist; she then stepped forward.
Terror, Grief, Fear, and pale Insanity,
Who wore a twitching face, walked out with her;
She stood up at the entrance of the palace,
Now cursed forever, House of Aeolus,
Where beam and lintel trembled at her coming
And fell away from her; the burnished oak
Grew dark, the bright sun fled. Ino went mad
At what she saw; fear captured Athamas,
But as they tried to leave, the deadly Fury
Barred their escape: no exit from that room.
Vipers were darting bracelets round her arms,
And as she shook her head the waking serpents
Fell to shoulder, breast, spit blood and vomit,
And forked their hissing tongues. Then from her head
She plucked two snakes and aimed them with true art
At man and wife. The gliding creatures crawled
Over the breasts of both, kissing their lips,
Pouring black serpent's breath into their lungs;
Nor was their flesh seared, but their minds were pierced.

Nor were these all the Fury's gifts; she brought
More deadly ills: spittle of Cerberus,
Wiped from his open jaws, and Hydra virus
And fiery Apparitions born at midnight,
Amnesia and Tears and Love of Killing,
All stirred together with new-drawn blood, dosed
With green droppings from the dread hemlock tree,
All cooked in a brass pot. As both stood shaking
She tossed her broth across their naked breasts,
Where it burned inward to their very souls.
Then, clutching up her torch, she swung it high
Till all the air was lit with moving fires:
Her work was done and she sank back to Night
To put aside the serpents she had worn.

It was then the son of Aeolus went mad,
Screaming through palace halls, "Hello, my friends,
Come set your traps within this lovely forest:
I saw a lioness run out with her two children—"
And tracked his wife as though she were a beast
And as his son, Learchus, smiling infant,
Reached toward him, tore the child from Mother's arms;
As if he held a stone within a sling,
He smashed the child against a rocky wall.
The mother fell into increasing madness,
Either from Fury's broth or natural grief,
Screaming and witless and with tossing hair,
Stark naked, running with her infant son,
The child Melicertor, within her arms,
She cried out "Io Bacchus!" as she ran.
When she heard Bacchus' name, great Juno laughed;
She said, "I hope the child you nursed will save you."
Where Ino came there was a seaside cliff,
Deep-hollowed by the waves that rode against it
Into a shelter of waters free from storm;
There where the cliff-top reached high out and seaward
(For madness gave her strength) Ino climbed up.
All normal fears were swept out of her mind,
The child held fast, she dived far out to sea,
And where she fell grey waters rose in foam.

But Venus thought her grandchild badly treated,
And pleaded with her uncle, "O great Neptune,
Captain of seven seas, whose powers, except
The grace of heaven, rule the world, I ask
Large favours; show the measure of your heart,
Think, if you will, of my unfortunates
Who fell in the immense Ionian sea—
Place them among your demigods, your servants.
Since I am of the sea I claim a debt
Of family pride—among the Greeks my name
Recalls my birth in glittering white sea foam."
Then Neptune answered her and washed away
All mortal taint from Ino and her son:
The new sea god was then named Palaemon,
The new sea goddess sweet Leucothea.

The Theban women who had followed Ino
Climbed far enough to see her leap the cliff,
Nor did they doubt that she was truly dead.
In funeral tribute to the house of Cadmus,
They beat their breasts and tore their clothes and hair;
They railed against great Juno, saying she
Had been less just than cruel to the poor woman
Who had offended her. In her own rage
Against their charges, Juno said, "Dear ladies,
You'll make a monument of savagery."
Almost at once her wish came true: the woman
Who deeply loved mild Ino cried, "I follow
My dearest queen into the wild sea channel."
But as she tried to leap the cliff she stood
As if carved from the rock beneath her feet;
Another as she struck at naked breasts
Saw her arms fixed in air; another pointed
At the sea, and, as she turned to stone, her hands
Reached out forever leaning toward those waters;
Another, tearing at her hair, was held
In that wild gesture for the rest of time,
All as they were when Juno's spell came on them;
The rest were changed to birds, frail Theban women.
Who fly across the surface of that sea.

METAMORPHOSIS OF CADMUS

Cadmus knew nothing of the great sea-change
That made his daughter and her son divine.
Bewildered by ill luck that stormed upon him,
Frightened and awed by signs of further troubles,
He took flight from the city he created,
As though the place and not his own ill fortune
Were cause of all the grief upon his head.
After a long and winding journey north,
His wife and he came near Illyrian lands:
Sick with continual sorrows and old age,
They brought to mind a history of errors
That rained upon their house early and late.
Cadmus remarked, "Did my long lance pierce through
A magic holy serpent long ago,
That very day when I arrived from Sidon,
And sowed his teeth across the willing earth
Those seeds which gave us that queer race of men?
If this is cause of why the gods disown us,
Then let me be a snake with my poor belly
The length of half an acre —" As he spoke
He grew reptilian features everywhere:
His skin turned hard and scales swarmed over it
And shining spots glittered across his body;
He fell flat downward to the earth—his legs
A tail that whipped the ground beneath it.
Yet he had arms and power to reach them out,
And tears poured from his all too human face:
"Dear wife, O miserable wife, come near me;
While something of myself is left to call you,
Before the serpent swallows all of me,
Touch me and hold my hand within your hand—"
Though he had more to say, his tongue had split;
His words were sounds that hissed among tall grasses,
The only gift of speech that nature left him.
And as his wife struck at her naked breast,
"Cadmus, O stay with me, misfortunate,
Tear off your monstrous disguise," she wept,
"And what is this, where are your feet, your hands,

Your face, and as I speak, the whole of you?
And why, O gods who rule the heavens, why,
Am I not changed to serpentkind?" Cadmus
Then kissed her lips, then slipped between her breasts
As though his very life were nourished there,
As if he wished to hold her in his arms,
He glided from her girdle to her throat.
Those who looked on and saw them as they were
(For friends had come with them) grew terrified—
And yet their queen caressed the plumèd snake.
They looked again and saw them as in bed,
Their bodies joined as in a last embrace,
And yet, a moment after this, two serpents
Were seen that vanished deep in the green forest
Who neither feared nor fought with anyone,
Calm dragons that had cherished what they were.

PERSEUS

   Though changed, these two found solace in their
        grandson
Before whom India bowed, and templed Greece;
Only in Argos, through Acrisius, son of Abas,
And of his line, was one who shut the gates
Against Lord Bacchus; he, Acrisius, denied
Bacchus was son of Jove, nor would he say
That Perseus, the spawn of Danaë,
Conceived with joy beneath a shower of gold,
Was Jove's creation. Yet the very truth
Has its own strength, and bold Acrisius
Lived to regret denial of the god,
Nor recognized, as all men should, a grandson.
By this time Bacchus earned high rank in heaven
And Perseus carried as a proof of valour
A memorable prize—all that was left
Of a wild snake-haired creature, fought and won—
Through lucid air on strident, whirling wings,
Sailing for miles across the Libyan desert.
As blood from Gorgon's head streamed down to earth,
It generated snakes in ancient sands—
And that is why the desert swarmed with serpents.

Light as a cloud that drifts through winds at war,
He tacked to right and left across the skies;
Above the world, he saw its seas and mountains
Unfold beneath him like a map: three times
He saw the frozen Arctic gleam, three times
He saw the open Scissors of the Crab,
He tossed to east, to west, then back again,
And as day faded he feared to sail by night;
He steered to earth close by Hesperides
Where Atlas ruled and hoped to wait until
The morning star took fire from the dawn
And sun-bright chariot made its early start.
Here, tall as any giant, Atlas lived,
The blood of Iapetus in his veins,
He was the captain of World's End, and the master
Of that far sea that opened its cold waters
To cool the horses of the Sun and bring
To rest his well-worn blazing chariot. Atlas
Measured his wealth by several thousand sheep,
As many heads of steer, and various cattle
Who strayed the grasses of his broad domain,
Nor had he neighbours to contest his rights.
Among his treasures was a golden tree
Whose glancing leaves hid golden fruit and branches.
Said Perseus to him, "If noble heirs
Find glory in your eyes, I am Jove's son,
If you appreciate a man of action,
Whose works are miracles, then look at me;
I ask for shelter and a place to rest."
Atlas recalled an ancient prophecy
Which Themis of Parnassus told to him:
"Atlas, the day will come when your fine tree
Will lose its gold, and credit for that prize
Will go to no one else but Jove's own son."
Atlas had raised thick walls around his treasure
And set a dragon near the tree to guard it,
And if a traveller wandered past the gate,
The man was warned to go. Then Atlas turned
To Perseus. "Young man, you are invited
To go so far away that all the stories
Which you've been telling me seem true,

So far you'll get protection from your father!"
With this he tried to throw him out of bounds
While Perseus grappling with him tried to hold
Him off, to stay his anger with calm words,
Yet found himself outmatched (for who can stand
Against great Atlas?). Therefore he replied,
"Since you won't give the little that I ask you,
I have a most enduring gift for you."
He then turned round and with his back to Atlas
Lifted with his left hand Medusa's head
At which the giant turned into a mountain,
His beard and hair were trees, his shoulders, arms
Were mountain trails, plateaus, his very head
The frosted mountaintop, his bones were boulders,
Yet he continued growing everywhere
(Such was the will of gods) till heaven itself
And all its glowing stars had crowned his head.

Meanwhile the son of Hippotas locked up
The winds in their eternal caves and morning
Lucifer, that star that beckons all mankind
To daily rounds, came up the sky. Perseus
Clipped wings to heels and buckled on the curved
Sword that he carried and as quickly leaped,
Sailing at ease full speed through cloudless air.
He travelled over countless multitudes
Until he saw Egyptian shores below him
Where Cepheus was king, where unjust Ammon
Had ordered Andromeda to be punished
Because the poor girl had a foolish mother
Who talked too much. When Perseus saw her
Fastened to a rock, arms chained above the sea,
But for hot tears that rippled down her face
And swaying hair that fluttered in the wind,
He might have thought the girl a work of art,
Carved out of stone. Dazed by the sight of her
Fire was lightning in his veins; he could not speak;
Lost as he gazed he almost failed to beat his wings,
Then, as he landed near the girl, remarked,
"O, you should never wear the chains that hold you;
Wear those that lovers cherish as they sleep

In one another's arms. Tell me your name,
Why you are here, the place where you were born."
At first she did not answer, being modest;
She feared to talk to any bold young man,
And if her hands had not been chained behind her
She would have hid her face. Meanwhile her eyes,
Though free to speak, rained down her ceaseless tears.
Then, as he pressed her, to prevent his thinking
That she was guilty of some hopeless crime
She softly said her name, told who she was,
And how her mother bragged of her own beauty.
And as she spoke huge noises lashed the air,
Roaring from waves where a great dragon floated,
Riding the sea, and as it clambered toward her
The girl screamed while her parents, wild and harried,
Raced to her side, and though they beat their breasts,
Weeping their helpless tears, they knew her danger
And clung to her, while the young stranger said,
"There will be time for weeping afterward,
Yet time for rescue is a little space:
If I took to this girl as Perseus,
Jove's son and son of her who in a cell
Received Jove's favor in that golden rain
That filled her veins with life, if you will take me
As one who killed the snake-haired Gorgoness,
As Perseus who rides the air with wings,
You should be flattered by your daughter's prospects—
A worthy husband as your son-in-law.
With the gods' grace, I'll add to my distinctions
By helping you, and if your daughter's life
Is saved, she's mine." The parents took his terms
(As who would not?) and pleaded for the rescue;
And promised him rich lands as daughter's dowry.

Look out to sea! Swift as a diving, tossing,
Knife-sharp-nosed ship that cuts the waves, propelled
By sweat-soaked arms of galley slaves, the dragon
Sailed up while churning waters at its breast
Broke into spray, leeside and windward; plunging
It came as near to shore as a Balearic
Sling could send its shot. Perseus, leaping

From earth behind him, vaulted to mid-air;
The dragon saw his shadow on the sea
And plunged to tear at it. Then, as Jove's eagle,
When he has found a snake in a broad meadow
Turning its mottled body to the sun,
Falls on the unseeing creature from the air,
And as the bird, knowing the snake's forked tongue,
Grips its scaled neck and sinks his claws within it,
So Perseus dove upon the raging dragon,
Thrusting, hilt-deep, the sword into its shoulder.
Burning with its gaped wound, the dragon reared
Its bulk in air, then dived, veered like a boar
When it has been surrounded by quick hounds,
Loud with the kill. Perseus, dodging, swayed
Past snapping jaws on agile, dancing wings;
Then as the beast rolled its soft belly open,
Or bared its neck, his crooked sword struck in:
At back grown tough with sea-wet barnacles,
At flanks, or at the thin and fishlike tail.
The beast began to vomit purple spew,
And Perseus' wings, damp with salt spray, grew heavy;
He saw a rock that pierced the shifting waters
As they stilled, now curtained by the riding
Of the waves, and leaped to safety on it.
With left hand grasping on a ledge of cliff
He struck his sword three times and then again
Into the dragon's bowels. Then all the shores,
Even the highest balconies of heaven,
From which the gods looked down on Perseus,
Rang with great cheers; Cepheus and his wife,
Cassiope, called to their hero as a gallant
Bridegroom who saved the glory of their house.
And now the girl, chains dropped away, stepped forward,
The cause for which he fought and his reward.
As sign of victory he washed his hands,
Then, mindful of the snake-haired Gorgon's head,
To keep it free of scars in gravelled sand,
He set it down among sweet ferns and seaweed,
For the Medusa once was Phorcys' daughter.
At once these grasses drank in magic fluid
Of Gorgon powers; stem, leaf, and tendrils hardened.

Delighted sea nymphs gathered weeds by armfuls,
Throwing them near Medusa, for sight of magic
Where wilted greens turned into filigree
Of semi-precious stones; some tossed these twigs
As seeds to make more grow in distant waters;
Lifted to air the weeds are known as coral.

Then on the grassy shore Perseus raised
His triple altars to his favourite gods:
The left to Mercury, the right a tribute
To the warrior virgin, and then between them
A shrine to Jove. To his Minerva he
Offered a cow, to the wingèd god a steer,
And to the greatest of all gods a bull.
And with no mention of a future dowry
He took his Andromeda as his bride.
Hymen and Cupid shook the wedding torch;
The fires were lit and incense filled the air,
And through the streets houses were hung with garlands;
Behind each gate and lintel, song echoed to the flute,
All music of the joy that shone within.
Then great doors of the palace were thrown back
Where golden rooms showed gentles to a feast
And Cepheus' court joined in a celebration.

After they'd eaten well and hearts and minds
Grew large with heady draughts of Bacchus' vine,
Then Perseus asked his hosts of their own country,
Its habits and the temper of its men.
The prince, who gave him information, said,
"Now that you know us, tell what art you practised,
Bravery and skill, to take that snake-haired head."
Perseus, heir of Agenon, replied
That under freezing Atlas was a shelter
Carved out of rock, where at the open cave,
Two sisters lived, the children of old Phorcys.
These had between them but a single eye;
They loaned it to each other, hand to hand,
And as it passed, Perseus snatched it up
For his own use, then vanished out of reach.
He ran through unknown ways, thick-bearded forests
And tearing rocks and stones, until he found

The Gorgon's home. And as he looked about
From left to right, no matter where he turned,
He saw both man and beast turned into stone,
All creatures who had seen Medusa's face.
Yet he himself glanced only at its image—
That fatal stare—reflected in the polished
Bronze of the shield he wore on his left arm.
When darkest sleep took hold of dread Medusa,
Even to the writhing serpents of green hair,
He struck her head clean from her collarbone;
From that thick blood, as though it were a mother,
Quick Pegasus and Chrysador were born.

Then Perseus told the story of his travels,
Their trials and conquests, wonderfully true,
What lands, what oceans he saw under him,
And how his fluttering wings had brushed the stars.
And when he stopped, they waited for still more
Till one prince asked him why only Medusa
Of those three sisters wore snakes in her hair.
Perseus replied, "That too is a good story,
And here it is: Once she was beautiful,
Pursued by many lovers, and best of beauties,
She had glorious hair, as I heard said by one
Who claimed to know her. As the story goes,
Neptune had raped her in Minerva's temple,
A scene that shocked the nerves of Jove's pure daughter,
Who held her breastplate up to shield her eyes;
As if to warn the girl of carelessness
She turned her hair to snakes. Today Minerva
To keep bold strangers at a proper distance
Wears snakes on the gold shield across her breast."

# V

# BOOK V

Perseus' Battles • Pallas Athena and the Muses • Death and Proserpina • Arethusa • Triptolemus • Metamorphosis of the Pierides

*The story of Perseus continued from Book IV introduces us to one of the greatest of Ovidian heroes. His rescue of Andromeda chained to a rock, his killing of the sea monster sent to devour her may be read as a prevision of Saint George's slaying of the dragon. Nowhere is Ovid more skilful in the telling of complex adventures than in his recital of the Perseus-Medusa incidents. Cellini's famous statue of Perseus is the nearly perfect image of Ovid's hero, young, ruthless, beautiful to look at. The image also illustrates the proximity of Ovid's imagination to baroque art; at the very least, Cellini successfully recreated Ovid's Perseus. One could say that the amoral Italian Cellini understood the capricious Roman poet, that their visions of the world were not unlike. Ovid's wild battle scenes show a taste for the letting of blood. Readers of Cellini's* Autobiography *know that he was not averse to the sight of it.*

# BOOK V

As Perseus, brave son of Danaë,
Talked of his famous trials and victories
Before a crowd of African commanders,
The palace halls began to echo turmoil:
Not noise and music of a wedding feast,
But racket that precedes a storm of war.
And, as a hurricane lashes quiet seas
Into a roaring tumult of the waves,
So the gay feast itself became a riot.
The storm was led by raging Phineus,
King's brother, who thrust a bronze-tipped ash-plant up
And shook it in the air. "I've come," he said,
"To claim my stolen queen. Not even wings,
Nor Jove, nor that faked shower of gold shall save
You now!" He aimed his spear while Cepheus shouted,
"Brother, have you gone mad? Is this your courtesy
To him, our guest, his earned reward and dowry
For valour and the rescue of his lady?
If you wish truth, it was not Perseus
Who stole her from you, but the scaled and crowned
Ammon, sea-dragon-god of swimming Nereids
Who'd come to eat the child of my own loins.
You lost your claims when she was left to die—
Perhaps you wished her to, and, sharing in my sorrow,
To ease your own. Since you saw her in peril,
In chains, yet never stirred nor came to help her,
You, her dear uncle and her promised husband,
Sulked, and now envy him who rescued her.
What are you looking for? That girl who seems
So glorious in your eyes? You should have freed
Her from the rocks where she was held; let him who
Saved her take her, who also rescued me

117

From being childless as I grow old—then have
Him keep what he has won, his bride, his wife
Through his own merit and my word of honour.
And he, your rival, was not favoured here;
He came between you and the choice of death."

And Phineus said no more; his shifting glances
Turned to his brother, and back to Perseus,
Nor did he know at whom to thrust his spear,
Then for a moment gathered breath and charged it
With all the forces of his hate at Perseus;
Yet it went wild and struck a bench near by.
At which, as quick as ever on his feet,
Perseus tossed back the spear so aimed it would
Have pierced his enemy's heart, but Phineus weaved,
Dodged, turned behind the altar, safe and shameless,
While the swift spear went through young Rhoetus' face;
Flailing the air he fell, and the spear, torn
From joint and skull, released his blood's red fountains
On tablecloth and feast. Then the crowd's temper
Opened in flames: some threw their spears, some said
Cepheus should die as well as Perseus.
Yet the king had vanished to a safer place
Calling on Faith and Justice to look down,
And prayed to gods of hospitality,
Saying the quarrel took fire against his will.
Then war queen Pallas came to shield Perseus,
And gave her brother spirit for the battle.

From India there was a boy named Athis
Whom it was said his mother brought to birth—
Since she was creature of the river Ganges—
Beneath the waves of Ganges' purest waters.
He looked like a young god just turned sixteen,
Which made him seem much handsomer than ever;
He wore a purple cloak fringed with deep gold
As though he were a king of ancient Tyre,
A gold chain at his throat, a gold tiara
To bind his hair which smelled of sweetest myrrh.
At javelin toss he struck the farthest targets;
Yet as an archer he had greater gifts,

And as he drew an arrow to his bow
Perseus plucked up a heavy smoking torch
From the lit altar and with one quick blow
Smashed the boy's face into a net of bones.

When Lycabas of the Assyrian kingdom
Saw the boy fall, saw the sweet face of friend,
Bride, lover, changed to a blood-soaked horror
At his feet, he moaned aloud for Athis,
Whose last breath sighed through fissures of his wound.
He then snatched up the bow that Athis dropped
And shouted, "You have me to fight, my friend,
Nor long fame follow murder of this child
Which brings you greater shame than your poor valour."
And as he spoke, his arrow snapped from bowstring,
Yet merely pierced a fold of Perseus' cloak.
At which Acrisius' grandson charged at him,
Waving the sword that brought Medusa's death,
And drove the scimitar into Lycabas' heart.
And yet Lycabas, dying, eyes in darkness,
Sought out his Athis as he fell beside him
Down to death's shades, where they were one forever.

See how Phorbas from Syene, Metion's son,
And Amphimedon of Libya wild to fight,
Rushed, slipped, and fell on blood-wet floors, then, rising,
Met Perseus' sword, which pierced the side of one,
Then, flashing, cut the naked throat of Phorbas.

Yet when Eurytus, son of Actor, swung
His double axe, Perseus had dropped his sword;
He raised above his head a huge wine urn,
Embossed with gold and brass and silver facings,
And flung it at Eurytus, who fell dying
To earth in blood, his body throbbing against
The floor. Then in quick order Perseus
Felled Polydaemon of Semiramis,
And of her house Caucasian Abaris,
Lycetus, who had lived near Spercheos,
Then Helices of the long flowing hair—
And Perseus walked over the dead and dying.

Now Phineus feared to close with Perseus,
But with a wild thrust tossed his javelin,
Which wounded to the quick bystanding Idas
Who did not choose to fight, yet blazed his eyes
At Phineus to say, "O Phineus,
Since I must fight, then you must take me now
As bitterest of all your enemies.
Exchanging wound for wound, I'll come at you!"
But as he raised the spear drawn from his side,
He fell, his veins, his body drained of blood.

Then Hodites, vice-king to Cepheus, fell,
Struck down by Clymenus, while Hypseus
Had cut down Prothoenor, then Lyncides
Hypseus. Yet in that fighting mob was one
Who stood alone, ancient Emathion,
Who also stood for piety and decorum.
Too old to carry arms, he fought with words,
And stepped up to protest unholy warfare.
As trembling with old age he clung at altar,
Chromis struck off his head, which dropped straight down,
The tongue still crying doom among the flames
Until it perished in the altar fires.

Then Phineus chopped down Ammon and Broteas,
Two brothers whose gloved hands had never failed them
At rounds within a ring. But what were gloves
Against the steel that Phineus raised? Then Ampycus,
The kindly devotee of Ceres, perished,
His priestly forehead sealed with a white ribbon.
Even Lampetides, whose voice and lyre
Made him unsuited to the sight of war—
He who'd been called to bless the wedding feast
And lead the marriage choir with his song—
Heard Pettalus shouting as he raised a sword,
"Finish your song among shades of Hell,
Play on, play on!" And as he spoke his blade
Ran through the left side of the singer's face.
Lampetides staggered; as he sank to earth
His dying fingers swept across the strings
And filled the air with deep and deathly music.

Nor was his death in vain: Lycormas,
Frenzied at what he saw, tore out the bar
That held a doorway at the right and crashed it
Against his killer's neck. Pettalus, dazed,
Was struck to earth like a new-butchered bull;
Meanwhile, Pelates, who'd come north from Cinyps,
Leaped up to tear the left side of the lintel
To find his right hand fixed there by a spear
Thrown by Corythus, king of Marmarida,
While Abas plunged a sword into his side;
He could not fall, but rather swung to die.
Of Perseus' company, Melaneus was killed,
And Dorylas, millionaire of Nasamonia,
No one as rich as he in land or spices,
Heaped up in mountains over his estates.
Thrust from one side, a spear pierced through his groin—
A deadly spot. When Halcyoneus, who threw
The spear, heard Dorylas sigh and saw his eyes
Roll up, he said, "Here where you lie are all
The lands you own," and left the heavy corpse.
Perseus, quick for revenge, drew out the weapon
Warm from the bloody sheath of Dorylas' belly
And thrust it through his killer's nose, as if
It were a hot spit, boiling down his throat and back.
Fortune ran quick with him, he struck down Clytius
And Clanis, brothers of a single mother,
Yet both killed neatly with a different wound,
One with an ash spear through the thigh, the other
With an arrow between his teeth. Then also
Celadon of Mendesia was killed,
And Astreus, got by a Syrian mother,
A nameless father, and Aethion, once apt
At knowing what's to come, now fooled and broken
By false designs, and Thoactes who carried
King's battle-dress to field, and the ill-famed
Agyrtes, known for murder of his father.

    Still others pressed on weary Perseus,
All against one and from all quarters rising,
All who denied his loyalty and great valour.
At Perseus' side were ranged his helpless allies;

The father of his bride, his bride, her mother,
Who filled the chamber with their fearful cries
Among the louder crash of shield and spear
And moaning of the men about to die.
Meanwhile Bellona, goddess of all wars,
Rained blood on the protectors of the household
And where the fighting ceased restored its fire.

When Perseus saw a thousand crowd against him,
Headed by Phineus and a swift storm of spears,
As dense as winter's hail, fly left and right
Past eyes and ears and everywhere around him,
He backed himself against a thick stone column;
Shielded behind, he stood to face the battle.
Then from the left came Molpeus, warrior
Of Chaonia; from the right, full tilt,
Charging the hall, Arabian Ethemon.
Then as a tiger cat, half starved, hears lowing
Of two herds, each within a separate valley,
Can't make her choice, though wild to tear at both,
So Perseus paused to strike on right or left.
Molpeus he crippled with a sharp leg wound
And saw him limp away, but Ethemon
Gave little time for breath, and drove his sword
As if to thrust one blow through Perseus' neck,
Yet too much strength and bad aim splintered it
Against the heavy pillar where Perseus stood;
One edge flew back and lodged in Ethemon's throat,
Yet this was not enough to kill him outright,
Rather he stood with open, helpless, pleading arms
While Perseus hooked him with Cyllenius' scimitar.

When Perseus saw his energy no master
Of the great horde that still came hard against him,
He cried, "You've forced my will, and waked this horror,
The deadliest help of all. If friend is near,
O turn your face away!" Then he swung up
The dreadful Gorgon's head. "Warn others of
Your miracles," cried Thescelus, who raised
A fatal javelin in plangent air,
Yet stayed in motion as though carved in stone.

Then Ampyx plunged his sword straight at the breast
Of the great-hearted hero, Perseus, yet
As leaning toward the blow, his right hand stiffened
Nor moved at all. Then Nileus, who had falsely
Said he was son of seven-lipped Nile and wore
Its image bossed in silver and in gold
Across his shield, cried out, "Look, Perseus,
Think who my fathers were—which should be pleasure
To brag of in the silence of Death's shades!
What fame shall greet you to be killed by me!"
Even his words froze as spoke, his lips hung open.
Eryx then shouted at the two who turned to stone,
"It is your fear and not the Gorgon's head
That makes you stand as if you were asleep;
Wake up with me and cut this monster down,
This boy who talks of magic spells and weapons."
He charged, but as he lunged, floor gripped his feet;
He turned to granite in full battle-dress.

All these had earned the treatment they deserved,
Yet there was one, Aconteus, Perseus' man
At arms, who fighting for his hero, glanced
In his direction at the Gorgon's face;
He was himself in stone. Astyages,
Who thought the man alive, raised his long sword
And struck him with it—then he felt the clang
Of iron against rock. Astyages, dazed,
Stood fixed in the same trance, carved with a mask
Of wonder on his face. To tell the names
Of all who died would take too long: two hundred
Came through the battle fearful yet alive;
Two hundred saw the Gorgon and were doomed.

By this time Phineus had his own regrets
Of fighting without reason or just cause.
But what to do? He saw his warriors
All poised for action as he called their names.
Could he believe his eyes? He touched the nearest,
And knew at last that all were monuments.
He turned his face from Perseus, spread his fingers
As if admitting his defeat, and cried,

"O Perseus, you have truly conquered me,
Put that monstrosity away, Medusa-Gorgon
That changes men to stone—whoever she,
Whatever it may be, take it away!
Nor was it hate of you but wild ambition
That made me fight, and fight for her who should
Have been my bride. You have the greater valour,
And I the elder promise she was mine.
Now I want nothing except the right to live,
O powerful and brave! All else is yours."
He feared to look at Perseus, who replied,
"Dear timid Phineus, put aside your worries.
I have a gift, a great gift too, to raise low spirits,
I will not let you perish by the sword,
And you shall be a monument forever,
Here in the palace of my fond in-laws,
Where my young wife can look at you with ease—
The perfect image of a future husband."
At this he swung the Gorgon's head to face
The terror-haunted and averted eyes
Of Phineus, whose neck at once grew rigid,
And tears of onyx hung upon his cheeks.    •
Here, as if fixed for all eternity,
Were weeping features and a beggar's gaze,
Hands reaching out for mercy in despair.

Though his grandfather scarcely earned that honour,
The conquering Perseus and his new-made wife
Entered the fortress of his native city
To war on Proetus, who usurped his brother
With fire and steel. He held the fort, Acrisius,
Grandpère of Perseus, was thrown out, yet neither
Armed men nor stone-built walls could hold a siege
Against the deadly stare of snake-crowned Gorgon.

Yet Tyrant Polydectes of Seriphos
Ignored the boy's spectacular successes,
His bravery, his trials; he turned steeled hate
And everlasting anger at the hero.
He could not praise him and he thought aloud
That dread Medusa's death was storytelling.

"We'll give you ample evidence for that,"
Perseus replied. "Now shield your eyes," and wild
Medusa's face turned Tyrant into granite.

### PALLAS ATHENA AND THE MUSES

   Meanwhile Athena stood beside her brother,
Whose birth came from a stream of golden rain.
Draping an empty cloud across her shoulders,
She flew from Seriphos the short-cut over
Sea, past Cythus and Gyarus on her right,
To Thebes, then Helicon, where Muses lived,
And made safe landing on Parnassus Mountain.
She spoke directly to the gifted sisters,
Saying, "I've lately heard of a new spring
Kicked into liveliness by the edged hoof
Of that winged horse, the weird child of Medusa.
That's why I'm here—to look upon the creature,
For I was witness at his blood-soaked birth."
Urania then said, "Whatever mission
Brings you—welcome, Goddess, for you are always
Near to us in spirit, our threshold always
Open to your tread. What you have heard is
True: the winged horse Pegasus created
A new fountain." At this she guided Pallas
To that fair spring where the calm goddess rested,
Stared with a smiling wonder at clear waters
Struck into being by a lightning hoof,
And out beyond them saw an ancient forest,
Grottoes and grasses spread with brilliant flowers.
She said the daughters of Mnemosyne
Were happy in their arts and place to stay,
And one replied, "O Pallas, gifts you own
Would find you here among the best of us,
Had you not more important things to do;
Yet you are right in naming our good fortune—
Our arts, our home. It's true, we should be happy,
If we were more secure—but fear (such is
The temper of the times) destroys our rest,
And many things unhinge the virgin mind.
The sight of Pyeneus, horrid creature,

Haunts us by day; I feared the man myself.
This Tyrant with his marching Thracian army
Has stormed through Daulis and Phocian meadows
And has usurped the province that he holds.
One day, as we were going up Parnassus
To worship at the temple of our souls,
He saw us. With deceptive piety
He called out—for he recognized us all—
'O daughters of Mnemosyne, come here,
My house has shelter from the stormy sky.'
(It had begun to rain.) 'The very gods
Have taken rest within a poorer place.'
Spurred by his invitation and the storm,
We stepped inside, only to see rain vanish,
The South Wind conquered by the North, and dark
Clouds in retreat across the sky. But as
We turned to leave his house, he locked the doors
And charged at us, at which we strapped on wings
And flew to safety in the open air.
But he, as if to follow us again,
Raced to the highest of his balconies
To shout, 'Where you adventure, so shall I!'
As though he had gone mad, he leaped and fell
And stained the earth with scattered bones and
            blood."

While the Muse talked, the fluttering of wings
And words of salutation reached the ear;
They seemed to drop out of trees' highest branches.
Jove's daughter glanced up at the leaves above her,
Certain she heard the words—a human voice;
She saw a bird. And then she counted nine,
All talking crows, complaining in high voices—
Which imitate whatever noise they choose—
Of their sad fate. Minerva seemed surprised.
In lowered speech, as if goddess to goddess,
The Muse explained. "Of recent date these creatures
Have taken a sharp fall and now are birds;
They are the daughters of landowner Pierus
Whose millions came from the rich estates in Pella;
Their mother was a girl from Paeonia—

Her name, Euippe, brought to bed nine times,
And nine times called for aid from great Lucina
To bear a child. Because these foolish sisters
Were so many—and made a crowd—they thought
Themselves superior and rare, and toured
All towns of Thessaly and Achaia
To challenge us in stupid competition.
'Why try to fool the ignorant?' they said.
'We mean the silly mob, with your attempts
At poetry and songs? Unless you fear us,
Come sing with us, O Thespian goddesses,
And may the best girls win; we are as many
As you pretend to be—and count us: nine!
We shall outsing, outplay, outdance all comers:
And if you lose, we claim Medusa's spring
As well as the Boeotian Aganippe's,
And if we lose, you'll get those pretty acres
Across the north frontier to Paeonia
And half a mountain with its head in snow.
We'll have the Nymphs as jurors for our trial.'

    "It was disgrace to think of singing with them,
But greater folly to let them brag forever;
The Nymphs swore by their rivers and sat down
As proper jurors on green sandstone benches
Then she who spoke the challenge opened up—
Nor were lots drawn for those who should sing first—
And sang of war between the gods and giants,
And praised the giants with small valour to the gods.
She sang how Typhoeus sprang from earth
And shook the gods of heaven into fear
Until they showed their backs to him and ran
Far down in Egypt to the seven-lipped Nile;
With Typhoeus after them they wore
(As if to hide) false faces: 'Jupiter,'
She said, 'became a ram, leader of sheep—
Ammon of Libya wears his crooked horns—
Apollo was a crow, Bacchus a goat,
And Phoebus' sister then became a cat,
And Juno a great cow, white as a snowdrift,
Venus a fish and Mercury an ibis.'

"That was the song her voice sang to the lute
Which we Aonians were forced to answer—
But are you bored?" "Of course not," Pallas said,
"Tell me your story as it should be told,
From the beginning to the end." The Muse
Continued. "Then we chose Calliope
To lead us, one for all. She stood with ivy
Crown to dress her hair then plucked the lute and swept
Her hand across the strings—so she began:
'Ceres was first to break the earth with plough,
First to plant grain, and first of all to nourish
Natural things, she the creator of
All natural law—all things in debt to her:
Of her I sing, if I am fit to do so,
A goddess who deserves the best of songs.

DEATH AND PROSERPINA

"'The land of Sicily, that great green island
Had fallen on the giant, Typhoeus,
He who had hoped to climb to highest heaven.
He tried to move, to clamber to his feet,
But his right hand was crushed by cape Pelorus
His left by Pachynus, his legs held fast
By Lilybaeum, and his head by Aetna.
Held on his back beneath the weighted mountain
Wild Typhoeus spits out flames and cinders
And shakes the earth; from time to time, he strains,
Turns, tosses to lift up the weight of cities,
Plains, mountainsides, and forests from his breast.
Earth rolls and cracks and groans; even the tyrant
Of the silent kingdom, world under world,
Feared that the splitting earth would send a shaft
Of daylight terror down to shades below.
As if to save his dark unhappy kingdom,
He travelled upward into Sicily
Mounted behind his charging flint-black horses.
When he discovered earth's foundations firm
His mind grew quiet, but as he made his rounds,
Venus of Eryx in her mountain temple
Looked down and saw his rapid wanderings.

At this she took her son into her arms.
"My dear, my Cupid, my life, my heart, my will,
And my right hand, go take your flashing arrows
Which never, never fail and fire them straightly
Into the heart of that dark god to whom
The last part of our triple empire came.
My dear, your power sways the will of Jove,
Gods of the sea, and even he who rules them,
Why spare the lands of Tartarus alone?
Why not increase my empire and yours? One third
Of the whole world shall be your prize. In heaven
We've lost prestige and with loss comes the failure
Of love itself—surely you know Diana
And even Pallas are aligned against me:
If we allow her, Ceres' daughter will remain
A virgin till she dies, for even now
Her models are the moonlit deities.
If you respect the kingdom which we share,
Marry the youthful goddess to her uncle."
So Venus spoke; and at his mother's word
Cupid unlocked his quiver and from a thousand
Arrows took one, the keenest and best fitted
To his bow. Then, aiming from his knee, he sprung
The shaft that pierced the center of Death's heart.

"'Hard by the town of Henna was a lake,
Pergus its name; nor even Cayster's waters
Held in their echoes sweeter songs of swans.
A forest crowned the hills on every side
Where even at sunstruck noonday the cool shores
Were green beneath a canopy of leaves,
The lawns, the purling grasses bright with flowers,
And spring the only season of the year.
This was the place where Proserpina played;
She plucked white lily and the violet
Which held her mind as in a childish game
To outmatch all the girls who played with her,
Filling her basket, then the hollow of small breasts
With new-picked flowers. As if at one glance, Death
Had caught her up, delighted at his choice,
Had ravished her, so quick was his desire,

While she in terror called to friends and mother,
A prayer to mother echoing through her cries.
Where she had ripped the neckline of her dress,
Her flowers had slipped away—and in her childish,
Pure simplicity she wept her new loss now
With bitter, deeper sorrow than her tears
For the brief loss of spent virginity.
He who had raped her lashed his horses on
To greater speed, crying the names of each,
Shaking black reins across their backs and shoulders;
He stormed his way through waterfalls and canyons
Past the Palici, where fiery thick sulphur bubbled
From split earth to the narrows where men came
(Corinthians who lived between two seas
And followed Bacchus) to set up a city
That rose between two jagged rocky harbours.

"'Between Cyane and the spring of Arethusa
There is a bay, a horn-shaped stretch of water
Contained by narrowing peninsulas.
Here lived Cyane, nymph of Sicily
Who gave the place a legend with her name;
Waist-high she raised herself above the waves
And at the sight of childlike Proserpina
She called to Death, "Sir, you shall go no farther,
Nor can you be the son-in-law of Ceres
By right of conquest and the use of force;
The child deserves a gentle courtly marriage.
If I compare a humble situation
With one of highest birth, then let me say
I once was courted by my lord Anapis,
And gave in to his prayers, but not through terror."
With this she spread her arms and barred his way—
Yet Saturn's son lashed at his furious horses
And swung his sceptre overhead, then struck
Through waves and earth as his dark chariot
Roared down that road to deepest Tartarus.

"'Cyane grieved at Proserpina's fate,
Her own loss of prestige, her waters tainted

By the wild capture of the youthful goddess,
Nor was consoled; she held her wounds at heart.
Speechless, she flowed in tears, into those waves
Where she was known as goddess. There one saw
Her limbs grow flaccid and her bones, her nails
Turn fluid; and her slender gliding features,
Her green hair and her fingers, legs, and feet
Were first to go, nor did her graceful limbs
Seem to show change as they slipped in cool waters;
Then shoulders, breasts and sides and back were tears
Flowing in streams and then her living blood
In pale veins ran to clearest, yielding spray—
And nothing there for anyone to hold.

    "'In all this time the anxious frightened mother
Looked for her daughter up and down the world;
Neither Aurora with dew-wet raining hair
Nor evening Hesperus saw her stop for rest.
She lit two torches at the fires of Aetna
And through the frost-cloaked night she walked abroad,
Then, when good-natured day had veiled the stars,
Kept at her rounds from dawn to setting sun.
Spent with her travels and throat dry with thirst
(Nor had her lips touched either brook or fountain),
She saw a cottage roofed with straw and knocked
On its frail gate at which an ancient woman
Ambled forward, who when she learned the goddess
Wanted drink brought her a draught of sweetest
Barley water. And as the goddess drank
An impudent small boy stared up at her,
Made fun of her, and said she drank too much,
At which she took offense and threw the dregs
Of barley in his face. The boy grew spotted;
His arms were legs; between them dropped a tail;
He dwindled to a harmless size, a lizard,
And yet a lesser creature. The old woman
Marvelled at what she saw, then wept, then tried
To capture it; it fluttered under stones.
It took a name that fitted to its crime,
Since it was covered with star-shining spots.

"'It would take long to list the many names
Of seas and distant lands that Ceres travelled,
But when she found no other place to go,
She turned her way again through Sicily
And on this route stood where Cyane flowed.
Though she had much to say and wished to tell it—
Would have told all—Cyane had no speech
But that of water, neither tongue nor lips,
Yet she could bring sign language to the surface,
And tossed the girdle Proserpina dropped
Before her mother's eyes. When Ceres saw it,
It was as if the child had disappeared
Today or yesterday: the goddess tore
Her hair and beat her breasts—nor did she know
Where the child was, but cursed all earthly places
For lack of pity and ingratitude,
Saying they had disowned the gift of grain,
And worst of these the land of Sicily
Where she had seen the water-drifting ribbon
That Proserpina wore. With savage hands
She smashed the crooked ploughs that turned the soil
And brought dark ruin down on men and cattle;
She then gave orders to tilled field and lawn
To blight the seed, betray their duties, and
Unmake their reputation for rich harvest.
Crops died almost at birth, from too much sun,
Or withering rain; even the stars and wind
Unfavored them; birds ate the fallen seed,
And weeds and brambles thrived in starving wheat.

"'Then Alpheus' daughter, Arethusa, rose
Lifting her face from the Elean waters.
She shook her streaming hair back from her eyes
And cried, "O mother of that lost girl, the child
That you have looked for everywhere, mother
Of fruit and field, come rest awhile with me.
Forgive this pious land that worships you—
This countryside is innocent of wrong;
It had been forced to welcome rape—nor do I,
Pleading its cause, claim it my native land.
Pisa is mine, my ancestors from Elis,

And as a stranger came to Sicily—
Yet I have learned to love this countryside,
This island more than any place I know.
Here is my home—O gracious goddess, bless
The place I live; a proper time will come
To tell you why I came to Sicily,
Steering my course beneath uncharted seas—
A time when you are smiling down at me.
Earth opened to me down to deepest dark,
And floating through its underwater channels
I raised my head as if to turn my eyes
Toward stars almost forgotten to my sight,
And as I drifted through the Styx I saw
Persephone herself; she seemed in tears,
Even then her face still held its look of terror,
Yet she was like a queen, true wife, regina
Of that dictator who rules underground."
When the mother heard this news, she stood half-dazed
And stared as if she had been turned to stone,
But when her sorrow turned to active grief,
She stepped aboard her chariot and flew
To heaven itself; there, with dark features
And wild hair, flushed, passionate, she stepped
To Jove. She said, "I come to speak aloud,
To plead a case for your child and my own.
If you disown the mother, allow the child
In her distress to move a father's soul,
Nor think the less of her because I gave
Her birth, the long-lost daughter who has now
Been found—if one calls finding her sure proof
That she is lost, or if to find is knowing
Where she's gone; I can endure the knowing
She was raped—if he who has her shall return
Her to me. Surely any child of yours
Should never take a thief for her true husband."
Then Jupiter exclaimed, "She is our daughter,
The token of our love and ours to cherish,
But we should give the proper names to facts:
She has received the gift of love, unhurt,
Nor will he harm us as a son-in-law.
And if he has no other merits, then

It's no disgrace to marry Jove's own brother,
For all he needs is your good will, my dear.
His great fault is: he does not hold my place,
His lot is to rule over lower regions
But if your will is fixed on her divorce,
The girl shall rise to heaven on one condition—
That is, if no food touched her lips in Hades
For this is law commanded by the Fates."

"'He had his say, and Ceres was determined
To claim their daughter, yet the Fates said No.
But Proserpina, guileless, innocent,
Had taken refuge in Death's formal gardens
And, as she strolled there, plucked a dark pomegranate,
Unwrapped its yellow skin, and swallowed seven
Of its blood-purpled seeds. The one who saw
Her eat was Ascalaphus, said to have been
The son of Orphne—she the not least known
Among the pliant ladies of Avernus,
And by her lover, Acheron, conceived him
In the grey forest of the Underworld.
The boy's malicious gossip worked its ill
Preventing Proserpina's step to earth;
Then the young queen of Erebus in rage
Changed her betrayer to an obscene bird:
She splashed his face with fires of Phlegethon
Which gave him beak and wings and great round eyes;
Unlike himself he walked in yellow feathers,
Half head, half body and long crooked claws,
Yet barely stirred his heavy wings that once
Were arms and hands: he was that hated creature,
Scritch-owl of fatal omen to all men.

"'Surely he earned his doom through evil talk,
But why are Acheloüs' daughters wearing
The claws, the feathers of peculiar birds—
And yet they have the faces of young girls?
Was this because, O Sirens of sweet song,
You were among the friends of Proserpina
Who joined her in the game of plucking flowers?
However far they travelled, land or sea,

They could not find her; then they begged the gods
To give them wings to skim the waves of ocean,
Renew the search again. The gods were kind,
And quickly Siren limbs took golden feathers,
But human, girlish faces did not change,
Nor did their voices cease to charm the air.

   "'But Jove (with equal justice to his brother
And to his stricken sister) cut the cycle
Of the revolving year; and for their claims
Six months to each, with Proserpina goddess
For half the year on earth, the other half
Queen with her husband; then at once her face
And spirit changed, for even dark Death noticed
A weary sadness spreading through her veins,
Now changed to joy; who, like the sun when held
Behind grey mist and rain, now showers down
His light through clouds and shows his golden face.

ARETHUSA

   "'Then Ceres, all at ease and generous,
Her child at last secure in her return,
Asked why the lady Arethusa came
To be the spirit of a sacred fountain;
And while their goddess rose from her deep streams,
Wringing green hair with her pale hands, the waters
Fell to quiet murmuring, so the old
Legend of River Elis' love could be
Distinctly heard. "I was a nymph," she said,
"Of Achaia; none were more active in the chase
At beating thickets or at laying traps
Than I. Though I was bold enough I never
Tried to excel among the local beauties,
Yet I was known for being beautiful.
My looks, though praised, refused to give me pleasure;
Most girls would find them a sufficient dowry—
I blushed as red as any farmer's daughter
To get that kind of praise; I felt it wrong
To tempt and then allure. After a day
(If I remember rightly) tired and spent

With chasing through a tangled Thracian forest,
The heat was fearful and a full day's work
Had made it twice as hot. I saw a brook
So clear it seemed to run without a ripple,
Nor was there any murmuring, so clear
That one could count the smallest stones that lay
Beneath the brook that scarcely seemed to stir.
Willow and poplar, shaking silver leaves
Whose roots drank at the stream on either side,
Rose from the green and gentle banks below them,
The river stilled as if in nature's shade.
At first my feet slipped in, then up to knees;
Nor this enough, I tossed all I was wearing
On yielding willow boughs, naked I dived
Curving a thousand rings within the waters.
And as I thrashed my arms I seemed to feel
A voice beneath the stream. Then terror took me,
And I had climbed the near bank; from his waters
Alpheus cried, 'Where are you, Arethusa?'
I climbed the nearest bank while Alpheus
Himself called from the waves, 'Where are you running,
Arethusa, so fast, so fast, where do you run
Away?' So echoes of his deep sea voice
Came at me, while I, my shift, my dresses
Left across the stream, ran naked as if ripe
For him to overtake me. I ran, I fluttered
As the dove runs and shakes its wings; he hot
And racing as the hawk, flew after me
Cross field and brake, past Orchomenus,
Psophis, Cyllene, and the gulf Maenalus
And frost-tipped Erymanthus and far Elis,
Nor could he show more speed than I, yet I,
Less hardy than his strength, began to fail
While he could hold the pace of a long track.
Through prairies and hilled forests, down cliffs and rocks,
Beyond known trails I ran, the sun behind me,
My follower's shadow growing with each step longer
Before my eyes—my eyes, or fear's. I heard
His foot-beat sound like terror in my veins,
And felt his lung-deep breath sweep through my hair.
Half dead with running, I called out, 'O goddess

Of the hunting snare, I am trapped, sunk, bound,
Unless you save me; it was I who carried
Your bow, your arrows; you must save me now!'
The goddess heard me; then a dense white cloud
Of dew—no eye could pierce it—fell over me.
The river god paced round me through the fog,
Blind in white darkness, crying, 'Arethusa,
Arethusa,' twice near around me stepping
Close, then nearer. And how did I, sad creature,
Feel or care? Was I a lamb who hears the baying
Wolf cry round the herd? Or a stilled hare sheltered
Under the thorns, who fears to tremble when
It sees the fatal jaws of dogs clip near?
Nor did he leave me, for he saw no footprints
Beyond the cloud; he stood and stared at it.
Then freezing sweat poured down my thighs and knees
A darkening moisture fell from all my body
And where I stepped a stream ran down; from hair
To foot it flowed, faster than words can tell.
I had been changed into a pool, a river;
Yet in these streams Alpheus saw and knew
The one he loved, and slipped from man's disguise
To water flowing toward me as I moved.
My Delian goddess opened up the earth,
And I, a cataract, poured down to darkness
Until I came to island Ortygia
Blessed by my goddess' name and which I love,
And here I first returned to living air."


                                                        TRIPTOLEMUS


    "'So Arethusa ended her brief story
And Ceres, goddess of life-giving earth,
Harnessed her constellation of the Dragons,
The bit between their teeth. She rode midair
Until she landed at Athena's city
Where, giving her swift car to Triptolemus,
She ordered him to rain the seeds of harvest
Upon raw earth as well as fallow soil.
The boy sailed over Europe into Asia,
Steering his way to Scythia where Lyncus

Sat as a king—and there he crossed the threshold
Of the great palace. The king then asked the purpose
Of his visit, his name, what land he came from.
The boy replied, "My home is famous Athens
And I am Triptolemus, nor did I sail
The sea, nor walk the earth; the air itself
Gave up its roads to me. These are the gifts
Of Ceres that I carry, which if you
Scatter across your lands will bring a harvest
Free of all weeds and thorns." The savage king
Received this news with envy; thinking he
Should take the credit of a gift from heaven,
Made his guest welcome, lulled him off to sleep,
And then picked up a sword. But as the blade
Touched Triptolemus' breast, Ceres had turned
The king into a lynx; then she commanded
The Greek boy ride her dragons through the sky.'

### METAMORPHOSIS OF THE PIERIDES

"This to the last word was my sister's song,
And all the nymphs in concert gave the honours
To us, the goddesses of Helicon.
While the defeated sisters cursed and railed
I said, 'It was a criminal disgrace
For you to think of singing songs like ours
But now you add an insult to the crime;
Even our patience cannot last forever,
And you shall be well paid for what you've earned.'
The Pierides began to laugh and chatter,
But when they tried to talk, to thumb their noses,
They saw quick feathers spread across their hands,
Across their arms; they saw each other's faces
Grow into profiles like stiff beaks of birds;
They had become new birds within the forest,
And as they tried to beat their breasts, their wings
Were black, their bodies swung midair. They were
Gossips in trees yet all had human voices—
A fearful noise, they talk, talk, talk forever."

# VI

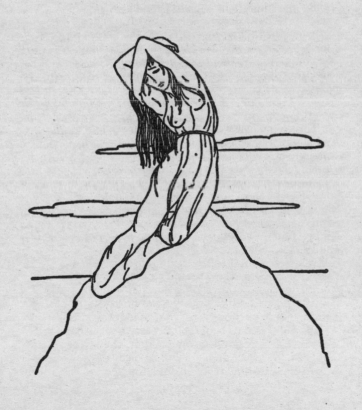

# BOOK VI

Arachne • Niobe and Latona • Marsyas • Pelops • Tereus,
Procne, and Philomela • Boreas and Orithyia

The stories of Arachne and of Niobe are among Ovid's
commentaries on the workings of Divine envy. His story
of Arachne may be read as a parable of the craftsman (or
woman) who attempts to rival divinely inspired artists. But
Ovid's way of telling the parable is important; the reader's
sympathy veers in Arachne's direction. Her stubborn pride
is foolish enough; she is not too attractive, yet Pallas Athe-
na's punishment of her is deadly cold. Ovid's Italian atti-
tude toward Pallas is not without interest: as Athens' patron
goddess, she might well represent cold-blooded Greek in-
tellectual passion. As Ovid shows, her prudish virginal fury
transformed Medusa's hair into a nest of snakes. Envy is
among her servants. She is attractive only on her visit to the
Muses. Can we say that Ovid had a deep-seated distrust of
highly formulated intellectual conduct? Perhaps. He loved
wit, but kept a shrewd, half-doubting eye fixed on deliber-
ated wisdom.

# BOOK VI

Tritonia, or Pallas as some called her,
Accepted what the Muses had to say,
Assured them that their rage against Pierides
Was in good faith, and then she praised their music.
"But praise," she thought, "is poor return for merit;
I mean true virtue, and if so, let me
Praise even myself; my dignity demands
Respect, and those who snub me shall be made
To suffer." Then she thought of young Arachne,
The girl of Maeonia, and what doom
Would come upon her, for Arachne dared
To rival Pallas at the loom, to think
Herself superior in art. The girl
Had neither family nor proper place;
Her art alone had given her rewards:
Idmon of Colophon, who was her father,
Tinted raw wool for her with Phocis purple—
Her mother dead, and both of poor estate.
And yet Arachne in a wretched home,
A cottage in the village of Hypaepa,
Was famous for her art in Lydian cities.
To see her fashion marvels on her looms
The nymphs would leave their vineyards of Tmolus,
And rise out of the waters of Pactolus,
Not merely to admire work that's done,
But to enjoy the sight of making it—
She was so light, so swift, so all at ease;
So apt at guiding raw wool with her fingers,
Rolling it in a ball, weaving her hands
From distaff through soft clouds of wool to strain it
In long threads with a quick thumb at the spindle,
So artful with her needle that one knew

No less than Pallas was her inspiration.
Yet she denied the goddess was her teacher,
And took offence when art was called divine.
"Let her compete with me," she cried. "If she
Does better, I shall give up everything."

    Then Pallas put on years and a grey wig,
Leaned on a stick to hold old legs upright,
And spoke as follows: "My dear girl, remember
All things that elders say should not be spurned.
Wisdom arrives with years—take my advice:
Accept your reputation among mortals
For artful tricks with wool, but give your goddess
Grace for your gifts and ask her to forgive
The thoughtless speeches of a foolish daughter;
You'll be forgiven if you say your prayers."
With a wild look Arachne held her fists
As though about to strike and, flushed with anger,
Said to the mask that Pallas had assumed,
"You've come to see me with a feeble mind;
Old fool, your curse is having lived too long.
Talk to your daughters or your sons' wives, if you
Have them, and I'll advise myself; nor shall I
Argue 'gainst gratuitous remarks; we are
Agreed. If you're concerned, where is your goddess?
And why is she afraid to rival me?"
The goddess answered, "She is here," and dropped
Her mask—Pallas revealed. The Thracian women
And the nymphs fell to their knees. Only the girl
Defied her, yet she stirred; as when Aurora
Flushes the sky with red and the sky pales
To gold when sun goes up, so was Arachne's
Face, her manner cool and fixed; she, foolish,
Ready to show her skill, raced to her fate.
Nor did Jove's daughter plead delay, nor warn
The girl. They set up rival looms across
The room, stretching the weblike threads from beam
To beam and, where the reeds divided them,
Flashing their shuttles through with ardent fingers
While the toothed heddles beat the nap in place.
Stoles tight across their breasts, their bare arms weaving,

They took delight in speed and craftsmanship;
And there upon the looms Tyrian purple
Shaded to lavender and violet-rose,
As though one saw the sun strike passing rain,
Its rainbow like a ribbon across the sky,
A thousand colors streaming light within it,
Each melting into each where no eye sees
One fade into the other, yet both far ends
Colors of distant hue—gold thread to bind them,
To weave the story of long years ago.

      Pallas restored Cecrops, the mount of Mars,
The ancient quarrel of naming land below it,
Twice six Immortals with Jove at the center
High on their thrones, each to the life and godlike
And Jove the very image of a king;
There God of Ocean struck the rock-grown cliff
With his long trident where salt water gushed
To name the place his own; Pallas herself
Head cased in helmet, and aegis at her breast—
These to defend her while her spear pierced earth
Down where a silver-glancing olive tree
Shot up heavy with olives on its boughs;
Athena's victory while the high gods marvelled!
So that the girl may see what waywardness
And fury can undo, Pallas sketched in
At the four corners of her design four trials,
Set off as small scenes in their own true colours:
One showed Rhodope of Thrace along with Haemon,
Now barren mountains who were mortal creatures
Who took the names of gods; another showed
The miserable doom of Pygmy's queen
(Of dwarfs undone by Juno): she turned into
A crane, then sent to war against her people;
Then next Antigone, who held her mind
Against the wife of Jove himself, and how
Queen Juno changed her to a bird: Troy could not
Help her, nor Laomedon, her father—
She was a stork, dressed in white feathers, snapping
A great long yellow bill; and last of all,
Cinyras, clasping stone steps of a temple,

The steps that once were knees of his lost daughters—
Helpless he lay and looked as though he wept.
Around all these she wove the olive leaf,
A sign of peace, her tree: the work was done.

    Arachne wove the story of Europa,
Who was seduced by image of a bull.
The bull, the churning waves were true to life;
One saw her gazing back to shore and almost
Heard her cry to friends for help, her fear
Of rising waves, her shy feet shrinking back.
Asteria captured by the wrestling eagle
Came next, then Leda on her back beneath
The swan; then Jove, seen as a satyr,
Piercing at once the lush Antiope
To fill her up with twins; then Jove as husband
To innocent Alcmena, a golden shower
To Danaë, a tickling flame of fire
To Aegina, a happy shepherd boy to
Mnemosyne, a writhing spotted snake
To Deo's daughter. After Jove came Neptune
Changed to a lively bull to take Canace;
Then as Enipeus he conceived two giants,
And as a ram he took Theophane;
Mild Ceres had him as a horse, and snake-haired
Mother of the winged horse received him wildly
As a bird, Melantho as a dolphin.
Arachne sketched these figures as they were:
Phoebus as though he lived outdoors, hawk-feathered,
Or with a lion's mane; then as a shepherd:
How he had played with Isse, Macareus' daughter,
How Bacchus hidden in a bowl of grapes
Had tricked Erigone; how Saturn, changed
Into a horse, conceived the man-horse, Chiron—
Arachne weaving swiftly round her loom
Framed the entire scene with flowers and ivy.

    Not even Pallas nor blue-fevered Envy
Could damn Arachne's work. The gold-haired goddess
Raged at the girl's success, struck through her loom,
Tore down the scenes of wayward joys in heaven,

And with her shuttle of Cytorian boxwood
Slashed the girl's face three times and then once more.
Nor could Arachne take such punishment:
She'd rather hang herself than bow her head,
And with a twist of rope around her neck
She swung, and Pallas with a twinge of mercy
Lifted her up to say, "So you shall live,
Bad girl, to swing, to live now and forever,
Even to the last hanging creature of your kind."
And as she turned away she sprayed her features
With droppings from dark herbs of Hecate;
Hair, ears, and nose fell off, the head diminished,
The body shrivelled, and her quick long fingers
Grew to its sides with which she crept abroad—
All else was belly, and the girl a spider,
The tenuous weaver of an ancient craft.


NIOBE AND LATONA


    All Lydia stirred with rumours of the story
And Phrygian cities echoed them again
Until its moral was heard round the world.
Meanwhile Niobe, who had known Arachne—
The two were neighbors in Maeonia
And lived as children near Mount Sipylus—
Ignored the teachings of Arachne's doom.
She thought of heaven slightly if at all,
The lady had too much that gave her pride:
Yet all her husband's gifts at making music,
And both their claims of kinship to the gods,
Their wealth as rulers of a state (though pleasant)
Were less than the bright joy that came to mind
When she recalled her splendid progeny.
She would have been the happiest of mothers
If she herself had not been sure of it.
Manto, the daughter of Tiresias,
Gifted with second-sight, was passing by,
And as she, tranced by heavenly inspiration,
Walked through the streets of Thebes, called to all comers:
"Ladies of Thebes, go to Latona's temple;
Offer the goddess and her twins your prayers,

And don't forget to bind your hair with laurel—
Sacred Latona speaks these words through me!"
The Theban women followed her command,
Wove laurels through their hair and burned sweet spices
And chanted what they knew of holy sayings.

But look! The tall Niobe came surrounded
By crowds of her retainers, she herself
Dressed in a purple cloak, threaded with gold;
Handsome as angry women sometimes look,
She shook her graceful head until her hair
Had fallen like a veil on either shoulder.
Then still and standing taller than before,
She turned round eyes upon the crowd and shouted:
"Is everybody mad? To primp and pray
To heavenly creatures that no one has seen?
Why is Latona praised at altars here,
And my divine right to these prayers ignored?
Tantalus, my father, was the only mortal
Fit to eat dinner with the gods; my mother
Sister of the Pleiades; strong Atlas
Who wears heaven on his shoulders my grandfather,
My other grandfather is Jove; I glory
In speaking of him as my husband's father,
And all my country looks to me in awe.
I rule the House of Cadmus, and my husband
By playing on his harp built up these walls;
The people know us as their king and queen,
And when I look about me in the palace,
I see the signs of luxury everywhere.
I know I am as handsome as a goddess,
But more than that, look at my seven daughters,
Look at my seven sons, all fit to bring me
Daughters- and sons-in-law. These are the reasons
For pride, and you may share them, placing me
Above that Titaness (daughter of Coeus—
But who was he?) Latona, fugitive,
Who scarcely found a place for lying-in.
Nor heaven nor earth nor sea would welcome her,
Exiled from everywhere, till Delos said,
'Even earth won't take you and I'm lost at sea,'

And gave her shelter on a trembling island.
There she had twins, while I've had seven times
As much as she. Of course I'm very happy
(Can you doubt that?). I am too rich in making
Boys and girls, too rich for Fortune to outwit
Me now: if she takes many, I have more;
My wealth so great I have no fear of loss.
If I lose several of the brood I made
I won't be robbed or left with two poor infants
Which were Latona's harvest—all she had
To keep herself from total barrenness.
Your prayers are done; go home and you may strip
The laurels from your hair." The women dropped
Their wreaths, the ritual broken; they turned to go,
And, as they left, murmured their goddess' name.

Then sacred Latona became indignant
And, rising to the very top of Cynthus,
She spoke to the twin deities who ruled it,
To her Diana and the young Apollo:
"I am your mother and you are my pride,
No one but Juno is a greater goddess,
And even now someone presumes to doubt
The sacred power of my gifts and name.
Unless you act, my dears, the altars raised
To me will fall in ruins, nor is this fate
My only cause for grief: that spawn of King
Tantalus (noble daughter!) says that her
Children deserve more praise than you, that I
Am barren. May this boasting knock her down!
She is as blasphemous as her loose-tongued father!"
After these words she would have pleaded further,
But "Stop!" said Phoebus, "for a long recital
Merely delays the payment made for crime,"
And Phoebe echoed him; swifting through air,
In clouds they stepped to earth near Cadmus' fortress.

Beneath those walls there was a levelled field,
Worn bare and hard by racing hoofs and wheels.
There Amphion's seven sons trained their great horses;
Dressed in Tyrian purple, they rode straightly

And steered their prancing creatures with gold bridles.
One of their number, first-born Ismenus,
Speeded the track, spray at his horse's bit.
He cried, "It's me"—an arrow pierced his heart,
Reins slipped from dying hands, he toppled toward
The beast's right shoulder as he slid to earth.
Then as he heard through the still air the whine,
The whistle of the flying arrows, Sipylus
Gave rein, and like a captain of a ship
Who feels a storm rise at his back and spreads
Full sail to catch the lightest wind, so he
Gave greater freedom to his horse for speed,
Only to take the arrow none may 'scape—
Pierced through his neck, the point beneath his chin—
Shot forward over mane and horse's head,
Tossed down to colour earth with his hot blood.
Unlucky Phaedimus and that poor boy who had
The name of Tantalus from his grandfather
(Since they were done with all their daily chores)
Drifted into a boyish turn at wrestling,
And as they came together, breast to breast,
Swift from the bow, an arrow ran them through,
And made them one: they groaned together, fell
Together in one twisting fatal wound—
The same last look from dying eyes, the same
Last gasp of breath. Alphenor saw them fall,
Struck at the heart that almost tore his breast,
Then ran to lift their cold dead bodies up;
Yet in this pious act, he tripped, Apollo
Thrust death's edged iron hot between his ribs
Which when its hooks were drawn, out came his lungs;
His breath, his blood, his life flowed into air.
Nor did a single wound strike down Damasichthon;
One arrow cut through the calf of his right leg
Between the muscles where the flesh seemed soft,
And as he stooped to pluck it out, another
From point to feather shot through jugular veins:
Blood spouted from that wound in a red fountain.
The last was Ilionous, arms thrown wide
In their surrender with a hopeless prayer—
"May all the gods on high spare, pity me!"—

He did not know he need not speak to all!
This was too late to ward Apollo's aim,
And yet the god of arrows felt his prayer;
The boy fell and the arrow grazed his breast
Which tore the flesh but did not strike his heart.

News of disaster, the sad faces of the people,
Tears of her friends brought home to Niobe
Quick sight of ruin; she stood lost in stupor,
Flushed with dark rage at what had come upon her,
And marvelled at the power of the gods.
Husband Amphion fell by his own hand,
Sword thrust within his heart; dying he brought
An end to life, to grief. O what a change
Was this Niobe from that Niobe
Who turned the people from Latona's shrine,
Who walked through streets, the envy of her friends,
And now the pity of her enemies!
Now tossed on the cold bodies of her sons,
Raining last kisses on dead wounds and lips and eyes,
And from her knees raised purple bruisèd arms,
Crying to skies, "Then drink my tears, Latona,
Eat of my sorrow: gorge your bloody heart!
With seven sons I die my seven deaths;
Take pleasure in your dirty victory!
But have you won? Even in my loss, my grief,
I have much more than what you've made or own:
After my many deaths, there's victory!"

Even as she spoke one heard the bowstring's music
Which frightened all except distraught Niobe
Whose very madness cleared her mind of fear.
Her daughters, dressed in black with hanging hair,
Stood where their brothers fell. One drew an arrow
From the loins of a dead boy, then stooped as if
To kiss him; faint and dying, there she fell.
One tried to soothe the wretched mother, failed,
Doubled with pain flowing from a hidden wound,
Her mouth tight-lipped until her spirit passed.
One tried to run away, an arrow tripped her,
One perished as her arms embraced the body

Of a dead sister, one crouched as if to hide,
Another trembled as she stood in view:
So six had died in various attitudes
Of various wounds. Only the last remained.
Her mother leaned above her with spread cloak
And body shielding her. "O not this smallest,
The youngest one," she cried. "Leave her to me—
Of all my many, leave this last, this one!"
And as she prayed the one she prayed for died.
Then like a stone the childless matron sat—
Around her the dead bodies of her sons,
Her daughters, and her husband. There no motion
Of the wind stirred through her hair, her colour gone,
Bloodless her melancholy face, her eyes
Stared, fixed on nothingness, nor was there any
Sign of life within that image, her tongue
Cleaved to her palate and the pulse-beat stopped:
Her neck unbending, arms, feet motionless,
Even her entrails had been turned to stone.
Yet eyes still wept, and she was whirled away
In a great wind back to her native country,
Where on a mountaintop she weeps and even now
Tears fall in rivulets from a statue's face.

Then without doubt all men and women trembled
At this clear signal of Latona's rage;
Then even greater awe and fear were shown
When they sang praises of the twin gods' mother.
Touched by the story of Niobe's fate,
People began (and this was natural)
To think of earlier legends about Latona,
And one recalled the incident which follows:
"Long, long ago in fruitful Lycia,
Peasants ignored the goddess to their regret.
This strange tale is unknown because its victims
Were men of poor estate and of no honour.
I saw the lake where miracles took place;
My father was too old to walk that far,
So he had ordered me to drive fat cattle
Home from that country and gave me a native
To act as guide. There where the man had led me

Through a jungle, I saw a lake and at
The middle of it an old altar, charred
With smoke and fire of many sacrifices,
And round it was a growth of shaking reeds.
Then the man stopped and murmured as in prayer,
'Have pity on me!' and I echoed after
Him, 'Have pity!' I asked him was this raised
To worship Naiads or perhaps King Faunus,
Or any other god of this domain.
He said, 'Young man, no mountain god lives in
This shrine. It is She who has it; She who
Was exiled by the very queen of heaven
Out of this world, where floating Delos hardly
Heard her prayers to give her room upon a
Tossing island. There in the shade, cradled
By palm and olive 'gainst the will of their stepmother,
She had her twins. From there the young Latona
(It was said) still ran from Juno's rage,
And carried at her breast her infant gods.
At last she reached the home of the Chimaera,
The outskirts of the land called Lycia,
There where the sun poured down his fiery heat
Across the plains the goddess sped, worn out
With her long journey, even her breasts milked dry
Where eager infants fed, lips cracked with heat
And thirst. She had stumbled near
A little lake, set down within a hollow
Where peasants gathered willows and marsh-grasses.
There she, daughter of Titans, knelt to drink,
But as she stooped to taste the cooling waters
Peasants thrust her aside, and, pleading with them:
"Why grudge me water—water the pleasure
Of everyone to drink? Nature has not
Made sun, air, and vivacious water gifts
For few alone. I ask a public want—
And still I ask it as a special need.
I've not come here to sink my tired body,
My hands, my face, my arms into this pool,
But for a drink because my throat is dry,
My tongue, my mouth are burned; I scarcely speak.
Water is nectar to me, my source of life,

And you will give me life if I may drink.
Or let these children move you—their frail arms
Reach from my breasts to beg." And at that moment,
Their arms reached out; and who could not be touched
By the sweet mildness of the goddess' words?
And yet the peasants still denied her want,
Telling her to leave or they would beat her,
And to this added curses and abuse.
Nor were these words enough: with evil pleasure
They plunged hands, feet in, danced, darkened the pool
Until the surface floated streams of mud.
Then rage came before thirst; and Coeus' daughter
Could bend no more, nor beg, nor speak with less
Authority than any goddess. She
Raised open hands to heaven and called out,
"Then you shall live forever in this pool!"
And so they did—quite as the goddess ordered:
It was their joy to live in water, dive
Deep, or show their heads, or skim the surface,
Or on the reeded banks to sit, then leap back
Into cold glistening waters of the lake.
Even now as then they speak a dirty language:
They try to croak their underwater curses,
Their voices rough and deep—their flabby throats
Swell into bags and all their quarrelling makes
Wide mouths grow bigger; and as they stretch their faces
Necks seem to disappear; their backs are green,
A filthy whiteness is their underside,
Which is the larger part of their round bodies;
As newly fashioned frogs they dance in mud.'"

MARSYAS

   When the anonymous narrator had told
How the Lycian peasants were undone,
Someone recalled the story of a satyr,
A creature whom the son of Latona
Had beaten at a match of piping music,
The reeds of Pallas played, and caused his doom.
"Why do you strip myself from me?" he cried.
"O I give in, I lose, forgive me now,

No hollow shin-bone's worth this punishment."
And as he cried the skin cracked from his body
In one wound, blood streaming over muscles,
Veins stripped naked, pulse beating; entrails could be
Counted as they moved; even the heart shone red
Within his breast. The natives of those hills,
The forest gods, fauns and his brother satyrs,
Olympus (whom he loved, even to the last),
The nymphs and every shepherd, those who grazed
Their sheep or wide-horned cattle near the mountain,
All rained with tears for him until rich earth
Drank them away into her deepest veins.
She gave the tears to vapours of the air
Which raced down gentle banks to open sea,
To take the name of Marsyas, that quick river,
The clearest stream in ancient Phrygia.

PELOPS

Then all turned from old stories to the new,
And wept for Amphion and his lost children;
All said the mother was the cause, yet Pelops,
Her brother, had a tear for her, and tore
His vest to show a plaque of ivory
Set in a spot that covered his left shoulder;
At birth both shoulders were of fleshy color,
But when his father had dismembered him,
(So rumour said) the gods repaired the damage,
All parts restored, except a missing part
Between a jugular vein and left arm joint;
There ivory took its place: Pelops was whole.

TEREUS, PROCNE, AND PHILOMELA

Since all the princes of those lands were gathered,
The cities asked their kings to send condolence
To Cadmus' walls. Argos and Sparta joined,
Then came the Peloponnesian Mycenae,
Then Calydon—all cities that had not waked
Diana's envy; fruitful Orchomenos,
And Corinth, noted for its art in bronze,

Brave Messene, Patrae, obscure Cleonae,
Pylos, Troezne, before Pittheus came,
And all the rest, enclosed by Isthmus,
The land between two seas and cities seen
From there across two channels. Only you
(And who'd believe it?), Athens, sent no word;
For war had severed diplomatic ties—
Barbarians from across the seas were storming
Its walls once fortified by Mopsopius.
Tereus fought them back with his battalion
That raised the siege which gave him greater fame.
Since he was rich and had his own stout army,
And fortunate also in having noble blood
From Mars himself—King Pandion of Athens
Took him as son-in-law, husband of Procne.
But Juno, chosen as the bride's own goddess,
Hymen, and the three Graces were not there
To bless the wedding—and the Furies came
With torches stolen from a funeral pyre;
They made the bridal bed, and a scritch owl
Howled from the rafters of the wedding room:
And with these blessings Procne took Tereus
And in their presence they conceived a child.
All Thrace joined in a general celebration
And praised the gods: first when King Pandion's
Daughter received her lord and their great tyrant,
And second on that day Itys was born—
So are the fortunes of our lives concealed.

Now through five autumns Titan turned the years,
Then Procne, as she flirted with her husband,
Said, "Dear, if I am sweet to give you pleasure,
Let me go home to visit with my sister,
Or rather, bring her here to visit us;
Promise my father that her stay is short—
For if I see her, that is my reward."
Swiftly Tereus mounted sail and oar;
Steering through Cerops' harbor he set foot
On Piraeus and took the king's right hand:
Good cheer and welcome!—then began to talk
Of why he came, his wife's desire, and said her

Sister would be returned almost at once
To her own home—when look! the girl walked in,
Young Philomela, dressed like any queen
But richer underneath her clothes her beauty;
So as one hears of water nymphs and dryads
Moving among the green shades of the forest,
It was the way she seemed—that is, if they
Were dressed as fine as she. With one look at her
Tereus was in flames—the kind of fire
That sweeps through corn, dry leaves, or autumn hay
Heaped in a barn. Of course the girl was worth it,
But all his natural passions drove him on;
Men of his country were well known for heat—
Their fire took root within him as his own.
His impulse was to bribe her maids, her nurse,
Or with his riches make the girl a whore,
Even at the price of losing all he ruled,
Or rape her at the cost of war and terror.
Stormed by the heat of love, nothing could stop him,
Nor heart hold back the flames within his body.
Nor could he wait: he made his wishes seem
Procne's desire; love made him quick of speech,
And when he talked too fast, too eagerly,
He said he took instructions from his wife
And at her inspiration begged and wept.
Great gods! What darkness fills the human heart!
As he built up his plans Tereus got
Credit for being kind, soft, pious; he
Was loudly praised for criminal intentions,
And more than that, unwary Philomela
Shared his impatience; with her soothing arms
Around her father's neck, she begged to go,
To see her sister for her own good health—
But, if she knew, against it; still she pleaded.
As Tereus looked at her, he had a vision:
The girl was in his arms. Then as she glided
Her arms around her father's neck and kissed him
All this increased his fire; he saw himself
Taking her father's place—if he had done so,
His flushed desires were none the less unholy.
King Pandion at last gave way to both;

Tereus' wishes were no less obscene,
His hopes were no less evil. Then the King
Gave way to them. His daughter danced with joy
And thanked her father for herself and Procne,
Unlucky fool!—which brought despair for both.

Day's journey of the Sun had nearly ended,
Westward his horses steered behind Olympus.
Royal supper served, red wine in golden vessels,
Feasted and drunk, the palace fell asleep,
But not Tereus—though he went to bed,
His mind still boiled with thoughts of Philomela,
Her glance, how she moved her feet and hands—
And what he had not seen he well imagined,
Which fed his furnace high and drove off sleep.
Daylight arrived and Pandion wrung his hand,
And weeping gave his daughter to his care:
"My loving son, benevolence has won me;
Since both my daughters wish to see each other
(And that is your desire, my Tereus)
I trust this girl to you; and by your faith,
Our kinship and gods' will, take charge of her
As with a father's love, and in brief season
(Which is long to me!) send the girl home again,
For she's the last delight of my old age.
And as you think of me, my Philomela
Come back to me at once (even your sister
Is far away)." These were his last instructions:
He kissed his child with swelling tears, then asked
The two to keep their promises by taking
His right hand, and joined theirs to seal the contract,
Nor to forget to bring from him warm greetings
To Procne and her son; at this his voice
Gave way; he shook with weeping and thick tears
Through his good-byes. He feared what was to come.

With Philomela on his painted galley,
Waves curled and tolling under its swift oars,
Land falling out of sight, then stout Tereus
Cried, "Now, I've won the answer to my prayers!"
His barbarous heart held cheers, and he could barely

Hold back his naked gladness; his eyes shone at her
Never to leave her face; he, like Jove's eagle
When the bird has clawed then dropped a shrinking
Rabbit in a high nest and the spent creature
Has no chance of an escape—Tereus gazed,
And gloried at the prospect of his feast.

The wave-tossed ship soon struck the shores of Thrace,
Then the barbarian king seized Pandion's daughter,
And where old forests hid a small stone cottage
He thrust her in and turned to lock the door;
The girl, pale, frightened, shaken with tears, asked where
Her sister was, while he disclosed his need
And mounted her. Like any helpless girl,
Trapped and alone, she cried out for her father,
Then her sister, but, more than these, she called
The names of gods. She trembled like a lamb,
Which, torn and fearful, clipped by a grey wolf
Does not believe itself alive, or as a pigeon
Blood-winged and throbbing from the claws that pierced
        it,
Still fears the tearing of its beating veins.
When her mind cleared she plucked her hanging hair,
Tore at her arms like one who had seen death,
Then with her hands reached out she said,
"What have you done to me? O beast, O savage horror!
Have you undone my father's will, his words,
His tears, my sister's love, my innocence,
The laws of marriage? And all changed to madness!
I am a whore that turns against her sister,
And you are married to us both; now even Procne
Is my enemy; why don't you kill me?
O liar, liar, false! I wish you had,
Even before this happened; I'd be a ghost,
Bloodless and pure among the shades. If those
Who live above the earth look down, if there are gods
Who see and know this room, my fate, my terror,
If all things have not perished where I turn,
The day will come, or late or very soon
When you shall find just payment for your crimes.
I'll tell the world how you have ravished me,

And if you keep me here within the forest,
I'll make each rock, each stone weep with my story,
And if God lives, heaven and He shall hear it."

    At which the tyrant's anger rose in flames,
No less his fear; quickened by both, he drew
Sword from its scabbard at his side, and seized
His mistress by her hair and pinned her arms
Behind her as he bound them. Philomela
Saw the sword flash before her eyes and gave
Her neck to meet the blow, to welcome death;
Instead he thrust sharp tongs between her teeth,
Her tongue still crying out her father's name.
Then as the forceps caught the tongue, his steel
Sliced through it, its roots still beating while the rest
Turned, moaning on black earth; as the bruised tail
Of a dying serpent lashes, so her tongue
Crept, throbbed, and whimpered at her feet. This done
The tryant (it was said; we scarce accept it)
Renewed his pleasure on her wounded body.

    Carrying his guilt he entered Procne's rooms,
And when his wife asked where her sister was,
He lied and sobbed, spoke of her sister's death:
His very tears made what he said seem true.
Then she ripped off her gold-embroidered cloak
And dressed in black. She raised a sepulchre
In memory of her sister and the false image
Of an absent spirit took prayers and lentils.
It was not proper that her sister's fate
Received this kind of honour or its grief.

    Twice six times in the courses of the year
Phoebus rode through the wheeling Zodiac.
And how could Philomela spend her days?
A spy was kept in arms outside her door;
Around the cottage was a stout stone wall;
Her silent lips could not tell tales of loss.
Deep sadness turns to help from mother wit,
And misery generates a subtle shrewdness.
She strung crude country wool across a loom

(The purple threads pricked out against the white);
She wove a tapestry of her sad story.
When it was done she gave it to her servant,
The one poor maid she had, and with dumb show,
Begged her to take a present to the queen.
Not knowing what it was, the frail old woman
Delivered the rolled gift to Procne's hands
And when the monster's wife undid the package,
She read the fearful story of her betrayal.
Then she was silent (which was a miracle!);
Grief closed her lips, held back the words that stormed
To speak her anger; and there were no tears,
No thought of right or wrong—only her fury
With all her being speeded toward revenge.

This was the time, once every other year,
When Thracian women held a feast to Bacchus
(Night joined their mysteries: at night Rhodope
Clanged, and all air trembled with the noise of brass).
It was at night the queen slipped from her house:
She wore the dress of Frenzy; vines that hung
Down from her hair, the deerskin flying at her
Left side, the light spear carried on her shoulder.
There with her retinue, like one gone mad with grief,
She raced the forest (O the perfect actress
Of your passion, great God Bacchus). She had come
To Philomela's hidden cottage door,
Crying the name of Bacchus, smashed its bars,
And decked her sister as a wild Bacchante,
Her face green-draped in ivy and ripe vines,
Swept her half-dazed into her own apartments.

When Philomela saw where she had come,
The house of curses and of nameless sins,
The luckless girl went white with shock and horror.
Then Procne found a room to quiet her,
Unwound the vines that hid her guilty face,
And held her in her arms. The trembling girl
Could not look at her sister; she felt shy
At being cause of Procne's injury.
Face turned to earth she wept and longed to call

Gods down to prove her sins were not her will;
Speechless, she raised her hands to speak her prayers.
But, turned to fire, Procne scolded her
And cried, "Now is no time for tears; we need
Good steel, something that has a bolder strength
Than iron, and with a keener edge, my dear.
This is my day for crime, to take a torch
To all rooms of the palace, to push Tereus,
Who made us what we are, into its flames,
Or clip away his tongue, tear out his eyes,
Cut off the genitals that injured you—
And then still gaping with a thousand wounds
Whip from that body breath of its damned soul.
My heart is fixed upon some major plan,
But what or where I'm still of several minds."

As Procne spoke, young Itys sauntered by;
The sight of him became an inspiration;
She glanced down at him with unfeeling eyes:
"How much," said she, "the boy looks like his father,"
And said no more, yet her blood boiled with rage—
Then she began to plot her new design.
But when he came to throw his arms around her
And kissed her with a sweet, curt boyishness,
Her anger vanished; she became all mother.
Though she resisted them, tears filled her eyes;
Then when she saw her plan less clear and shaken,
And she herself becoming more maternal,
She stared back at her sister, then her son,
And looked at both: "Why does one speak so sweetly,
While the other's lost tongue cannot say a word?
Why can't she call me sister? He cries mother.
I am the child of Pandion, a king,
Must I recall whose wife I am? Tereus?
Honour his bed? Such honour is perversion
In my blood!" And no more words—she caught up
Itys, and as a tigress carries off
A poor teat-sucking fawn down the deep forests
Of the Ganges' side, so she took Itys,
Far to a lonely room of the huge palace.
The boy saw death within his mother's face

And screamed, "O mother, mother!" reached his hands
As though to throw his arms around her neck,
And Procne, with no change of eyes or feature,
Ran a quick knife below his beating breast.
The boy died with one thrust, but Philomela
Stabbed through his throat; the body warm, still breathing,
Was cut and pared: some pieces turned on spits,
Others boiled in a pot. The room ran blood.

This was the preparation Procne made
For the high supper served to bold Tereus
Who in his ignorance took each dish from her hands,
She saying it was his ancient privilege
To eat the feast alone, servants and slaves
Dismissed—and she his maid in waiting. So
He sat as on a throne for a state banquet
And eagerly ate flesh of his own flesh;
Blind as he was to what his wife had done,
"Bring Itys here," he called; and she, bright with
Mad joy to be the first to let him know
His fate, cried out, "You have the boy inside."
Again he turned to ask her where he was,
And as he called a third time, Philomela,
Spotted with blood of Itys, her wild hair
Flying, leaped up to him, tossing the boy's
Blood-dabbled head into his face: at no time
Had she the greater need for words of joy
She felt at serving him. Then with a cry
The Thracian tyrant kicked away the table,
And hailed the snakehaired Furies from Hell's pit.
Now, if he could, he'd cut his breast in two
And from it tear the body of his son.
Weeping he called himself his son's sad tomb;
Then with a naked steel he paced the floor
To trap, to strike down both of Pandion's daughters—
Who flew, as if on wings, ahead of him.
In truth, they were on wings: one took to forest,
The other fluttered to the roof. Even now
Such birds have stains of murder on their breasts
In flickering drops of blood among their feathers.
And he himself in flight, spurred by hot grief

Changed to a bird, his crown spiked quills, his beak
A long spear pointed toward revenge, slow-winged,
He was a red-eyed plover, armed for war.

Sadness drew Pandion's days to a swift close
And brought him to the shades of Tartarus
Before he walked the length of his old age.
His land, his sceptre, came to Erechtheus,
Well-known for justice and a potent army;
He had four sons, four daughters of which two girls
Were of surpassing beauty: one had made
(And this was you, O Procris) Cephalus,
Grandson of Aeolus, a happy husband.
Because of Tereus and cold Northern Thrace,
Boreas was disliked and not encouraged
To make a match with his much-loved Orithyia,
Nor did he press too hard; his words were prayers,
Yet when he found his gentleness meant nothing
He whipped up anger in his usual style
And said, "I've earned defeat, for my true manner
Is one of wildness and cold rage, and threat
Of horror. And of what profit are mild words
To me? The way I live is force that drives
Dark clouds, turns sea to tempest and uproots
Great oaks, snow into ice, and rain to hail
That storms the helpless earth. Then when I meet
My brothers in the sky—my field of war—
I fight them with such rage the heavens thunder
And fire comes roaring out of empty clouds.
And that is how I tear through every hollow
Of the earth; my backside harries every crack,
Each crevice, down to the lowest caves where ghosts
Take fear, and, like the whole world, shake with cold.
That's how I should approach my wedding day.
Nor should I plead my way with Erechtheus,
But force him to make me his son-in-law."
With these remarks and others not less stormy,
Boreas raised his wings and with their beating
Clapped a great blast on earth and tipped wide ocean;

He trailed his cloak across high-peakèd mountains,
And swept the ground. Then in his shroud of darkness
His dusky wings encircled Orithyia
Who was all terror as he caught her up
And held her as a lover in his arms.
And as he sailed, his cold heat turned to flames,
Nor did he drop to earth until they reached
A northern country with its savage people;
And so it was that an Athenian princess
Married the ice-flamed king of the Cicones.
She had twin sons like her in every feature,
Except for wings: some say these did not grow
Until their short beards matched wild yellow hair
And both the faces of Calais and Zetes
Were ruddy as their father's wind-tanned cheeks—
Then both had wings clipped to their sides like birds'.
When they grew up they joined the Argonauts
In the first ship that sought the Golden Fleece.

# VII

# BOOK VII

Jason and Medea • Minos Wars Against Aegeus • The Myrmidons • Cephalus and Procris

*Ovid's Medea is far more bloody, more savage in her behaviour than the heroine conceived by Euripides. Ovid makes her an archetypal sorceress, a priestess of Hecate and all the evil forces of night. Her image survives in tales of witchcraft, and her chariot, drawn by dragons, became transformed into a broomstick. Ovid invests her with the full trappings of superstitious horror. He accents the melodramatic elements in her story, and enlarges the range of her deliberated crimes. Her last act is an attempt to poison Theseus. As an Ovidian figure she loses the tragic potentialities of Euripides' heroine and very nearly all semblance of human character. Like incestuous Myrrha of Book X, she belongs to Ovid's world of night, a figure of* nightmare *in its original meaning; she is Medea as a female incubus. Her murder of old Pelias by making his stupid daughters the instruments of his death is like a scene enacted in a dream. Her magic of restoring youth and potency to old age also belongs to the night world of desire known in dreams. No central figure on the stage of the* Grand Guignol *is more spectacular than she.*

# BOOK VII

Now in a ship that had been built at Pagasae
The Argonauts cut through the restless waves.
And on their way they saw blind Phineus,
His pitiful old age in endless night;
Sons of the North Wind came to drive away
The girl-faced vultures plucking at his lips.
This scene was one of many swift adventures
Shared by the Argonauts, led by bright Captain Jason,
Who steered them safe at last; the ship was beached
Within the rapids of the mud-brown Phasis.
Officers and crew had come to take the fleece
Stolen by King Aeetes (as his gift
From Phrixus) nor would this hard-driving king
Give up the fleece without harsh terms and trials.
As the dispute ran high, the king's own daughter,
Sharp-eyed Medea, burned with quickening heat.
She fought against her fever: it was madness;
Nor could she cool her brains with hope of reason.
She cried aloud, "Medea, wits are futile
Against this heat. Some god's bewitched my senses,
Chained my will. Is this called love? Why do
The trials my father offers these young men
Seem difficult and cruel? His price is high:
Why do I fear the death of one I've seen
But for a moment and for the first time only?
What lies behind this fear? Then come, Medea,
Tear out the flames that scorch your innocent heart,
You poor, unlucky child! Brace up, my darling,
Be yourself again: O if I could, I would,
But now against my will an unknown power
Has made me weak: heat sways me one way,
And my mind another: I see the wiser,

167

Yet I take the wrong. And why do you, king's
Daughter as you are, grow hot with love because
You see a stranger? To seek a wedding bed
In an alien world? There's much to love
At home. And if he lives or dies? Gods' will
Takes care of that. And yet I hope he lives!
Let me hope, pray for him, and yet not love!
What harm has Jason done? It is inhuman
Not to be moved by Jason's manliness
That shines like summer's day, and his green vigour,
Even that clear line of his gentility;
If nothing else, look at his lovely face!
Surely he stirs my heart! Now to his rescue:
Great bulls will burn him blind with fiery breath,
And from the seeds that fall from his own hand
An army sprung from earth will strike him down
And he'll be fed as carrion to a dragon.
If he's destroyed, his very death shall prove
That I'm no more than a mad tigress' daughter,
My heart a bloodless weight of iron and stone.
Why can't I look down at him as he falls?
Why is that vision tainted in my eyes?
Why don't I order great bulls to charge, armies
To cut him down, and spur the watchful dragon
Who never sleeps? These questions are not answered
By a prayer; they call for action now—and yet
Shall I betray my father's kingdom, crown,
To shield an alien hero in my bed,
Then see him set his sails and make away
With some new bride? And I, Medea, pitiful,
Alone? But if another woman takes
His love, he's earned his death. No, no—his manly
Look, aristocratic air, his poise, his grace
Deny my foolish fear of being tricked.
And should I help him, I shall have his promise;
Even the gods shall witness our premarriage—
Then why be fearful if the way is certain?
To thrust aside delay, one must act now.
Jason shall be in debt to you forever,
And shall be yours in gravest matrimony;
Great crowds of women from every town in Greece

Would know your name as one who saved their hero.
Then shall I leave my native gods? Leave brother,
Sister, father? This country runs wild and rough,
My father savage, my brother a mere boy.
My sister would encourage me to go,
And, more than that, a godlike power rules me,
Greater than all the gods! Nor shall I leave
The very best behind, but journey toward it:
My fame shall be of one who rescues heroes,
Young Greeks, and shares with them a better country,
Cities so brilliant their reflected glory
Shines on these shores, and with them art and learning.
And, more than all these gifts, I'd hold a man
I would not trade for the round world itself
And everything within it, the Son of Aeson
Standing at my side, the man my husband,
And myself the choice of heaven; even now
I seem to walk among the stars. But what of
The mountains rising from 'mid seas at war?
Even brave sailors fear rock-caved Charybdis
Who drinks the waves, vomits them out again,
And Scylla with her barking dogs around her
Churning the waves that circle Sicily.
Yet holding what I love and Jason's arms
Around me, I shall have no fear, or if I
Tremble, that will be fear for him, my husband,
Him alone. But wait, Medea, do you call
Heat marriage, and give a fancy name to your
Desires? Look to the next day and the next.
Look at your longings for what they are, leave them
To die"—this to herself. And Daughterly
Affection, Modesty, Right Thinking shone;
Defeated Cupid nearly flew away.

Then toward the shrine of Hecate she turned,
An ancient altar in a deep-leaved forest,
Her mind made up, her ardour almost dead.
And as she walked, she saw the son of Aeson;
The dying fires of love were waked again.
She flushed up to her eyes, her face was lit,
An inner radiance spread within her veins

And as pale embers hidden beneath grey ashes
Fanned by a little breeze are stirred to flame,
Crackling and swelling to its former heat,
So now her languid love took life again
As the young hero stepped before her eyes.
It happened that young Jason looked refreshed,
More handsome than himself; one could forgive her
For being overwhelmed, he was so fair.
As if she had not seen the man before
She stared with both eyes fixed upon his face,
And in a trance she saw him more than mortal,
Nor could she turn her shining gaze away.
And as the foreigner began to speak aloud,
To prison her right hand in his, to sigh
His need of her and promise marriage, tears
Flowed from her eyes like rain; quickly she said,
"I see what I am doing. I know the truth,
For it is love that brings me to your side.
Even my arts are here to save your life;
Only be sure your promises are kept."
Then by the three-faced goddess, Hecate,
By all the mysteries of the shaded forests,
By father of his father-in-law to be—
Yellowed-eyed Saturn who looks on everything
By his own trials and hard-won victories,
Jason swore that his hand was hers forever.
She took him at his word: then gave him straightly
A spray of magic herbs, and he, delighted,
Strode through the woods back to his sleeping quarters.

When dawn had cleared the stars from the pale sky
Crowds filled the arena of the field of Mars,
Then climbed the hills to watch the coming battle;
And at their centre sat the king in purple
Who held a golden sceptre in his hand.
Look! Now bronze-footed bulls charged to the field,
Whose steel-ringed nostrils poured a blast of fire;
Grass withered at their feet. As flames within
A raging furnace roar, as limestones splashed
With water in a kiln splutter and steam,
So roared the thunder in bulls' chests while Jason

At his ease came at them marching. The bulls
Turned up their furious faces at him, iron-
Tipped horns in air, the earth cut into dust
Beneath them, the echoing hills stormed back
Their fiery groans. The frightened Argonauts
Stood stark with terror, yet Jason still advanced
Nor seemed to fear or feel that fiery breath—
Such was the power of magic drugs upon him.
He stroked the creatures with a steady hand,
Caressed their dewlaps, and as quickly tossed
A harness over them; startled, they drew
A plough across the trampled untilled campus.
The Colchians rose in wonder at the sight;
Argonauts cheered and spurred their Captain forward.
Then Jason thrust his hand in a bronze helmet
And sowed the serpent's teeth behind the plough.
Snake's-spittle-green the seeds dropped to quick earth,
And, as men in their mothers' wombs unfold,
Nor are made whole until they gasp and fall
Crying into the world, so from earth's belly
New creatures stepped, full-armed, miraculous,
And every man clashed weapons that he wore.
When young Greeks saw them aim their spears at Jason
Their mouths fell open and their hearts grew heavy.
As she saw Jason turn (one man alone)
To meet that army, even she, Medea,
Grew white and cold with fear, as if the herbs
She'd given him were futile. Then she chanted
(As if at prayer) a spell of deeper magic
Than her dark arts and gathered herbs revealed.
Meanwhile young Jason threw a side of rock
That struck the centre of that charging army,
Which made it rage, each man against the other—
Earth's sons gone mad in their own civil war.
Within the field of fallen warriors
The Greeks hailed Jason for his victory,
Hugged him and made him flush with their embraces.
You would have done the same, savage Medea,
If thought of gossip had not held you back;
You were discreet—you gazed at him and shone
And thanked the dark gods with your silent prayers.

The next trial was to meet the Sleepless Dragon,
To close his eyes; one held that beast in awe
(The creature had to guard the Golden Tree)
Because of his great plume, his triple tongue
And fangs, yet Jason sprayed him with green liquor
Distilled from Lethe's herbs, and said three times
The words that cause mild sleep, to soothe and quiet
Mountainous seas and rapid river falls;
And sleep closed eyes that never slept before—
Then Son of Aeson plucked the Golden Fleece!
Big with his loot and at his side the woman
Whose arts had charged him with the skill to take it,
Jason and bride and crew sailed to Iolchos.

To celebrate return of sons and heroes
Aged fathers and Greek matrons brought rich gifts
(Which they had pledged), incense, a gold-horned bull
For sacrifice; and many altars blazed
In Grecian temples. But Aeson did not join
These happy crowds: under the weight of years
He sank near death; therefore his son said, "Wife,
Dear wife, you who have saved me, whom I owe
More than I dreamed (and if your arts have done
All this, what can't they do?), take living years
Out of my life and resurrect them in
My father." Jason's face was wet with tears.
Medea, stirred by what she saw in Jason's face,
Love for his father, made her think of home
And old Aeetes left behind, yet she
Said nothing of this thought, but cried aloud,
"What blasphemy is this, my gallant husband?
How can I give another man one day,
One hour of your precious life? Hecate
Would scarcely listen to my prayers, nor can I
Ask for crimes of that description.
In spite of this I may do something better
Than cutting short your days. I may have arts
That will revive, increase the many years
Your father has to live. If Hecate
Will help me at this trial, then all is well."

After three nights had passed and Luna's horns
Joined in their circle to flood earth and sky
In silver splendour, loose-cloaked and barefoot,
Hair fallen over naked breasts and shoulders,
Medea stepped abroad in silent midnight.
Men, beasts, and birds were locked away in sleep;
No rustle of a whisper through the forest.
The leaves were voiceless and moist air was still,
And only stars flashed in moonlight above her.
Three times she raised her arms to stars and sky,
And three times wheeled about and three times splashed
Her hair with moonlit water from a brook.
Three times she screamed, then fell upon her knees
To pray: "O night, night, night! whose darkness holds
All mysteries in shade, O flame-lit stars,
Whose golden rays with Luna floating near
Are like the fires of day—and you, O Hecate,
Who know untold desires that work our will
And art the mistress of our secret spells,
O Earth who gives us bounty of weird grasses,
Your wandering winds and hills and brooks and wells,
Gods of the dark-leaved forest and gods of night,
Come to my call. When you have entered me,
As if a miracle had drained their banks and courses,
I've driven rivers back to springs and fountains
I shake the seas or calm them at my will;
I whip the clouds or make them rise again;
At my command winds vanish or return,
My very spells have torn the throats of serpents,
Live rocks and oaks are overturned and felled,
The forests tremble and the mountains split,
And deep Earth roars while ghosts walk from their tombs.
Though crashing brass and bronze relieve your labours,
Even you, O Moon, I charm from angry skies;
Even Sun's chariot (which my grandfather pilots)
Grows dim when my enchantments fill the air,
And flushed Aurora takes a greenish pallor.
O Hecate, who answered my last prayer
To still the smoking breath of fiery bulls,
And tamed the beasts who never ploughed a field,

And spurred wild warriors of the serpent's teeth
To fall in their own blood, who charmed the Sleepless
Guardian of Golden Treasures while Jason took
That famous shield to Greece, now, I need more,
A magic, potent drink that dissipates
Old age and fills old veins with manly blood—
Nor shall you fail me; even the distant stars
Have bowed their shining heads at my command,
And here's my chariot with its winged dragons."
Then from night's heaven her chariot floated near;
First she caressed the arched necks of her creatures,
Then leaped aboard and shook their flickering reins,
And with that signal sailed through moonlit air.
As she glanced over lovely Grecian valleys
She steered her team toward neighbourhoods she knew:
She searched the foliage that Ossa wore,
Steep Pelion, flowering Othrys, and fair Pindus,
And Mount Olympus who leaned over it.
She took her choice among the plants that pleased her,
Some, roots and all, others she trimmed as one
Might cut a flower, clipping them neatly
With a bronze scimitar; she plucked rare grasses
From the sides of Apidanus, from waters
Of Amphrysus, nor forgot Enipeus;
Peneus and Sperchus gave their share,
And the reed-crowded shores of slow Boebe;
At Anthedon she clipped the vital mosses
Known for their powers to increase the span of life,
But yet unknown as the weird food that changed
Glaucus the fisherman to a sea god.

Nine days and nights looked down on her adventures—
Medea in her chariot of dragons;
Then she steered home, the dragons safe, yet fumes
From evil-smelling herbs had scorched them:
They sloughed the scales they'd worn for many years.
She left the chariot outside her gate and swiftly
Turned from her husband's arms and stayed outdoors.
She made two mounds of earth: the right to Hecate,
The left to Youth—these were her altars, decked
With the boughs she'd gathered from near forests,

And at their sides she dug a little moat.
At one thrust of her knife a black sheep fell
Whose veins were emptied at her altars' trough
And into blood she stirred warm milk and wine.
Meanwhile she chanted spells to deepest earth
And said a prayer to Dis and his fair bride
(The unhappy girl he'd stolen from her mother),
And begged them not to steal the breath of life
From the grey breast of Jason's dying father.

When she had soothed the tempers of her gods
By repetitious prayers, she told her servants
To bring old Aeson's dying corpse outdoors,
Then with a lullaby she closed his eyes,
And laid him, as one might stretch out the dead,
Helpless upon a mat of herbs. She ordered Jason,
His servants and her own to leave the spot,
Nor look with curious eyes at holy magic.
When they were safely out of sight, Medea,
Wild-haired Bacchante at her flaming altars,
Thrust forked divining boughs in pools of blood
And lit these blood-stained branches at altar fires.
Three times she purged the old man's flesh with fire,
Three times with water, three times with smouldering
         sulphur,

Meanwhile in a bronze pot her liquor simmered,
Steamed, leaped, and boiled, the white scum foaming hot:
There she threw roots torn from Thessalian valleys,
Seeds, flowers, plants, and acid distillations,
And precious stones from the far Orient,
And sands which the spent tide of Ocean washes,
The whited frost scooped under the full moon,
Wings of the weird scritch owl and his torn breast,
Bowels of the werewolf which shudder and twist
Into a likeness of mad human faces,
The scaled skin of a thin-hipped water snake,
Liver of a long-lived deer, foul eggs,
And battered head of a crow that outlived
Eight generations. And with these a thousand things
Without a name. When wild Medea smelled

The unearthly brew, she dipped a wither'd wreath
Torn from a tree that once hung rich with olives
Into the pot—and look, even dry stems turned green,
Then leaves crept out, and, as they flowered, the wreath
Became an olive bough grown thick with fruit!
And where hot foam dripped from the boiling pot,
The earth was like a garden plot of flowers
And green between them sprang new ferns and grasses.
And when Medea saw her brew was ripe
She flashed a knife and cut the old man's throat;
Draining old veins she poured hot liquor down,
Some steaming through his throat, some through his lips,
Till his hair grew black and straight, all greyness gone.
His chest and shoulders swelled with youthful vigour
His wrinkles fell away, his loins grew stout,
His sallow skin took on a swarthy color;
And Aeson, dazed, remembered this new self
Was what he had been forty years ago.

     Meanwhile God Bacchus, sitting in the sky,
Looked down and saw Medea at her work,
And from her got a promise she'd restore
His early nurses to their youthful beauty.

     To keep her evil wits as sharp as ever
Medea faked a bedside quarrel with Jason
And went on pilgrimage to Pelias' door;
Since the old king was bowed with years, his daughters
Received her as a guest. These innocents
Were soon tricked into friendship by that lady.
She spoke of her great arts, how she revived
(Which was her shining proof of recent wonders)
Old Aeson to the semblance of his youth,
And Pelias' daughters, listening to her story,
Began to think their father (by such skill)
Could be a young and handsome man again.
Whatever she demanded they would pay:
At which she seemed to hold doubts in her mind,
And kept them waiting for her grave decision.
At last she seemed to clear the air by saying,
"To give you true assurance of my powers

Bring me the eldest sheep of all your herds,
And see how quickly he'll become a lamb."
Straightly the girls led out a thick-wooled, tottering,
Battered old ram, his huge horns curved in whorls
Around his head. And then with one flash of her
Thessalian knife the sorceress had slit
Its withered neck in two, nor was the blade
Stained with such thin unhealthy blood; as quickly
She tossed the poor remains in her brass kettle
And with them poured her brew of vital sauces.
They saw its carcass dwindle and its horns
Boil into nothingness, and as they vanished,
So the quick vapour melted years away.
A bleating noise was heard, and as they listened,
A lamb leaped out and ran to milk a ewe.

Dazed by this miracle, Pelias' daughters
Urged, begged the sorceress to serve their father.
Three days went by, three times bright Phoebus' horses
Dipped into Ebro's waters and were unharnessed;
On the fourth night, when stars flamed in the sky,
The evil daughter of Aeetes poured
Pure water in a blazing pot and stirred
A brew of pale, impotent weeds. By then
King Pelias, charmed by her spells, had fallen
Into a sleep like death, his body flaccid;
So had his guards. Led by Medea, his
Daughters came to his bedside while their leader
Shouted, "Why stand in doubt, you fools; take out
Your knives, open his throat while I pour through it
New life, the blood of youth, down empty veins.
Your hands, your very knives hold the quick secret
Of an old man's journey out of death to life;
If like true daughters you respect your duty
(And if your frail hopes are not futile dreams)
Then at a single thrust pierce through old age,
Let his thin blood carry his years away."
Stirred on by love not to commit a crime,
They stepped into the deepest crime of all;
As knives were poised to strike they closed their eyes,
And with blind hands plunged at his helpless body.

Veiled with his blood, the old man lifted up
Head, shoulders on the prop of a crooked arm
And sighed, "O Daughters, what is this strange doing?
Why are you armed to the very death against me?"
As courage fell, knives dropped from shaking hands.
It was Medea who slit the old man's throat
Then tossed his torn remains in boiling water.

Medea's crime would not have gone unpunished
If her winged chariot had not swept by,
Lifting her over shade-draped Pelion
Where Chiron lived, and over Othrys where
The neighbourhood was known for old Cerambus
Who'd been swept up by nymphs above the flood
In Deucalion's day when heavy earth
Fell under roaring waves. And on the left
Where she sailed by stood a huge writhing serpent
Carved out of stone, and near it Ida's forest
Where Bacchus as he hid a stolen ox—
His son the thief—changed that slow beast
To the illusion of a swift-paced deer.
—Over the shallow sands where the spent father
Of Corythus lay in dust, where Maera,
Waking in terror, barked unearthly noises—
Above the town of old Eurypylus
Where Hercules retreated and the women cows
Grew horns like cattle above the isle of Rhodes
(That Phoebus loved) where lived the Telchines
Whose eyes blasted earth and everything they saw,
Till Jove, who hated them, swept them off earth
To flounder in the waves of Neptune's oceans.
She sailed past the great walls of old Carthaea
On island Cea where fatherly Alcidamas
Was yet to see, half dazed and shocked, his daughter
Deliver a mild dove from her heaving body.
Next she saw Hyrie's lake near that rough valley
Well known for Cycnus' shifting to a swan,
Where Phyllius, charmed by the boy, had brought him
Wild birds to play with and a roaring lion
Which he had mastered for the boy's delight;
Then the boy told him to tame a raging bull,

Which Phyllius promptly did, but felt annoyed
That the spoiled darling did not yield to love
And hid the gift, which made the boy reply,
"Now you'll be sorry for what you have not done,"
And leaped from a high ledge of stone. It seemed
As though Cycnus had killed himself, yet falling,
Become a swan swaying in air that held him,
Through which he floated on his snow-white wings.
Ignorant of her son's escape from death, his mother
Hyrie melted into a lake of tears.
Near by was Pleuron, where Ophius' daughter
Flew from her murderous sons on trembling wings,
Beyond that city Medea saw an island,
Calaurea, blessèd for Latona's sake,
The place that witnessed how their king and queen
Were changed to birds. Then on Medea's right
Came Cyllene, damned by King Menephron
Who like a beast had shared his mother's bed.
Medea then looked down on Cephisus
Who wept because Apollo changed his grandson
Into a sleek-haired seal; and there below her
The house where old Eumelus lived and grieved,
His son, a bird, hovering in salt sea air.

    At last Medea, sailing serpent wings,
Landed at Corinth where green Neptune's daughter
Was keeper of a living sacred spring:
There, so an ancient legend said, men grew
From rainswept fungus. There Medea found
Jason remarried, and with her deadly spells
She burnt his bride to ashes while two seas
Witnessed the flames that poured from Jason's halls.
Even then her blood-red steel had pierced the bodies
Of their two sons; yet she escaped the edge
Of Jason's sword by taking refuge in her
Dragon's car, those flying monsters born
Of Titan's blood. With these she stormed the gates
Of Pallas' fortress sailing wing by wing,
Entered the city flanked by floating eagles,
Just Phene, old Periphas, and granddaughter
Of Polypemon trying out her new-

Winged flight in air. Medea was received,
Welcomed by Aegeus; as if this foolishness
Were not enough, he took her as his wife.

Meanwhile young Theseus came in full disguise;
Not even Father Aegeus recognized him.
He, a soldierly young man, had forced
Peace on that strip of land between two seas.
Set to destroy him, Medea poured a drink,
A deadly mixture, made up long ago,
Imported from the shores of Scythia.
This medicine they said came from the spittle
Of mad-dog Cerberus who guarded Hades.
The dog lived in a cave, dark-tunnelled, sloping
Down a long-necked channel. When Hercules
Came there he trapped the dog with chains
That held it fast, then dragged the twisting creature
Up to the cave mouth while its great eyes turned
Inward and down, blinded against the blazing
Light of day. Then Cerberus in his rage
Filled hell, earth, heaven with triple-headed
Howling; this while the white foam from his teeth
Dripped to green mosses at his feet. Some say
The spittle grew from dank ground where it fell
And turned to evil growth between veined rock,
The kind of plant that people of that country
Called wolfbane. This liquorish poison, stirred
Within a drink by shrewd Medea, was raised
To Theseus' mouth, but when his father saw
The family crest engraved in ivory on
The hilt of his son's sword, Aegeus struck
The cup from the boy's lips. Meanwhile Medea,
'Scaping her own death, vanished in a cloud,
Dark as the music chanted in her spells.

Though Father Aegeus took high pleasure at
His son's release from danger, the old king
Was touched by horror at the narrow chance
That spared his life; therefore to praise the gods
He lit huge altars, sacrificed prize bulls
Who fell with garlands twisted round their horns.

For many years that day of celebration
Lived in the memories of all who shared it.
Elders and countrymen joined the feast
And songs were sung quickened by wit from wine:
"All Marathon rejoices, O brave Theseus,
Who killed the Cretan Bull, who freed the country
Of a mad boar raging across tilled fields!
And it was you who conquered the club-swinging son
Of Vulcan while the Epidaurian plain
Witnessed your skill. Even the river Cephisus
Reflected your killing of the murderer
Procrustes, while Ceres, little village
Of Eleusis, saw how you threw the deadly
Cercyon to his own death. Then you struck down
The giant Sinis, who bent swaying trees
To his own will—those blasting catapults
Of the pine forest that aimed and hurled men
Into the sky. The road is clear up to the walls
Of Alcathoe, now that our Theseus
Has disposed of Sciron: Sciron whose bones
Even earth threw up and all the seas refused,
But it was said that since they could not rest,
They bleached and stiffened into chalk-white cliffs
That took the name of Sciron. O sweet Theseus,
If we could number things we praise you for
These would be more than years which tell your age;
Therefore we raise your health in draughts of wine
To show the world how much we honour you."
The palace rang with cheers: throughout the city
No shade of sadness fell within its walls.

### MINOS WARS AGAINST AEGEUS

And yet (for it is always true that pleasure
Conceals the shadows of anxiety) Aegeus'
Reception of his new-found son was tempered
By the hidden fears of war. Minos stood armed:
Strong as his forces were in men and ships,
Paternal anger held deeper threat.
He had a righteous use for sword and spear;
The Greeks had killed his son, Androgeos.

With this in mind, Minos had gathered allies;
And since his strength was in a swift-winged navy,
He looked for friends among the sea-borne kingdoms
(And won Anaphe by large promises
And Astypalaea by threat of war)
Beyond these he secured wave-washed Myconus,
The chalk-isled Cimolus, thyme-growing Syros,
And flat-topped Seriphos and marble Paros;
And that isled kingdom Arne had betrayed
For love of money and became a jackdaw,
Night-winged, night-footed bird who hoards up gold.

Yet nations that were rich in olive groves
Oliares, Didymae, Tenos, Gyaros,
And Peparethos refused to help King Minos.
His fleet turned to the left, toward Oenopia,
The ancient kingdom that Aeacus ruled,
And named Aegina after his loved mother.
And as King Minos landed, a great crowd
Gathered to meet a famous man of war;
The king met the three sons of Aeacus,
Telamon, Peleus, and Phocus, each in turn
The younger son, and after them their father,
Bent with age, who asked Cretan king why he
Had come. The question caused the king to turn
His mind back to his grief, and as he spoke
He sighed: "I ask for what arms you can spare
Against my enemies who killed my son.
Join my crusade as in a holy war
To rest the spirit of the sacred dead."
Aeacus answered him, "How can you ask me
For what I cannot give? No country has
A closer union with our fate than Athens
And we have signed the treaty that shall bind us."
"No treaty is of greater price to you,"
Said Minos as he sadly turned aside,
Who thought it better to hint of future war
Than spend his time in fighting unripe battles.
Although the Cretan ships still rode at anchor
And stood in sight of island city walls,
A Greek ship briskly sailed between their prows

And steered to shore within a friendly harbour;
The ship brought Cephalus: good will from Athens!
And though they'd not seen Cephalus for years
The sons of Aeacus knew him as a friend,
Took his right hand and led him to the palace;
Then as he came all eyes saluted him,
And saw him beautiful and straight as ever,
Wearing the olive branch as one might hold a sceptre,
And at his left and right two younger Greeks,
Clytos and Butes, who were sons of Pallas.

After this company renewed its friendly greetings,
Bright Cephalus recited terms from Athens,
And in the name of common ancestors
And elder treaties held between two nations,
He asked for help against the king of Crete,
And warned that Minos looked toward far-spun
        conquest—
Not only Athens but all lands of Greece.
When Cephalus had had his say, Aeacus,
His left hand at the hilt of his bronze sceptre,
Straightly replied, "O Athens, take what's ours;
This island shall be yours without the asking,
And all my kingdom, even men at arms.
I've men enough to frighten enemies,
And—gods be praised!—the times are very good.
There's no excuse for me to break my treaties."
"I hope all this is true," said Cephalus,
"And may the numbers of your kind increase;
From shore to palace I was glad to see
A generation of young men to greet me
And yet I missed the many elder faces
That on another day had welcomed me."
Aeacus drew a deep breath and said sadly,
"There was a bad start to our better fortunes,
I wish the best had come without the worst;
And with the fewest words of introduction,
I'll tell you each in turn: men you remember
Are bones and dust, and half my people perished
With their death. A plague struck at us through the heat
Of Juno's anger and she hated us

Because our island had her rival's name.
At first the plague seemed of an earthly source,
And while it seemed so, we called in physicians;
Yet soon enough it had outwitted us,
And spread destruction till it dazed our arts.
Skies seemed to fall on us in darkest heat:
Four times the moon's horns grew to their full circle,
And four times dwindled to their slender shape;
Yet the South Wind poured deadly heat upon us,
And all that time the evil sickness entered
Our springs and wells. In every field a thousand
Serpents writhed and poured green spittle in our rivers:
First dogs, wild game, birds, cattle were struck down,
And luckless farmers stumbled at the plough
To see their teams fall sick within the furrow;
The wool-clothed sheep fell naked to the ground,
Their bodies dwindled into bones and skin.
Race horses lost their spirit on the track,
Forgot their victories and, trembling, whinnied
Toward death within their darkened stalls.
The wild boar lost his rage, the deer his swiftness,
The bear his will to fight 'gainst stronger creatures.
Lank sickness held them all; forest and road
Piled up with dead whose stench poisoned the air.
Even dogs, grey wolves, and vultures kept away,
While rotting filth spread sickness on the wind.

"Then countrymen were struck down to their doom
And the Great Sickness walked through city walls:
At first men's bowels were filled with flames, blood rushed
To throat and face; the tongue grew thick and thick
The fiery breath, and swollen lips fell open
To gasp its tainted air. Nor could the sick
Take coverlet or sheet, but threw themselves
To earth to gasp at coolness from damp ground
Only to feel coolness grow hot beneath them
And earth take fire from their feverish bodies.
Nor could one stay the Sickness; its disease
Took the physician while his arts increased
The feverish agonies of those they touched,
And those who nursed the sick at once fell dead.

As life's hopes left them, the diseased snatched pleasures;
Where nothingness becomes the only promise
Then the worse vices are the best. The sick fell
Naked at their drinking troughs and fountains. Nor was
Their thirst relieved as long as they had life;
Dying as they drank they tainted every well.
And as they leaped out of plague-ridden beds
Some rolled to earth and died, while others ran
From homes, and since the cause of death remained
Unseen, even the least of shaded shelters
Seemed like doom. Some half-dead creatures walked
To death along the highways, others sat
Weeping their lives away. Still others turned
Glazed, sightless eyes to heaven, while their neighbours
Reached up their futile arms to darkened skies.
Each went to death, however death had caught him.

   "And as I looked on this, what was my temper,
How did I feel? Did I not have the right
To hate all things and life itself, and join
The fate of those who were my friends? Wherever
I looked I saw dead bodies fallen as though
They were ripe apples dropped from a tossed bough,
Or acorns fallen from a wind-swept oak.
Look up, and see a temple rising there,
Up many steps to sacred Jupiter!
How many times were prayers unanswered there?
A husband for his wife, father for son,
Still praying for mercy from a silent altar—
The pilgrim dead, the unlit incense fallen
From his hand. How many times the bull was led
By priests and as his horns were wet with wine,
The bull fell dead before the raised knife touched him.
There on that hill I sent my prayers to Jove:
This service for myself, my sons, my people.
The sacrificial bull was at my side;
With fearful groans the beast fell to the ground,
Though my raised knife had scarcely grazed his throat.
With fearful groans the beast fell to the ground,
The plunged blade clean; pale blood dripped from it,
And the torn bowels no sign of prophecy

Nor message from the gods, for plague had eaten
The very entrails of all living creatures.
Meanwhile the dead were fallen all about me,
Even at temple doors, at smouldering altars,
Where the foul smell of death seemed to betray
All sacredness and duty. And in this horror,
The charnel house of prayer, some hanged themselves,
To kill the fears of death by death's own hand.
Nor were the dead interred by usual rites:
Too many funerals crowded temple gates;
Stale bodies either rotted into earth
Or were heaped up on common funeral pyres,
Nor any reverence for dead and dying.
Some fought to die within the common flames
And perished like poor thieves, and none were left
To weep their loss; unwept the souls of matrons,
Of brides, young men and ancients—all vanished
To the blind wilderness of wind. Nor earth to hide
Plague-spotted bones and flesh, nor wood for fire.

### THE MYRMIDONS

   "Drunk in this sea of grief I prayed to Jove:
'O Jupiter! If rumours do not lie—
If it is true your arms enfold Aegina,
Daughter of Asopus, and you, great father
Of our house, deny the shame of having us,
Your children, here on earth—give back, O lord,
My people to my land, or let me follow
The dead I loved into their sepulchre.'
His answer was a bolt of fire and thunder.
'And this is your reply,' I said, 'I take it
That your will toward us is good will, so shall I hold
You to a sacred promise.' As I spoke,
I saw an oak spread branches over me,
The talking oak of Jove-Dodona's kind.
And there we noted that a trail of ants,
Each with a grain of wheat between his lips,
Marched in a single file through wrinkled bark.
Dazed at the sight of creatures beyond number,

I said, 'Great Father, fill my empty cities,
Give me as many people as this army.'
As though a storm had burst in windless air,
The great oak shuddered and my body shook
With fears that made my flesh and hair rise up;
Falling, I kissed the oak down to its roots,
Nor dared to hope aloud, but kept thought hidden
In some dark channel of my mind. Night came
And with it sleep possessed our anxious bodies.
In that deep senselessness I had a vision:
There was the oak, as many-leaved as ever,
As many ants among its many branches—
The great tree shaken by a sudden tremor
While ants dropped to the grasses at its feet,
Then seemed to grow, to stand upright, to lose
Their shadow thinness and their black complexion
In human forms: I saw stout legs and arms.
When I awoke the vision seemed unreal;
I wept at lack of mercy from the gods,
And yet I heard strange noises in the palace,
Voices of men that had grown unfamiliar;
I thought they were another trick of sleep.
Then Telamon came running to my door
And cried out, 'Father, more than any hope
Or dream now walks before us. Threshold waits
For you to step outside.' And as I followed,
There was the multitude I saw in sleep
Who welcomed me and hailed me as their king.
Then I praised Jove and gave to my new people
Parts of my kingdom that had been deserted,
And called that army 'Human Myrmidons,'
Nor was I wrong, for you have seen their strength.
They keep to habits of their early being:
They are hardworking, thrifty, honest creatures,
Who harvest every grain of wheat they sow;
And they shall serve you in the wars to match
Their youthful energy with youthful courage.
They wait at your command and you shall have them
As soon as the East Wind that brought you here
Gives your ships over to his Southwest brother."

CEPHALUS AND PROCRIS

    With casual talk they spent the declining day,
Feasted at supper, and with night came sleep.
Yet when the golden morning sun grew bright,
The East Wind held Cephalus' ships in harbour.
The sons of Pallas went to join their captain,
And all three visitors walked to the palace.
The king still slept, while Telamon, assisted
By one brother, gathered recruits for war;
And Phocus, youngest son of old Aeacus,
Received the guests. The friendly Greeks were led
Across a courtyard into rich apartments
Where all sat down, and quick as Cephalus
Strode to his seat young Phocus saw he wore
A gold-tipped javelin of curious make.
After a few remarks that seemed to wander,
The young man said, "I love the forest and the arts
Of capturing wild game: what is the secret
Of that lovely spear you carry? The wood is rare.
If it were ash it would be saffron yellow;
If cornel, it would be both gnarled and grey,
But what it is has made me curious.
My eyes have never seen a better weapon."
And a young Greek replied, "If you but knew
How marvellously it works, you'd like it more
Than what your eyes can see of its strange beauty:
It never fails to strike the thing it aims at,
And it returns with proof of blood upon it
Back to the hand that threw it." The young Phocus
Burned hot with eagerness to know its story
And the true source of all its secret power.
At first the hero answered a few questions,
But scarcely dared to tell the price he paid
At owning this rare gift; then Cephalus,
Weeping, held in his mind his lost young wife
And sighed, "O goddess' son! Can you believe
What I have yet to say? The very thought
Of it shall fill my eyes, however long
The Fates spin out the legend of my days.
Here is the gift that killed my wife; it were better

That I had never carried it at all.
Her name was Procris, yet it's far more likely
You've heard her sister's name, Orithyia—
The beauty who became the North Wind's mistress.
Procris was better-looking of the two,
And far more tempting to the wicked eye.
Erechtheus her father gave her to me,
And it was love alone that joined our hands.
My neighbours took me for a happy man:
Happy I was and would be so today
If gods above us had not changed their will.
Some fifty days after my wedding night
I laid my nets to trap the antlered deer;
There on the top of flowering Hymettus
Gold-haired Aurora, who dispelled night's shadows,
Had caught me up and carried me away.
Goddess forgive me if I tell the truth!
But truly as the rose shines from her lips,
As truly as she guards both day and night
And sips sweet nectar on the hills of heaven,
By all these truths I loved Procris alone,
She in my heart, her name upon my lips.
Always I praised our first, our wedding night.
The goddess was annoyed: 'Are these the thanks
I've earned for sleeping with a thoughtless boy,
Who is a critic of all I am and do?
Then keep your Procris! But if I read the future,
Someday you'll wish you never saw your wife.'
Briefly she raged, then sent me back to Procris.
On my way home my weary mind recited
The warning that the goddess forced upon me;
And was it true my wife was always faithful—
Even a girl so beautiful and young?
And she was good. Yet I had been away
A long, long time, and she with whom I stayed
Had been the very queen of faithlessness.
(True lovers hold their doubts of everything!)
I looked for reasons of dark faults in Procris,
And hoped to tempt her chastity with bribes.
To make my playing of the jealous husband
A part that carried weight, Aurora changed

My looks (and I felt strange). In this disguise
I entered Athens straightly, then to my house:
Nothing misplaced indoors, except the gloom
A house has while it waits an absent master.
Then by a thousand lies at last I came
To that far chamber where Erechtheus' daughter
Looked up at me, and when I saw that lady
I almost dropped designs of testing love;
Rather I wished to take her in my arms,
To kiss those very lips I knew so well.
No girl more beautiful than she in sadness,
Where she was grief itself without her husband.
Think, Phocus, of how beautiful she was,
How well she wore an anxious veil of sorrow;
And when I tried to force her lips to yield,
How many times she set aside temptations!
At each she said, 'I am given to one man—
Wherever he may be. I'm his alone.'
Who in his right mind would dispute her claim?
Or ask for further proof of chastity?
Yet I heard nothing and went on. At last
After wild promises I thought I saw
A look of doubt tremble across her features,
Then, conquered by my own deceit, I cried,
'O you are cursed; I am your only husband,
But now disguised as your adulterer.
Look! You have stained your bed—I am your witness!'
Silent with shame for me, the girl ran from me,
The traitor-husband, and his hateful bed.
All men she hated, and she chose to follow
Hillside and forest ventures with Diana.
Since I was left alone love burned within me
Until I feared my flesh would turn to ashes.
I begged her to forgive me, said my sins
Were all my own, that I would yield to half
The very gifts and bribes I promised her.
When I soothed her pride and closed her wounds
She came to me and for a few short years
We shared the sweetness of another marriage.
As though to give herself were not enough
She came with gifts for me: one was a hunter,

A brilliant dog that Cynthia gave to her,
And as she gave it, said, 'This creature's swiftness
Outraces every creature of its kind';
The other was this precious javelin.
Both gifts were mine—but would you care to hear
The entire story? Perhaps it moves the heart;
At least there is a touch of wonder in it.

     "One day the son of Laius, Oedipus,
Answered the question no one understood.
Her secret all undone, dark-winged and broken,
That emptied prophetess fell into sand.
A second monster was sent down to Thebes;
In spite of all his kindness gentle Themis
Would not allow a human victory,
Therefore the beast he sent into that country
Struck fear across the land to men and cattle,
And we, the young men of the cursèd region,
Set trap to catch the monster as she ran.
However high our nets were spread, she leaped them—
At which our dogs (unleashed) ran after her.
Such was her speed, a hundred dogs seemed slow;
She tricked and doubled like a plunging bird.
Then those who knew me quickly called out, 'Tempest'
(Which named the dog my wife had given me),
And since he strained the leash, I let him go.
Then no one saw the creature anywhere;
The hot dust held his footprints—that was all—
As though he were a spear tossed into air,
A shot of lead whirled from a sling, an arrow
That took its aim from a Gortynian bow.
Above the plain there was a grass-grown hill,
Where I climbed up and saw a marvellous race:
The beast forever seeming to be caught,
And just escaping as the dog came at her.
She ran a doubled course that wheeled and turned
Beyond the dog's quick leap, then, pace for winding
Pace, jaws snapped at empty air. Then I took up
The precious javelin in my right hand
And as I slipped my fingers through its thong,
I glanced aside. O marvellous!—I saw

Two marble figures in an endless race
Yet fixed upon the plain, the hunter still
To capture the pursued. If gods had seen them,
Surely some god had set a spell upon them,
Neither defeat nor victory for both."
As Cephalus fell silent, Phocus said,
"But what harm came to you beyond this story?
What evil entered your fair javelin?"
Then Cephalus resumed his narrative.

    "My pleasures were the prelude to my grief,
But Phocus, first of all I'll speak of them.
Even now, O son of Aeacus, I remember
Those early years my wife and I enjoyed:
Small worries and great raptures held us fast,
Nor would she barter Jove's love for my kiss,
Nor naked Venus tempt me from her arms.
The single flame of love burned in our hearts.
When morning mountaintops grew bright with gold
I took the hunter's way through field and forest.
Nor did I need the company of friends,
Or horse or dog, or net or trap; I had
This magic javelin, which was enough
To make me certain of a day's reward—
Wild fowl or deer. Then to cool shades I ran,
Making my way where soothing valleys waited,
Where little winds stirred every leaf and covert,
And there I seemed to court a gentle breeze
Whose breath cooled my quick heat: she was my fancy
Who calmed and rested me. 'Come to me, Aura,'
As I remember saying, 'and press your lips
Against my heated breast; look how I burn!'
Perhaps I said (for Fates were leading me),
'You are my dearest love, my sweetest comfort,
Because of you I love the shadowy forest—
To drink your breath between my lips forever—'
Someone who heard me read ambiguous sense
Within my words and thought the name of 'Aura'
Called out the name of some frail girl I knew.
That teller of tall tales then went to Procris,

Reciting in a whisper what she'd heard.
True love I know has ears for everything—
Procris (so I was told) fell in trance,
And when she woke she cursed herself for being
The most ill-fated woman she had known,
And turned against me for betraying her;
She wept against a name, the flying shadow
Of words upon the wind, and saw the image
Of a living girl. Then she would throw herself
In doubt, reject the gossip she had heard,
And claim I had been faithful to her always—
She'd have to see what I had done and hear me.
When pale Aurora drove the night away,
I left my bed for hunting in the forest,
And after some success at stalking game,
I lay on grass and cried, 'Come, Aura, come;
I am all fire, cool me with your breath; Come,
O precious dearest, take me as I burn.'
At this I heard a stirring of dry leaves:
A beast perhaps. I threw my javelin—
And there was Procris with a wounded breast,
Who cried, 'O by my grief I am undone!'
That was her voice; myself gone mad with terror
Rushed where it came. Her torn dress stained with blood,
I saw her dying, and O what pathos there
To see her hands still try to tear the gift—
Once hers to me—out of her yielding breast.
I raised her body in my arms and, folding
Her torn dress where she bled, I held her fast,
Nor could I stop the flow of blood. I prayed
She would not leave me tainted with her death.
Though she was growing weak, she raised her voice,
Thus, a last effort with a failing breath:
'By our sweet marriage, by the heavenly gods,
And by the household gods who kept me pure,
By all I've given you, even this love within
A last, a closing hour which brings my death,
Do not let Aura share my wedding bed.'
Then I knew well the error of my fancy,
Told her the truth—but what good was truth then?

She fell back in my arms, life drained away,
Yet her last breath was felt against my lips—
Something like joy had crossed her dying face."

    The hero closed his story with flushed tears
And Aeacus came by with his two sons:
The mercenary troops were now at hand
And Cephalus accepted their brave arms.

# VIII

# BOOK VIII

Minos, Nisus, and Scylla • Daedalus and Icarus • Meleager
and the Boar • Althaea and Meleager • Acheloüs • Baucis
and Philemon • Erysichthon

Ovid's version of the Minos legend is remarkable for its
implied motivation of King Minos's fall from power. His fall
is all the more effective because we see him first as the shin-
ing warrior loved by Scylla, who through her love for him
betrays her father. His loss of self-confidence begins with his
queen's adventures with a bull, and his concealment of the
Minotaur is further progress in his decline until at last we see
him fearing the presence of young men at his court. In these
scenes Ovid probably revived historical fiction as well as
mythological legend concerning the rise and fall of Crete's
great ruler. His technique in the recital of King Minos's story
rivals Plutarch's life of Theseus, which was written about
three generations later than The Metamorphoses. Book
VIII also shows Ovid's genius in the interweaving of several
related stories into a flowing narrative. Book VIII caught the
imagination of the masterly Flemish painter Peter Paul Ru-
bens (1577–1640), whose Feast of Acheloüs is an enduring
and vivid interpretation of Ovidian colour and movement.
It is also one of the rare examples of how the living qualities
of a poet's work can be translated into plastic art. Book VIII
impressed several English poets, but none more notably than
Dean Swift, whose version of the Baucis-Philemon story is
among his masterpieces in the writing of verse.

# BOOK VIII

When white-starred Lucifer drove night away
And showed the world another day begun,
The East Wind dropped and wet clouds rose to heaven;
The placid South steered Cephalus and recruits
(The virgin army that Aeacus gave him)
To swifter passage than they hoped to find,
Harboured and safe almost before they knew it.
But while they sailed, King Minos had destroyed
The towns that ranged the coast of Megara,
And now had brought a siege against that city
Where Nisus ruled: among his royal grey hairs
He wore a purple plume of great distinction,
Source of his power and able statesmanship.

Six times had rising Luna shone white horns
And victory swayed on hovering dubious wings,
And where Apollo was said to rest his lyre
Music still sounded from the city's walls
From which a tall and graceful tower grew.
Before the war, the daughter of King Nisus
Used to climb up its stairs and drop small stones
Down its deep well to hear their echoing noises,
And as the war went on she climbed that tower
To get a clear view of the men in battle.
From here her eyes saw every Cretan hero;
She learned his name, his horse, his battle dress,
But most of all, and least to her own good,
She knew the features of Europa's son,
And when he wore a plumed, engravèd helmet
She was enchanted by the shining headpiece;
And shining Minos wore the brightest shield,
And when his bare arm threw a heavy spear,

The girl stood dazzled by his strength and art,
And when she saw him draw his deep-curved bow
It was as if she witnessed young Apollo
About to fill the air with glittering arrows.
But when in purple—and his head uncovered—
He sat erect on a white horse, and steered
The creature, foam at its lips, yet guided
By his hand, the daughter of King Nisus
Went almost mad with love. She thought how lucky
The reins he held, and if she could have done so,
She would have leaped down tower halls to run
Past Cretan battle lines to welcome him,
Or in her frenzy throw wide the city's gates
To let him in, to let him take of her
Whatever else a master may demand.
As she looked down at the white-tented army,
She said, "What shall I do? Or am I happy
Or weeping-sad at this unhappy war?
Minos is enemy of her who loves him,
Yet if there were no war, I'd not have seen
His face nor known his ways. If he would take me,
Hold me prisoner, then he'd give up this war,
And I would be the terms he'd make for peace.
And O, most fortunate of lovely women,
More beautiful than any girl on earth,
The mother of the man who fills my heart,
It's little wonder that the god who took you
Was fire itself to hold you in his arms.
If only I had wings to glide through air
Down to the Cretan king to tell him truly
How deep I burn for him and let him take
Whatever price he asks to make me wife—
Yet never let him ask me to betray
My father's city: let me sleep alone,
Nor ever hope to share a husband's bed.
Yet there are many who love to feel the weight
Of those who conquer them and take their pleasure
From a kindly master. And it is true
That Minos has an honest cause for war;
Both men and arms are joined in righteous battle

Because his son was killed—and we shall lose.
And if our city falls, why should his iron gloves
Tear wide our gates which my sweet love would open
Without a siege or loss of his own blood?
Nor should I fear an arrow through his breast,
For who, if he were sane, would strike down Minos,
Even with a spear that has nor heart nor pity?"
This reasoning seemed good enough to her:
She set her mind to sacrifice her home,
Her dowry—anything to end the war.
Yet her persuasive will was not enough:
"The doors are guarded and my father holds
The keys which keep us locked within the city:
If only I'd been born without a father
Who makes me timid, who undoes my will,
While every creature feels the right to be
Himself, herself alone: Good Fortune turns
Away from trembling prayers. A girl whose heart
Burns with a love like mine would be all fire
That sweeps through everything that bars its way.
And why should others show more strength than I?
Even now I'd gladly walk through sword and flame,
Yet neither's in my way. All that restrains me—
More valuable than any gift of gold—
Is in the purple plume of father's hair,
The talisman whose charm will make me blessed."

　　While these thoughts filled her mind, and night closed
　　　　round her,
The night that stills anxiety and fears,
And as its shadows fell, her bravery flourished;
Then in the early hours of darkest sleep—
The day-worn heart finds peace in weariness—
The girl came gliding where her father slept,
And clipped (O fatal error of her will!)
The purple plume whose secret was his life.
Wearing that plume (since she was sure of welcome)
She strode to Minos' camp and stood before him.
"Love guided me," she said, "my name is Scylla,
Daughter of Nisus. Here's my heritage,

My country's wealth and honours—all is yours;
And all I ask is, take me in your arms.
This purple plume is my true sign of love.
It's yours, this shock of hair clipped from the center
Of an old man's skull, more than his life to him,
My father's treasure." And with guilt-tainted hand
She thrust it toward him while King Minos shuddered,
Drew back at this new horror in his eyes,
And said, "I hope the very gods in heaven—
O darkest monster of the age we live in—
Send curses on you from both land and sea,
Nor shall you rest in Crete, my world, my island,
The sacred nursery of infant Jove!"

      This said, just Minos gave the land of Nisus
New laws, released the hawsers of his fleet;
And manned the oars of all his brass-bound ships.
When Scylla saw the fleet sail from the harbour,
And all her prayers undone, herself neglected,
Even her crime ignored, wild madness shook her.
With flowing hair and upraised hands she cried,
"Where have you gone to leave me here alone
Who gave you all you've won, even my country?
To what direction will your sails take wing,
Your victory that is my crime, my glory?
Does all mean nothing to you, nor the gift,
The sacrifice of love, my hopes, my life?
Now the dark world is desert in my eyes,
Where shall I go? Home to my city? No,
Its walls are fallen and if they stood again,
What I have done bars every gate to me.
Nor can I face my father's eyes again,
And all my countrymen have cause to hate me,
Even neighbours see me as a symbol of
Dishonour and disgrace. In all the world
Crete is my only haven: if you say
You leave me to this wilderness I own,
Then white Europa never gave you birth
But quicksand Syrtis who devours men,
Or the Armenian tigress of the hills,

Or stormed Charybdis where the South Wind rages.
Nor are you son of Jove, nor was your mother
Betrayed by him in likeness of a bull;
That was a lie: your father was a beast,
A steaming bull who never loved its kind—
Then whip me, punish me, O Nisus, father!
And you, the very walls of my dead city
Take glory from my sorrow and these tears,
For I have earned my death. Let Hatred come,
Let those whom I've betrayed take toll of me;
Then why should you whose victory was mine
Bring down a curse on me? My crime destroyed
My country and my father: my gift is yours.
Your wife was more than proper wife to you,
That creature who disguised herself in bark
So she could kneel to let a bull mount on her
And carry in her womb half-man, half-bull.
And do you hear me? Or does that same wind
That tears my words away to empty sound
Lift up your sails into the farther seas?
Nor was it marvellous that Pasiphaë
Thought you more beastly than a roaring bull.
Then look at me, while that thankless Minos
Orders his men to put on speed! I hear
Oars strike the waves, while there pale lands and I
Recede and disappear; yet this escape
Shall not mean you'll forget me: look, I follow—
My arms cling to curved sides of stern and rudder,
Dragged through the wake of ships in this broad sea."
And as she spoke she dived beneath the waves.
Love gave her strength, and with a driving stroke
She reached the stern of Minos' Cretan ship
Where like a hated spirit she held fast.
Her father, floating over waves above her
(He had been changed into a sun-gold eagle),
Tore at her hair with his hooked beak and claws.
She lost her hold; she seemed to fall, then sway,
Hovering in air as if she were a feather.
Scylla became a bird that some called Ciris,
A name that brings to mind clipped locks of hair.

## DAEDALUS AND ICARUS

When Minos landed on the coast of Crete,
He bled a hundred bulls to mighty Jove,
And decked his palace with the spoils of war.
And yet strange gossip tainted all his honours:
Proof that his wife was mounted by a bull
Was clear enough to all who saw her son,
Half-beast, half-man, a sulky, heavy creature.
To hide this symbol of his wife's mismating
He planned to house the creature in a maze,
An arbour with blind walls beyond the palace;
He turned to Daedalus, an architect,
Who was well known for artful craft and wit,
To make a labyrinth that tricked the eye.
Quite as Meander flows through Phrygian pastures,
Twisting its streams to sea or fountainhead,
The dubious waters turning left or right,
So Daedalus designed his winding maze;
And as one entered it, only a wary mind
Could find an exit to the world again—
Such was the cleverness of that strange arbour.

Within this maze Minos concealed the beast,
And at two seasons placed nine years apart
He fed the creature on Athenian blood;
But when a third nine years had made their round,
The monster faced the season of his doom:
Where other heroes failed, the son of Aegeus,
Led by young Ariadne, walked the maze,
And, winding up the thread that guided him,
Raped Minos' daughter and sailed off with her
To leave her on the island shores of Dia.
The helpless girl was lonely and distraught
Till Bacchus came to wipe her tears away,
And then, to make her shine among the stars,
Gave her a crown as she rose up to heaven.
When she ascended through pale vaults of aether,
The jewelled tiara flamed with dancing fires,
And yet retained the likeness of a crown.
It took its place between the Kneeling Hero
And Ophiuchus, whose great hands held serpents.

Weary of exile, hating Crete, his prison,
Old Daedalus grew homesick for his country
Far out of sight beyond his walls—the sea.
"Though Minos owns this island, rules the waves,
The skies are open: my direction's clear.
Though he commands all else on earth below
His tyranny does not control the air."
So Daedalus turned his mind to subtle craft,
An unknown art that seemed to outwit nature:
He placed a row of feathers in neat order,
Each longer than the one that came before it
Until the feathers traced an inclined plane
That cast a shadow like the ancient pipes
That shepherds played, each reed another step
Unequal to the next. With cord and wax
He fixed them smartly at one end and middle,
Then curved them till they looked like eagles' wings.
And as he worked, boy Icarus stood near him,
His brilliant face lit up by his father's skill.
He played at snatching feathers from the air
And sealing them with wax (nor did he know
How close to danger came his lightest touch);
And as the artist made his miracles
The artless boy was often in his way.
At last the wings were done and Daedalus
Slipped them across his shoulders for a test
And flapped them cautiously to keep his balance,
And for a moment glided into air.
He taught his son the trick and said, "Remember
To fly midway, for if you dip too low
The waves will weight your wings with thick saltwater,
And if you fly too high the flames of heaven
Will burn them from your sides. Then take your flight
Between the two. Your route is not toward Boötes
Nor Helice, nor where Orion swings
His naked sword. Steer where I lead the way."
With this he gave instructions how to fly
And made a pair of wings to fit the boy.
Though his swift fingers were as deft as ever,
The old man's face was wet with tears; he chattered
More fatherly advice on how to fly.

He kissed his son—and, as the future showed,
This was a last farewell—then he took off.
And as a bird who drifts down from her nest
Instructs her young to follow her in flight,
So Daedalus flapped wings to guide his son.
Far off, below them, some stray fisherman,
Attention startled from his bending rod,
Or a bland shepherd resting on his crook,
Or a dazed farmer leaning on his plough,
Glanced up to see the pair float through the sky.
And, taking them for gods, stood still in wonder.
They flew past Juno's Samos on the left
And over Delos and the isle of Paros,
And on the right lay Lebinthus, Calymne,
A place made famous for its wealth in honey.
By this time Icarus began to feel the joy
Of beating wings in air and steered his course
Beyond his father's lead: all the wide sky
Was there to tempt him as he steered toward heaven.
Meanwhile the heat of sun struck at his back
And where his wings were joined, sweet-smelling fluid
Ran hot that once was wax. His naked arms
Whirled into wind; his lips, still calling out
His father's name, were gulfed in the dark sea.
And the unlucky man, no longer father,
Cried, "Icarus, where are you, Icarus,
Where are you hiding, Icarus, from me?"
Then as he called again, his eyes discovered
The boy's torn wings washed on the climbing waves.
He damned his art, his wretched cleverness,
Rescued the body and placed it in a tomb,
And where it lies the land's called Icarus.

As Daedalus gave his ill-starred son to earth,
A talking partridge in a swamp near by
Glanced up at him and with a cheerful noise
The creature clapped its wings. And this moment
The partridge was a new bird come to earth—
And a reminder, Daedalus, of crime.
For the inventor's sister, ignorant
Of what the Fates had planned, sent him her son—

A brilliant boy and scarcely twelve years old.
The boy studied the backbone of a fish;
This image in his mind, he made a saw
And was the first to bolt two arms of iron
In a loose joint: while one was held at rest,
The other traced a circle in the sand.
Daedalus, jealous of his nephew's skill,
Murdered the child by tossing him head-first
Down the steep stairs that mount Minerva's temple,
Then lied by saying the boy slipped and fell.
But Pallas, who rewards quick-witted creatures
Restored him with the feathers of a bird,
Saved in midair. The quickness of his mind
Was in his wings and feet; he kept his name.
Even now the bird does not take wing too high,
Nor makes her nest in trees or up a cliff,
But claps her wings in shallow flight near earth;
Her eggs drop in thick brush, and not forgetting
Her ancient fall, she fears high resting regions.

### MELEAGER AND THE BOAR

Aetna in kindness sheltered Daedalus,
The old man in distress and worn and broken.
King Cocalus took his case, defended him
With show of arms; and praise to Theseus—Athens
No longer paid blood tribute to King Minos.
Warlike Minerva's temple was a wreath
Crowned with gay flowers to the sky, while Jove
And other gods received their tributes piled
High up in sweetest incense and rich gifts,
And at their altars blood of sacred bulls.
Swift-flying Fame carried the name of Theseus
Through every city in the land of Greece,
And people of that wealthy countryside
Begged for his services in time of danger.
Although Meleager was their local hero,
The frightened and oppressed of Calydon
Sent up their ugent prayers for Theseus' help:
That land was troubled by a giant pig,
A wild boar who ate everything in sight

And took his orders from an angry goddess—
Diana, who had cursed all Calydon.
The story was that Oeneus, its king,
Had praised the gods for a successful year,
Gave grain to Ceres and sweet wine to Bacchus,
And to fair Pallas golden oil of olive:
Appropriate gifts were made to all the gods—
To gods of earth as well as those of heaven—
And yet Diana's altar stood neglected.
Sometimes the gods are moved by fits of rage;
Therefore Diana said, "An oversight
Like this won't be forgotten; if I'm slighted,
No one can say that I've gone unrevenged."
At which she loosed the boar in Oeneus' kingdom.
He was a creature huger than the bulls
Who feed on grass-grown plains of Epirus,
And bigger than the beasts of Sicily.
Both blood and fire wheeled in his great eyes;
His neck was iron; his bristles rose like spears,
And when he grunted, milk-white foaming spittle
Boiled from his throat and steamed across his shoulders.
Only an elephant from India
Could match the tusks he wore, and streams of
          lightning
Poured from wide lips, and when he smiled or sighed
All vines and grasses burnt beneath his breath.
One day young shoots of wheat were trampled under,
The next a luckless ploughman saw his crops
Fall into dust, and on the following morning
Whole fields of ripened grain were cut to ruins;
Silos and barns lay empty to the winds.
All vines went down; even the hardy olive,
Whose leaf forever shows its silver green,
Was a torn wilderness of blackened boughs;
Nor did the raving beast spare living cattle
And neither dog nor shepherd could defend them,
Nor wary bulls their cows. The people scattered
And ran for refuge under city walls.
At last Meleager raised a troop of boys,
All ripe for glory in the list that follows:
Tyndarus' twins—one was a boxing hero,

The other was a genius on a horse;
And then came Jason, first to make a boat,
Then Pirithous and Theseus, two great friends,
Two sons of Thestius, two sons of Aphareus,
Fleet Idas and Lynceus, then Caeneus,
The girl who had been changed into a boy,
Then fighting Leucippus, and swift Acastus,
The matchless warrior with his javelin;
Hippothous and Dryas and young Phoenix,
And Actor's pair of sons, and Phyleus,
Then Telamon, and sire of great Achilles,
Who came with Pheres' son and Iolaus,
And after him swift-acting Eurytion,
Followed by Echion, unrivalled runner;
Wild for a fight came Lelex and Panopeus,
Hyleus, Hippausus, eager as they,
Then Nestor in the best years of his life,
And from the ancient town of Amyclae
Old Hippocoon had sent his gallant sons;
Then came Ulysses' father and Ancacus;
The son of Ampycus, who read the future,
And Amphiaraus, yet to be betrayed
By a false wife; and last came Atalanta,
The heroine of the Arcadian forests;
A smartly polished brooch held her loose cloak,
Her hair was drawn back in a single twist;
At her left shoulder swung an ivory quiver
Which as she walked echoed a bell-like sound
Of arrows striking time; in her left hand
She held a bow: this was her costume, graced
By all the beauty of simplicity.
Her lovely face seemed boyish for a virgin
And yet was far too girlish for a boy,
And when the Calydonian hero saw her,
Love at first sight had turned his heart to fire.
God was to intervene, forbidding it.
"O fortunate young man," he cried, "if she
Finds him a lover fit to hold her hand."
He said no more: the moment was not ripe
For thoughts of love. There were great things to do,
And he was urged to face a larger battle.

Before them rose an ancient virgin forest,
So deep it had become a wilderness
Which overlooked the plain and a short valley.
The young men, eager to waylay the beast,
Set up their nets and traps, unleashed their dogs,
While others took a trail that led toward danger.
Edged by the forest lay a swamp, rainwater fed,
Where willows, reeds, and watery grasses grew,
And from this shelter the wild boar leaped out;
And like a bolt of fire from black clouds
The beast tore through the shaded underbrush.
There was a tearing noise and blasts of thunder
When great trees fell, and half the grove went down.
The young men raised a cry, nor feared to aim
Broad iron-headed lances at his snout;
And yet the beast charged where the dogs ran thickest
To tear him down. He tossed the yelping creatures
Left and right, each fallen with a deadly
Sideswipe thrust. Echion's first spear-shot
Went wild and glanced a thick-boled maple tree;
The next, if it had not had too much power,
Might well have struck the beast's broad back and felled
        him,
But overshot its mark, Jason the thrower.
Then Mopsus shouted; "O my patron Phoebus!
If ever you have heard me, hear me now!
Give me a perfect shot with my true spear!"
The god then did his best; the spear struck home,
But as it flew, Diana tore away
Its iron head; only the splintered shaft
Had found its mark, harrowed the beast to rage.
The creature burned with hotter speed than lightning;
White flames shone from its eyes and seared its breast.
Then, as a boulder from a catapult
Storms through the air against a thick-manned wall
Or armoured tower, weighted for the shock,
So with his deadly bulk the beast charged down
To tear a passage through the troop before him.
To the far right young Eupalamus stood,
And with him Pelagon, yet both were toppled over
By the blow. Friends helped them to their feet,

But as they ran, the son of Hippocoon,
Paralysed with fear, had turned his back,
Only to feel the monster with one stroke
Tear through his loins before he fell to death.
Nestor himself might never have lived to see
The walls of Troy if he had not spear-poled,
Quick-vaulting to the branches of a tree
Where, looking down, he saw the raging temper
Of what he fought and how he had escaped.
The beast sharpened his tusks against an oak,
And with fresh energy charged at Hippaus,
And at one pass ripped through the giant's thigh.
Then (this was long before they took their place
Among the stars) Castor and Pollux rode up,
Twin brothers mounted on their snow-bright horses—
They shone above the rest—and flashed their spears
That filled the air with trembling silver death.
But as they came the wild-quilled monster vanished
Deep to green glades where neither horse nor spear
Could pierce the forest. Telamon leaped forward
To take the chase, but too much eagerness
Had sent him sprawling where a tree's root tripped him.
As Peleus raised him to his feet, bold Atalanta
Speeded a flaming arrow from her bow
Which flashed through bristles on the monster's back,
Drew blood, and pierced the flesh behind its ear.
Nor was she happier than her friend Meleager,
Who was the first to see her hit the target,
To show it to his friends, to cry aloud,
"Honour to her for bravery and skill!"
Flushed, half ashamed at their own backward stance,
The young men drove themselves to wilder courage,
Shouted, and threw their lances in the air,
Which hindered their advance until Ancaesus
Swung at his fate with a huge two-winged axe
And cried out, "Boys, I'll teach you how to hunt,
How far a manly blow outdoes a woman's.
Here's work for me; although Latona's daughter
Cover that beast with a fine net of arrows,
Although the lady calls herself Diana,
My good right hand 'll cut the beast in two."

Grown like a tumour in his vanity,
Loud-mouthed and big, he swung his heavy axe,
As though he held a crowbar in both hands;
Stretched at full height, he waited for attack.
The creature threw his weight at this bold talker
And by a clever stroke dodged certain death.
His double tusks had pierced the underbelly
Of the unwary man; so Ancaeus perished,
Blood and intestines emptied to the ground.
Then Ixion's son stepped up, bearing his lance,
About to fire it from his true right hand,
While Theseus shouted, "O my dearest heart,
Who's half my soul forever, steer away.
Even a brave man fights at proper distance;
Only a careless fool like poor Ancaeus
Makes courage seem his doom." Then Theseus
Tossed out his own bronze-weighted spear,
Which seemed a perfect shot; yet as it grazed
The thick-leaved branches of a winter oak
It swayed to earth. Then Jason took his try,
Only to see his lance pin down to earth
Some poor dog who deserved a better fate.
Meleager's hand had other turns of luck:
His first shot grounded but the second flew
To the live center of the monster's back.
The beast fought death in circles, reeling, spinning,
Bright blood and spittle boiling from its lips;
His ardent killer pressed it on to fury,
Then with a shining stroke of his swift lance
Brought beast to earth, the last thrust through its shoulder.
Cheers stormed the air and all Meleager's fellows
Came round to shake his hand, to look, to marvel
At the great monster that lay still, yet covered
Half the earth they knew; it was as if they feared
To touch the beast—but as he walked around it,
Each hunter gravely stained his lance with blood.

With one foot resting on the monster's head—
The very jaws that once breathed deadly fires—
Meleager spoke aloud to Atalanta:
"Dear huntress of the far Arcadian mountains,

Take half of what I've won and share my glory."
At which he placed before her the stiff-quilled
Beastly hide, and that ferocious head where great
Teeth glittered in its open jaws. The gift
Amused her and she liked the giver too,
But some felt she was getting more than hers.
A murmur of dissent ran through the crowd.
Waving their arms, two sons of Thestius
Rushed up and shouted, "Girl, these gifts are ours;
We won't be fooled by your good looks or lover,
And shall see to it he keeps his distance."
They snatched the spoils from her and damned Meleager,
While the hot son of Mars boiled up with rage
And cried, "I'll show you thieves the greater distance
Between a feeble threat and men of action!"
At which he thrust his bright and wicked steel
Straight through the chambers of Plexippus' heart,
And the boy died before he knew what happened.
And as Toxeus wondered what to do—
Fearing his brother's fate, yet hoping for
A moment of revenge, Meleager left
No time for doubt, but warmed his blade again,
Still feverish red with the first brother's heat,
In the fresh blood that poured from Toxeus' side.

### ALTHAEA AND MELEAGER

In a great temple sacred to the gods,
Althaea praised them for her son's success,
Then turned, saw the bodies of her brothers.
She beat her breasts, and all the city streets
Grew loud with her wild tears and cries of sorrow;
She tore away her cloak of twinkling gold
And dressed herself in cloth of darkest night;
But when she heard of how her son had killed them,
Love's tears gave way to hate, grief to revenge.

When Althaea lay in childbirth with Meleager,
The three Fates tossed a bit of fuel to fire,
And as they spun the taut-bound threads of life
They chanted, "Just as long as this wood burns,

So long, O precious child, your life shall last."
When the three goddesses had had their say
And disappeared, Althaea seized the stick,
Now flaming like a torch, and killed its fire
In a fresh stream of water that ran by.
For many years she hid the thing away—
And O, young man, that secret saved your life!
But now she brought the charred remains to light
And told her servants to prepare a fire,
To pile it high with pine knots and small shavings,
To make the evil flames grow in a tower.
Four times she swayed the charred stick toward the flames
And four times drew it back. Mother and sister
Fought nearly equal battles in her soul;
Even the names of both tore at her heart.
Her face grew pale with what she planned to do,
Then feverish red rage lit up her eyes;
One moment all her features turned to evil,
The next she looked like someone pleading pity,
And as the heat of anger dried her tears,
Still tears rained down again. She, like a ship
Caught between wind and tide and tossed by both,
Dispels her rage and makes it leap to flames.
At last her pride of family heritage
Has greater will than motherly affection,
And all the shades of ancient ancestors
Demanded toll of blood from blood relations,
So she turned pious with impious will.
And when the fatal fire she built grew hot,
She cried, "Here fall the ashes of my flesh!"
Then, standing with the charred stick in her hand,
The unhappy woman faced her flaming pyre.
"O triple goddesses," she sighed, "O ancient
Furies who haunt the living to avenge
The murdered dead, witness my sacred oath
To kill the one who kills, of death for death.
Then see a murderous house go down to ruin!
Should I stand still while happy Oeneus
Takes pleasure in the glory of his son—
And this while sons of Thestius fall dead?
It's better for both houses to learn grief.

My brothers' ghosts smile gaping wounds at me
To take the fateful gift my womb delivered.
In what direction do I seem to speed?
O brothers, do you understand a mother?
Look at me now: my hands deny my will,
And yet I know my son has earned his fate.
But how can I become his murderer?
Shall he be careless, proud of his success,
And, big with pride, rule over Calydon?
And you poor ghosts are but a fall of ashes
Shaken with silver cold among the shades.
No, that is not my will: let him go down,
Down with his father's hopes, his wealth, his throne.
Is this the way a mother thinks aloud
And takes religious pleasure in her duties?
And what of those ten months I carried him
And gave him to the world with so much pain?
O child, whose life should have been spent and lost
In that first fire from which I saved your life,
Now you have earned the death of all you've done.
I gave you life at birth, then a new being
When I drew out this blackened torch from fire:
Two lives are now the price I ask of you,
Or I'm one more within my brothers' tomb.
Where shall I turn? My eyes have seen the blood
That pours forever from my brothers' wounds;
The very name of mother breaks my will.
O brothers, look at me: I am undone.
Your victory's my curse and you shall win—
And my last solace is to follow you!"
She turned her head away, and shaking hands
Dropped the charred torch of fate into the flames
And as it fell it seemed to speak or groan
Until it vanished in slow-burning ashes.

    Unknowing of his fate and miles away
Meleager carried heat of those same fires:
Deep in his sides he felt the secret flames
Mount through his entrails till they reached his breast;
And though he mastered pain he saw before him
The agony of dying far from glory,

And envied Ancaeus' wounds and called him lucky
To die still fighting as he fell. Meleager groaned
And as his breath grew short he cried aloud,
Naming his ancient father and his brothers,
His gentle sisters and his wife; perhaps
Even his last word seemed to echo "Mother."
Fire and pain flared up, then both turned chill and grey,
And as red embers fell to smouldering ashes,
Slowly his spirit wandered into air.

High Calydon had fallen: young and old,
The vulgar and the proud wept at its fall,
Women who lived where Euenus river flowed
Let down their hair and wailed while the old king,
Meleager's father, lord of Calydon
Fell face to earth and scoured his head with dust.
And as guilt pierced her mind, the hero's mother
Took self-revenge in death; her hands had thrust
A quick knife upward through her yielding thighs.
Not even if a god from high Olympus
Gave me as gift a century of tongues,
A master's genius—all that Helicon
Confers upon a dedicated poet—
No words of mine could tell you half the sorrow
Nor half the grief Meleager's sisters knew.
Forgetful of decorum the poor creatures
Bruised naked breasts, and while their brother's body
Lay out in state they kissed and smoothed its limbs;
They kissed the cloth that covered his remains
And when his flesh had been consumed by fire,
They gathered up his ashes to their hearts;
They lay upon his tomb and where his name
Was carved, they filled the crevices
With tears. At last Diana, sure that she'd
Undone the house of Calydon, planted feathers
Across the naked shoulders of the girls—
But spared two sisters: one was handsome Gorge,
The other girl was wife to Hercules.
Long wings were spread across their languid arms;
Their weeping noses and their sulky lips
Were twisted beaks. Diana sent them flying.

ACHELOÜS

Theseus, relieved from combat with the boar
And duties of a leader among men,
Set out for Athens where Erechtheus ruled;
But as he travelled roads were washed away,
For Acheloüs, big with heavy rains,
Turned field to flood, and Theseus' swift return
Came into paths more difficult and slow.
"O famous son of Cecrops, stay with me,"
Smiling Acheloüs cried, "nor risk your life
Among those hungry waves that crowd my waters.
They've whirled away great trees and giant rocks,
And where my banks have been I've seen barns, fences,
Sheep, cattle, horses uprooted and outpaced,
The torrent roaring. Down these mountainsides
I've seen snow turn to streams that swept away
Hardy young fellows, seen them disappear
Where churning waters made a darkening well.
Better to wait with me until this flood
Subsides into a shallow-glancing river."
Said Theseus, "I accept your invitation,
Your shelter, and advice," and crossed the threshold
Of Acheloüs' house, a shaded palace
Carved out of lava-rock and grey-lipped pumice,
The floor a yielding carpet of wet moss,
The ceiling a mosaic of purple shells.
When Sun, the son of old Hyperion,
Had blazed his journey through midafternoon
Theseus and friends were urged to rest awhile,
To take their ease stretched out on cots and benches.
The son of Ixion was there, and Lelex,
The Trojan hero, famous for his poise,
Whose dignity was marked by iron-grey hair,
And there were others worthy of attention.
The genial river god of Arcady
Was glad to welcome guests of such distinction;
His naked nymphs gave service to their needs.
A feast was set before them; after that,
Rare drinks went round in cups of jade and crystal.
Then Theseus, gazing out across the flood,

Pointed a finger at the scene before him
And asked, "What do you call that place out there?
Is it an island or a group of islands?
It seems to be a single rise of green."
The river god replied, "Not quite. The view
From here makes several look like one;
There are five islands resting on that sea.
You will be less surprised at their strange story
If you remember how Diana acts
Whenever that fine lady feels offended.
Not long ago these islands were pretty nymphs,
Who after killing off ten head of steer
Prepared a banquet for the local gods.
All were invited to that dancing party
Except myself, and as the nymphs grew gay,
I swelled with anger and grew big with flood;
And when I lose my temper, torrents rage.
Orchards dismembered, pasture lands destroyed,
The nymphs, who then remembered my existence,
Went down, even where they danced, and the place with
        them.
My floods and rivers tore the land apart
Into the five Echinades that rise
Floating like forests of green hair above those waters.
But try to see their last faint touch of green,
The little island I love best beyond them.
The sailors call that place Perimele:
I loved her dearly and I took away
The right for other men to call her virgin.
Her father, Hippodamas, turned to fury
And killed the girl. I saw her body fall,
Thrown from high rocks that overhung the sea,
And then too late I took her in my arms
To lift her floating limbs above those waters.
'O trident-carrier,' I cried, 'whose destiny's
To rule that world which lies so close to earth
Down even to the smallest careless wave that stirs—
Hear me, and let me speak for one whose father,
More merciless than any human creature,
Damned her to drown beneath your restless waters!
Give her a home on earth, O god of ocean,

Or let herself become a green-haired island.'
Then as I prayed I saw earth close around her
And that fair island was her second being."

BAUCIS AND PHILEMON

    At last the river's words fell into silence
And still his marvellous story charmed them all—
All except Ixion's son, who laughed aloud
At what the rest believed, and it was true
His thoughtless spirit had no faith in gods.
"You have a gift for fiction, Acheloüs,"
He laughed again, "a touch of superstition,
But who believes the gods have secret powers
To change the very things we know and see?"
The others disagreed with what he said
And grew uneasy at his blasphemy,
Particularly Lelex, who was wise,
Mature in years as well as wit and feeling.
He said, "The powers of heaven are eternal,
Not to be measured by our time and space,
And what the gods decide, their will is done:
Meanwhile in the foothills of Phrygia
There are two trees, a lime tree and an oak
That grow within the ruins of a wall.
I've seen the place, for Pittheus had sent me
To that far country where his father reigned;
And near the place I saw there is a moor,
Once pasture land, but now half sunk in swamp,
And near those ruins is a no-man's-land,
Half mere, half swamp, once pleasant countryside
But now a region of wild ducks and reeds.
Long, long ago, Jove in his mortal dress
Came to this country with his lively son—
The one who stemmed from Atlas, a brisk boy
Who'd dropped his wings but held a magic wand.
They knocked for shelter at a thousand homes
And learned a thousand gates were locked against them.
At last a cottage roofed with straw and grass
Swung its doors wide. Within these shabby walls
Wife Baucis and old Philemon survived,

Equal in age, both pious and reserved.
When they were very young and gay and married,
They chose the little cottage as their home,
And there they lived till they'd grown old; the couple
Made light of being poor by making certain
The little that they owned was truly theirs:
The two were servants and their own sweet masters.
So when the heavenly visitors arrived
And bowed to enter the low-ceilinged door,
Philemon rose to offer them a seat,
Dusted a bench, and smoothed a rug across it,
While thrifty Baucis stirred a dying fire,
Threw twisted leaves and bark among the coals
And blew them into flames with withered breath.
Then from the rafters overhead she gathered
Up sticks of kindling neatly
And broke the sticks in two to place them under
A copper pot that waited near the fire.
She trimmed a cabbage that her husband cut
Within a kitchen garden close at hand;
Then the old man, raising a forkèd stick,
Fetched down a side of bacon from black rafters
And cut small parings of the precious fat
To toss them where they steamed in boiling water.
To please their guests they kept small-talk in motion,
And as they bowed and smiled put things in service:
An ancient woven willow bench appeared
(For this occasion as for holidays);
A grass-filled mattress was draped over it,
And over that a gaily colored cloth.
Next came a table, ancient as the bench.
The gods sat down: then pinning up her skirts
Elderly Baucis became a proper waitress
To set her three-legged table in good order.
One leg was shorter than the rest; she propped it,
And though her hands shook as she worked she thrust
A broken cup beneath the splintered foot.
And as the table seemed to right itself
She polished it with green, fresh-smelling mint.
Then food was served; first came Minerva's fruit,
The ripe brown olive and September cherries

Spiced with a measure of sweet wine, new lettuce,
Creamed cottage cheese, pink radishes, and eggs
Baked to a turn; and all were handed round
On plates of country-fashioned earthenware—
And of the same make came a large bowl, then
Small wooden cups, all lined with amber wax,
The service for the soup poured at the hearth;
Then came the table wine and the next course.
Set to one side, nuts, figs, and dates, sweet-smelling
Apples in a flat basket, grapes just off the vine,
The centerpiece a white comb of clear honey.
But happier than the simple meal itself,
A halo of high spirits charmed the table.

    "When the huge bowl drained dry, it filled itself,
And empty flasks still spouted running wine.
Old Philemon and then his timid Baucis
Threw up their hands and eyes and said their prayers;
Shocked by this miracle the couple begged
Their guests to let them make a better meal
And ran to catch a goose (who'd been the watch-dog
Of their small farm) but that sly-witted bird
Showed more speed flapping wings than they could run
And seemed to dodge for shelter in Jove's lap.
'Don't murder the poor goose; we're gods on earth,'
The two gods cried. 'This un-god-fearing country
Shall be condemned, but you, my dears, shall not;
Leave home at once, and we'll climb up the mountain.'
Staggering on crutches Baucis, Philemon
Took the long path uphill, and when they'd reached
An arrow's flight from where the top loomed high,
They turned to see the land they'd left below them:
A flood rose over everything in sight,
Except their house. Bewildered by the change
They wept aloud for their lost neighbourhood,
Even for their house that had been much too small,
But now looked grand enough to be a temple—
For such it had become: great marble pillars
Stood where forked branches held the shaky gables
And, where the grass roof slanted, a gold dome.
The barnyard was a handsome marble terrace

Enclosed by gates of artful bas-relief.
Then Saturn's son said in a quiet voice,
'What gift would suit a good man and his wife?'
After she whispered to old Philemon
Shy Baucis spoke to him, 'Our dearest wish is
To be your servants in that marble temple,
And since we've lived together all our lives,
So may we share the moment of our death.'
And then the ancient Philemon continued,
'I hope I never see my dear wife's grave,
Nor may she see earth cover my remains.'
Their wishes were respected; many years
They took charge of the temple. When at last
In frail old age they stood at ease before
The temple's doors and spoke of years gone by,
Philemon saw Baucis shake green leaves around her,
And she herself saw Philemon wear leaves.
Around their faces branches seemed to tremble,
And as bark climbed their lips as if to close them,
They cried, 'Farewell, good-bye, dear wife, dear husband.'
In Thrace the natives show their visitors
Two trees so close together that their branches
Seem to grow upward from a single trunk.
The story that I told you came to me
From a respectable old man who had no motive
In telling lies, and I myself have seen
Memorial garlands hanging from those boughs,
And I've refreshed them with new wreaths of flowers.
I said, 'Those who respect the gods come near
To being gods themselves: they've earned our praise.'"

    At this the story closed. The teller of it
Had charmed his listeners—Theseus most of all,
Who wished to hear of further miracles
Inspired by the restless will of heaven.
Then leaning forward on one arm the father
Of Calydonian rivers turned to him:
"O best of heroes, I have known some creatures
Who have been changed but once, but then no more.
Others have been transfigured many times,
Like Proteus, who lives within the kingdom

Of that great sea whose arms encircle earth.
O Proteus, how many times your image
Comes to us as a young man from the sea,
Then as a lion, then a raving boar,
Or as a snake whom many fear to touch!
Horns change you to a bull, or you might be
A sleeping stone, a tree, or water flowing,
Or fire that quarrels with water everywhere.

ERYSICHTHON

    "This kind of power to change also possessed
Autolycus' wife and Erysichthon's daughter—
Her father was of irreligious temper,
Nor would he burn sweet tribute to the gods;
Then on a certain day his axe invaded
The forest that was Ceres' sacred temple.
Among those ancient trees there was an oak
That gathered strength for many countless years
And was a hallowed temple of its own.
Memorials of prayers swayed from its boughs;
Ribbons and written vows and crowns of flowers;
And wood-nymphs joined their hands to dance around it,
Circling the trunk that measured fifteen yards,
And that great tree had climbed above the others
As far as they out-topped the ferns and grasses.
But wild Triopas' son, Erysichthon,
Saw nothing here to stay his axe; he called
His servants to cut down the tree, and since
They wavered as they stepped on holy ground,
He plucked an axe from someone's timid shoulder
And cried, 'Though this is Ceres' sacred oak,
Though she herself may be alive within it,
I'll strike its topmost branches down to earth!'
And as he raised the axe the oak of Ceres
Trembled and sighed; its leaves and acorns paled,
And its long arms took on a grey-white colour.
But when the vicious stroke fell, blood gushed like
A fountain from the neck of a great bull
Who falls before the altars of the gods.
At sight of blood the crowd stepped back in horror,

Except one who had less fear than the rest
And leaped in Erysichthon's way to stop
The blasphemous swinging of the axe; he halted.
His master faced him, roaring, 'Here's reward
For your fine manners and your piety!'
And at one blow sheared off his victim's head.
Then as he hacked the vitals of the oak
A voice came from the centers of its body:
'I who was once a nymph of Ceres' forest,
Blessed by her grace, had made this tree my home,
And I foretell, even when breath grows faint
And death surrounds me, you who murder me
Shall find true punishment beyond my grave.'
Nor did her warning end his ruthlessness;
At last the tree, shaken by countless blows,
Dragged down by ropes, swayed its tall heaviness
Toward earth and crushed the forest where it fell.

    "Dazed by destruction of the home they cherished,
A sisterhood of dryads dressed in black
Took their complaints to Ceres and implored her
To do her very worst with Erysichthon.
At this the lovely goddess bowed her head,
And all the golden fields of ripened grain
Bowed as she tossed the sunlight from her hair.
She then turned in her mind a punishment
That would bring fear to every living creature,
And yet no one would weep for Erysichthon:
This was to torture him with cursed Famine.
But since the Fates would not allow their meeting,
Ceres gave orders to a local nymph
And one who ruled the flowering mountainside:
'Where Scythia freezes in the farthest north,
There is a land of dark and sterile pastures.
Nor grain nor tree grows there, and in that waste desert
Cold makes her home and with her deathly Pallor
And next to her is Fear and wasting Famine.
Go there, tell Famine to slide in the veins,
The very entrails, of damned Erysichthon;
Tell her no feast on earth shall ease that hunger,
And prove she can out-eat my world of riches.

To make that journey seem less far and fearful,
Ride through the air; my dragons at your service.'
The nymph took flight in Ceres' dragoned car
And sailed to Scythia where near the top
Of a stark mountain range (the Caucasus)
She pulled up short, unhooked the fiery dragons,
And stepped abroad to take a look at Famine.
She turned her gaze across a stone-ribbed waste,
And there was Famine squatted to the ground,
Her claws and teeth tearing stray shreds of grass,
Hair lank, eyes fallen in, and face the colour
Of dead moonlight, lips grey, and her arched neck
Was raw with open sores; skin stretched so thin
One saw her vitals through it, and thighbones
Came curving outward over empty loins,
And where her belly should have been was nothing.
Her breasts (perhaps her ribs) clung to her spine;
Her wasted body made joints monstrous—
Her knees and ankles big as cancerous tumours.

   "While from far off the nymph looked down at her
(Nor could she face the horrid apparition),
She raised her voice to call out Ceres' orders
And then stepped back. Although her stay was short,
She felt the chill of Famine in the air
And ran to take her seat behind the dragons
To steer them high and home to Thessaly.

   "Though two opposing forces shape the powers
Possessed by Famine and enjoyed by Ceres,
Famine set out to do as she was told
And sailed the winds toward Erysichthon's palace.
Then where the irreligious king lay sleeping
(The time was night) she climbed into his bed
And mounted him to give him all she had,
Kissing his throat, his empty heart, and dreaming lips,
And breathing through his pores she planted hunger,
The kind of hunger that is never stilled.
Knowing her orders had been well accomplished,
She left the world where Ceres poured her riches
For house and desert where she felt at home.

"Meanwhile the placid wings of sleep still fluttered
Above the head of night-filled Erysichthon
Who dreamed that he was at a banquet table;
He worked his lips and ground his teeth on air,
Which gave his belly room for strange delusions.
Then when he waked he felt a wild desire
To eat as he had never done before.
With shrinking stomach and with jaws on fire
He roared for all that earth, air, sea could give
To set before him at one meal; yet as he
Pursued his way through half a dozen courses,
He spoke of hunger gnawing through his sides,
And midway through one feast called for another.
What would have fed a city or a nation
Was not enough for him who ate alone:
The more he ate the more he craved to eat.
As ocean swallows rivers of the earth
Nor overflows with waters near or far,
And as a raging fire eats up fuel
In countless logs or anything that burns
And both take more as more falls into them,
Hunger increased by all they've had before,
So blasphemous and greedy Erysichthon
Took down each meal and filled another plate.
To him all food became just cause for hunger;
Great eating led to greater emptiness.

"In that deep well where Famine dug her pit
He poured the wealth of his inheritance,
Yet she was hungry and his greed unchecked.
At last when what he owned had been devoured,
His daughter (who deserved a better father)
Was all he had to sell. He sold her promptly.
The girl had spirit and escaped her buyer,
And running raised her hands at ocean's shore.
'O Neptune, I shall never be a slave;
You know me well, for you have ravished me'—
Which was the truth, for Neptune had possessed her
And could not even now deny her prayers.
Although the man who bought her saw her run,
The god had changed her dress and made her seem

Like any fisherman who strolled the beach.
And as her master glanced at her he said,
'My friend who is so clever, I mean you,
Who hides a small hook covered with small bait
And in still waters drops a slender line
To catch an unsuspecting little fish—
And did you see a girl go by this way,
One in a tattered dress and flying hair?
I saw her standing here—and footprints end.'
She knew at once the god had answered her
And that his trick had worked, so she replied,
'Whoever you may be—I beg your pardon—
My eyes are on the waters at my feet,
And my attention to the craft of fishing.
If it is true that a great god has helped me
To make an art of what I choose to do,
Then no man has been here except myself,
Nor for that matter, any other woman.'
But when her father learned she had the gift
Of being anything she wished to be
He set her up for sale to many a man,
And sold her as a mare, a cow, a bird,
A doe—all at a price that bought another meal—
But kept his greed alive. At last when Famine
Exhausted even the girl's resourcefulness,
And food increased his ravenous disease,
The old king's teeth tore at his wasted body
And in despair he ate himself to death.

      "Why talk forever of the fate of strangers,
When I myself take on so many changes?
But O, my dear young men, my range is small:
Sometimes you find me as I am today,
Or I'm a green snake winding through a meadow,
Or a chief bull charging forward with my horns—
But one—look at my forehead—disappeared."
At which he closed his story with a sigh.

# IX

# BOOK IX

Acheloüs and Hercules • Hercules, Nessus, and Deianira
• Hercules' Birth • Dryope • Themis' Prophecy • Byblis
and Caunus • Iphis and Ianthe

In Beatrice Chanler's Cleopatra's Daughter (1934), there
is a passage describing the invasion of Egyptian cults into
Rome. The immediate scene was in Mauretania at Caesarea
before the Temple of Isis: "Blowers of trumpets dedicated
unto mighty Serapis gave forth a ditty proper to the temple
and the god; and now at last did Berbers in Mauretania—
like Ovid at Rome—hear that shrill music of the sistra and
for the first time see the strange animal gods of Egypt. The
priests, leaders of the sacred rites, bore the relics of all the
most puissant gods: a golden lantern shining forth with a
clear light; a palm tree with leaves cunningly wrought of gold;
a round vessel of gold in the form of a breast from which
milk flowed." In telling the story of Iphis, Ovid showed how
he was charmed, like other Romans of his day, by the cult of
Isis, which roused the disapproval of Augustus, who caused
Cleopatra's son by Julius Caesar, Caesarion, called "King of
Kings" by Antony, to be put to death. Naturally enough, Au-
gustus wished to stamp out all signs of Cleopatra's influence
in Rome. C. P. Cavafy, the best of twentieth-century Greek
poets, has a memorable poem "On the Alexandrian Kings"
which revives, like Ovid's story of Iphis, that moment when
an Alexandrian splendour shed its mysterious light through-
out the Mediterranean world.

# BOOK IX

Theseus (some looked on him as Neptune's son)
Asked why the god made moan, and why he wore
A deep-cut living scar above his eyes.
The river thrust lank reeds around his curls
And said, "It's a sad story, hard to tell—
Which one of us likes to talk about his failures?
I'll tell the truth and nothing but the truth,
For if one does fail, there's a touch of glory
In having tried at all. The one who overthrew
Me had more than brutal strength, that fact, that thought
Is sop to vanity. If you have heard
Of Deianira, then you know that of
All girls she was the beauty, she the hope
Of countless yearning lovers who pursued her,
Myself among them, to her father's house.
'Make me your son-in-law, Oeneus, here's
My hand,' I said. Hercules said the same,
And all the rest gave way to two of us.
He said Jove was his father, and named the trials
He suffered at the whim of a stepmother
And took them in his stride. Then I insisted
It was a dirty crime to let a man
(This was before the gods made him immortal)
Be given favours that a god deserved—
'For I am god of all the many rivers
That make your kingdom green as fields in heaven.
And if I take your daughter, she'll be given
To someone who is not a foreigner,
But one who knows each foot of land you own.
It's to my credit Juno does not hate me;
No trials are forced on me through her disfavour.
It's true enough that you're Alcmena's son,'

229

I said to him. 'You say that Jove's your father,
And if he is, your mother's a fine bitch,
Yourself a bastard or a cheerful liar.'
As I went on, his half-shut eyes glared at me,
Then lightning fire flashed, and these few words
Were all he said: 'My hands make better speeches
Than my tongue. Go try to win a battle
With your talk!' And then he lunged at me.
I'd said enough, too much, nor could I turn
Away; so dropping my green cloak I took
My stance, fists, elbows at the level of my breast,
My body taut and spare—at which he scooped up
Sand and showered me with it and the yellow
Dust flew back and covered him. One moment
He was at my throat, then snatching at my feet,
Then seemed to tear each muscle in my body.
Yet my weight saved me; I stood as stolid
As a cliff where waves eat at its sides. Quickly
We had squared off—then lunged, both swift, both certain
The other would give way, feet grappling feet,
Hands interlocked, head thrust at forehead, all
My weight against him. So I've seen in battle—
A fat cow to the winner—bulls storm each other,
And while the fight's in doubt, the cattle shake
With fear. Three times Hercules tried to toss
Me from his breast and three times failed, but at
The fourth—a side-blow from his fist—he broke
My grip. (I'll try to tell this story as it
Happened.) He swung me round and leaped upon
My back. (I do not make him stronger than
He was to make myself a hero too.)
It was as if a mountain came upon me.
Sweat pouring from my arms I slipped his grasp,
Yet he had winded me—nor time for breath
Before he had me at the throat and threw me,
Teeth gritting dust. Nor was I any match
For him at all. I turned to my old arts,
Became a long-tailed snake that wheeled and rippled
Through his clasping fingers. But when I coiled
And thrust my tongue out at him, he laughed aloud
As if my magic were a foolish art.

He shouted, 'It's child's play for me to watch you,
For in my crib I used to murder snakes.
If you were the biggest monster of your kind,
You'd be a single snake against the hundred
That used to flourish from the Hydra's torso;
As one head was cut off, two heads grew up;
They sprouted like the branches of a tree
That got their strength through pruning and destruction.
I took the Hydra's measure and destroyed her.
And you, poor imitation of a snake,
What will become of you, frail arms and legs
Concealed in that long tail, that mere disguise
That wriggles to escape?' And as he spoke
He seized my throat, and as my jaws fell open
I felt his iron hands. I sloughed my skin
To take my third disguise—a raging bull
That charged him where he stood. At my left side
He threw an arm around me, kept in step
As though he raced a circus course with me,
Then with full weight he heaped himself upon me,
My neck bent double, the left horn fast in earth,
My left side buried in the sand. Nor was he done.
His murderous right hand plucked at my right horn
And tore it root and bone from my poor forehead.
One day the girls who blessed my streams and waters
Picked up my relic and filled it with gay fruits
Wreathed with sweet flowers pouring from its lips,
And now the fertile goddess carries it,
Her harvest flowing from my sacred horn."

### HERCULES, NESSUS, AND DEIANIRA

Then since the river god had told his story
One of his nymphs came tripping into view;
The slender girl was naked as Diana,
Green hair undone and flowing down her sides.
And in her arms she held the Horn of Plenty,
Harvest of Autumn's fruits—and after it,
A second round of apples, the health of life.
Then when grey daylight came and Sun's first rays
Glanced over hilltops of the distant range

The young men took their way, nor would they wait
Until the stormy river eased his course.
And as they left him, native Acheloüs
Concealed his weather-beaten face, his wound, his scars
Beneath the surface of his rising waves.

Except for the deep scars across his forehead
(For they reminded him of loss and sorrow,
And which he covered with a wreath of reeds)
He was unharmed. But what of fire-filled Nessus,
The Centaur with an arrow in his back,
Doomed by his love for the same girl, Deianira?
As Hercules, returning with his bride,
Advanced upon the town where he was born,
He came to the swift waters of Euenus,
Still wild with winter rains which overflowed it;
Its furies seemed impossible to cross.
As for himself, he did not fear the passage,
But feared his wife could scarcely swim across.
As he stopped short, Nessus rode up to him
And said, "I'll trot her to the other side;
You keep your strength to swim yourself to safety."
The Theban Hercules looked at his bride
(Who trusted neither Centaur's back nor river
And paled at both) and he, though heavy with
His lion's skin and quiver (for he'd tossed
His club, his bow across the brawling stream),
He dived and shouted, "Waves are enemies,
Look how I conquer them." He swam cross-current
And fought the waves; then as he came to shore
He heard his wife call out and at a glance
Saw Nessus mounting her. Hercules cried,
"Don't think you'll get away with all your speed,
You fornicating fool, half-man, half-beast,
Nor shall you get your fill of what is mine.
And if you're not afraid of what I say,
Your father's turning wheel should be a warning;
Go, gallop like the wind, there's no escape;
No wind runs faster than my fatal arrows."
Then from his bow an arrow pierced the Centaur

And like a spit ran through his back and breast.
As Nessus tore it out, the arrow dripped
With Hydra's venom and his own life's blood.
Under his breath he sighed, "My death has come,
But not without revenge." His poisoned shirt
Still wet with blood he gave to Deianira,
Told her that all who wear it are possessed,
Seized by the magic of reviving love.

 Time passed: the famous trials of Hercules
Were known around the world—stepmother Juno
And her undying hatred known as well.
After his victory at Oechalia,
He stopped at Cenaean to pay respect
To Jove, to ask his blessings at an altar.
Then quick-tongued Rumour came to Deianira
Ahead of Hercules; Rumour, who mixes
Frail truth with lies, began to tell a story
Of how Amphitryon's son was all too eager
To spend his time (and preferably at night)
With Iole, captive daughter of a king.
His wife believed the fiction she had heard,
But after fits of weeping asked a question:
"Why all these tears? The girl my husband sleeps with
Should be well pleased at making me unhappy
And since she's on her way, it's very late
For me to know exactly what to do,
How to uproot that woman from my bed.
Shall I say nothing, or sit down and whine?
Or go to Calydon? Stay here and suffer?
Or face them at the door—if nothing else?
Meleager (since I am your own true sister!)
Give me the strength to work some horrid plot—
And let me kill her; she at least shall know
How a true woman takes her stand against her."
She wavered between many things in mind:
At last and best she thought of Nessus' shirt,
Still thick with blood and virulent as ever—
The perfect gift for Hercules to wear,
To make his love (grown pale for her) show life.

Mindless of building up her future sorrow,
And with sweet words, instructions where to go,
She gave the shirt to Lichas, who in turn,
Was ignorant of what the thing could do,
And told the boy to take it to her husband.
Lichas obeyed; undoubting Hercules
Was glad to wear the Hydra-poisoned shirt.

As Hercules sent up his praise to Jove,
Incense, red wine poured on the marble altar
To make its flames grow brighter in devotion,
The altar's heat increased the hidden fires
That burned within the shirt and spread their flames
Until they seemed to pierce the hero's bones.
In manly fashion, still much like himself,
His groans and sighs were silent and withheld,
Yet when the pain was more than he could bear,
He tore the altar from its base and filled
Long miles of Oeta's forest with his cries.
Then as he tried to strip the shirt away,
His flesh came with it. Horror to his sight,
It seared his bones and clung or stripped them bare;
Like white-hot rods thrust into icy water,
His blood steamed with the heat of Hydra's venom,
Its flames burned inward to his vital parts,
And darkened sweat poured from the restless
          furnace
That covered lungs and belly, even the marrow
Of bones turned into steaming, brackish water;
And all his limbs turned black with hidden fires.
He raised his hands to heaven as he cried,
"Saturnia, eat your fill of ruined flesh,
Look down at me from your high throne in heaven
To feed the barbarous sinews of your heart.
If I deserve the slightest sign of mercy—
And that from an immortal enemy—
Take, take this burden from me, which is life,
That is no more to me than hopeless labour,
Long hours of disease and agony.
And what you take shall be a gift to me,
The only grace a stepmother can give.

This my reward for killing Busiris
Who tainted temple walls and sacred places
With blood of wanderers in search of Jove?
I who unmanned the giant Antaeus,
Destroyed the power he gathered from his mother?
Who had no fear of Spanish triple faces,
Nor feared the triple-headed Cerberus?
Was it for this reward that my hands ripped
The bull's horn from its socket? Surely Elis
Knows how these hands have worked, what they have
            done—
So do the watchful waters of Stymphalus,
The very trees of the Parthenian orchards—
These hands that fought the Amazons in battle,
And won the golden girdle of their queen,
And filched the apples of Hesperides
In full gaze of their dragon's sleepless eyes.
Is this because Centaurs could not outwit me,
Nor the Arcadian Boar? Or because I seared
The ever-double-growing heads of Hydra
Until their magic power was undone?
Was it not I who saw fat Thracian horses,
Their stables filled with stench of human blood,
The very floors wet with poor, murdered flesh—
Was it not I who killed them and their master?
And did my arms embrace the Nemean Lion
Till he fell dead? And did my shoulders carry
The ever turning skies of night and day?
Perhaps the savage wife of Jove is sleepy,
Has strained her mind inventing labours for me,
Which even now I'm willing to attempt—
Yet I can feel a new death creep by fires
Through veins and limbs, not to be shaken off
By naked strength, nor force of sword and shield.
Even my lungs breathe out destroying fires
That burn within my veins, but Eurystheus
Is still spared. O Earth and Heaven!
And are there some who think the gods exist?"
Then like a bull who wears a fatal shaft
Piercing his sides (after his enemy
Has run away) Hercules stormed the trails

Of highest Oeta; even as you look up
You'll see him tearing half his flesh away,
Uprooting giant cypresses and pines,
Groaning and roaring with the wind, or see
His hopeless hands raised to his father's heaven.

Turning his head the hero saw poor Lichas
Fearful and shuddering in a shallow cave;
With anger caused by ceaseless agony
He shouted at the boy, "Now I have found you—
The one who brought me this disease I wear,
The murderer, the cause of early death."
The boy turned pale and feeble in his terror,
Made limp excuses for his innocence,
And hid his face against the hero's knees,
At which Alcmena's son seized the boy's feet,
And swinging him in circles overhead
He catapulted him toward the far waters
Of the Euboean Sea. As rain turns hail,
Then snow in Northern winds, so this frail boy
Sailing, blood chilled by fear in middle air,
Had turned to ice (so ancient legends say)
Then to flint rock. Euboean sailors tell
Of a rock island that's the body of a man,
That seems to float half-drowned between the waves
And though it's senseless stone, they fear to land.
Still touched with awe they called the island Lichas.
Meanwhile the son of Jove tore down the trees
That peopled Oeta's thick-grown mountaintops,
And with them built a mammoth funeral pyre,
Then told Philoctetes to light the fire;
And for his services the hero gave him arrows,
Their sheath (which he had worn) both fated
To return to fields of Troy. As the huge pyre
Welcomed its hungry flames Hercules draped
The Nemean Lion's skin on crackling boughs
As though they made a bench and stretched it neatly
And at one end for headrest placed his club.
As though he dined with red wine and red roses,
He took his ease upon a bed of flames.

Soon racing fires grew around his body
And ate away indifferent head and limbs—
This, while the gods on Mount Olympus feared
The hero's death would leave the Earth unguarded,
Even themselves a prey to wayward dangers.
Jove (who knew well the tenor of their feeling)
Grew glad and took this line of discourse with them:
"I'm happy you have Hercules in mind,
Happy to be the father of you all;
It is my pleasure still to be a king
Of gods who show their loyalty to a master,
To know my sons are shielded by your care,
That Hercules receives your kind approval.
I'm flattered by the compliment you pay
The memory of everything he's done,
And I'm in debt to every one of you;
Therefore be free of panic and small worries,
And even now don't underestimate
The heat, the cleansing powers of his flames;
Yet as he won his way through earthly trials,
He has the power to overcome their doom.
Only his mortal flesh (his mother's gift)
Shall be consumed in flames of Vulcan's fires;
The rest can never die—that comes from me.
No flames of Earth or Heaven can destroy it,
And as his charred corpse pays respect to Earth,
I plan to welcome Hercules in Heaven.
I think this gift of mine has your consent,
But if a single one of you regrets
The presence of young Hercules as god,
Or he or she may hold to an opinion,
Yet shall be forced (since he has earned his title)
To take him as he is." To this the gods
Agreed; even Queen Juno sat unmoved,
Except for Jove's last words, which seemed to carry
A warning to her, and her eyes looked sad.
While Heaven gave its honours to Jove's son,
The flames had purged (with Vulcan at their center)
The mortal features of the earthly hero;
All that his mother gave him burned away.

Only the image of his father's likeness
Rose from the ashes of his funeral pyre;
Then as a snake sloughs off his elder skin
And glories in new dress with glittering scales
So Hercules stepped free of mortal being,
And took on greater stature with his honours,
And with an air of gravity and power
Grew tall, magnificent as any god.
Then Jove, the Father, circled him with clouds,
Riding him skyward, drawn by four white horses,
To throne his son among great shining stars.

HERCULES' BIRTH

   Worn Atlas felt the weight of Hercules,
Eurystheus no less angry at the sight—
His hate of Hercules had turned to spite
Against the hero's heirs and near relations.
Grown prematurely old with family worries
Alcmena told Iole all her cares,
Gossip of women's illnesses, complaints,
As well as all the Trials of Hercules.
At Hercules' command, his young son Hyllus
Took willing Iole to bed, and in due time
The girl was big with child, for like his father's,
Young Hyllus' gift to girls was swift and large.
Then elderly Alcmena spoke to her:
"May the great gods be kind to you and make
Your labours short and clean—do take the trouble
To pray to Ilithyia; she takes care
Of girls who fear the trials of lying-in.
She was the one whom Juno turned against me.
When I came near my time with Hercules—
It was the tenth moon and the boy was heavy,
So big I knew at once Jove was his father—
I thought he'd tear each muscle in my belly
And break my bones. What fearful cramps I had!
Even as I think of them cold sweat covers my body;
Seven nights and days they held me in their horrors,
Then, spent with pain, I opened arms to Heaven,
And groaning like deep Earth I called Lucina

(As well as the three deities of childbirth).
Lucina came; but she had promised Juno
At once to murder me. She locked her fingers
On her right knee crossed over her left leg
And sat crouched on the altar at my door.
As she delayed the birth of Hercules,
Perhaps she liked to listen to my groans.
Meanwhile she sang a spell that kept the child
Deep-locked within me. I went mad with pain:
I cursed Jove and his mischief, begged for death
So pitifully even stones would weep.
To soothe me, housewives of the neighbourhood
Stood at my side and prayed for my relief.
A red-haired peasant girl (my best-loved servant)—
Her name Galanthis—guessed vindictive Juno
Had put a curse on me; as she slid past
Lucina at my door, she noted quickly
Tight fists and tight-crossed knees, and with a grin
Said, 'I don't know you, but stand up to cheer
My mistress who's delivered of a boy!
Alcmena's prayers are answered by the gods!'
At this, Lucina, shocked, leaped to her feet,
Hands spread in wonder that her charms had failed.
I had relaxed; the boy fell from my womb.
Then (it was said) the naughty girl laughed at
Lucina, and as Galanthis doubled up
With laughter the indignant goddess seized
Her rich red hair and held her to the ground
Until her arms were forelegs of a beast.
Her pretty hair retained its reddish tint;
Her cheerful habits were the same—she smiled—
And yet the girlish creature was a weasel.
Because Galanthis lied in helping me,
She gives birth to young weasels through her lips,
As in the past she makes my hearth her home."

DRYOPE

Remembering the fate of her fond servant,
Alcmena's heart shed tears, and as she wept
Her daughter-in-law replied in soothing words,

"Dear mother, you are weeping for the loss
Of a delightful girl who was a stranger.
What if I tell you of a queer mischance
That fell upon my own beloved sister?
Even as I talk sobs gather in my throat.
She was her mother's only child (for I'm
The daughter of my father's second wife).
She was the famous, lovely Dryope
Who gave her maidenhead to gold Apollo,
Yet honest Andraemon was glad to take her,
And both lived happily as man and wife.
One day she strolled the banks of a small lake,
A charming landscape spread with grass and myrtle;
Nor did she know the history of the place,
Its strange fatality and curse (I tell you this
To wake a sympathetic touch of anger).
She'd come to pay devotion to the nymphs,
To weave them wreaths of myrtle and crisp daisies,
And at her naked breasts she held her son
Who took sweet pleasure from the milk she fed him.
At the stilled edges of the little lake,
The floating lilies and bright lotus grew.
To make the baby smile, she plucked the lotus
(I being with her stooped to do the same)
Then in her hand I saw blood drip from petals,
The torn stalk shake as if possessed by terror.
As you may know, plain-minded country people
Tell how a girl named Lotis got away
From the mad chase of naughty Priapus—
She changed into a flower which took her name.

    "My sister did not know that ancient legend,
Nor what it meant, but, frightened, she stepped back,
Whispering a prayer to keep herself from harm.
Then as she turned to run, her feet were caught,
Held into earth and grass, and as she swayed,
Only her arms and shoulders were swung free.
Rough bark crept up her legs, her thighs,
And as she felt it creep, she tore her hair,
Only to find her fingers full of leaves.
The boy Amphissos (for the child was named

As grandfather Eurytus specified)
Felt his young mother's breasts grow rough and dry.
O sister, sister, it was I who saw
The doom, and I more helpless now than then,
Hoped to delay the fatal spell; I threw
My arms around your waist, clung to your branches;
(Shall I admit this sin?) I longed to bury
All of myself within your tree-grown prison.

"Listen, then came Andraemon, her poor husband,
And with him came her poor unlucky father,
To look for Dryope. I pointed where she stood—
A lotus tree. They ran to it and kissed
Its warm rough bark, her body, to its roots;
Only her shadowed face was seen 'twixt leaves
That fluttered where her tears dropped through their
            branches,
And as her pale lips moved in that green darkness,
They heard her raining voice through the stilled air:
'If promises, if truth from those in wrong
Are ever heard on earth, then let me say
I did not earn this punishment, this doom.
In innocence I spent my waking hours,
And innocent my passion and my loss.
If these last words are lies, then wither me,
Twist leaves in heat, toss branches in the fire,
To make me die without a memory.
Take care to drive my child from these poor boughs,
And let him nurse at other breasts than mine—
Yet, if all's well, then give him greenest shade
Beneath these branches where there's room to play,
And as he learns to speak, then have him whisper,
"My mother lives within a lotus tree—"
And warn him of the lake, nor let him tear
At flowers or trees' branches; each hides a nymph
In her last fair disguise. Good-bye, dear husband,
Sister, and kindly father. If you love me,
Let neither steel nor tooth break through these boughs,
Nor senseless cattle eat away my leaves.
Since I can't stoop to kiss, rise to my lips,
Raise up my son to take his mother's blessing.

Even now my throat grows rough—nor can I speak;
No need to close my eyes, for night has come;
Nothing but darkness in this tree-green cell.'
Her last words spoken, she was tree itself,
Swaying in air, yet many hours after,
Her graceful body held the warmth of life."

THEMIS' PROPHECY

As weeping Iole told her tale of wonders,
Her story done, Eurylus' daughter wept;
To show her sympathy, the elder woman
Caressed her cheeks and stroked away her tears.
Then both were startled by a fresh surprise:
They saw a young man in the shaded lintel,
Iolaus, looking like a boy, the beardless image
Of all he used to be. In answer to
The prayers of Hercules, Hebe (his wife
In heaven and Juno's daughter) had worked her magic
For husband's sake and gave his dearest friend
(Grown old) his youthful energy and strength.
She thought, "I'll never do this thing again."
At which Themis (the soul of justice) cried,
"Look down at Thebes gone wild with civil war:
Only the hand of Jove can stop Capaneus;
Brothers are bent on murdering each other.
A king (possessed of second sight) will see
His ghost fall through the gaping floors of earthquake;
His son (both loyal and cursed) will go insane;
Haunted by both his mother's ghost and Furies
He'll stray in exile till his wife demands
A gift cursed by the Fates, a gold-wrought neckpiece
While Phegean steel drips red with his cousin's blood.
Then Acheloüs's daughter, Callirhoë,
Shall plead with Jove to make her boys grown men
Swift to undo their father's enemies,
And Jove with Hebe's help shall grant her wish."

As visions of the future flowed in words
That poured from Themis' mouth, each god in Heaven
Demanded favors for their protégés:

Pallantis said her husband was too old
For any kind of pleasure on Olympus;
Ceres (whose words were always understatements)
Complained that Iasion wore a long white beard;
Vulcan said Erichthonius needed vigour;
Venus insisted that her ancient friend Anchises
Was not the upright lover she enjoyed—
A draught of youth would make him new again.
Each backed a friend, the racket grew so dense
No one was heard at all, until Jove spoke:
"Where's your respect for me?" he roared,
"Where do you go from here in all this noise,
And have you any manners left at all?
Come, don't deny the laws that make you gods
Or Fate that made Iolaus young again
And Callirhoë's sons climb overnight
From childhood (nor was this what they desired)
To fighting men. And if you need my words
Of consolation, remember that the Fates
Rule over all of us, including me.
If time ran as I willed it, years would make
Old Aeacus' back, loins, legs grow straight again;
Rhadamanthus would be a boy forever,
And Minos would not be a poor old king,
Heavy with years, his reign a weary story."

    Jove's words had moved the hearts of all the gods,
For if one thought of time-worn Rhadamanthus,
Old Aeacus, or what Minos used to be,
Jove's argument was not to be denied.
When Minos was in golden middle age
All nations feared the mention of his name,
But now he'd grown so impotent, so feeble
He shied away from proud young Miletus,
The forward son of Phoebus and Deione;
Though Minos half-suspected Miletus
Had eyes upon his throne and framed a plot
To make a palace revolution, he feared to act,
To sign the papers for his deportation.
Therefore when Miletus had sailed away,
Crossed the Aegean to the shores of Asia,

To found a city that still bears his name,
He left home by his own determination.
There as he strolled the banks of the Meander,
That river that coils its way against its source,
He met Cyane, daughter of the river,
Whose sinuous body gave him deathless pleasure
And of their meeting came the twins, Byblis and Caunus.

### BYBLIS AND CAUNUS

When Byblis fell in love (That is a story
Of how girls should not fall in love at all)
She had immoderate heat for her twin brother,
The fair and glittering grandson of Apollo.
At first she did not think such heat was love.
Although her greatest pleasure was to play
A game at kissing him, her arms around his neck,
She thought these gestures sisterly affection.
Slowly these careless pleasures turned to fire;
When she strolled by his rooms she was her best,
Her face made up, her clothes as if she were
Her brother's mistress at a palace feast,
And yet more radiant with a flash of jewels—
And she grew jealous if he looked at girls.
Yet all these signs of how she felt were vague;
She could not read them clearly, nor admit
These were the wavering joys of love itself,
That hidden fires glowed within her blood.
Then (to herself) she called him Lord of Life,
Hated the name of "brother" when she said it,
And thought a word like "sister" cold and thin;
She wished he took the hint to call her Byblis.

Throughout the day desire fell half-asleep
But when night came and she grew warm in bed,
It waked to float in raptures through her dreams.
And though she slept as if in sleep forever,
She blushed and felt her brother's weight upon her,
His thrust as she received his quick embrace.
Knowing this to be a dream, when she awoke,

She seemed to melt, to fall in dreams again;
Then her mind swayed from daylight into darkness,
From dark to light. "Unhappy me!" she said,
"To wake at morning from my lovely sleep;
Yet that's not what I mean! My lord is
Beautiful in daylight too; his enemies
Find him rapturous to look on; he charms
The world. And I could love him if he weren't
My brother; it's my curse to try to be
His sister every day, not let him mount me,
Drag me into bed. Yet I can sleep
And have the best of him in dreams again;
No one need know what I do in my dreams,
And nothing's wrong with little secret pleasures.
O Venus, playing with small-winged Cupids,
What joy I had! Like you, I seemed to melt,
Floating in glory with the night around me—
But it was all too brief. The night grew jealous;
It was impatient at my great delight.

"O Caunus, if my name were not 'Your Sister,'
And I was other than I am, not I,
What a sweet daughter I would be to your dear father,
What a great son-in-law you'd be for mine:
All things in common would be ours to share—
But our grandparents, for I'd want you born
Far better bred than I! Someday, perhaps,
You will be someone's husband, straight, upright,
More beautiful than anything on earth—
And yet to me, you'll be no more than brother;
That's the misfortune of my birth and yours,
That's what we share—and yet the meaning of my dream?
And is it true? May all the gods say 'No!'
Yet many gods were glad to sleep with sisters.
Ops became Saturn's wife; Tethys shared bed
With Oceanus, Juno, the wife of Jove, and he
The king of all Olympus. True, the gods
Have other laws than ours; how can I balance
My human Fate with theirs? This heat shall leave
My heart if I grow cold and I may die

Before I give way to desire. I shall be laid,
White on a pyre; my brother's lips will join
To mine in a last kiss—two wills as one:
In pleasing me, will this seem wrong to him?

"Yet Aeolus' sons took sisters to their beds—
Why do I try to emulate their sisters,
Who're they to me, what do I know of them?
Where do I drift? Let all these floating fires
Drop from my mind—and now I'll love my brother
Like a devoted sister, five years old.
Let him be loveless; if he makes advances,
I'll almost put him off with a cool smile;
Rather, I'll make love to him first—since I
Never could say 'No' to his wants, desires.
Love gives me orders and I follow them;
If I'm ashamed to speak, I'll write a letter."
Her last thought brought her wavering will to rest;
She propped herself in bed on her left arm.
"Now let him see me, naked as I am;
Both of us gone insane. What darkening heat
Has gathered in my mind?" was in her thoughts.
With trembling hand she wrote what impulse guided;
Right hand held stylus, left, the sheet of wax.
She wrote, then stopped, then shocked at what she wrote,
Erased, began again, crossed some words out,
And hoped to find the right ones, stopped, then threw
Her tablets to the floor, then picked them up,
She doubting everything she wrote, or right
Or wrong, or spelled correctly, her face flushed
With guilt, yet mouth set firm. She had just written
        "sister,"
Then crossed it out and wrote, "Good wishes, darling,
If you return them, they are mine; if not,
I'll take them anyway, to keep them for you—
Yet know that they are yours from one who loves you.
Though she's ashamed to give her name, she hopes you
        know
What she needs most—her name's Anonymous,
Ready at last to die within your arms,
Nor am I Byblis till your arms disarm me.

You might have guessed at much of what I write:
My beating heart that scarcely dared to beat,
My face grown thin, my eyes that filled with tears,
My kisses and my arms around your neck—
These, if you noticed them at all, were more
Than sisterly respect for handsome brothers.
And now though ceaseless fires burn within me
(God knows I've done my best to put them out)
I've held my pride to keep from going mad;
Wild with unhappiness, and yet demure,
Pregnant with greater heat than girls can carry.
Now that I'm broken, hear me talking in a whisper,
Frail, timid, saying, 'Darling I am yours,'
And only you can save me from myself,
Or save or damn the mistress who adores you.
The choice is yours; I'm not your enemy,
I'm of your kind who longs to make us one.
Let our dry elders talk of right and wrong,
And keep the letter of an ancient law.
Venus is kind to creatures young as we;
We know not what we do, and while we're young
We have the right to live and love like gods.
My dear, our father is an easy man;
We have no fame to lose, no reputation,
No fears, no nothing in the way. Though we
May think of being chaste and coy in public,
Remember, dear, we'll act like relatives,
Loving and sweet, and as we drink at dinner
We'll kiss and fall into each other's arms.
And are there further pleasures you desire?
I'll give them to you when we meet at night.
Have mercy on me—take the girl who tells you
Of her love, yet would rather die than speak
Of it aloud. But she has lost her mind;
Look, she is dying, nor let these words be written,
My epitaph upon a moss-grown tomb:
'Here lies the girl who died for love of Caunus.'"

    When these last words were written (foolish words
That brought her grief) she had filled the sheet,
Then stamped it with her seal; because her tongue

Went dry her tears sealed up the letter.
She blushed and called a servant to her side,
Then whispered, "Take this to"—her voice grew faint,
Trailed into space and trembled—"to my brother."
The sheet slipped from her hand—the kind of omen
That she feared, yet could not heed. The servant
Had her letter and was gone. Then the man waited
Dead-still until his master saw him—then gave
The letter to his hand. Meander's grandson
Glanced down the sheet and threw it to the floor,
Red with his fury smashed the servant's face.
"Run like a fool before I cripple you,
You Goddamned idiot and pimp—get out!"
He cried. "If this weren't blackmail and my ruin
I'd murder you!" Breathless the slave returned,
And when his mistress got the drift of Caunus' threats,
She turned as pale as ice; yet when her blood
Came back, her veins ran hot with her old madness.
"It's all my fault," she whispered to herself,
"To write what should be said with lips and hands
In a dark room in bed with him alone.
I should have tested him with double-talk;
Waited in harbour till the wind blew fair,
Then reefed my sails and steered a course to shelter.
Full-bellied, I sailed into unknown winds,
Torn on the rocks, wrecked, floundered, lost
In storms of ocean where no shores return.

   "An omen warned me not to write of love:
The sheet dropped from my hand. A stupid whim
Prevented me from calling back that fool
Who tells me that my hopes are nothingness.
Should I have waited for another day?
If I had not gone mad I could have read
The warning of the gods in that brief omen;
I should have sent myself and not the letter,
Not trusted love and all I hoped to live for
To little words in wax that fade away.
Caunus should see my face, my tears, and hear me,
Should know the love that cares for him alone.
All this is more than words that I can write.

Then we would kiss; I'd close my arms around him,
And if he'd throw me off, I'd faint away
Like a poor girl who's dying, droop to the floor
To kiss his feet, beg for my life, and clasp his knees.
I should have done all things at once to win him;
My stupid slave undid me, took the wrong moment
When Caunus, out of spirits, turned against me.

"My errors play against me, for dear Caunus
Is not a tigress' cub, nor is his heart steel-bound
Or cut from rock, nor did a lioness
Give him her breast to suck. Now I must talk,
Talk to him till my last breath leaves my lips.
There's no undoing what I've said before,
But second best to win back what I've lost
And make a fresh beginning of my case.
But if I drop him now he won't forget
How far I've gone, and yet not far enough;
If I neglect him, he may think me faithless,
Or that I tried to test, to tempt, to trap him.
Whatever he may think, will he believe
I've been inspired by the god who fills
My very blood with heat beyond all telling?
Nor can I quite undo what's gone before;
I've written that in foolishness, but true—
If I do nothing more I'll show mere guilt,
Or prove that I'm ashamed. I've nothing now
To lose—but O so much to hope for when
I see him holding me within his arms!"
So the disorder in her mind ran on;
She knew her weakness, yet resumed her way,
Pleaded with Caunus, begged him to seduce her;
As often as he turned from her she clung,
Till he left home and built a foreign city,
A place called Caunus in far Caria.

Then Princess Byblis, daughter of Melitus
Tore off her clothes to cool her breasts, her body.
To those who looked at her, she showed her cuts and
        bruises.
To those who listened (and as if to wake their pity)

Told how the Fates deprived her of true love.
O Bacchus! She'd gone mad as wife or virgin
Touched by the thyrsus in a noonday heat,
Mad as a dancer in thrice-yearly celebrations—
And that was how the good wives of Bubassus
Saw her run screaming through their peaceful meadows,
Through Caria, and beyond them, armed Leleges.
From there she wandered where the Lycians lived
And steered past Cargos, looming overhead,
Then down through Limyre to the Xanthus River,
There where the dreadful Chimaera looks down—
Fire-breathing lioness's head and claws,
And yet the creature wears a dragon's tail.
Beyond this forest mountain range she ran,
Till spent, she fell—O Byblis!—face to earth,
Half buried on a plot of stones and leaves.
The girls who guarded native streams and rivers
Then tried to lift her up, to carry her,
To tell her hopeless love could be dispelled.
She lay unhearing, careless where she fell,
Tore at pale grasses, watered them with weeping.
(Some say the naiads filled her veins with tears—
What else had they to give to cool disorder?)
As sap runs from the sides of new cut pine,
Or tar spurts from a fissure of hot earth,
Or west wind floating under April's sun
Turns ice to water in a frost-bound well,
So all of Byblis melted into tears,
And is that fountain in a distant valley,
A stream that has her name, that rises, falls,
And flows beneath a dark-leaved ilex tree.


IPHIS AND IANTHE


The story of how Byblis loved her brother
Would have been gossip in a hundred towns
If Crete had not produced another legend,
A miracle in the changed face of Iphis.
Once on a time near Gnossus, the royal seat
Of Phaestia, there was a man called Ligdus,

A modest freedman, simple and unknown,
Nor was his wealth enough to make him famous;
His one distinction—he kept out of jail.
One evening when his wife was big with child,
He said to her, "Two things I pray the gods:
One is that you may have an easy birth,
The other that the baby is a boy!
Girls cause great trouble in their bringing up;
Fortuna makes them delicate and wayward.
Therefore (and Heaven forbid!) if it's a girl
(I dislike saying this; it sounds unholy),
Then let the creature die." Both wept, for he
Got from his wife a promise to obey him.
Meanwhile, by night, by day, soft Telethusa
Begged him forget the promise she had made,
But he would not; Ligdus was mild, yet stubborn.
As her time neared, at midnight in a dream
She saw great Isis walking toward her bed,
And with her all her sacred company.
Upon her forehead shone the crescent moon,
Halo of golden wheat above her head
That flashed and glimmered with supernal light;
And at her side strolled the dog-faced Anubis,
Holy Bubastis, polycolored Apis,
And Harpocrates, finger at his lips
As though to summon up eternal silence,
The sacred rattles, and the God Osiris—
For whom no search is ever deep enough—
The Egyptian asp, her rolling body thick
With poisoned sleep that drifts to sleep forever.
Mazed Telethusa seemed to be awake,
To see all things more clearly than at noon,
To hear as if awake the goddess speak:
"O Telethusa, dearest child of mine,
Forget your troubles and your husband's error,
When good Lucina helps you through your labours,
Protect and nurse your child, or boy or girl.
I'm one who answers prayers of those who love me—
Nor have you called on an ungrateful goddess."
At this the goddess vanished in night air.

Still glowing with the joy her dream inspired
The Cretan Telethusa left her bed,
Slipped out of doors, and lifted pious hands
To thank the stars, to pray her midnight vision
Was truth beyond a dream and things on earth.

   The child was born, and though it was a girl,
The father happy with misinformation
Heard his fond wife tell nurse to feed the boy
(The nurse was in the secret of that birth).
The dazzled husband chose a name, his father's,
The family name of Iphis, neutral gender,
Which gave the pious mother pure delight,
And made her feel the name was not a lie.
The midnight inspiration to deceive
Remained a secret kept in midnight's grave.
Dressed like a boy, the girl was slight and pretty,
A beauty of her kind—or either sex.

   When thirteen years slipped by, blind Ligdus found
A golden-haired Ianthe for his son—
And of the girls whose beauty made the land
Of Phaestia a place to spend the night,
This girl, daughter of Cretan Telestes,
(And hoped-for bride) was best and fairest.
The two were of an age, Iphis, Ianthe;
They shared their teachers, alphabets together.
Their hearts made way for love with the same fervour,
The same reverses and the same surprise.
Yet what they hoped for was not quite the same:
Ianthe looked toward marriage and a man
Who practised noble husbandry in bed;
Iphis (perhaps) loved more unselfishly,
And with a deeper, closely guarded flame,
A girl who sought another girl for love,
Her loss the loss of pleasures known to wives.
She scarcely held back tears: "What will I do,
Possessed by wayward love unknown to men?
A stranger's love where earth turns upside down;
And if the great gods keep me as I am,
Why don't they rescue me from hope, yet terror,

And if destroy me, send me common weakness,
The kind of madness others understand?
Cows have no love for cattle of their gender,
Nor mares for mares; the ram leaps on the ewe,
The frail doe runs her mazes toward the stag,
So birds in airy flight meet, male to female,
Nor any creature couple kind to kind.
If only I were not a girl—yet Crete
Has many legends of peculiar nature:
The daughter of the Sun took on a bull,
Delighted in the welcome that he gave her,
A female who enjoyed male ruddiness—
I have more madness in my love than hers.
For pleasure she pretended she was cow;
Only her willing lover fooled himself.
Though Cretan marvels happen day by day,
Though Daedalus fly home to us again,
What could he do for me? Could his shrewd art
Make me a boy? Or change my sweet Ianthe
Into more charming beauty than her own?

  "There, Iphis, keep your head above your shoulders,
And put your heart back where it ought to be.
Unless you'd fool yourself as well as others,
Remember what you were when you were born,
Love as most girls were first inspired to love;
And hope of love returned keeps it alive,
Yet Nature by her sleight of hand deceives you—
And yet and yet no chaperon guards your darling,
No envious husband, no forbidding father,
And she is open to your arms. But you can't take her
As so many girls are used. Both gods and men,
All things smile down upon you—you alone
Are left where darkness gathers in your heart.
Even now my prayers have seemed to bring me pleasure:
The gods are kind and give what's theirs to give,
Both fathers, hers and mine, have what they will—
But Nature, only Nature turns against me
And undoes all the promises of men.
The hour is almost here; Ianthe, bride,
Seems to be floating through that hour and me—

Yet she's not mine; and now adrift and lost
Riding an ocean of a million waves
We die of thirst. Then why is Juno here
And torches lit and Hymen at her side?
Where no man takes a woman to his bed?"
The voice within her thoughts trailed into sighs.
Meanwhile Ianthe checked her own impatience,
And prayed that Hymen would not wait too long.
Fond Telethusa, knowing all and fearing
The disappointments of Ianthe's bed,
Pretended to be ill. She forced delays
And said wild omens brought bad luck to weddings,
Until at last the marriage eve had come.
Then she unbound her own, her daughter's hair
And held her trembling body to the altar:
"O Isis, Queen of ancient Paraetorium
And of eternal Mareotic Meadows,
Goddess of Pharos and the sevenfolded Nile.
Come to our call to keep us clear of wrong.
I saw your glory on a far midnight,
Your holy ministry, the signs of moon and star,
The torches lit—I heard the sacred sistra,
Nor in these years was anything forgotten,
No word of yours betrayed. Here is my daughter,
Whom you gave light of day, your child and mine;
Merciful goddess, give us hope and pity."
Tears flooded her last words. The goddess moved,
The altar shook while temple doors swung wide;
Blue flames of lightning struck her crescent crown,
And in the darkness warning sistras sounded.
Still touched with nameless worries and yet cheerful,
The woman turned toward home and Iphis followed.
The girl stepped forward with a mannish stride;
Her skin grew darker and her face looked firm;
Lithe hidden fibres seemed to guide her body.
Her hair, though still disordered, seemed much shorter.
Now as she walked the girl stepped into manhood.
Now to the wedding feast with careless ease,
To consecrate the altars with sweet prayers,
And there to place a tablet written large:
"Here was the tribute manly Iphis made

Which as a girl he promised to the gods."
The early Sun came up to praise the Earth,
Valley and hill and stream in golden glory,
While Juno, Venus, and their consort Hymen
Joined hands to dance a turn at wedding fires,
And youthful Iphis took his bride Ianthe.

# X

# BOOK X

Orpheus and Eurydice • Cyparissus • Ganymede • Apollo and Hyacinthus • Pygmalion • Cinyras and Myrrha • Venus and Adonis • Atalanta • Metamorphosis of Adonis

*The cycle of stories in Book X is clearly post-Homeric. Among other things Homer's two great epics reflected a moral order established on Mount Olympus, which was re-enforced by the masters of Greek drama, Aeschylus and Sophocles. That order had drifted far into Greco-Roman decadence; how far is dramatically revealed in Ovid's version of the Orpheus legend, in the stories of Ganymede, Pygmalion, and Myrrha. Ovid hints broadly enough of the homosexual elements in Orpheus's character, in Jove's through his love for Ganymede; a miracle of self-love is deftly turned in his version of the Pygmalion legend—that of the artist who falls in love with a work of his own creation, which is one of the finest examples of Ovid's intuitive wit. These stories show another world than earlier scenes of Greco-Roman heritage. One detail of the Myrrha story has curious significance; that is in the portrait of Myrrha's indulgent nurse, who helps Myrrha in her invasion of her father's bedroom. Myrrha's old nurse "spoils" her as lavishly, as foolishly as Juliet's nurse "spoils" her darling in Shakespeare's play. Both nurses are examples of maternal senility. It is possible that Shakespeare drew hints from Myrrha's nurse in his marvellous creation of Juliet's nurse in* Romeo and Juliet.

# BOOK X

ORPHEUS AND EURYDICE

When his farewells were said at Iphis' wedding,
Hymen leaped into space toward blue uncharted skies,
His golden-amber colours gliding up,
Till he sailed over Thrace where Orpheus hailed him
(But not entirely to his advantage)
To bless another wedding celebration.
Though Hymen came to help him at the feast
And waved his torch, its fires guttered out
In coiling smoke that filled the eyes with tears.
Then on the morning after, things went wrong:
While walking carelessly through sun-swept grasses,
Like Spring herself, with all her girls-in-waiting,
The bride stepped on a snake; pierced by his venom,
The girl tripped, falling, stumbled into Death.
Her bridegroom, Orpheus, poet of the hour,
And pride of Rhadope, sang loud his loss
To everyone on earth. When this was done,
His wailing voice, his lyre, and himself
Came weaving through the tall gates of Taenarus
Down to the world of Death and flowing Darkness
To tell the story of his grief again.
He took his way through crowds of drifting shades
Who had escaped their graves to hear his music
And stood at last where Queen Persephone
Joined her unyielding lord to rule that desert
Which had been called their kingdom. Orpheus
Tuned up his lyre and cleared his throat to sing:
"O King and Queen of this vast Darkness where
All who are born of Earth at last return,
I cannot speak half flattery, half lies;
I have not come, a curious, willing guest
To see the streets of Tartarus wind in Hell,

259

Nor have I come to tame Medusa's children,
Three-throated beasts with wild snakes in their hair.
My mission is to find Eurydice,
A girl whose thoughts were innocent and gay,
Yet tripped upon a snake who struck his poison
Into her veins—then her short walk was done.
However much I took her loss serenely,
A god called Love had greater strength than I;
I do not know how well he's known down here,
But up on Earth his name's on every tongue,
And if I'm to believe an ancient rumour,
A dark king took a princess to his bed,
A child more beautiful than any queen;
They had been joined by Love. So at your mercy,
And by the eternal Darkness that surrounds us,
I ask you to unspin the fatal thread
Too swiftly run, too swiftly cut away,
That was my bride's brief life. Hear me, and know
Another day, after our stay on Earth,
Or swift or slow, we shall be yours forever,
Speeding at last to one eternal kingdom—
Which is our one direction and our home—
And yours the longest reign mankind has known.
When my Eurydice has spent her stay on Earth,
The child, a lovely woman in your arms,
Then she'll return and you may welcome her.
But for the present I must ask a favour;
Let her come back to me to share my love,
Yet if the Fates say 'No,' here shall I stay—
Two deaths in one—my death as well as hers."

     Since these pathetic words were sung to music
Even the blood-drained ghosts of Hell fell weeping:
Tantalus no longer reached toward vanished waves
And Ixion's wheel stopped short, charmed by the spell;
Vultures gave up their feast on Tityus' liver
And cocked their heads to stare; fifty Belides
Stood gazing while their half-filled pitchers emptied,
And Sisyphus sat down upon his stone.
Then, as the story goes, the raging Furies
Grew sobbing-wet with tears. Neither the queen

Nor her great lord of Darkness could resist
The charms of Orpheus and his matchless lyre.
They called Eurydice, and there among
The recent dead she came, still hurt and limping
At their command. They gave him back his wife
With this proviso: that as he led her up
From where Avernus sank into a valley,
He must not turn his head to look behind him.
They climbed a hill through clouds, pitch-dark and gloomy,
And as they neared the surface of the Earth,
The poet, fearful that she'd lost her way,
Glanced backward with a look that spoke his love—
Then saw her gliding into deeper darkness,
As he reached out to hold her, she was gone;
He had embraced a world of emptiness.
This was her second death—and yet she could not blame
        him
(Was not his greatest fault great love for her?)
She answered him with one last faint "Good-bye,"
An echo of her voice from deep Avernus.

    When Orpheus saw his wife go down to Death,
Twice dead, twice lost, he stared like someone dazed.
He seemed to be like him who saw the fighting
Three-headed Dog led out by Hercules
In chains, a six-eyed monster spitting bile;
The man was paralyzed and fear ran through him
Until his very body turned to stone.
Or rather, Orpheus was not unlike
Lethaea's husband, who took on himself
The sin of being proud of his wife's beauty,
Of which that lady bragged too much and long,
Yet since their hearts were one (in their opinion)
They changed to rocks where anyone may see them
Hold hands and kiss where Ida's fountains glitter.
Soon Orpheus went "melancholy-mad":
As often as old Charon pushed him back,
He begged, he wept to cross the Styx again.
Then for a week he sat in rags and mud,
Nor ate nor drank; he lived on tears and sorrow.
He cried against the gods of black Avernus

And said they made him suffer and go wild;
Then, suddenly, as if his mood had shifted,
He went to Thrace and climbed up windy Haemus.

    Three times the year had gone through waves of
        Pisces,
While Orpheus refused to sleep with women;
Whether this meant he feared bad luck in marriage,
Or proved him faithful to Eurydice,
No one can say, yet women followed him
And felt insulted when he turned them out.
Meanwhile he taught the men of Thrace the art
Of making love to boys and showed them that
Such love affairs renewed their early vigour,
The innocence of youth, the flowers of spring.

    One day while walking down a little hill
He sloped upon a lawn of thick green grasses,
A lovely place to rest—but needed shade.
But when the poet, great-grandson of the gods,
Sat down to sing and touched his golden lyre,
There the cool grasses waved beneath green shadows,
For trees came crowding where the poet sang,
The silver poplar and the bronze-leaved oak,
The swaying lina, beechnut, maiden-laurel,
Delicate hazel and spear-making ash,
The shining silver fir, the ilex leaning
Its flower-weighted head, sweet-smelling fir,
The shifting-coloured maple and frail willow
Whose branches trail where gliding waters flow;
Lake-haunted lotus and the evergreening boxwood,
Thin tamarisk and the myrtle of two colours,
Viburnum with its darkly shaded fruit.
And with them came the slender-footed ivy,
Grapevine and vine-grown elms and mountain ash,
The deeply wooded spruce, the pink arbutus,
The palm whose leaves are signs of victory,
And the tall pine, beloved of Cybele
Since Attis her loyal priest stripped off his manhood,
And stood sexless and naked as that tree.

Then came the cypress with its cone-shaped fruit:
The tree was once a boy loved by Apollo,
God of the twanging lyre and the bow.
And at that time there was a stately deer,
Worshipped by nymphs who shared his neighbourhood,
A pretty pasture called Carthaean Field.
His eyes were shaded by broad-branching antlers
Which shone in burnished gold, and at his throat
A collar breathed of many coloured jewels;
Even at his birth he wore a silver crown,
And glinting round his head and from his ears
Were strung the daintiest of Orient pearls.
The creature had instinctive faith in man;
He walked in homes where strangers kissed his forehead.
All seemed to love him, but beyond all others
His sweetest lover was young Cyparissus.
Daily he led the deer to greenest pastures,
To drink at fountains in Carthaean meadows.
He gathered violets and pinks and daisies
To dress deer's antlers in a wreath of flowers,
And then as if the boy were a bold rider
He'd mount the creature's back or stroll beside him;
Like a proud master with a dancing stallion,
He fashioned reins and bit of purple silk
To lead the deer, caressing his soft lips.

At noon one summer's day—it was the hour
When the beach-yearning Crab stretched wide its claws
That turned to fire in the sun's white heat—
The deer sank down to rest, to wet his lips
At a cool spring flowing in a wooded covert.
Not knowing that the deer had strayed so far,
And glancing carelessly through shuttered leaves,
The boy thrust a quick spear through the deer's side,
And when poor Cyparissus gazed and saw
The blood, the open wound, the dying deer,
He knew his love was lost and wished to die.
Phoebus said everything he could to cheer him—

What did he leave unsaid? Nothing at all:
He told him too much grief makes sorry faces,
To save his tears for deeper wells of sorrow;
But no, the boy said all he wished to do—
May Heaven help him!—was to cry forever.
Tears drained the manhood from his slender thighs,
His fair white body took a greenish tint;
The waving hair that used to hide his forehead
Grew upward like a green and thorny tower.
He was a tree whose shapely topmost branches
Stared at the stars across the circling night.
Apollo sighed, his own eyes filled with sadness,
"You whom I weep for, shall share grief with others,
And you shall stand wherever mourners are."

## GANYMEDE

These were the trees of miracles and wonders
That Orpheus' music made into a forest;
Encircled by wild beasts and fluttering birds,
He tuned his lyre with a delicate hand.
He leaned an ear—"Harmonious enough,"
He thought, yet certain notes are pitched too high,
Others too low. Then he began to sing:
"From Jove, as well as my maternal Muse
(For Jove is ruler of the World and all things in it)
I ask a gift to guide the themes I sing.
Though I've praised Jove in accents fit for Heaven,
His power, his glory, and his rolling thunder
That drove the Giants from Phlegraean meadows,
I ask a lighter touch, a softer strain.
My theme is pretty boys whom gods desire,
Of girls who could not sleep unless they sinned—
All paid the price of loving far too well.

"One day the very king of all the gods
Took fire when he looked at Ganymede.
Then, O, he wished himself less masculine—
Yet he became a flashing, warlike eagle
Who swooped upon the boy with one swift blow
And clipped him, wing and claw, to Mount Olympus,

Where much to Juno's obvious distaste,
The Trojan boy serves drinks to Father Jove.


APOLLO AND HYACINTHUS


"Phoebus himself was charmed by Hyacinthus,
And if the Fates had given him more time,
And space as well, Apollo would have placed him
Where stars break out in heaven. Anyhow,
The boy became immortal. Now as often
As spring rides down the frosted reign of winter,
And leaping Ram runs after diving Pisces,
Frail Hyacinthus rises from green earth.
My father loved the boy; he thought him sweeter
Than any living creature of his kind
And Delphi, capital of sacred glory,
Was like a tomb, deserted by Apollo.
The god went ranging after boyish pleasures
And strolled suburban Sparta, field and river.
Bored with the arts of music and long bow,
He found distraction near his lover's home.
Humble as any mountain guide or shepherd,
He carried bird nets, tended dogs and leashed them,
And joined the boy in day-long mountain climbing.
This native life stirred Phoebus' appetite
And made the boy more charming now than ever.
When Phoebus-Titan came at noon, half way
Between grey morning and the evening's pallor,
The lovers, naked, sleeked themselves with oil,
And stood at discus-throw. Phoebus came first,
And like a shot he whirled the disk midair
To cut a cloud in two. It disappeared;
It looked as if the thing had gone forever—
And eager to retrieve it, Hyacinthus
Ran out to meet it where it seemed to fall.
Then like a ricochetting wheel of fire,
It glanced a rock and struck the boy full face.
As pale as Death itself, the god rushed toward him,
To fold the shrinking creature in his arms,
To bind his broken features with sweet grasses,
To cure his ragged lips and sightless eyes.

But all of Phoebus' healing arts were useless:
As in a garden, if one breaks a flower,
Crisp violet or poppy or straight lily
Erect with yellow stamens pointed high,
The flower wilts, head toppled into earth,
So bent the dying face of Hyacinthus,
Staring at nothingness toward breast and shoulder.
'Even now, my child, your hour is passed, is run,'
Cried Phoebus, 'and my hand your murderer,
And yet its crime was meeting yours at play.
Was that a crime? Or was my love to blame—
The guilt that follows love that loves too much?
You should have lived forever in my sight,
Your life well-earned, and my life given for it—
But this runs far beyond the laws of Fate,
Yet certain accents of your name shall echo
"Ai, Ai," within the music of my lyre
And shall be printed letters on frail flowers.
And Ajax, hero of a time to come
Will wear a name that calls your name to mind.'
As God Apollo spoke his prophecies,
The blood that filled the grasses at his feet
Turned to a brighter dye than Tyrian purple,
And from its lips there came a lily flower,
And yet, unlike the silver-white of lilies,
Its colour was a tinted, pinkish blue.
Nor was this miracle enough for Phoebus;
He wrote the words 'Ai, Ai' across its petals,
The sign of his own grief, his signature.
And now, the very gentlemen of Sparta
Give honours to the memory of their son,
And like their ancestors, each year they gather
To make a feast on Hyacinthus day.

     "But if you go to Cyprus, home of Venus,
And ask the city of Amathus whether
She cares to honour the Propoetides,
She would say 'No,' she has no use for whores,
Nor does she like to think of the Cerastae,
Named after serpents who wear crooked horns.
In front of city gates there used to be

A shrine set up to hospitable Jove;
But of the time I speak, a careless stranger
Unwary of the things that happened there,
Would think that calves and ewes of Cyprus stained it,
And not the blood of guests who spent the night!
Shocked by these signs of murder and disgrace
Venus prepared to leave her island cities;
Then said, 'Should these white walls and pleasant houses
Take all the blame? What have these temples done,
The streets, the squares? But O, look at the people!
They're scarcely fit for death or deportation;
They're worse than brutes; I'll show them as they are!'
And while she stood in doubt, she longed to curse them;
She saw their horns—which told her what to do.
She changed them into stupid roaring bulls.

"Nor were the women more attractive cattle:
They went to bed with anyone who'd take them,
And laughed at Venus when her back was turned;
And since they could not blush, their faces paled;
It was no wonder that they turned to stone.

PYGMALION

"Pygmalion knew these women all too well,
Even if he closed his eyes, his instincts told him
He'd better sleep alone. He took to art,
Ingenious as he was, and made a creature
More beautiful than any girl on earth,
A miracle of ivory in a statue,
So charming that it made him fall in love.
Her face was life itself; she was a darling—
And yet too modest to permit advances
Which showed his art had artful touches in it,
The kind of art that swept him off his feet;
He stroked her arms, her face, her sides, her shoulder.
Was she alive or not? He could not tell.
He kissed her; did her lips respond to his?
He spoke to her, then slipped both hands around her
And felt a living whiteness move; then, frightened,
He hoped he had not stained that perfect beauty.

He whispered at her—look, he brought her toys,
Small gifts that girls delight to wear, to gaze at,
Pet birds and shells and semi-precious stones,
White lilies, flowers of a thousand colours,
And amber tears wept by Heliades.
He dressed her like a queen, rings on her fingers,
Or diamonds and gold or glancing rubies;
A shining collar at her throat, pearls at her ears,
And golden chains encircling her small breasts.
All these were beautiful enough, yet greater beauty
Shone from her nakedness in bed; he called her
His bride, his wife, the fair white creature sleeping
On cloth of purple, as if she shared his dreams,
Her head at rest upon a feathered pillow.

"Meanwhile the Feast of Venus had arrived
And all of Cyprus joined in celebration:
Golden-horned cattle lay at smoke-wreathed altars,
Blood pouring from white throats in sacrifice
In honour of a blessèd holiday.
Pygmalion, after paying his devotions,
Began a prayer, then shyness overcame him;
He whispered, 'May the very Gods in Heaven
Give me a wife'—he could not say outright,
'Give me the girl I made.' He stammered,
Then went on: 'But someone like—'
He cleared his throat, then said, 'Give me a lady
Who is as lovely as my work of art.'
The prayer was scarcely heard, yet golden Venus
(Who on that day had come to join the feast)
Was well aware of what Pygmalion longed for:
Three times his altar burned in whitest fire;
Three times its flames leaped floating into air,
Six friendly omens of her good intentions.
Then he ran home to see, to touch again
The ivory image that his hands contrived,
And kissed the sleeping lips, now soft, now warm,
Then touched her breasts and cupped them in his hands;
They were as though ivory had turned to wax
And wax to life, yielding, yet quick with breath.
Pygmalion, half-dazed, lost in his raptures,

And half in doubt, afraid his senses failed him,
Touched her again and felt his hopes come true,
The pulse-beat stirring where he moved his hands.
Then, as if words could never say enough,
He poured a flood of praise to smiling Venus.
He kissed the girl until she woke beneath him.
Her eyes were shy; she flushed; yet her first look
Saw at one glance his face and Heaven above it.
Venus came down to be their guest at wedding
And blessed them both. Less than a year went by—
Scarcely the ninth moon filled her slender crescent;
A girl was born to them—Paphos they called her,
And from that child a harbour takes its name.

CINYRAS AND MYRRHA

"Cinyras was Paphos' son; if he'd been childless
Some would have called the prince a lucky man:
Even to speak of him (I'm going to sing his story)
Is warning of how everything goes wrong.
If fathers wish to leave me now, they may,
And so may daughters who have curious dreams,
Girls of unsettled minds and morbid tempers,
Or if they wish to stay for their amusement,
I'll let them disbelieve the plot, the horrors.
But if they think perhaps the story's true,
Then they must hear it as a fatal warning.
Since Nature (when she lives in other lands)
Permits queer customs and disgusting habits,
As well as crimes we seldom think about,
Let us be thankful we are men of Thrace,
Far from the worst of places on the map.
One of these countries is rich Panchaia,
Arabia of cinnamon and spice,
Sweet-smelling herbs and holy frankincense,
Of lovely flowers growing everywhere,
And where a new tree grew, sweet-smelling myrrh,
Whose marvellous birth was hardly worth the cost.
Cupid insisted that his fatal darts
Had never touched the sleeping Princess Myrrha,
Nor had the wildest flames that lit his torches

Entered her veins. It must have been a Fury
From darkest Styx with serpents in her hair
Whose smoking torch gave Myrrha heat and fire
(If it is wrong to hate a doting father,
It's twice as indiscreet to love him madly).
Meanwhile young Myrrha had her choice of princes;
Young men from every Oriental kingdom
Gave her the chance to share their wedding beds,
Yet for the joy of spending nights in love,
One man alone held her imagination,
And though she knew her wayward choice was wrong,
She sighed, 'Where am I drifting, what's my mind
That drives me toward peculiar hopes and fears?
O may the gods in Heaven pity me,
And may the sacred laws that guide my parents
Keep me from evil thoughts—if they are evil.
And who am I to know what's right or wrong?
The animals, of course, have Nature's law;
A cow takes pleasure when her father mounts her—
So does a mare; and when the mood is on him
The grey goat takes his daughters with delight;
Even the birds enjoy that kind of play,
And birds are happy creatures everywhere.
Only our laws deny what Nature loves;
I know of lands where mothers sleep with sons,
And daughters welcome fathers to their beds;
Domestic love becomes a double wedding.
Why was I born or anywhere but here,
Unlucky, hopeless me? Why do I hope
For things I cannot know, and dream all day
Of things I cannot do? Surely my father
Deserves a love as great as his great name,
And if I weren't his daughter, he and I
Would sleep together in a single bed.
Yet as things are, he's mine, and yet not mine;
Though half my love is lost by living near him,
Yet if I were a stranger in his house,
Would I be happier than I am today?
Perhaps if I left home my mind would clear,
But unrequited love keeps lovers chained:
Here Cinyras stands before me every day.

I smile into his face; I touch him, kiss him—
This much at least Cinyras can give to me—
But what else do you want, ungracious girl?
Then things are all confused: you'd be at war
With your own mother in her husband's arms,
Your father's whore, the sister of your son,
Your brother's mother. Have you lost the fear
Of snake-haired Sisters who wave raging torches
In front of poor damned souls? Yet you've done nothing,
Then why spend all your thoughts in thoughts like these?
Why don't you turn to natural desires?
Of course you wish you could—that's what you yearn for;
Yet facts are facts, not what you wish they were.
Father is virtuous and has a pious mind—
O how I wish he were possessed like me!'

"These were her words, but thoughtful Cinyras had
Another matter to consider: which
Of all the lovers asking for his daughter
Was fit to take her? He made up a list
Of those he thought were best, then read it to her
For her advice. She paused, and with large eyes
That stared at his, she seemed in doubt and wept.
Cinyras concluded this was girlish fear;
He stroked her face and kissed his daughter lightly.
Then Myrrha brightened; when he asked her whom
She'd like to marry now, she whispered shyly,
'Some one like you.' The king was pleased and flattered.
'How very daughterly,' he said. 'May I be blest
Forever with a daughter like my own.'
When he said 'daughterly' the naughty girl
Looked at the ground and turned aside her head.

"At midnight, when sleep seems to cure the body,
Impatient Myrrha's restlessness increased.
Heat filled her veins; she tossed; she prayed for love,
Then she became ashamed, grew hot again.
Her mind was like a tree, wavering before
The last fall of the axe, shaken and split,
Swaying from side to side. Death was her wish,
The last solution of her hopeless will.

She left her bed and reached across beams above her
And there she swung a noose made from her girdle;
Then passed the cord around her throat—and deathlike,
Pale as a ghost, she cried, 'Dear Cinyras, look,
You'll learn too late the cause of my good-bye!'

"Some say a servant overheard strange noises—
Myrrha's old nurse, who slept outside the door,
Had waked to hear her own beloved's voice.
She rushed into the room and saw Death near,
The white girl swaying from the high crossbeam;
Then as she screamed and tore at naked breasts,
She cut the noose, and held the fainting girl,
Took breath for tears before she asked a question—
Why did her child have any thought of death?
The girl stared at the floor and would not speak,
Regretting that she'd been too slow at dying
And had been caught before Death captured her.
The nurse let down white hair and showed her breasts,
Saying she swore by them, to learn the reason
For her poor child's dark-winged unhappiness;
And while pale Myrrha turned from her and sighed,
The nurse persisted with smooth promises:
'Old age is not unwise,' she said, 'I'll cure
Even your madness with sweet charms and grasses;
If wayward magic's worked a spell against you,
I've cures for that—or if the gods are angry,
Then we'll appease them gladly with rich altars;
And can you think of more that I can do?
Surely affairs at home are doing well—
Your father, mother in good health; they flourish.'
At the word 'father' Myrrha sighed again,
And though the nurse knew nothing of her secret,
Yet instinct told the woman to say more.
She held the sobbing child to her thin breasts,
'You're very deep in love; I know that much,
So deep I'll never let your father know it.'
The girl leaped from her arms to hide her face
Among the scattered clothes across her bed;
She cried, 'Get out—don't dare to look at me!'
And as the nurse leaned over her again,

'O go away,' she said; 'don't ask me how or why's
The way I feel—that's something you can't know,
It's worse than love.' The nurse fell at her feet,
Trembling with old age, terror, pity, hope;
She wept with promises, then turned to threats—
Said she would tell her sweetheart's father this:
His daughter put a noose around her neck—
Then turned to questioning more: who was the man?
Myrrha had filled her nurse's breast with tears,
Then hid her face within the woman's shawl
To cry out, 'Mother, happiest of creatures,
Your husband in your arms,' then said no more,
And sobbed. The nurse, half-petrified, knew all;
Even her white hair seemed to rise in frost.
She did her best to pacify the child,
To argue that her mind had gone astray;
The girl agreed and said her road was death—
Unless she took full measure of her love.
'Then live, live as you will,' replied her nurse,
'Go take your—' but she could not say aloud,
'Your father,' and sent silent prayers to heaven.

"The season came when Ceres had a feast,
And wheat-crowned wives went out in praise of harvest;
Then for nine days and nights all married women
Refused to let a man take pleasure of them.
Among the stately ladies at this meeting,
Queen Cenchries, wife of Cinyras, was the purest,
Nor failed to keep the letter of the law.
Since the king's bed grew cold with emptiness,
And since the king drank twice his share of wine,
The old nurse said she knew a girl who loved him,
And gave a name the king had never heard.
At this he asked how young the creature was;
Nurse said, 'As old as Myrrha' while the king
Told her to bring the beauty to his bed.
She ran to Myrrha's room and cried, 'We've got him,
The night is ours and now's the time to play!'
Yet Myrrha shrank; her heart was still divided,
Half filled with tears, half golden with delight.
It was an hour when silence fell to darkness,

Boötes turned his wheel between the Bears;
His way was slanted toward the nether Pole,
And Myrrha walked to meet her fateful trial.
Even the golden moon took flight from heaven
Where deepest clouds shut out the wandering stars.
All the familiar fires of night had failed;
Icarus had been the first to shield his face,
And after him white Erigone vanished,
Who gave her life in daughterly devotion
And rose to heaven among the brightest stars.
Though Myrrha stumbled three times on her way,
And three times heard the deadly scritch owl wail—
Though these were further signs of going wrong
(The dark made even her blackest guilt seem lighter),
Her left hand clutched the eager nurse, the other
Wavered through unseen halls and deeper shadows.
At last she entered where the king lay waiting.
Blood seemed to leave her veins; her knees were trembling;
She seemed to faint with fear toward her desire.
And as she turned aside, nurse drew her forward,
Saying, 'Here, Cinyras, take her as she is,
The girl is yours.' The king's great body took her;
Hands and endearing words stroked fears away;
She was so young he called his pet 'My Daughter,'
And she responded with quick cries of 'Father'—
Appropriate names to join their souls in hell.

    "Filled with the fruit of love between her thighs,
She left her father's bed and welcomed it
The following night, the next, until at last
Cinyras lit a lamp to see his treasure:
One look at her and he went wild with horror
And raised a sword that shone beside his bed;
But Myrrha, lithe in nakedness and swift,
Slipped free and coursed her way through night beyond
                him,
Gliding through open fields and palm-tree shadows,
Leaving her native country far in darkness.
After nine moons of wandering foreign sands,
Heavy with child and spent, she scarcely knew
Which way to take. Her life was weariness,

Her fear was death. She prayed, 'O gods in Heaven!—
If any god would care to hear me now—
I've earned my fate, but if I go on living,
My life's a curse on all who look at me.
Or if I die, even the dead will damn me.
Nor place on Earth or in Death's Kingdom home;
Make me a thing that neither lives nor dies.'
Some god (who's nameless) overheard her prayer,
And as she spoke Earth seemed to rise around her;
Roots sprouted from her feet to hold her fast,
Her body upright while her bones grew strong;
Treelike, her arms became crooked heavy branches,
Rough bark encased her sides—she was all tree
That covered her thick belly, breasts, and throat.
Impatient for her doom she thrust her face
Downward within the rising tree. She wept
And hot tears poured along her straining sides.
Yet weeping trees are rare and some grow famous:
The myrrh tree's tears were known all time to come.

    "The child conceived in darkness still survived
And swelled the womb within the coarse-limbed tree.
Though groans of labour are not phrased in words,
Their moaning echoes reached Lucina's ears;
And true enough, the tree belled like a woman
Who knew her time had come; she swayed and sweated
While kind Lucina blessed her ceaseless labours.
At last the tree gave way; a boy was born,
And dryads washed him with his mother's tears.
They wove a crib for him of leaves and grasses;
Envy herself, caught at an honest moment,
Would sigh, then call him pretty as a picture,
Painted as one of Venus' boy babies,
Perhaps a twin, naked and sweet as Cupid,
Nor could you tell which boy was which unless
One held an arrow and one stood empty-handed.

                                        VENUS AND ADONIS

    "Time slipped away: there's nothing more elusive
Than Time in flight, more swift in flight than he

Who steals our years and months, our days and hours.
Son of a sister whom he never saw,
Son of a grandfather who cursed his being,
Child of a tree, Adonis grew to boyhood—
And lovelier than any man on earth.
When Venus looked at him, his mother's guilt
Seemed like an old and half-forgotten story,
And on that day as Eros stooped to kiss her,
His quiver slipped, an arrow scratched her breast;
She thrust her son aside and shook her head
While that swift cut went deeper than she knew.
She found Adonis beautiful and mortal
And lost her taste for old immortal places:
The shores of Cythera, the sea-green harbours
Where Paphos floated like a jewel-set finger,
Cnidos, the rocks where wheeling fishes spawn,
Even Amathus streaked in rich gold and bronze,
And she was bored with living in the skies.
On Earth she took Adonis for an airing,
An arm around his waist, and thought this better
Than golden afternoons on Mount Olympus.
Before she met him she used to lie on grasses
To rest in shade and wreath herself with flowers,
But now she walked abroad through brush and briar,
Climbed rocks and hills, and, looking like Diana,
She wore short dresses, poised as a mistress out
To lead the hunt—yet she sought harmless game,
The nervous rabbit and high-antlered deer.
Her rule was to keep shy of savage brutes—
The lunging boar, the wolf, the bear, the lion—
All those who lived by killing men and cattle,
Who smelled of blood. Adonis had her warning,
If any warning could have held him back.
She told him, 'Save your valour for the timid—
The wild and large are much too wild for you;
My dear, remember that sweet Venus loves you,
And if you walk in danger, so does she.
Nature has armed her monsters to destroy you—
Even your valour would be grief to me.
What Venus loves—the young, the beautiful—
Mean less than nothing to huge, hungry creatures

Who tear and bite and have wide, staring eyes:
The boar whose crooked teeth are lightning flashes,
The stormy lion and his raging jaws.
They have my fears and hates; I know them well.'
And when Adonis asked her why, she said,
'I'll tell you how I know: there is a story
That has a fearful end, and there are wonders
For you to hear. I've walked too far today,
At your quick pace. Look, there's a willow tree
And under it a bed of grass and clover;
We'll have our rest within that charming shade.'
They slipped to earth, her head upon his breast,
And when from time to time she sought for words,
She raised her face to his and kissed his lips.

ATALANTA

    "'Perhaps you've heard the legend of a girl,'
Said she, 'who could outrun all human kind,
Or girls or men. That legend was no lie;
She did outrun them and her reputation,
For she was swift as she was beautiful.
Meanwhile the girl came of an age to marry
And went to get oracular advice.
The god who heard her said, "O Atalanta,
Run from the thought of sleeping with a man;
You shall be caught with one, and yet alive,
Lose all that's yours, nor ever get away."
Turned wild with fear she lived within a forest,
Untouched by men, and when young lovers came,
She sent them home or said, "I'm not your kind;
Only the man who wins a race against me
May take me in his arms, but if he loses,
His gift is death. These are the terms I've made;
Take them or nothing. You have heard me speak."
The girl seemed heartless, yet her beauty fired
Brash lovers who saw danger as delight—
They came in crowds to win the race or die.
Young Hippomenes sat at ease to watch them
And said, "Look at the pretty fools, the sheep—
Who'd try to get a girl and lose his life?"

But when he saw how neatly she was made—
Her face, and glimpses of her thighs and shoulders
(She was as beautiful as both of us,
As you would be, if you were not a man)—
Even he was dazed, reached out his hands to say,
"Forgive me; I was wrong. How could I know
What beauty fires your hearts to win the race?"
At this he felt his own heat mount and hoped
That no one would outdo her; even now
His heat was spurred by jealousy, by envy.
"Why can't I take my chances with the others,"
He thought, "for God has always helped the brave?"
As Hippomenes asked himself the question,
The girl flew past him as if feet were wings,
And to the boy from Helicon her speed
Was like a Scythian arrow's flight through air,
And she, of course, more beautiful than ever.
Her grace in flight had magic of its own:
Ribbons at feet and knees whipped by swift motion,
O glorious hair like wings across white shoulders;
And as a purple curtain hung at doorways
Flushes its light on stone, so her swift body
Seemed to take colour as it glanced beyond him.
She'd won the race and wore the winner's garland,
Indifferent to the boys who went to death.

   "'No less unmoved by loser's fate than she,
Young Hippomenes looked at her and said,
"Why play at honour against slow-footed fools?
Come, set your pace with mine; if gay Fortuna
Gives me crowns you wear, you'll have my glory—
A lucky loser to a gallant man.
Megareus of Onchestus is my father,
Grandson of Neptune, which makes me (with honour)
Great-grandson of the ruler of the seas.
And for myself, as well as family pride,
I claim my own distinction: if I lose,
Your name is famous overnight; you've won
From whom? The undefeated Hippomenes!"
The king of Boeotia's daughter, Atalanta,
Looked softly at him. As she heard him speak,

She veered between her hopes to win, to lose,
And, half caught up in both, she answered him:
"Is there a god who has a touch of envy
For handsome boys who wish to marry me,
And therefore sends this lovely one to death?
Dear god, however much I love myself,
That dreadful price is much too high for me.
No doubt his beauty moves me—say it does;
But not for that alone—for he has charm—
But rather he's so young, so very young,
And has a certain fearlessness of dying,
And of good family, kinship to the seas.
He loves me, says that death means nothing to him
Unless he marry me? Dear boy, go home.
You come from foreign places—there is time
To leave now; while you can, please go away.
Escape a marriage that is poised with murder
And fixed by Fate; another girl will take you,
A clever girl who has more brains than I.
Why do I look at you—so many lovers gone?
Let him die if he wishes, since he knows
How others ran toward death. Or life or death—
Look, he's indifferent! But to let him die
Only because his fancy turns to me?
If I should win I shall be greatly hated,
Yet I am not to blame. Please leave me now—
Or if you have gone mad, I hope you win.
Sweeter than any girl's is that sweet face,
And O, my dear unhappy Hippomenes!
For he was made to live and love forever;
If all were well and Fate had not said no
To dreams of marriage, he alone could take me,
To share my bed, to hold me in his arms."
So for the first time she was touched by love,
But innocent of all she felt and said,
She scarcely knew how swiftly love had trapped her.

     "'The king, her father, and his court—the people—
Had grown impatient for the race to start,
Then Hippomenes, like a son of Neptune,
Called for my help as if his voice were prayer:

"May Cytherea bless me at my side,
To help me with the love that she inspires,
To make me brave in what I hope to win
And greet me with her smiles." A gracious wind
Swept up the prayer which somehow touched my heart,
Yet there was little time to answer it.
There is a meadow people call Tamasus,
The choice estate within Cyprian country,
Which many years ago they gave to me
And where my temples gathered Cyprian treasures.
Among these riches grew a golden tree,
And since I came away from it that hour,
I held three golden apples in my hands.
Invisible to all but Hippomenes,
I gave him brief instructions how to use them.
Horns blew the signal for the race; both boy and girl
Were set, were on the mark and flashed through air
As though their feet had never touched the track,
You'd think their speed had made their feet so light
That they could sail the waves through dancing waters
Or skim the tops of silver growing wheat.
From side lines came the cheers for Hippomenes—
"On, on, you'll make it, now's the time to sprint,
Don't drop behind, go on, you're going to win!"
It's hard to say if this gave greater spirit
To Megareus's son or the king's daughter;
Or once or twice she could have swept beyond him,
And yet held back—and when she saw his face,
Half-heartedly, she took the pace ahead.
As Hippomenes ran—the finish tape
Was still a mile beyond him, far in sight—
His throat went dry; he struggled for his breath—
At last he rolled an apple toward the girl.
She caught the glitter of its golden light,
Then swerved to pick it up, while he, with cheers
Rising from crowds behind him, passed beyond her,
But half a moment later she outstripped him.
He tossed a second apple at her feet;
Again she stopped; again she flew beyond him.
The last stretch of the track rose up before them;
He cried, "Now bless me, Goddess, with this throw,"

And then he tossed the third far out of bounds.
When Atalanta saw the golden arc
Fly through the air, she seemed to draw her breath,
Uncertain whether she would risk the race—
And I inspired her to pick it up,
An impulse that I knew would make the burden
Of weighted gold undo her speed. And now
To make my story fit the race itself,
I'll cut it short—swift-footed Atalanta
Became the joyful bride of Hippomenes.

   "'And do you think, Adonis, Hippomenes
Had learned the grace to thank me for his bride?
He had forgotten all he owed to me;
I lost my temper at his waywardness
And planned to make his memory improve,
To make him and his bride a common case
For those who do not take my deepest warnings.
One afternoon the two young people walked
Deep in a forest where an ancient temple
Had been erected by Echion's men;
It was a sacred shrine to Cybele.
Fired by my heat, hot Hippomenes turned
His mind to love, a bed, a place of shelter
Beside the temple stood a holy chapel
Carved out of rock where elder priests had placed
Grave wooden images of gods. Impatient
Hippomenes led his fond bride to rest
Within the welcome darkness of the grotto;
They had their pleasure at full length; the gods,
Though they were wooden images and old,
Were shocked and turned their faces to the wall.
At first the high-crowned mother of the gods,
Dread Cybele herself, had the intention
Of tossing man and wife beneath the Styx,
But changed her mind—they needed sterner warning:
At once a yellow mane flowed round their shoulders;
Their fingers changed to claws, their arms to legs.
Their breasts grew heavy; both wore tufted tails
That swept the floor, and when they talked they growled;
When they made love they sought deep-wooded places.

As angry lions other creatures feared them,
Yet for her service, thoughtful Cybele
Put bits between their teeth and drove them smartly.
These beasts, like others of their kind, attack
Breast forward, tearing at all things they meet
And you, Adonis, should keep far away
Whenever lions roar across the path.
Your efforts to be brave will find no glory;
Your death will be an end of both of us.'

### METAMORPHOSIS OF ADONIS

"Since she believed her warning had been heard,
The goddess yoked her swans and flew toward heaven—
Yet the boy's pride and manliness ignored it.
His hunting dogs took a clear path before them
And in the forest waked a sleeping boar;
As he broke through his lair within a covert,
Adonis pricked him with a swift-turned spear.
The fiery boar tore out the slender splinter
And rushed the boy, who saw his death heave toward him.
With one great thrust he pierced the boy's white loins
And left him dying where one saw his blood
Flow into rivulets on golden sands.
As Cytherea sailed midair near Cyprus,
She overheard, as from far distance, echoes
Of her beloved's voice; swiftly she steered
Her circling swans above the boy's pale body.
She stepped to earth and when she saw his blood
She cried against blind Fate, then slowly said,
'But even Fate shan't have eternal will;
My sorrow shall have tribute to its own.
Each year will bring memorials of this death,
And where its blood has stained the earth, a flower.
Do I remember this? Persephone
Once had the gift of Heaven to change a nymph
Into a plant that's called sweet-smelling mint—
And if she held that gift, it's mine as well.'
She cupped her hands and poured bright streams of
          nectar
Above the pale remains of Cinyras' son,

And as low fountains spring from yellow sands,
The drops of nectar seemed to move, and flutter,
Red as the pomegranate seed in fruit.
Soft echoes of the wind—'anemone'—
Are in the flower's name; yet at one touch,
The fading petals scatter—all too soon."

# BOOK XI

*No better version of King Midas's story exists than in Ovid's high-spirited recital of his foolishness. The barbarous king is both generous and greedy; he has the manners of a provincial Italian gangster. As in Book V, when Pallas visits the Muses on Mount Helicon, Ovid in the Midas story makes clear his respect (and with great cheerfulness) for divine standards of art. Here his taste is of urban Apollonian quality. Midas's error in wishing to turn all things he touches to gold is less grave in its consequences than his admiration for Pan's country piping. One might say that Ovid would have little sympathy for those who too ardently find pleasure in square dances, folk songs, and primitive improvisations of jazz music. Pan was able to impress only Midas and a group of not-too-sensitive country girls. Ovid treats this scene with admirable good humour; a pedantic lover of fine music might show anger, but not he. Book XI also has the memorable passage of drowned King Ceyx's image rising at his wife's bedside in her restless dream. It is one of the best of Ovid's domestic scenes. Preceding it his elaborate presentation of Sleep's dominion serves as a companion piece to his description of Envy's home in Book II, and it is likely that both passages served as precedent for Spenser's art of personification in the writing of* The Faerie Queen.

# BOOK XI

The songs that Orpheus sang brought creatures round
    him,
All beasts, all birds, all stones held in their spell.
But look! There on a hill that overlooked the plain,
A crowd of raging women stood, their naked breasts
Scarce covered by strips of fur. They gazed at Orpheus
Still singing, his frail lyre in one hand.
Her wild hair in the wind, one naked demon cried,
"Look at the pretty boy who will not have us!"
And shouting tossed a spear aimed at his mouth.
The leaf-grown spear scratched his white face,
Nor bruised his lips, nor was the song unbroken.
Her sister threw a stone, which as it sailed
Took on his music's charm, wavered and swayed;
As to beg free of its mistress' frenzy,
Fell at the poet's feet. At this the women
Grew more violent and madness flamed among the crowd:
A cloud of spears were thrown which flew apart
And dropped to earth, steered by the singer's voice.
The screams of women, clapping of hands on breasts and
    thighs,
The clattering tympanum soon won their way
Above the poet's music; spears found their aim,
And stones turned red, streaked by the singer's blood.
No longer charmed by music now unheard,
The birds, still with the echoes of Orpheus' music
Chiming through their veins, began to fly away—
Then snakes and wild things (once his pride to charm)
Turned toward their homes again and disappeared.
Now, as wild birds of prey swoop down to kill
An owl struck by a blinding light at noon,
Or as when dawn breaks over an open circus

287

To show a stag bleeding and put to death by dogs,
Such was the scene as Maenads came at Orpheus,
Piercing his flesh with sharpened boughs of laurel,
Tearing his body with blood-streaming hands,
Whipping his sides with branches torn from trees;
He was stoned, beaten, and smeared with hardened clay.
Yet he was still alive; they looked for deadlier weapons,
And in the nearby plains, they saw the sweating peasants
And broad-shouldered oxen at the plough.
As they rushed toward them, peasants ran to shelter,
Their rakes and mattocks tossed aside
As the maddened women stormed the helpless oxen
To rip their sides apart, tear out their horns.
Armed with this gear they charged on Orpheus
Who bared his breast to them to cry for mercy
(A prayer that never went unheard before);
They leaped on him to beat him into earth.
Then, O by Jupiter, through those same lips,
Lips that enchanted beasts, and dying rocks and trees,
His soul escaped in his last breath
To weave invisibly in waves of air.

The saddened birds sobbed loud for Orpheus;
All wept: the multitude of beasts,
Stones, and trees, all those who came to hear
The songs he sang, yes, even the charmed trees
Dropped all their leaves as if they shaved their hair.
Then it was said the rivers swelled with tears,
That dryads, naiads draped their nakedness
In black and shook their hair wild for the world to see.
Scattered in blood, and tossed in bloody grasses,
Dismembered arm from shoulder, knee from thigh,
The poet's body lay, yet by a miracle the River Hebrus
Caught head and lyre as they dropped and carried them
Midcurrent down the stream. The lyre twanged sad strains,
The dead tongue sang; funereally the river banks and
        reeds
Echoed their music. Drifting they sang their way
To open sea, and from the river's mouth
The head and lyre met salt sea waves that washed them up
On shores of Lesbos, near Methymna: salt spray in hair,

The head faced upward on strange sands, where a wild
        snake
Came at it to pierce its lips and eyes, to strike:
Phoebus was quicker, for as the snake's tongue flickered
He glazed the creature into polished stone,
And there it stayed, smiling wide-open-jawed.

The poet's shade stepped down from earth to Hades;
To stroll again the places that it knew,
It felt its way toward fair Elysium.
There Orpheus took his Eurydice, put arms around her
Folding her to rest. Today they walk together,
Side by side—or if they wish, he follows her, she, him,
But as they move, however they may go,
Orpheus may not turn a backward look at her.

Lyaeus could not let the killing of Orpheus
Pass without revenge on his mad murderers.
Angered by loss, he captured Thracian women
Who saw him die, trussed them with roots,
And thrust their feet, toes downward, into earth.
As birds are trapped by clever fowlers in a net,
Then flutter to get free, drawing the net still tighter
Round wings and claws, so each woman fought,
Held by quick roots entangling feet and fingers,
Toenails in earth, she felt bark creeping up her legs,
And when she tried to slap her thighs, her hands struck
        oak;
Her neck, her shoulders, breasts were oak-wood carving;
You'd think her arms were branches—you're not wrong.

MIDAS

Nor was this all that Bacchus sought to do,
Nor was he done. He left his Thracian vineyards, hills,
Dells, valleys, and chose a better crowd of followers.
He went to his own mountain Tmolus
And to Pactolus River for his pleasure.
This was before the river got its fame
For being golden and some envied its rich sands.
Satyrs and happy drunken naked women

Surrounded Bacchus—all there except Silenus,
For the old man weighed half a ton with wine;
His years had made him heavy with his drinking.
The Spartan peasants tripped him up and caught him,
Twined vine leaves round his head and carried him
Before their famous king, unwary Midas.
Not many years ago Orpheus had taught
The joys of Bacchus to the Spartan king,
And in like fashion pleased the King of Athens.
When Midas saw the old man was Silenus—
They had been filthy drunken good old friends—
He ordered up a dozen rounds of drinks,
Then more and more, and drank ten days and nights.
When the eleventh dawn streaked hills with red
And drove reluctant stars behind the sky,
Midas, still cheerful-drunk, took gay Silenus
The road to Lydia, nor did he stop till he delivered
The old man to the ruler he loved best,
His foster child in drink, the young God Bacchus.

Then Bacchus, glad to see the old man home,
And like a good adopted son, thanked Midas,
Gave him the choice of making a wish come true:
What would he have? Midas was always sure
To make the worst of every good occasion—
Of turning glory into desperate ill—
So Midas said, "Make everything I touch turn gold."
Bacchus gave him the golden touch, yet thought
"What foolishness; it almost makes me sad." Meanwhile
The Hero Midas danced on his way, and touched all things
That flashed before his eyes. Could he believe this?
Yes! He plucked a green shoot from a tree—
It was all gold, pure gold, had the right weight and colour;
Then a handful of wet clay—he had but to touch it
And it was gold. His trembling fingers plucked
A head of wheat—it might have been the promise
Of golden harvest—and next he took an apple from a tree,
And in his hand it shone as though it were a gift
Transported to him from the Hesperides.
He touched a standing beam that held the roof;
Look sharply now! It was a pillar of gold.

And as he dipped his hands in running water,
A stream of gold rushed out that could have raped Danaë.
Midas' imagination, his hopes, his dreams grew big with
          gold:
He called his slaves to bring a feast before him,
From wine to meat to bread to fruits to wine.
And as he broke bread, that rich gift of Ceres,
It did not break but was of gold itself,
Beautifully hard, not stale, and as his teeth
Ate into meat, the meat was gold, too
And he could not close his jaws. As he poured
Water into wine (Bacchus' own wine) red, sunset colour,
And raised them to his lips, both turned to gold.
Dazed, damned by gold, a golden terror took him,
Midas began to hate his wealth, tried to escape
The very riches that he prayed for. However large
The feast laid out before him, he went hungry,
And though his throat burned dry, no drink could wet it.
By his own choice gold had become his torture.
He lifted glittering hands and arms to heaven:
"O Bacchus, Father of your unlucky son!
I have done wrong, wrong from the start, wrong, wrong
          forever,
But take away your gift that shines in gold.
It's damned—it curses me." Because he seemed to learn
His way was error, the gods took pity on him.
Bacchus reversed him to what he was before;
He said, "Through your own foolishness you wear
A golden coffin, your very body is a tomb of gold;
Go to the river that winds past Sardis city,
Walk up the Lydian hills to its high source,
In that pure font be birthday naked, head to foot
To wash your guilt away." The king obeyed;
And gold fell from him to the waters that ran gold.
Even now the golden touch has stained the river,
And the soil it waters is as hard as gold.

     Midas, no longer lured by dreams of riches,
Took to the woods, became a nature-lover;
He worshipped Pan, uphill then down to caves
Under the mountains. His wits did not improve;

His mind was fated to undo new masters.
He lived where tall Mount Tmolus looked out far
Above the sea, one side a deep cleft down
To Sardis city, the other to Hypaepae.
As Pan sang to the country girls around him
(The girls were young, wide-eyed, and ignorant)
He held the tune by piping on his reeds.
During intermissions, he would tell them how
Much better his voice was than Apollo's;
Nor could Apollo whistle on his lyre.
In this way, with Mount Tmolus as the judge,
He entered an unequal competition.

Tmolus, both judge and mountain, was an ancient
Who took his seat on high, shaking his head
To free his ears of leaves from tallest trees;
An oak wreath held his dark green hair in order,
While acorns dangled round his cloud-white forehead.
Down, down he glanced at shaggy, goat-heeled Pan,
Then coughed. "Your judge is here," was all he said,
And Pan began to whistle country airs
Which Midas overheard and stood enchanted
Hearing them rock and roll and scream and moan.
The noise was of a kind that pierced the head
And Pan was done. Then Tmolus quickly turned
His face to Phoebus, and with him all the forest
Faced the god. Apollo's golden head shone through his
          laurels,
His cloak swung from his shoulders to the earth,
And 'gainst the purple folds the ivory lyre,
Flashing with diamonds, was held in his left hand,
The plectrum in his right. He was the very image
Of the artist, all poise and pose;
He touched the string and Tmolus gazed down at him;
He then told Pan to throw his pipes away.
The show was over: only echoes filled the air;
Tmolus had spoken and the lyre won.

Tmolus was cheered by everyone who heard—
And who would have his say against a mountain?
Only poor foolish Midas raised his voice

To speak for Pan. Apollo Delius
Knew well enough that Midas' ears were not
The kind of ears that human creatures wore—
So he enlarged them, made them grow grey hair,
And as they twitched, they wheeled for better hearing.
Midas looked like a man, except for ears—
Which were the property of mules and asses.
Even Midas felt a loss of dignity
And wrapped a purple turban round his head,
Which spared his vanity and held his secret.
Only the slave who trimmed King Midas' hair
Knew what another slave would love to know.
The story burned his lips—where could he tell it?
He kneeled as if to pray and with quick fingers
Thrust hand in earth, his lips above it whispered,
"King Midas has ass ears," then closed his voice
Within the hole he made, covering it up
With large handfuls of moist earth. Then frightened,
He ran away. But whispering reeds grew up
Around that spot and through the earth beneath them
The imprisoned voice came whispering to the wind,
Then all the world learned of King Midas' ears.

### THE BUILDING OF TROY

Since his revenge on Midas was assured
Phoebus Apollo and Latona's son
Left Tmolus sailing his course through spray-bright air,
Nor was his route across the straits of Helle,
Yet he dropped safely where Laomedon reigned.
Between peninsulas of Sigeim and of Rhodes,
An ancient altar stood; it was the shrine
To Jove-the-Voice, the Word, the Thunderer.
It was there Apollo saw Laomedon
At work to build the walls of a new town,
(Armies of men were needed to build Troy);
Help was demanded here, therefore Apollo
Called up the Father of the Seas and the two gods
Disguised as men made terms with Laomedon
To be paid off in gold. The contract signed,
A short time later the job was done, the fee unpaid;

The king denied he owed them anything:
Why should he pay them? But Neptune said, "You'll hear
Much more of this," and threw a storm of waters
'Gainst walls of faithless Troy: farmlands and city
Floated beneath the waves—and the king's daughter
As a feast to a sea dragon. Chained to a rock,
The girl was rescued by young Hercules,
Who had been promised (if he freed the girl)
A brace of stallions for his skill and courage.
The king refused to pay. Then Hercules
Marched through and took twice-faithless walls of Troy,
And Telamon, companion of the hero,
Got, for his share of conquest, Hesione,
King's daughter, who'd been saved by Hercules.
Peleus, another captain of that war,
Had his reward by marrying a goddess;
Peleus had double glories: grandson of Jove he was,
And now, with Thetis in his bed, Jove's son-in-law.

## THETIS AND PELEUS

   Old Proteus said to Thetis, "Now's the time,
O goddess of the waters, for your embrace
To make you mother of son whose fame outreaches
Even his father's glory; greater than all the arts
His father knows of war and chivalry
Shall this child know." Though Jove still felt
Blood stirring in his veins for love of Thetis
He stayed away from her, fearing that a son
Who had more brilliance on earth than he
Would rival him or make his godship fail.
Therefore he told his grandson, Peleus,
To take his place in Thetis' bed, godlike in love,
His victory, the virgin of the sea.

   On shores of Thessaly there is a bay
Shaped like a sickle, two arms reaching from it.
And if the waters of the bay were deeper
They would float ships within a lovely harbour.
The sea washed lightly over its pale sands,
Nor was the hurried traveller delayed

By seaweed tripping him on his swift way
From shore to shore. A myrtle grove grew near,
Hung with sweet fruit of parti-coloured berries,
And in the grove there was a cave or grotto—
But was it made by nature or by art?
Many believed that human hands contrived it.
To this fair haven, riding from the sea,
Sailing her dolphins, naked Thetis came,
And laid herself upon its bed to sleep.
There, as she slept, young Peleus came at her,
And tried to force his way with arms around her—
For if she had not taken other forms,
He would have found his rest on her at once.
One moment, so it seemed, he held a bird,
The next, a green ash tree, the next, a leopard
(This last was terror breaking through desire)
Which he let go. He thought of prayer, and with a cup of
        wine
Tossed on the waters he called the sea gods,
And lit a fire at a nearby altar, offered to it
The entrails of a lamb and smoking incense.
Then he saw Proteus rise upon the sea
And heard him say, "O son of Aeacus, go make
A net to trap your sleeping bride; her dreams transform her,
But if you bind her you may lie upon her."
So Proteus spoke, and as he vanished, waters
Rose where he stood, and closed above his voice.

    As Titan-Phoebus swung his chariot down
To ride the Western sea, Thetis came home,
Undressed herself for sleep. Scarcely had Peleus
Mounted her, she changed, or tried to change,
Yet she was open to him, limbs bound fast.
At last she moaned, "Some god made you undo me."
Then she gave way and Peleus held his Thetis,
And got his son on her, the great Achilles.

                                                    DAEDALION

    So Peleus grew happy in his marriage
And with his son—that is if one forgets

The later story of his brother's murder.
Peleus had killed him and went into exile;
Stained with his brother's blood, he sought escape
In Trochis. Here Ceyx ruled—he was the son
Of Lucifer and one could see
His father's radiance shine from his bright face;
But for the moment he was not himself:
He dressed in mourning for a far-lost brother.
Heavy with guilt and his long journeying,
Peleus came up to meet him; in his train,
Only a few loyal servants walked behind him,
His cattle herded in a shaded valley
A mile or two outside Ceyx' citadel.
Approaching Ceyx, he bore an olive branch
Wrapped round with wool, told who he was,
His heritage, what he had done (except
The murder on his hands), and begged to stay.
The king was kind and offered kingly friendship:
"My country, Peleus, is generous to all;
Even the poor find hospitality.
You have our friendship and a famous name,
Descendant from great Jove. Do not waste time
By asking favours of me—all is yours!"
Then Ceyx began to weep. When Peleus
And his servants asked him why, he wept again:
"O Peleus, it may please you to believe
A certain bird of prey—look at him there—
Who frightens all and lives by killing others,
Has always been the creature he is now.
But that's not true. The creature was a man,
Upright in war, loyal to his men, ready to fight,
Named Daedalion. Both of us were sons
Of him who wakes the sky in night's last hours,
And is the last star seen when daylight rises.
As for myself, I always sought for peace,
Domestic peace as well, to please my wife.
But raging war became my brother's will;
His courage conquered kings and levelled kingdoms—
Today, masked as a bird, his mad blood harries
Thisbe's mild doves. He had a lovely daughter,
Chione, who had won a thousand lovers.

One pleasant day Phoebus and Mercury
Strolled in from Delphi and tall Cyllene.
Both saw the girl and knew they were in love:
Apollo thought of meeting her that night,
But Mercury could not wait till evening came.
He passed his silver wand across her face;
As she fell sleeping in his arms he took her.
When night came with a million shining stars,
Dressed as an old nurse, Phoebus had pleasure with her.
In due time she gave birth to Autolycus,
A son of Mercury, wing-footed, as if born
With all his father's cleverness and speed,
He made white look like black and black like white.
His twin was Phoebus' son, named Philammon,
Known for his voice—how well he played the zither!
Proud as she was by giving birth to twins,
The girl was charmed at having two gods mount her,
And she herself descendant of a star.
Yet what was all this worth? Too much of glory
Carries ill fortune and a curse to many,
Bad luck for her. Since she had found herself
More glorious than Diana, she said the goddess
Was less attractive than she used to be.
Diana, white with rage, restrung her bow
And said, 'I'll please you with a silent answer.'
Her arrow pierced dark-guided tongue and throat,
Even as the girl gasped to talk, life's breath went out,
Gone with her blood that flowed against my breast,
For it was I who like a father ran
To hold her in my arms, and I who tried
To quiet my brother's madness in his grief.
He heard me as high rocks hear waves below them,
Saw nothing but the loss of his fair daughter,
And when her pyre burned, four times they held him back
To save him from destruction in that fire.
He was a bull, like one stung by wild bees,
Lunging blood-blinded into wilderness.
Faster than human feet could carry him
('Destroy myself' was all he wished or knew)
He climbed his way to cloudy-topped Parnassus,
Where fair Apollo gave him godlike pity,

For as Daedalion leaped from cloud-swept rocks,
Apollo gave him wings to break his fall,
A hooked beak, and crooked claws—made him a hawk
As strong as any man, as wild, as fearless
As Daedalion felt himself to be,
And merciful to none—he tears at others
To make them know the pain that burns his heart."

PELEUS' CATTLE

When Lucifer's son brought end to that sad story
Of grief and miracles that doomed his brother,
The overseer who guarded Peleus' cattle,
Came up and cried "O Peleus, Peleus,
Murder is in the air, and death and terror!"
"Then what has happened?" Peleus returned,
While his new friend King Ceyx had his own fears.
Then the man went on: "This noon I took our beasts—
Poor tired creatures—to a stretch of water.
Some, looking out toward the calm sea, kneeled down to
        rest,
Some walked through shallows while the others swam,
Their shoulders in the waves. I saw a temple
(Nor gold, nor marble there, nor precious stones)
Of solid wood, hidden in shade-hung trees—
Sacred to Nereus and the Nereids
(This I had learned from an old fisherman
Sewing his nets, who sat beside me on the shore).
And near that temple was a waste-land bog
Where willows grew, reflected in sea water.
As I looked up, I heard a roar tear through them:
Then a great red-eyed sea-wolf, streaked with mud,
Came at us, tearing at cattle as he ran to kill them,
Nor stopped to eat; evil he was, not starved,
As though he plunged and tore for love of killing.
He killed my men as well as beasts, blood pouring
To the sea—but even as I talk, to wait
Is further death, death everywhere; go armed to meet
        him."
Yet Peleus seemed strangely still: his fate had come;
His brother's death was on him; his beasts were sacrificed

To Phocus' mother, the Nereid would take them
For her loss. Meanwhile King Ceyx ordered
His men to take their deadliest swords, light arms,
And spears, while Ceyx himself picked up his shield.
At all this noise, Ceyx' wife, half dressed, half naked,
Loose-haired and tearful, rushed toward him, crying
Him not to go, send others, save himself,
His life and hers. Then Peleus stepped forward:
"O Queen, your fears are queenly fears, but do not
Fear me. I'm not unmindful of the king. No one
Should lose his life because of me, nor fall
Before a monster that has doomed me. I
Must send up prayers to Goddess of the Sea."
There was a lighthouse high above Ceyx' fortress,
Where all climbed up to see the dead, the maimed.
Scattered in blood, in waves along the shore—
Saw the great sea-wolf, matted with blood, still wild
In his destruction everywhere. Peleus
Reached toward the sea and prayed to Nereid,
Mother of Proctus slain, yet she ignored him
Till Thetis, speaking in her husband's name,
Got favour for him. The wolf, though called away,
Had the insane salt taste of blood upon his tongue
And went on killing. And as he leaped
To the throat of a young cow, Nereid caught him,
Transformed him to senseless wolf in marble,
A harmless statue of a beast in stone.

Yet Peleus could not stay in King Ceyx' kingdom;
The Fates had ordered him to Magnesia,
Where Acastus purged him of his guilt of murder.

### THE JOURNEYS OF CEYX

Meanwhile King Ceyx still had a troubled mind—
Nor did his brother's fate alone cause worry;
He feared the threat of supernatural things,
The miracles he could not understand.
Therefore he planned to take a long sea journey
To hear the oracles of the Clarian god,
For gangsman Phorbus, henchman of Phlegyans

(People who lived by robbing shrines and temples)
Had made the road to Delphi hazardous.
As he told his wife, Alcyone, his intentions,
She turned the colour of a boxwood leaf,
As pale and grey; tears ran; three times
She tried to speak, her raining face turned toward him,
Then through her sobs she said, "What have I done,
My darling, to earn this? What made your mind
Shift into that direction? I was your care,
Above all else—and now you wish to leave
Your Alcyone? You want to leave me
For an endless journey, so that your love
May grow for me again? If you were thinking
Of the way by land, I should be full of tears,
Bored, restless, lonely—and unafraid—
But the dark face of the sea brings terror to me.
A day or two ago, and on the beach, I saw
Wreckage from ships, and near that shore
I read men's names carved over empty tombs.
Do not have too much hope that Hippotes
(My father and your father by our marriage)
Can hold the winds forever barred with
His fort—once they're at sea, nothing restrains them,
Or on land or sea, they harass clouds of heaven,
And as they quarrel, they burst red lightning
Across the sky. The more I see of them,
(And I have known them in my father's house),
The more I know they should be feared; and now,
If you must go, my love, then take me, too.
Both shall ride waves and meet the darkest storm."

When she said this, her husband, son of stars,
Lord of her love, felt his heart stir,
Nor did it flame less brightly in his breast
Than hers, nor could he change his mind,
Nor would he let her share his unknown dangers.
With calmness and soft words, he tried his best,
Yet could not get her word to let him go,
But his last effort won her slow consent:
"Each hour I spend away from you will seem
A million years of empty hours, a waste

Of all my life in darkness and alone,
Yet swearing by your father's deathless fires—
Fate willing—I shall return before two moons
Grow wide with light within a silver sphere."
This promise gave his wife a hopeful doubt,
And he at once manned ship to leave its harbour.
When Alcyone saw his readiness
(As though her love held darkness of the future)
Her body trembled and tears came again.
As she enfolded him she said, "Good-bye,"
Then her mind swayed into unconsciousness.
Though Ceyx made causes for delay, his oarsmen
Churned harbour waters into oar-sprayed foam.
Then Alcyone, veiled in tears, caught sight
Of Ceyx mounting the curved high after-deck.
His hand up, flickering, star-lit, to wave good-bye,
While her white scarf waved answer to his going.
And for a time she gazed (how could she measure time?),
The ship receding and her love's figure growing
Small, then smaller, till it fell from sight,
And yet she gazed, staring at mast and sails
Till they at last fell to the grey horizon.
Since these were lost, she turned her way toward home,
Entered the empty house, and saw her bed
Whose emptiness still told her he was gone,
Only her body filled its waste, and her spent tears.

   As Ceyx' ship left the harbour, a great wind
Seized stern and hull, and ropes on deck made loud
Both hold and cabin. The captain drew in oars,
And ran yard up the mast to make full sail.
Midsea the ship was, land to either side,
And as night dropped, white rolling waves appeared;
The winds, taking their lift, began to blow.
"Lower the yard and fasten sail," the captain ordered,
His shouting lost in the wind's cry overhead.
Some men drew in their oars and closed the ports,
And one or two drew in the sails; another
Tried bailing sea back to the sea; one man
Made fast the spars, and every action caught
In sliding panic as the wind drove down

Among waves' wilderness on every side. The captain
Saw darkness only and ship's bearings lost,
And less than useless orders given from his lips.
Destroying winds were masters of the ship,
Thundering above men's voices, rolling chains,
Waves mounting decks and crashing through the hull.
Water ran high enough to meet the clouds,
To reach at heaven in sea-rooted fountains.
From sand sea-floor to spray, the sea churned upward
In yellow waters, then to black waves rising
As dark as night in channels of the Styx.
Over it all white sheets of foam broke through,
Where the ship, like a toy ship, wheeled, swayed and
          shuddered.
The ship on waves swung high as tallest mountain
Rising from valleys, even the abyss of Acheron,
Then sunk where blackest waters swirled around her,
Where one looks up to heaven from deepest hell.
Like a siege engine's ram in iron against a fort,
So the waves struck port and starboard of the ship.
Or as great lions charge at hunters' shields,
So waves that rode the wind crashed the ship's sides,
And mounted at their will. Then decks began
To crack, pitch, wax, and ropes gave way, boards broken,
Sides gaping while Death's sea poured in the hold.
Rain fell in curtains from black clouds; you'd think
The very heavens had joined the sea, or that
The sea flooded night skies that swayed above it.
The sails hung like pale sheets of sea and rain;
The starless night above them closed in darkness,
And from that dark came ragged lightning flashing
Red fires that danced across the waves; then sea
Poured, rippling over each foot of deck and hull.
And as a soldier, quicker than his fellows,
Attempts to scale the wall of a sieged city,
Leaps up at last, to be the first in glory,
One man above the thousand men behind him—
So a ninth wave came scaling ship's side, after it
The tenth, nor spares the ship, then leaps within.
And now the sea made ready for invasion,
The crew in panic like lost citizens,

Who have tried to hold the gates of a sieged city,
Some blowing up its walls, others the gates,
However brave some were, saw in the waters
As many deaths as waves come down upon them.
One sailor could not stop his tears from flowing,
Another lost his voice, another prayed
To die, to be consumed on funeral pyres;
One lifted helpless hands to unseen Heaven
For mercy of the gods; one called upon
His brother and his father, another spoke
Of home, his hearth, his children—and all of them
Remembered the fair world they left behind.
But Ceyx held to a single thought alone,
And on his lips her name was Alcyone—
How glad he was that she was far away.
He wished to turn his face in her direction,
But storming night and sea obscured the sky,
Nor did he know which way his eyes should turn.
Rudder and mast were gone, and one last wave,
Rising as if to throw Pindus and tall Mount Athos
Into the sea, so came this wave upon them,
And the ship was gone, deeper than sight could follow.
Most of the crew went down beyond all hope,
Beyond all light of days. A few still held
To fragments of the wreck. Ceyx with one hand
(That once held sceptre in its fist) clung fast
To what had been a section of the deck.
He called for help, crying his father's name,
Then his wife's father's, but oftener than these
The name of Alcyone filled his lips.
He prayed the waves might lift him to her side,
That he might be interred by her own hands;
The while he kept afloat and waves allowed him,
He cried her name aloud. Look, then a wave
Rose higher than the rest, came at his head,
And drowned it in an eddy of white foam.
That morning Lucifer's face was wrapped in clouds,
So unfamiliar none knew it was his.

   Ignorant of loss at sea Alcyone
(Daughter of Aeolus, keeper of the winds)

Counted each night that passed, and wove a cloak
For Ceyx to wear and dresses for herself,
All to be worn the day of his return—
A day of light that she would never know.
She paid her services to all the gods,
But frequently she sent up prayers to Juno,
Praying for him who Juno knew had perished,
To keep him safe from harm, to bring him home,
Only her last prayer had a blessed answer.
At last Juno could hear such prayers no more—
Sad prayers of innocent hopes for one who died—
Nor could her altar bear funeral worship
Of pitiful clinging hands and falling tears.
She ordered Iris to her side and whispered,
"My dear, my faithful friend, who runs all errands,
Go to that heavy-eyed place where Sleep is bedded,
Tell him to send Ceyx' ghostly image in a dream
To Alcyone—let her know of his death—
And go at once." Iris slipped on her cloak,
And in that thin embrace of shining colours
She was a rainbow fleeting through the skies
To find the hidden chambers where Sleep reigned.


                                              SLEEP


    Down where Cimmerians lived a mountain's cave
Concealed the home of Sleep where Idleness,
Langour, and Listlessness slept side by side,
And all at rest in rooms of shadowed ease.
No Phoebus entered there with morning light,
No noons nor reddening twilights touched the floors;
Only fog-breathing Earth held Sleep in her arms,
In shades where cock-crow never wakes the dawn.
Nor does the watchdog waken Sleep with warnings,
Nor does one hear the cry of geese whose noises
Have sharper cleverness than barking dogs,
Nor sound of beasts, nor low of wandering cattle,
Men's voices nor the quick-tongued voice of leaves.
Beneath the cave the flow of Lethe's waters
Calls out to Sleep in sleep that sleeps forever.
And it is where dream-haunted poppies grow,

Hanging their heads above wet ferns and grasses,
Where mossy herbs distill sleep-gathering wines,
Breathing their fragrance to the night-filled land,
And weighted eyelids close each day to darkness.
These chambers have no doors, no hinges turning;
No watchman calls the hour to waken Sleep.
There in the innermost chamber of dark halls,
Draped in black velvet, stands the Sleeper's bed.
The god of Sleep, stretched on the coverlet,
Lies there, his figure languorous and long.
Around him drift the shapes of empty dreams,
As many images as ears of grain in autumn,
As leaves on trees, as sands along the beach.

As Iris stepped within the chambered cave,
She swept aside vague dreams that veiled the air,
The dark was somewhat lighted by her rainbow
Which led her to Sleep's bed. His heavy head
Rolling against his breast, Sleep forced his eyes
To open, to look toward her. It was as if
He had to tear himself out of himself
To give her welcome (for he recognized her),
And as he leaned his weight upon his elbow,
He asked her why she came. Iris replied,
"King Sleep, the gentlest god of all the gods,
Who brings the gift of peace to all on earth,
Who cures the soul, and in his deepest draughts,
Drives dreams to darkness, and our worries vanish,
Who brings us rest to give us strength to rise—
Dear Sleep, make a true image of a king,
A certain king who ruled the land of Trachis,
A region that great Hercules made famous.
Show this true likeness to his widowed queen,
Picture his death at sea—for my request
Is Juno's inspiration and command."
Then Iris, almost overcome by Sleep
Ran from his cave and briskly took her way—
Arched like a rainbow, went the path she came.

Sleep had a thousand sons, and of that number
He made the choice of waking Morpheus.

He was an actor; no one had more skill
At walking like a man, at looking like one,
At dressing like a man in all his fashions,
And when he spoke—no ghostly noise or chatter—
One heard a man about to make a speech.
And all his business was of men alone;
One of his brothers was an expert at
Zoology; he could be bird or beast,
And he could writhe like any long-tailed snake.
Gods named him Icelos (which means "like" in Greek);
Men call him Phobetor (in Greek the word
Means "fear") which was in tribute to *his* acting.
As for Phantastos, still another brother,
He imitated rocks, stones, waterfalls,
Trees, rushes, things that a nobleman
Might see at night, while other natural things
He chose haunted the worthy common people.
Sleep passed them by and fixed on Morpheus
To do the work commissioned him through Iris.
This duty done, Sleep sank to sleep again,
His head fell back upon his velvet pillow.

#### METAMORPHOSIS OF ALCYONE

On gliding wings (one could not hear them stir)
Morpheus made way to Alcyone's city.
He dropped the wings and took the mask of Ceyx;
Naked as Ceyx in bed and pale as death,
He leaned above the widow where she slept;
His heavy hair and beard dripped salt sea waters,
And from his eyes one saw the flow of tears.
Then came Ceyx' voice: "Dear wife, sad wife," it said,
"Now do you know me? Is my face disfigured,
My body wasted by the pall of death?
Then look at me—I am your husband's ghost,
A luminous shade that gleams against the wall,
Nor could your prayers have saved me; I am dead,
Beyond your hopes and mine. Auster plucked up
My ship from that Greek sea and crushed her sides
Against the wallowing waves and buried us.
And as I moved my lips to call your name

I drank the sea. Nor am I rumour's image,
Half truth, half lies, but naked as you see me
At your side, this thing is what I am;
I have come home to tell you of my fate.
Go dress yourself in clothes that widows wear,
O Alcyone, always weep for me!"
Since Morpheus caught the accents of Ceyx' voice,
The movement of his hands, and wept great tears,
The sleeping Alcyone moaned and turned
To hold him in her arms. But Morpheus vanished.
She cried, "O wait for me, where have you gone?
My feet will follow; we shall go together!"
Startled by her own voice, she was awake,
And looked about the room to find her husband.
The servants wakened by her cry brought lamps
Nor could she find her husband anywhere.
She tore her dress aside to beat her breasts,
And faced her nurse: "O Alcyone's gone,
She's nothing; she is dead, perished with Ceyx
At sea. Don't talk to me, for Ceyx is drowned;
I saw him, knew his face, yet when I moved
To take him in my arms, my love was gone.
He was a ghost, but my true husband's ghost,
His face less bright than what it used to be—
It was too ghastly pale—yet his, and there
He stood, wet, naked, dripping from the sea;
I saw him there for there was where he stood!"
And she looked to the floor to find his footprint.
"O my prophetic mind! I knew his fate;
It's what I've known and feared so many years;
O husband, how I begged you not to leave me!
Since you set sail for death, half my soul is gone,
Swallowed by waves and lost upon the seas.
And what is left is captured by those waters,
And yet the best is gone. If I live on
Beyond these days of sorrow, my poor heart
Would gather greater fury than the sea.
O my unlucky husband, how can I
Try to outlive your years? The very least
For me is: be your consort—if not entombed
With you, if my remains, poor bones and dust,

Are not to lie with yours, our names shall be
As one name written on a door of stone."
Her voice was lost in sobs. Her speech was done.

By this time it was morning. She stepped out
To walk the beach, the port he sailed away from;
The while she strolled, she whispered, half in tears,
"Here was the cable cast . . . and here he kissed me."
As she renewed the scene, she saw waves carry
What seemed to be the figure of a man,
As if it floated toward her. At this distance,
Without knowing who it was, she grew quite certain
It was a man who suffered death at sea—
Perhaps shipwreck—and she was moved, as though
All the anonymous deaths at sea had claimed her.
"Poor creature," so she thought, "pity your wife,
If ever you had a wife!" But at this moment,
The body drifted near her; what she saw
Resembled all she knew of her lost husband.
It almost washed ashore, then floated clear.
"It is he," she said, "he has come back to me."
She stripped herself, then ran upon a breaker
That caught the waves, and leaped as if broad wings
Took her to sea; even her cries were birdlike;
And as she neared the floating man beneath her,
She thrust her growing beak between his lips.
The story is: he raised his face to hers,
And I half think Ceyx did—if he had life.
The gods changed both to birds, and both were one,
Though love had given them a strange mutation.
Today they live and breed upon those waters
And for a week in winter, Alcyone
Keeps her brood warm within a floating nest,
Aeolus stills the winds that shake the waters
To guard his grandsons on a peaceful sea.

### AESACUS AND HESPERIA

An old man gazed at birds that flew in pairs
And praised their flight as faithfulness in love;
The habit seemed to show domestic ardour,

And long sustained through many generations.
Another elder (perhaps the same old man)
Shot out his finger toward a long-necked diver
To say, "Another bird of royal descent;
He sails the waves, flickering his legs behind him.
From what I know of genealogy,
His line is straight from Ilus, Assaracus,
And Ganymede (the boy whom Jove seduced),
Ancient Laomedon and bearded Priam
Who had bad luck at Troy. This bird descended
From Hector's brother's line; and if that brother
Had not turned bird too young, he would have been
A famous Hector too. While Hecuba
Gave birth to the first boy, Alexiroe
(So it was rumoured) came to bed
With Aesacus—and she, if I am right, was daughter
Of two-horned Granicus. Her boy disliked
The life at court, the gaudy palaces,
The streets of Troy. He took his pleasures
In primitive surroundings, up the mountains,
And seldom met the people down at Troy.
Yet he was not ungainly in his habits,
And somewhat delicate in making love.
He took a fancy to Hesperia,
The youthful daughter of the River Cebran,
Who as she sat close to her father's river,
Bleached her long hair beneath a noonday sun.
The boy surprised her and the girl ran from him,
As if he were a wolf and she a doe,
Or as a wild duck tries to escape a hawk.
The girl gained speed; he flew on wings of love,
While she, poor child, seemed to grow wings of terror.
But look! A snake came sliding through the grasses,
Snapped at her foot, and as she fell to earth,
His poison filled her veins, and flight was done.
Then her young lover seemed to lose his mind;
He put his arms around her: "O if I
Had not come at you, thoughtless, foolish, wild!
Your life was more to me than joy to take you.
The snake and I are brother murderers,
And I the cause of death far more than he—

And death shall be my comfort after all!"
With this, he tossed himself from a high cliff.
Tethys, who saw him fall, felt pity for him,
And as he fell, she covered him with feathers,
Then, floating seaward, he sailed free of Death—
Yet this was not the freedom he desired.
Up, up he clambered, flapping awkward wings,
Then threw himself to sea for Death to take him.
Such frenzied self-abasement made him slender,
His legs, his neck grew long—and the sea claimed him,
Kept him a curious bird and half a sailor;
They named him Margus, proper for a diver.

# XII

# BOOK XII

The Trojan War Begins • Caenis • Nestor's Tale of the Centaurs • The Death of Achilles

*Ovid's cycle of miraculous changes is beginning to turn in the direction of pro-Roman interpretation of the fall of Troy. Here, as in Book XIII, Ovid's manner is in great contrast to Virgil's. It is highly probable that he consciously stressed the difference of approach, holding to the characteristics of his style and to his theme of a continuing metamorphosis. One center of interest is in the story of Caenis in Book XII. Caenis is transformed from a woman to a man, whose name becomes Caeneus, not for love, as in the case of Iphis in Book IX, but for hardiness in battle. She becomes a supernatural warrior. Her last transformation is into a golden bird. The original cause of her desire to be a man has psychological interest; she was virginal in temper and was unwillingly raped by Neptune; she prayed never to fall by any sword held by man and her prayer was granted. Her rejection of contact with a man finds its analogy in sixteenth-century England in the legend of Elizabeth I. It is now believed that when Elizabeth was a child of thirteen, advances were made to her by Admiral Lord Seymour of Sudeley. Seymour was her Neptune—whether literally so or not is unimportant. Her fears made her a virgin queen; symbolically as queen and through Essex and Leicester she became a warrior. Ovid's miraculous psychology and his gift of fanciful invention seem to act as a prevision of behaviour in historical biography. It is also of interest that Ovid tells the story of Caenis with suspension of belief; it is told through the lips of an old man whose memory is failing, which warns us that Ovid regards the tale as fiction.*

# BOOK XII

Since Patriarch Priam still believed his son,
Aesacus, surely dead and not alive,
He wept for him, and held a funeral service,
Carved on an empty tomb Aesacus' name;
And there came Hector with his other brothers.
All paid their tribute to the lost, thought dead—
All except Paris, who a brief time after this
Eloped with a young bride, seduced her, stole her,
Which opened a long war against the Trojans.
A thousand ships and every living Greek
And their allies set sail. They would
Have won at once but they were crossed
By winds that stormed the sea and Boeotia held them
At fish-spawning Aulis. Here in the pious custom
Of Greek nations, they gave their thanks to Jove.
There, where the altar fires flashed through darkness
They saw a blue-green dragon climb a tree,
Whose highest branches held eight nested birds,
Their mother circling over them in terror.
The hungry dragon made short work of them;
All nine went down his throat, a single mouthful.
The Greeks were curious and ill at ease;
Thestorides, their prophet, had an answer:
"This means we win the war, my darling Greeks,
Troy shall go down, but not too soon. We have
A longer job than you might think." He read
Nine birds gone as nine more years of war.
The dragon, though still twined in green tree branches,
Turned into lapis lazuli, and hung
Preserved forever as a green-stone serpent.

Nereus still worried the Greek seas to violence,
Nor would he let the ships of war sail through them,

And some believed that Neptune, since he built
Troy's walls, wished to protect that threatened city.
Thestorides thought not; he knew the truth,
And always thought it better not to hide it:
He knew an angry virgin like Diana
Would need the solace of a young girl's blood.
When he began to feel that public duty
Was of more consequence than private virtue
(The politician over-ruled the father),
King Agamemnon, while her servants wept,
Took Iphigenia to a blood-stained altar
Where she was well prepared to give her life.
Even the goddess felt something go wrong:
She wrapped a fog around them, closed their eyes,
And as the scene grew slightly mad with weeping,
She placed a red-haired doe upon the altar—
So someone said—and spared Mycenae's child.
Then, since Diana had her share of blood,
For as she cooled, the sea itself grew calm,
The thousand ships took sail—and after many
Small misadventures reached Phrygian shores.

There, in the middle of the big round Globe,
Set at the center of space, between earth, sea, and sky,
Is where our triple World unites and spins.
There everything within the Globe is seen,
Everything said is heard, echoed, resounded
From those curved sides which might as well be ears.
Rumour, sometimes mistaken for great Fame,
More often dressed as Notoriety, lives there,
A mountain-round-house tower is her home:
Innumerable doorways all around it,
A thousand entrances, exits, arcades,
And none with doors. Or night or day
The place keeps open house, and its brass walls
Reflect the lightest word, the lowest whisper;
The place is never silent, never noisy,
Yet full of voices, like the sounds of waves
Heard from a lighthouse set a mile inshore,
Or like the stilled and trembling trail of sound
Jove's thunder leaves after black clouds collide.

Through tower halls the Many come to talk,
Lies twisted into truth, truth into lies;
All come and go, and gossip never ends.
Talk, talk, talk, talk fills many hundred ears
That empty as a story's told, rehashed,
And told to someone else, or fiction grows;
Each time retold adds what is heard
To what's been said before. And Innocent
Believe-It-All walks there, Deaf-And-Blind Error,
Pushing his way or runs and hides, and dear,
Foolish, Without-A-Leg-To-Stand-On Joy,
Mad Fear, Glib Treason, Confidential Whisper.
Rumour takes in all things at sea, on land,
And, at a distance, in the skies of heaven,
Everything heard or seen throughout the Globe.

Rumour told news of the Greek ships advancing,
Of their armed forces eager for the battle;
Therefore the invasion came without surprise.
The Trojans were prepared to meet invaders,
To resist a beachhead made upon their shores.
First Protesilaus fell, struck dead by Hector's
Well-aimed and lethal spear. These opening
Encounters taught the Greeks that Hector's
Skill at a rushing skirmish took its toll.
The Trojans also learned how bloody-handed
The Greeks could be, and soon the beach at Sigea
Turned red, and Neptune's Cygnus put to death
A thousand men while the Achilles burst
Like death-in-chariot through to cut them down,
Regiments with his Pelion-wooded spear.
In this thick fighting he kept his eyes alert
For Hector or for Cygnus, both or one:
Then he saw Cygnus. (Hector, as we know,
Was not met squarely till the war's tenth year.)
Then as his white-maned chargers champed the bit,
He let them tear full tilt at Trojan lines,
Waved his great spear, and cried, "Famous or not,
My boy, you'll get your fame and earn your honour
Killed by Achilles, prince of Thessaly,
An epitaph that no one shall forget!"

At this he threw his spear, the aim was faultless,
And yet it seemed to glance from Cygnus' breast,
Its iron-pointed cutting edge turned blunt;
The boy was scarcely scratched. Then Cygnus answered,
"I know you well; you're son of Goddess Thetis.
Rumour has told me who and what you are;
And you're surprised at seeing me unhurt?"
Achilles was bewildered. Cygnus said,
"Look at my helmet bright with its sun-coloured
Horse-hair at the top, and this great shield
That nearly knocks me down to carry it;
They may be pretty, but they don't protect me.
Mars wears his iron to make himself look smart,
Impressive as he takes the field; so I.
But not for any damage you can do.
It may be useful to be son of Thetis,
Daughter of Nereus and a noble family;
I find it not half bad to be the son
Of him who has command of Nereus,
His daughters, and all the waters of the world."
At this he tossed his spear at the Achilles
Which drove through brass and nine sheets of bull's hide,
Then stopped. Achilles shook it off his shield,
And with a greater force aimed the next spear
To see it strike then fall from Cygnus' body.
Though Cygnus put his shield aside, a third shaft
Glanced from his breast and trembling fell to earth.
Then as a bull charges a flickering red rag
Around the ring, gone mad because his horns
Cannot destroy it, so the Achilles stormed.
Was the spear broken? No, he saw its iron head
Still there. "Or has my hand gone wrong," he cried,
"Too frail to fight, and all my strength like water?
Not long ago I stormed Lyrnesus' fortress
And ruined it, Tenedos, Thebes, Eetion—
All drowned in their own blood; the Caicus
Turned purple with the blood of all who lived
Too near, and Telephus was badly wounded;
My spear had hooked him twice; he knows it well.
Even in this battle where so many fall to death,
The dead along these shores show what my hand

Has done—a good right hand that flourishes
Its power." Then—for he seemed to doubt himself—
He swung his spear full tilt at Menoetes,
One of the lesser breed from Lycia,
Who fell, pierced in the breastplate and the ribs;
And as the man went down, head first to earth
The Achilles tore the spear from its hot flesh
And said, "This hand—look at it—and this spear
Are what is needed for a victory.
Now let them work against the man before me!"
With this he lunged for the fourth time at Cygnus,
A true thrust of the spear, which landed,
Sounding a dull clang as it struck, where Cygnus
Turned a left shoulder open to the blow;
Then it bounced off, as from a cliff or wall.
Yet the Achilles saw Cygnus stained with blood,
And for a moment cheered; but no wound came;
Menoetes' blood had splashed Cygnus' left shoulder.
Then the Achilles leaped from his chariot,
To swing his sun-edged sword against calm Cygnus
Who stood unharmed, even as his helmet, shield
Were slashed and cut. Then as the sword-edge touched
His body, it turned dull and the Achilles
Clanged, beat at Cygnus' headpiece with a sword-hilt,
Cygnus retreating, backing from the blows,
Until fear took him; and black shadows came
To make him blind, to make him stumble backward
Over an unseen rock, while the Achilles
With a last thrust was on him, tearing at
Helmet where laces held it to the throat,
And the Achilles' iron hand cut off his breath.
Cygnus seemed dead, but as half-spent Achilles
Stripped off the armour, nothingness was there;
A white sea bird flew into air above it,
For Neptune made him bird which took his name.

CAENIS

        Following this scene an armistice was called
Which lasted many days; both Greeks and Trojans
Put arms aside, Greeks placing sentry near

The Trojan walls while a sharp Trojan guard
Paced near Greek lines. To break the boredom
A feast day came to celebrate the Achilles'
Defeat of Cygnus; a great cow to Pallas
Was offered up, smoked tripe and giblets
Roasted on altars—perfume to the gods!—
Rose in blue clouds to heaven, while below
Broiled steaks and joints made many soldiers happy.
Their captains washed down meat with draughts of
        wine,
Nor zither, flute, nor singing kept them cheerful,
They filled the night with talk, with glorious fables
Showing how bravery was the better part of man.
They talked of war and the respective merits
Of enemies, themselves and their best friends,
Repeating all the dangers they went through,
How bravely they surmounted each disaster,
How they rose to each occasion as it came.
The great Achilles talked of nothing else,
And how could others speak of lesser things?
More than all else, they covered, blow by blow,
The Achilles' recent strength in beating Cygnus:
It was a wonder that the boy's white body
Took punishment it did, nor iron-headed
Lance nor keen-edge sword strike through, all weapons
Blunted, grazing breast and shoulder.
Nor any Greek nor the Achilles knew his secret;
Then Nestor spoke: "In your day, Cygnus only
Could take the thrust of sword-play, lethal damage,
But many years ago I saw that marvel,
The Thessalian Caeneus, or rather,
Caeneus of Thessaly who used to live
High up Mount Othrys, who was great at fighting—
The wonder was that he was born a female."
This last remark made listeners curious;
They asked him to tell how and why and where.
The Achilles said, "Old man, you have a story—
You have an ancient gift of tongues; speak up.
We are all ears: who was the hero Caeneus?
And why did he—or she—change to a man?
How was *that* done? On what field did you meet him?

Who was the enemy? And if he fell,
Who brought an end to him? We want to know."
The old man said, "Old age and Time make vague
So many things I wish I could remember,
Yet much remains, and of what happened, either
In peace or war, the fate of Caeneus haunts me.
I've lived—now, let me see—two hundred years,
No, more than that, and if long living means
I've seen enough, and more, then here's my story:

    "Elatus had a daughter he named Caenis,
Beautiful girl, the best in Thessaly,
In fact the best in all that neighbourhood
(And this includes the city, dear Achilles,
Where you saw light). You should have seen young men
Who yearned for her. How many? Who can tell?
And Peleus was one? Perhaps, but he
Had either taken your mother or approached her.
But Caenis had turned blank all thoughts of marriage.
Then, so I've heard, she took a walk one day
Upon a private beach where no one came—
Except the God of Sea, who mounted her
Before she caught her breath. He was well pleased
And thought that she was too; he made an offer:
'I'll give you anything you wish, my dear'
(I heard this detail from reliable sources).
Caenis replied, 'Then make your gift a large one,
For I shall never take a man again;
I pray, I hope I cease to be a woman,'
And as she spoke her voice turned baritone—
Neptune had given her a mannish figure,
And to make sure that no one entered her,
He made her flesh impervious to sword.
Glad of her gift, she took up male gymnastics,
And as young Caeneus roamed through Thessaly.

### NESTOR'S TALE OF THE CENTAURS

    "Pirithous took as bride young Hippodame;
To celebrate the day, tables were set up
And couches placed for greater luxury

Beside them in a green, well-arboured grotto.
Among the guests were centaurs, rugged creatures
(Half horse, half man, conceived in clouds, they say),
Myself, and noblemen of Thessaly.
The palace shone and everyone was gay;
The wedding fires danced and songs were sung,
And through an archway came the bride, and with her
Young wives and matrons. O the bride was lovely!
Then we began to say how sweet the bride was
(This to her husband), but our good intentions
Began to bring ill fortune to the wedding.
Eurytus, craziest of rough-hewn centaurs,
Grew hot with wine, but when he saw the bride
Was that much hotter: tables were rocked,
Turned upside down, then tossed away.
Someone had seized the bride and mounted her,
Holding her head back, one hand in her hair;
It was Eurytus, while the other centaurs
Took women as they pleased, first come, first taken,
The scene was like the looting of a city.
The sound of hoofs and voices, women screaming—
Among these noises, we leaped to our feet
And Theseus shouted, 'Eurytus, you're mad;
Insult to Pirithous is my affair;
If you offend him, you're my enemy,
Two men against you and you're half a man!'
At which great-hearted Theseus charged through
The drunken centaurs and caught up the bride,
Nor could Eurytus find a ready answer
(He could not make a plea of innocence),
But made a rush with right and left fists driving
Swift raining blows on Theseus' face and chest.
At which Theseus swung high an ancient urn,
Rough-weighted with its fill of wine
Across the centaur's face. Through eyes and lips
The creature's brains burst from its broken skull;
Streaked with its blood, Eurytus fell to death.
Eurytus' fall was drunken call to battle;
Wine flasks and urns went crashing through the hall,
No quarter asked nor given in this war.

"Then Amycus centaur seized the lamps, the torches
That hung above the shrine and swept them down
As one might swing an axe to kill a bull,
Smashing the head of helpless Celadon,
Eyes torn, the cheekbones splintered as he fell.
Pelates in reply knocked down Amycus—
A table leg had served him as a club—
And with another swing caved in his jaw,
A drive that sent him down to Tartarus.

"Another centaur who stood near the altar—
Gryneus, whose distracted, bloodshot eyes
Caught fire from its flames, cried out, 'Take this!'
And threw the altar, swaying, tilted, falling
Upon the heads of two men in the crowd,
The two Broteas, and well-known Orios,
Whose mother, so I've heard, was Mycale,
Who when she raised her voice (and though the moon
Fought wildly, helplessly against that voice)
Tore the moon's horns down from sky to earth—
But this gave Exadius an idea,
Who cried, 'You're trapped; I'll find a way to get you.'
With that he plucked a gift to gods which hung
On pine-tree branches—antlers of a deer—
And pierced the centaur's brain. Its eyes fell out,
One on an antler's branch; the other, rolling,
Dropped to the centaur's beard and stared through blood.

"Look, Rhoetus seized a torch from altar fires
And plunged it in Charaxus' golden hair
Which turned to flames, swift-burning as a fire
That sweeps through fields of wheat in a dry season;
Then like a white-hot iron thrust in water,
The torch made a deep gurgling hissing sound;
Charaxus shook the fire from his head
And hoisted to his back the threshold-stone,
A load such as an ox-team draws with labour,
And overweight to toss at Rhoetus' head,
Yet it swung far enough to kill Cometes,
Charaxus' friend, who stood three feet away.

Rhoetus could not resist a smile at what he saw
And rushed on Charaxus to shout, 'I hope
Your crowd enjoys its bravery; here's my answer,'
And for a third time Rhoetus swung his torch,
And smashed the centaur's skull into its brains.

"Then Rhoetus turned on three: Euagrus,
On Corythus, on Dryas. Corythus was young,
His young beard like a threadbare veil of silk,
And as he fell, Euagrus cried, 'Brave Rhoetus!
Is all your glory in the killing of a boy?'
His mouth was open; Rhoetus answered him
By thrusting torch and fire down his throat
Until flames scorched his lungs. Then Rhoetus ran
Full tilt at rugged Dryas, but the chase did not
Bring as he ran, swinging the torch above him,
Another easy killing at one blow.
Dryas let fly a spear of charred wood, steering
Its way through Rhoetus' collarbone; he gasped,
Moaned, tearing his own flesh as he drew
The splinter out; stinking with blood and sweat,
He ran away. Orneus followed him, and Lycabus,
And Medon who felt blood at his right shoulder,
Thaumas and Pisenor, Mermeros who was swift,
But now limped bitterly from savage wounds,
Pholus and Menelaus, boar-chaser Abas,
And Asbolus the prophet who had warned,
Though no one heard him, all his friends
To give way, not to fight. He cried to Nessus,
'You need not run; you shall be saved till that
Fine day Hercules' arrow strikes your back.'
Yet Eurynomus, Lycidas, Areos,
And Imbreus all fell. Right-handed Dryas
Killed each before him—and though Crenaeus
Had turned tail, he turned again to meet
A javelin point between his arching eyebrows.

"Though noise roared over him, Aphidas slept,
Sleeping the sleep of ruby-coloured wine,
Stretched out, relaxed upon a bear-skin rug,
A cup in his right hand. While from a distance,

Phorbas aimed at him, not with proper focus;
At last his fingers gripped his javelin's bridle,
Then as he shouted 'Mix your wine with Stygian waters'
The iron-headed javelin hit its mark;
The head thrown backward showed a white-throat target,
And through it sailed the pointed javelin,
Nor did the boy awake; his wine cup caught,
As though it filled with wine to drink a toast,
A brimful measure of Aphidas' blood.

"I saw Petraeus straining at an oak,
An elder oak grown heavy-branched with acorns;
He swayed it right and left, then as he lifted
Its great trunk from the ground, Pirithous
Took aim and fixed his body to the tree.
It was reported that Lycus fell, then Chromis,
Both killed with much éclat by Pirithous,
Yet that great hero earned a greater honour
By killing off another pair of centaurs:
Helops caught a straight spearhead thrust through
          forehead
That entered his right ear to pierce his left;
Dictus, who ran from Ixion's son, met a high cliff,
And as the hero charged him, gaining speed,
Dictus fell forward, leaped the cliff, and down
He came, speared by the splinters of a tree.

"Aphareus stood there, eager to take toll
Of him who caused the centaur's death, and lifted
A sheet of rock ripped from the mountain's side,
Yet as he raised his arm, Theseus
Swung an oak branch that smashed his elbow bones,
And since he had no will to wreck him further,
The hero leaped on high-built Bienor's back
Which never held the weight of man before,
And as it reared, the hero dug his knees
Into its shaggy sides, his left hand seizing
Its long hair, and his right arm, as a flail,
Swung an oak club to beat the centaur's face.
With this same club he beat down Nedymnus,
And Lycopes who threw the javelin well,

And Hippasos who wore a breast-grown beard,
And Ripheus whose head topped tallest trees,
Thereus, known for skill at capturing bears,
Who carried them within his cradled arms,
Kicking and barking through Thessalian woods,
Until he brought them home. Demoleon,
Impatient at the news of Theseus' conquests,
Dug at a pine tree's roots to tear them free,
To make the tree a deadly guided weapon
At Theseus' head; but since he could not lift it,
He broke the trunk in two, and swung it wildly.
Meanwhile shrewd Theseus glided out of range;
He had been warned by Pallas, so he told us,
To let us know he shared Athena's favours.
If Theseus escaped the pine tree's dangers,
Not everyone stepped clear; the tree crashed down
Where Crantor stood—he was a tall young man;
It stripped his breast and maimed his white left shoulder.
He was your father's servant, dear Achilles,
Who held his shield and buckled on his armour,
Who, when Amyntor, King of Dolopes,
Took his defeat in battle with your father,
Was the king's gift, a guarantee of peace,
A handsome boy to guard off future wars.
When Peleus, even at a distance, saw
How badly maimed the boy was and half-dying,
He shouted, 'Here's the least that I can do,
My dear, to butcher meat to grace your pyre.'
And as he spoke his soul, his hand took aim
He shot an ash spear through Demoleon's ribs
Which trembled there within a cage of bones.
The centaur, with a superhuman effort,
And with both hands tore out the stubborn ash,
The iron spearhead held within his lungs;
His agony gave birth to blood-stained strength;
However deep the wound within his breast,
He charged and reared to trample Peleus under.
His hoofs struck shield and helmet,
And as he stooped, Peleus had drawn his sword,
And, rising with a quick touché, had flashed
Sword to the hilt through Demoleon's shoulder,

And with another lunge had thrust it where
Half-man, half-horse were joined in double breasts.
Not long before this and at awkward distance,
Peleus killed off Phlegraeos and Hyles,
And hand to hand cut down Iphinous
And with him Clanis; now he took another,
Strange Dorylas who wore a wolf-skin headpiece,
Horned like a bull's head—and the horns were deadly.

"I said to him (for I was growing brave),
'Look in my eye and test your bloody horns
Against the cutting edges of my spear.'
My javelin flew straight in his direction—
He was hemmed in and could not step aside;
He raised his hand fixed fast between his eyes
And I was cheered for perfect marksmanship.
Peleus stood at his side, and as my javelin
Struck home, he ripped the centaur's underbelly
Open and as the creature lunged at me,
His entrails spilled, his stumbling hoofs
Tore at them in a net; emptied, he fell.

"Nor did your glorious figure, Cyllarus
(If ever a centaur could be called good-looking),
Spare you from the disasters of that battle.
Cyllarus was handsome, young, and had a boy's soft beard
Glittering like golden threads upon his chin,
Long hair that waved like sunlight round his shoulders;
A lively face he had, and all his human features,
From throat to delicate hands, seemed to be made
As if Cyllarus were an artist's model.
No less artistic were his lower members,
Horse-flesh or human, all of him looked grand:
If upper half of him had been a horse,
The head, the mane, he would have been Black Beauty
Of Castor's choice, a perfect horse to ride,
An easy saddle and brave, rounded chest.
And black he was, and yet his tail shone white;
So did his feet. Girls of his centaur kind
Thought him adorable, and wished he loved them,
But of she-centaurs, he chose Hylonome,

The most attractive creature in that forest;
She was elusive, yet she had a way
Of helplessly admitting that she loved him,
Which kept him all her own. And her appearance
(As far as centaur girls are beautiful)
Was clean and fresh. She learned to use a comb;
One day she'd dress her hair with rosemary,
The next with violets, the third, red roses
And on the fourth or fifth, white bell-shaped lilies;
Then twice a day she washed her face and hands
In a bright waterfall that dropped from high green places
Above Pagasa, then for further beauty
(And twice a day) she bathed in that same water.
She had fine taste in dress, and draped a shoulder
Or a pointed breast with ermine, mink, or fox.
As much as he loved her, she cherished him,
And arm in arm they strolled through mountain passes
And slept together in a moss-hung cave.
Now to the battlefield at Lapithae
They came and joined the fighting, side by side.
From somewhere, somehow (no one knew who threw it)
A javelin struck and pierced through Cyllarus' breast;
His heart was scarcely touched, yet when the spearhead
Was plucked out, the heart stopped beating,
Faintness came over him, and cold death took him.
Hylonome threw arms around his body,
Then placed her hand over the wound to soothe it;
Her lips on his, she tried to breathe life in him
Or catch at least his last, his failing breath.
And when she saw his death, she spoke aloud
(But what she said I could not overhear;
The noise of battle swept her words away);
I saw her fix the spear that killed Cyllarus
Against her breast, and there she fell to earth,
Covering Cyllarus with her dying body.

    "Next I remember—even now I see him—
A centaur cloaked in six large lion skins,
Sewn like a tent to cover man plus horse.
He tossed a rough-hewn tree, the size of which
Would stagger—if they tried to haul it up—

A double ox team, at poor Tectaphos.
He rammed his head; and, as cheese in the making
Is forced through cloth, or like thick fluid drained
Through a rough screen, Tectaphos' brains poured
Through broken skull and nostrils, eyes and ears.
Even as the centaur leaped to rob the body—
Achilles' father witnessed this I know,
And he would say the same—I drove my sword
Into the centaur's thigh. Then I killed Chthonius;
Next, Teleboas. One had a whittled pitchfork,
The other, handy with a javelin
Which cut my face—look at that nasty scar!
Those days I could have taken Pergama
At one swift charge and then gone after Hector,
And if I could not hope to knock him down,
I could have stopped him if he tried to run.
Of course, at that time Hector was unborn,
Or if he was, he was too young for me;
And now I am too old. Come, must I tell you
How Periphas knocked down centaur Pyraethus?
Or how shrewd Ampyx with a broken lance
Pierced centaur Echeclus who rushed at him?
Macareus threw an iron rod which landed
Straight through the heaving chest of Erigdupus.
I can recall how Nessus, galloping,
Speared Cymelus in his left thigh.
And if you think that Mopsus was made famous
For prophecies alone, I can remember
How he speared and doomed centaur Hodites,
And how that creature fell without a word,
His tongue fixed to his jaw, his jaw to breast,
As though he wore a spit from face to middle.

   "By this time Caeneus had murdered five wild
           centaurs:
Styphelus, Antimachus, Elymus,
Pyracmos, who had swung an iron club,
And Bromus. Though I seem to know their names,
I can't remember how they looked when dying;
I jotted down their names somewhere, I think.
And now I see the giant Latreus,

Weighted with loot from killing Halesus;
Latreus was middle-aged but strong as ever,
A heavy brute, grey-haired and showy
With shield, sword, spear from Macedonia,
Prancing a circle, facing everyone,
And shouting through the crowd, 'Where is she, Caenis?
I mean that woman; does that girl remember
The creature that she was when she was born?
And what she had to do to get the gift
Of being changed to man? Know what you were,
Look back at what you've done, pick up your knitting,
Twist wool or card it, but let men
Fight through the wars.' As he raved on
Caeneus tossed a spear which ripped the centaur's
Left side as he wheeled swiftly to the right;
It cut the flesh where man became a horse,
And wild with pain, the centaur struck his lance
Full broadside 'gainst the young man's open face;
Yet not unlike hail bouncing from the eaves,
Or stones from a taut drum, the lance clanged backward.
Then at close quarters, the centaur tried his sword,
To cut his way through Caeneus' loins. 'I'll have you,'
Cried Latreus. 'Though my sword seems dull today,
It's sharp enough to cut you down; stand ready.'
His long right arm flashed toward Caeneus' thighs,
Then like the ring of steel against veined marble,
The sword struck flesh and splintered into air.
Bewildered Latreus gazed at Caeneus,
Who said serenely, 'Let me test your belly
With my poor steel.' Then at a single stroke
He drove the sword hilt deep through Latreus' side
And swayed it dialwise through his bleeding parts.
Then like mad centaurs which they were
The creatures stormed him, shouting, roaring, charging,
With sword, spear, javelin, hunting knife, and stones;
Yet Caeneus stood there quite untouched, unwounded.
This was a new being that the centaurs saw,
Nor could they say a word until Monychus
Opened his mouth to cry, 'Here's our despair,
A pretty picture of an entire race
Stopped by a monster who's not quite human,

Yet looks it. And we make our pitiful war
Against him and he stands there like a man.
And does it matter if we are
Twice what we might be, twice as strong as, swifter
Than anything on earth? Of course we are not
Sons of high goddesses nor Ixion's breed,
Yet his ambition had enough room in it
To hope to climb into great Juno's bed,
And we're defeated by one enemy
One creature who's half what he seems to be.
Since he is here and willing to receive us
We'll give him mountainfuls of trees and rocks,
To weigh him down a bit with high-hilled forests,
Leaves, branches by the ton to cover him.
I think these gifts will take his breath away—
If he is buried deep enough beneath them;
And weight will crack the corpse that dulls the sword!'
At his last words he saw a tree that fell,
Broken by the mad South Wind that tore its roots
And threw it where the centaur picked it up
To toss it like a forest bearing down
On Caeneus. The other centaurs stormed
The mountaintops, and soon green-bowered Othrys
And Pelion stood naked in the sun.
Against the weight of forests on his back
Caeneus lifted up great tons of oak,
Then sank because he could not catch his breath;
He stirred his head; the forests over him
Moved like an earthquake shaking tall-treed Ida.
How he met death is an uncertain story:
Some said the weight above him forced him down,
Still struggling in the abyss of Tartarus—
And yet a son of Ampycus said 'No,'
For from that mountain of branched leaves and logs
He saw a golden bird take wing to heaven,
A dazzling stream of fire to upper air—
I saw the thing myself, one flash of wings,
Then gone forever, but our comrade Mopsus
Claimed that he saw it circle overhead,
And heard it beat its wings in golden noises,
A golden rhythm that entranced his soul.

And with raised eyes he sang, 'Now praise Caeneus,
Glory of Lapithae, hero and bird,
None other like this wonder of the skies.'
Because of Mopsus' pious character,
His version of the story was accepted,
And we, enraged by loss of one great hero
Who took a multitude of centaurs to undo him,
Stormed at the creatures, killing half
Outright; others ran from us as they could,
The rest escaped as day fell into night."

When Nestor closed his story of how centaurs
Went into battle 'gainst the Lapithae,
Tlepolemus showed angry discontent
Because no word of Hercules was spoken.
"Old man," he said, "then what of Hercules?
The greatest miracle of all you've told us
Is that you have no word of Hercules,
Who, as we all know, as my father told me,
Destroyed more centaurs than he cared to capture."
Both sad and firm, old Nestor answered him,
"Why must you ask me to recall old grudges,
Old half-forgotten crimes, the scars I wear,
That make me curse your father? The gods are witness
To what he's done, some things of merit,
Which I am happy to forget. Do we praise Hector,
Deiphobus, Polydamas? What man on earth
Can praise his enemy? Your father ruined
Messene; he levelled, for no reason I could see,
Elis and Pylos and then destroyed my home.
He was a murderer, killing as he came
Eleven sons of Neleus, handsome boys,
And of the twelve sons I alone survived.
Some other murders may be half-forgotten,
And an unusual one, more notable
Than most, was Periclymenus,
For Neptune gave him powers of mutation,
The choice of being anything he wished.
After he tried a number of disguises,
He chose to be the bird of thunderbolts,
The king of birds loved by the king of gods.

He struck at Hercules, with wing, claw, beak,
And scratched our hero's face, then climbed the sky.
Then Hercules took aim (he never failed)
And shot the bird where flapping wings touched
              shoulders;
The cut was minor, but the wings fell helpless,
And the bird to earth, the arrow driven,
Body's weight on it, from left side to throat.
O handsome captain of the Rhodian ships,
Why should I praise your valiant Hercules?
All that I ask in payment of revenge
For my dear brothers' deaths is to forget
The very name of him who murdered them.
Yet you and I are friends; we'll drink together."

      After old Nestor's tactful story ended,
A night-cup went its rounds, the men got up,
And what remained of night was spent in sleep.

                    THE DEATH OF ACHILLES


      Yet he, the god whose trident swayed the waters
Mourned with a father's tears for his dear son,
That son whose features turned into a swan's.
Nor had his hatred of Achilles dwindled;
And as the days went on, it grew to madness.
The Trojan war was nearly ten years stalled,
When Neptune spoke to the rough-haired Apollo
(The deity of Asiatic nations)
To say, "O darling nephew of my heart,
Best of my nephews and my brother's sons,
Who joined me as we built the walls of Troy
(A labour that is now too soon undone),
What of Troy fallen with many thousand dead?
No tears for them who held the falling town?
Even now I have a glimpse of Hector dead,
His body circling streets of his Pergama,
The suburb where he lived. And yet Achilles
More heartless, violent than war, lives on,
He who undoes all that we hoped to do.

If he would step within six feet of me,
I'd show him how a trident gets to work
And has three points to every thrust in hand.
Yet it's beyond my power to face that hero;
It should be yours to cut him short, to take him
The quick way swifter than his eye can catch it,
The invisible arrow of death through soundless air."
The Apollo nodded yes; it was his pleasure
To join his uncle's wishes to his own,
And floating in the cloud he draped around him
He dropped to earth among the Trojan fighters.
There he saw Paris taking careless aim
At any Greek who happened to advance.
Apollo introduced himself to Paris,
And said, "Why waste your skill, your priceless arrows
On anyone you see? Think of your brothers,
And make short work of treacherous Achilles."
At this he showed the way where the Greek hero
Ploughed through a dozen Trojans with his spear;
He guided Paris' bow in that direction,
Then drew the arrow with his fatal hand.
At last—it was the first breath of true pleasure
Old Priam knew since Hector fell to death.
Then great Achilles who outfought the bravest,
Had fallen prey to one whose best performance,
Timid at the best, was stealing wives of Greeks!
If fate permitted you the strange misfortune
Of dying in a battle facing women,
How happily you'd take that last disaster,
Rather than this, and find your road to death
Where Amazons swung double axes at you!

    The fear, the horror of the Trojan people,
The pride of every Greek, my Lord Achilles
Was like the god who made him
Warrior that he had been, took him in fire.
The great Achilles came at last to ashes,
A scant half handful in a polished urn.
His splendour lives; it fills the rounded world,
And that is how the man should be remembered;
The splendour is himself, son of Peleus,

And Tartarus is not the place for him.
His shield still goes to war against the world,
And in his name all weapons go to war.
Nor are there others fit to carry them:
Nor Tydides nor son of Oileus
Came near them, nor less sturdy Menelaus,
Nor Agamemnon, elder than the others.
The sons of Telamon and old Laertes
Were the exceptions to this rule, and brave,
Had the temerity to claim such honour.
But Agamemnon, to avoid the issue
(Which might have brought a curse upon his judgment),
Called all Greek leaders to an open session
To choose between loud Ajax and Ulysses.

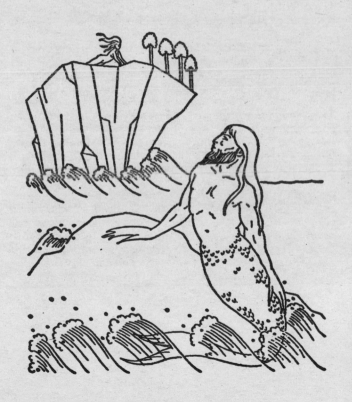

# XIII

# BOOK XIII

The Dispute over Achilles' Armour • The Fall of Troy •
The Sacrifice of Polyxena • Hecuba's Grief • Memnon
• Aeneas • Galatea and Polyphemus • Glaucus

The dispute between Ajax and Ulysses over the possession
of Achilles' armour reminds us that Ovid as a student of law
knew the arts of eloquence if not those of closely reasoned
logical debate. Ajax's speech actually damages Ulysses'
prestige (and in a way that would please Roman readers);
only the superior brilliance of Ulysses' intelligence, his well-
poised sophistries, his wit give him the right to carry Achil-
les' armour from the scene. Better than this, and more clearly
Ovidian, is Polyphemus's lyrical and grotesque courtship
of Galatea. In reading A Midsummer Night's Dream one
might suppose that Shakespeare transformed Polyphemus,
reduced in size, to Bottom and then gave him King Midas's
ears. It is possible that Shakespeare had Ovid's Polyphemus
in mind, reducing him still further, but retaining his irrev-
erence, when he created Caliban in The Tempest; both are
fabulous creatures of island earth; both are subhuman. In
The Metamorphoses itself we are prepared for Polyphemus
by Silenus's awkwardness and Pan's piping in Book XI.

# BOOK XIII

### THE DISPUTE OVER ACHILLES' ARMOUR

Then the Greek captains sat as judges at the trial
To hear what both would say; their standing troops
Had formed a ring around them, they the center
Of a great circus, and among that company
Ajax the bearer of the seven-tiered shield
Got to his feet and glared at Sigean beaches,
Right arm extended toward the ships in harbour.
"By God," he cried, "here, where our ships
Can hear my case, I'll tell my story,
And he who stands against me is Ulysses—
I mean the man who ran from Hector's fires,
Which did not stop me, and I saved the fleet.

"It's easier to talk, to tell a lie
Than fight. I am as shy at talking loud
As he is shy at fighting hand to hand;
In thick of battle I'm superior
But he can always find words that outrun me.
Dear Greeks, I need not tell you what I've done;
You've seen my work here, now and every day,
And since no one has seen Ulysses fighting—
Perhaps the night has—have him tell his story.
I know that I am asking a reward,
A great reward, and that the man who's standing
In my way takes—even to fight him—takes
Half of my glory as an unfit rival;
Ajax is less than Ajax if he wants
The very thing Ulysses wants to own.
Meanwhile Ulysses has his own reward—
After I've won it, carried it away—
In knowing that he shared the same ambition.

"And if my bravery were of dubious value,
My family has a better name than his:
Telamon conceived me, and with Hercules,
He conquered Troy, took ship, and sailed to Colchis.
Telamon's father is the famous Aeacus
Judge of the Underworld where Sisyphus
Still wrestles with a downward-rolling stone.
And great Jove says Aeacus is his son,
Which makes me third in line from Jove himself.
But O my brother Greeks, all this is nothing
Compared to kinship with the great Achilles,
The right to wear his breastplate, lift his shield;
He's my third cousin in a gallant line.
What claim has any heir of Sisyphus—
And very like him in his lies and treasons—
To carry what the great Achilles wore
And bring a foreign family name near mine?

"Is this because I practiced no deceptions,
Even from the first day when I went out to fight,
And therefore I deserve no proper arms?
And he who comes in last, superlative,
Always the last to fight?
Who claims that he's gone mad and dodges fighting?
Until, of course, someone with quicker eyes,
But more unselfish, and the son of Nauplius,
Shows up his lies and hauls this fightless hero
Into his battle-dress to wear a sword
That he's afraid to carry. Should he wear
The best because he hates to fight at all?
Am I to be disgraced, robbed of the gear
My cousin left for me—because, because
I'm always first to fight, to stand in battle?

"I wish he had gone mad or that no fool
Had shown us he was not, that this bland liar
Had not shipped with us to destroy the Trojans.
Then, Palamedes, you would not be doomed
To waste your life on Lemnos, that far island,
Where, so it's rumoured, he lies in a cave,
Where even rocks weep tears to hear him cry

Curses on our Ulysses, which he's earned—
And if the gods are still on Mount Olympus,
His cries are heard. He joined us for the war,
One of our captains, maimed by Hercules,
Sick, starved, is being dressed, fed by the birds,
And as he shoots down game he spends the arrows
That should have shot down half the men of Troy.
If he's alive, then he's escaped Ulysses,
Unlucky doomed and damned Palamedes,
Who would have liked to stay at peace, at home—
Then he'd be much alive and could have faced
Old age and death without the taint of wrong—
But for Ulysses who had not forgotten
How faked insanity had been discovered,
And stained Palamedes with charge of treason,
And hid gold to produce it as a witness
Of bribes that poor Palamedes accepted.
By sending some to exile, or by murder,
Ulysses drains the strength of good Greek forces;
There's the real danger of Ulysses,
Which shows the kind of fighting he enjoys.

       "Even I admit he talks a better story
Than faithful Nestor talking at his best,
Yet I cannot accept Ulysses' version
Of how he left the old man to his fate.
Nestor was slow, his gallant horse was wounded,
And he himself was crippled by old age,
He called for help upon his friend Ulysses
Who walked away. Tydides knows I tell
The truth, knows that old Nestor begged
Ulysses to stay with him, cursed him, called out,
'Ulysses, do not run away.'
There's your mock hero. But the gods are just;
They keep their eyes fixed on the ways of men;
Soon he who runs from them who need his help
Falls into helplessness and wants a friend.
As he left others, so he fell behind;
He made his own trap and fell into it.
Soon he was crying 'Help' to anyone—
Then I arrived to find him white as death,

Shaking because death seemed to crowd upon him;
My great shield over him where he had fallen
Protected him; of course I saved his life,
A useless life—I need no thanks for that.
And now, Ulysses, if you still oppose me,
We shall return to that old battlefield,
The enemy still at us, and you wounded,
And you as always deadly pale and shaking;
Take shelter from my shield; we'll fight behind it.
But when I'd saved him, he who could not stand
Leaped up (where were his wounds?) and ran away.

    "Then up came Hector with the gods behind him,
The battle bloody, nor Ulysses lonely
Even among brave men at being frightened;
Hector felt glorious, up to knees in blood,
And I by tossing a great sheet of rock
Tumbled him down, and when he rose, he chose me
To fight him clean and take the edge of battle.
The Greeks—or you, or you, called on the gods
For me to fight him and your prayers were answered.
And if you ask me how the fighting ended,
Hector could never knock me down; that much is clear.
And look, the Trojans brought both fire and steel,
Then Jove himself against the Grecian Navy—
Where was the talking hero, our Ulysses?
No one but I, my breast, my face, my shield
Stood out between them and our thousand ships
And our frail hope of getting home alive.
In the name of those fair ships, a thousand reasons,
I claim the gift of our Achilles' arms.

    "If for the sake of truth I speak the truth,
These arms have greater glory than I claim,
They cry out 'Ajax, Ajax,'
I do not go to them, they come to me.
Now let the man from Ithaca cast up
A balance between this and what he's done:
First Rhesus downed, then peaceful Dolon killed,
Then capture of Helenus, old Priam's son,
And then the walking off—the art of stealing—

With Pallas' statue hidden in his arms—
And even this with help of Diomede,
Nor nothing done in daylight, all in dark.
If you're rewarding charlatans and thieves
Give more than half these arms to Diomede.

"Why, why give your rewards to Ithaca,
Who has no use for battle-dress or armour,
Who is all tricks and sleight of hand, and best
When he can find the enemy asleep?
A golden helmet (if he wears it) shines too brightly
To keep him safely hidden in the bushes
Nor can his head, small as the little island
Where he was born, carry that weight of gold
That was a crown of glory for Achilles,
Nor can his right arm, weak, unskilled for fighting,
Lift that great spear that grew on Pelion.
Nor can his left arm with its quick light fingers,
(Hand of a brilliant thief) wear that great shield
With all the world reflected from its surface
Bewildering an army sent against it.
Why waste your strength, Ulysses, with the load
Of loot, of honour much too big to carry?
If with their good intentions, but in error,
The Greeks decide to hand this gear to you,
You'll be a great temptation to a soldier;
He'll strip you blind, and you who have a talent,
Retreating swifter than a man can run
Will learn that battle-dress Achilles wore
Will make you less than all of us in running.
Your shield is good enough, no scratches on it;
Seldom enough you've taken it to war,
But my poor shield carries a thousand wounds,
Hacked, rammed by steel-edged blows;
It's ready to give way to something new.

"And last of all, what good are words to us?
Action, my friends, the sight of us in battle!
The hero's battle-dress should go to war;
It should be worn by him who's fit to wear it,
Restored by him who wears recaptured glory."

The son of Telamon had had his say;
His last words roused the cheering of the crowd.
Then the heroic son of Laertes
Rose to his feet. As if to stress a pause,
His eyes glanced at the ground; a second later
He gazed straight at the captains come to hear him,
And with a courteous gesture he began:

"Greeks, if your prayers and mine had been effective,
There'd be no quarrel today concerning who's
Unfit for warlike valour: you, Achilles,
Would be with us, dressed in your glorious armour
But the fates, unequal in their favours,
Have taken him away from me and you."
(His hand then seemed to stroke away his tears.)
"Who's better fit to wear Achilles' shield
Than he who introduced him to the Greeks?
Are Greeks about to praise stupidity,
As if to cheer a man for lack of wit?
Dear Greeks, are you about to stand against me
Because my brains are always at your service?
Listen, my tongue can tell a story better
Than any speech I've heard; it speaks for me;
It always speaks for you. It should not make
An enemy today. Let every man
Put all his gifts to work, the best he has.

"As to my heritage, it's my conviction
That what one does—not what his family was—
Is measure of his value to the world.
Since Ajax drags the name of families forward,
And says that he's great-grandson of great Jove,
Jove is, of course, the father of my blood,
As far, as near as Ajax' heritage.
I am Laertes' son, his father Arcesius,
And Arcesius is a son of Jove;
Nor have I murderers within my family
Who've been exiled, sent off to Jove knows where.
My mother's line comes down from Mercury;
From both lines I inherit godliness.
My mother's noble birth, my father's innocence

Of guilt—he'd be the last man here to kill
His brother—these are not among the reasons
I have the right to claim Achilles' armour.
Whoever wins your vote, consider first
What he has done. Because our good friend Ajax
Reminds us Telamon and Peleus
Were brothers, do not give him praise for that;
This is beside the point. The question is:
Who is the better man in his own right
To carry honours that Achilles wore?
And if you look for heirs to wear his armour,
You'll find that Pyrrhus has a better claim,
For Pyrrhus is the son of Peleus,
And Peleus, of course, Achilles' father.
Then where does Ajax fit? Let's send these trophies
Either to Pyrrhus' home or Peleus'.
Teucer, like Ajax, is Achilles' cousin,
But have you heard him claim Achilles' armour,
And if you heard him, has he right to get it?
No, here's a case that rests on what we've done;
I've done so much, I half forget the details.
All I can do is put a few in order.

    "Achilles' mother, knowing what his fate was
That war would lead him toward an early death—
Had dressed him as a girl, which fooled the many,
And Ajax was among that company.
Meanwhile, nearby a box of costume jewelry,
And other girlish articles he wore,
I hid a few things that a fighting man would gaze at
And then the hero, still dressed as a woman,
Picked up a spear and shield to fondle them.
I said, 'Son of a goddess, Troy is damned;
She waits for you to rape her, tear her down.
What are you waiting for? That great doomed city
        trembles
For you to enter her and take her falling ruins.'
With this, I put my hand upon his arm,
And sent the hero to heroic duties.
In that sense all the work he did was mine:
Therefore, I wounded Telephus and cured him

With the same spear; he weeping, crying, broke.
Thebes fell to me, and so did Tenedos,
Chryse and Cilla, Apollonian cities,
Lesbos and Scyrus—all of them were mine.
In the same fashion (and through my inspiration)
Lyrnesus' walls went down in clouds of dust,
And—not to speak of other things I've done—
I chose the man who fought down savage Hector;
Through me the famous Hector fell to earth!
All that I ask for is the battle-dress
By which Achilles made his reputation;
The living man received my gift of arms—
Now that he's dead, I'll take it back again.

    "When Menelaus' tragedy struck home
To all the Greeks and a full thousand ships
Made ready on the eastern shores of Aulis,
The wind died down or forced its will against them.
Next, a bad-minded oracle declared
That Agamemnon offer his young daughter
As a stuck sheep on cold Diana's altar.
The father in him balked at this demand;
His blood ran hot and flamed against the gods;
Though he was royal, he had a father's temper.
At my persuasion, he was less a father
Than one who took to heart public affairs.
(May he forgive me as I make this late confession.)
I had a hard-wrought problem set before us,
An argument that swayed a sense of justice,
But for the sake of all—I mean the people,
His brother's welfare, and his own position
As general commanding all the Greeks—
By tact, by flattery I moved his mind
Against his instincts as a family man.
Then I went to his wife, the poor girl's mother,
Not to be won by reason, but by lies.
If Telamon's brave son had talked to her,
Our ships would still be windless in that harbour.

    "Then I was sent as diplomat to Troy—
To that high fortress where they sat in council

To meet the best of them, the men in power;
Nor did I fear them as I put before them
The argument, the claims all Greeks demanded.
I said that Paris was the worst of thieves—
He must give back both Helen and his loot,
And there I talked to Priam and Antenor
(Antenor always followed Priam's lead).
Paris, his brothers, and their friends who joined them
In any work that led to stealing wives,
Almost, not quite, laid dirty hands upon me
(A fact that Menelaus is aware of
And surely, Menelaus, you remember
The first day's dangers that I spent with you).

   "It takes too long to tell the things I did,
All for your sakes—advice and scenes of action,
The crowded incidents of a long war.
After the early skirmishes and forays,
The enemy hid behind the city's walls—
No hope of battle in an open field.
In the tenth year we settled down to fighting.
But in that time between, what were you doing?
I mean these men who know of nothing else
But hand-to-hand events on battlefield.
In all that time what did you think or do?
If you want facts from me about myself,
I planned disaster for the enemy:
Designed the trenches running round the city;
Cheered those who helped us—and they needed cheering
To break the boredom of an endless war;
I planned our commissary and went off
On secret operations, still kept guarded.

   "Then suddenly, fooled by a dream from Jove,
Our king, our Agamemnon, tried to tell us
To end the weary struggle of the war—
A war that we began—and backed his words
By telling what Jove told him as he slept.
Did I see Ajax take a stand against this,
Insist that Troy be ruined, and march to fight?
And did he stop the fools already turning

Toward ships for home? And did I see him stand,
Sword drawn, to bring deserters to his side?
—And this an easy job for one who loves
To speak only when he can praise himself,
Silent, except when on his feet for battle.
Of course he joined the crowd and ran away.
Ajax, I blushed to see you as you were,
Your back before my eyes, running to hoist
Your cowardly sails to treasonable winds.
Then I cried out, 'Has everyone gone mad?
O my dear friends—and you're deserting Troy,
The city that is falling to your hands?
Your cargo will be ten years of dishonour.'
Anger gave me especial gift of tongue;
I stopped them as they ran; they swayed, then turned,
And soon enough they came to let me guide them.
Meanwhile our Agamemnon claimed our allies,
And yet the son of Telamon stood silent.
Thersites made a racket; that maimed creature
Walked up to scold the king until I gave him
The kind of bitter treatment he deserved—
Then I stepped forward, and with fair language
Cheered up the timid souls among my friends—
Fresh manliness to others who stood by me,
Till all were fit to meet the enemy.
If Ajax fought well in the coming battles,
He owes a debt to me who brought him back.

      "Ajax, who chose you to be his friend?
Diomede took me and took his stance
By knowing that Ulysses's at his side;
And of the several thousand Greeks around us,
It's no disgrace to be the chosen friend
Of friend Diomede—nor did we join
By drawing lots for dangerous adventure.
We had no fear of night nor enemy;
That's when I killed Dolon, the Trojan spy,
Out on a secret mission like our own—
Nor did I kill him at first sight; I kept him
Twisting until he told me every scheme
That crooked Troy contrived against our siege.

That duty done—for I was done with spying—
I could have ventured home to get rewards,
But no, I saw King Rhesus' tents before me;
I killed him outright and his generals too.
Since I had won and I was thankful for it,
I drove my captured horses with an air,
Chariot and team, for I had earned that triumph.
Come take away Achilles' armour from me,
Return the horses to the enemy
To pay for one night's work and see if
Ajax, even at best, gave more than I.
And must I speak of Sarpedon, whose men
My sword went through as through a field of grain?
Here is a list of names of those who fell:
Coeranos and Alastor and Chromius,
Alcander, Halius, and Noemon,
Prytanis, Thoon and Chersidamas,
Charopes and Ennomos who was hounded
By fates. I do not count the lesser breed
I put to death below the city's walls.
Friends, I have wounds; I wear them where they should be,
Nor do you have my word for this,
Look at them!" And he opened wide his shirt.
"Look at my breast and see how well I've carried
The Greek war near my heart! Yet for ten years
This son of Telamon has never given
A single drop of blood to save his friends,
And not a single scar on that fair body!

       "And when he says he saved our good Greek Navy
Against the threat of Trojans backed by Jove,
What does he mean? I say he helped to save it,
For I'm not one to underrate a man,
To smear him, tear him down, and stand there smiling.
There were occasions when he did fight well,
But so do others, so did all, let him give honours
To all of you, for all of you deserve them.
The son of Actor in Achilles' image
Fought off the Trojans first; if he had not
Our navy and its captain would have perished,
Gone up in flames. But Ajax seems to think

He stood alone against great Hector. He forgets
Our king, king's generals, and, of course, myself;
He was the ninth man in that line of duty;
We all drew lots and he had luck that day,
The joy of meeting Hector hand-to-hand.
What happened after that, my dearest hero?
You met him—Hector left the field untouched,
Unscratched—and then the fight was over.

    "Even now I almost weep when I remember
The day Achilles fell—he was your wall,
O Greeks, remember this! Nor fears, nor weeping
Prevented me from stooping down to lift him,
To carry that dear body, fully armed,
And shoulder high, that is, across my shoulders,
The very armour that I ask to wear.
I took his dead weight and the armour with it.
And is there further question of my strength?
And what about my soul, my wit, my brains?
They know the honours you may give to me.
Achilles' mother, goddess of the sea,
Had high hopes for her son. Did she intend
These things he wore—and they are works of art—
To shield backside and front of a brute soldier?
How could he read the meaning of the shield?
And recognize the world engraved upon it?
Seas, continents, the midnight shining heavens,
Infinite stars, and then the Pleiades,
The Bears who must ride high of watery places,
The varied cities, and the radiant sword
Orion wears to guard unending night.
Poor Ajax wants what he can't understand.

    "And what of his remarks about my slowness,
My getting into battle much too late?
Does he know this? His very speech is libel
On great Achilles. If you call it wrong
To play at acting—acting is an art—
Then both Achilles and myself dissembled,
And used an actor's wit. I played for time—
If that was wrong, I was the first to sin.

A fond wife held me—as you know, Achilles—
Achilles had a most possessive mother;
We yielded to them first and then to you.
I do not fear what you may hold against me—
Not even if I can't defend myself—
Virtue or fault Achilles shared with me,
And he the greatest man I've ever known.
His genius was uncovered by Ulysses,
Ulysses' wit, and not poor Ajax' brains.

"Don't be surprised that Ajax' foolish tongue
Spits libel at us, you as well as me.
As for Palamedes—was I a villain?
Did I accuse the man on trumped-up charges?
And was your verdict, 'Guilty,' in good order?
The son of Nauplius could not deny the charge:
The crime was obvious, the proof before us,
Nor did you have to take my version of it;
You saw the evidence—the bribe itself.

"More: it is not my fault that Lemnos
Is now a prison for Philoctetes.
It's by your order he was exiled there;
Those were your wishes, but I must confess
I recommended that he take his leave
From scenes of war, the discipline, the fighting,
The journey eastward, all to ease his terrors,
His feverish agonies, and take a rest.
He took my words as wisdom—he's alive!
His life was saved, and all my good intentions
Had happiest results, but in this case
My good intentions show my loyalty.
But since our prophets say Troy cannot fall
Without the help of this great fighting man,
Go, call him to the wars, but don't send me;
No, better get the eloquent, tactful Ajax out
To charm him, and to curse his mind, his wounds,
Or by a clever bit of strategy to bring him
Back to our ranks to lead us into battle.
The Simois will flow from sea to mountain,
Ida itself will be a barren plain,

And Greece will fight against herself at Troy
Before the wit of muddle-headed Ajax
Would help the Greeks to better my commands.
O mad Philoctetes! What bitterness, what hate
You'd love to pour as flames of endless fire
Over the Greeks, their kind, and even me!
And though your curses try to bury me
From head to foot, and though you'd love to have me
Within arm's reach to drink my blood like wine,
I'd go at you, give you an equal chance
To have at me as you would have at me—
Jove save me—take you struggling as you are,
Back here. And I would take your fatal arrows,
If fortune's kind to me, out of your hands,
Just as I captured Helenus, who was
A prophet, as I also captured then
The secrets of the gods and fates of Troy—
In the same fashion, while all Troy marched round me,
I took the ikon of their own Minerva.
Does Ajax ever hope to rival me?
The truth is that the Fates themselves confessed
Troy could not fall unless we had the ikon.
Where's Ajax now? I mean the hero, Ajax,
Huge with heroic talk. Do I see him tremble?
Why did Ulysses on that darkest night
Glide past the guards, past naked swords in darkness
Through Troy, even to the heart of that vast fortress,
Even to the top—then, like a branch of lightning
Seize the goddess, the ikon of herself,
And bring her to her enemy, the Greeks?
Had I not done this even Telamon's brave son
Could not have fought with seven-bull-hides shield,
Worn into battle on his thick left arm.
That night I conquered Troy; I made the moment
When all of us could enter at her fall.

"Ajax, stop growling words beneath your breath,
Stop glancing up at me as if to say
Tydides helped me on that night in Troy;
The man has earned his praise and earned it well.
And when your shield defended our great navy

You did not stand alone; friends, men were with you—
And I stood with a single friend beside me.
If Diomede did not know that strong-arm fighters
Are less important than a man with brains,
He would step forward with his claims; so would
Another Ajax, less than you, and fierce
Eurypylus, Idomeneus, son of famous
Andraemon, and his neighbour Meriones;
Even Menelaus would claim Achilles' arms.
All these brave men, however strong and able,
Good as myself at fighting on the field,
Know my superior wit. A good sword arm
Is always of good use in any war,
But when it comes to strategy in fighting,
You need my leadership, my art, my brains.
Men may be brainless, yet have fighting power,
But my mind holds the warnings of the future.
And you, my Ajax, fight extremely well,
But I, I know the moment when to strike,
And tell our king. Your strength is of the flesh,
Mine in my head. The captain of a ship
Steers it and stands as far above his crew
As generals above the men beneath them,
And I'm your general and you my men,
For in this strange anatomy we wear,
The head has greater powers than the hand;
The spirit, heart, and mind are over all.

    "My lords, if you have gifts at your disposal,
Give them to him who guards you night and day.
For many, many years I've held our worries,
Our hopes, our fears, our fortunes, in my mind
And all I ask is honourable reward.
The work is done: obstinate fates removed;
I opened up tall Troy and we walked in.
By all our hopes, and by the very walls
Of Troy that are to fall as we march in,
And by the gods behind this captured ikon,
By what still holds of strategy and wit,
Should the risk of further war be needed,
And if you think the fate of Troy still sways

In balance—think of me! If I'm not worthy,
Then give the great Achilles' arms to her!"
And where Ulysses pointed stood a statue,
Image in marble of the Greek Minerva.

Ulysses' peers were moved, and as they yielded
They showed the force behind his gift of speech:
The man of words received the soldier's arms.
Then he who met great Hector single-handed,
Who walked through fire and sword so many times,
Even through lightning wrath of Jove, gave in to anger,
Madness defeated undefeated Ajax
And ripping out his sword, he cried aloud,
"Yet this is mine, or does Ulysses claim it?
This time I'll make it work against myself,
And if its steel grew stained with Trojan blood,
Today its iron will take a deeper colour,
The darker stain of him who carries it;
No one but Ajax can out-swordplay Ajax."
With this he drove the sword into his breast,
His open breast that never showed a scar.
Nor was there any hand that had the power
To pluck it out; only the fountain force
Of Ajax' blood behind it purged the steel.
In ancient times the blood-stained ground beneath it
Grew fertile with the blood of Hyacinthus,
Grass green and red gave birth to purple flowers,
Which were engraved for boy as well as Ajax,
"Ai, ai," the name of hero, cry of grief.

### THE FALL OF TROY

Where Queen Hypsipyle and famous Thoas lived,
Island of Lemnos and bad reputation,
An ancient place of murder and corruption,
Was where Ulysses spread his sails to go.
He came there to collect Tirynthian arrows,
And, having got them, brought them to the Greeks,
And these munitions closed the ten-year war.
Then Troy went under, Priam under it;
Priam's doomed wife became an animal

And where the Hellespont grew sharp and narrow
The poor she-creature barked and howled all night,
Which terrified that foreign atmosphere.
Troy burned, nor had its fires guttered out;
While Jove's shrine drank, a single draft of fire,
The last thin drops of blood old Priam offered.
Cassandra, priestess of Apollo's temple,
And though she lifted helpless hands to heaven,
Was hauled through half the city by her hair.
The Trojan women, clinging to their ikons,
The burning pillars of dismantled temples,
Were raped by Greeks—they made a priceless prize.
Meanwhile Astyanax was carried up
To that high look-out where he used to watch
His father (as his mother guided him)
Fight for the honour of their native city,
And from that tower the boy was tossed to death.
The North Wind gave the Greeks a hint of home;
It spoke aloud in fluttering sails and hawsers.
The captain gave his orders to hoist sail.
"Dear Troy, farewell!" unwilling whores cried out;
The women kissed their native shores good-bye
And turned away from that great smouldering town
That once held homes they knew. The last to leave—
O what a fearful sight—was Hecuba;
The Greeks had found her crouching in drear tombs,
The very tombs where all her sons lay buried.
And there she clung; she tried to kiss their bones.
The Greeks were forced to tear her wretched body
Out of the house of death, and yet she carried
Between her breasts that handful of spent dust,
Once Hector's ashes—that was all she had.
And on his tomb she scattered her grey hair,
These with her tears, the last small gifts she owned.

#### THE SACRIFICE OF POLYXENA

Across the way from Troy Bistones lived,
And there the wealthy court of Polymestor,
A king to whom Priam sent Polydorus,
To save this son of his from dangers of long war.

This was a wise idea—if Priam had not
Sent with the boy a chest of gold, rare jewels—
Treasures that always wake indecent hopes;
And if the soul is shrewd and avaricious,
They lead to murder. When the Trojan fortunes
Began to slip, the wicked Polymestor
Slit the boy's throat and then, as if this crime
Would disappear soon as the body vanished,
He tossed the boy's remains from a rock cliff
Down to the swirling waters of the sea.

There to the shores of Thrace came Agamemnon,
Anchored his navy till the sea calmed down,
Until the winds took on a new direction.
Suddenly as big as life and from that earth
Achilles' ghost walked through the mist and spray;
He looked as dangerous and fit for trouble
As when he drew a naked fiery steel
Against the Agamemnon long ago.
"And so, dear Greeks," he said, "you're leaving us;
You have forgotten me. Once I am buried,
I've drifted out of sight and from your minds—
That's my reward. But will you get away?
Not quite. My tomb shall have its proper flowers;
To please my ghost, bring Polyxena here;
Her body'll make a lovely decoration!"
Greeks took his word as law; the girl was ripped
Out of her mother's arms, she the last hostage
Of that woman's love, unlucky girl,
Yet brave, with more than girlish spirit
Walked to her pyre to grace Achilles' tomb.
She kept her poise, even facing the dread altar,
And knew that ceremony was her death,
Even as Neoptolemus held sword to strike,
And as her eyes met his, she said distinctly,
"Now is the time to take my gentle blood,
Your sword has choice of either throat or breast."
Then as she offered her breast and throat to him,
We may be sure that she'd be no man's servant.
"No, not by these means shall you please the gods,
Nor should my mother know the way I died.

Her sorrow makes my death less glorious;
My death is less her tragedy than life,
Her life that carries darkness all its own.
Then stand aside so my last breath will go
Straightly to waiting spirits underground,
And if I have the right to ask this favour,
Then no man has the right to touch my body.
If you're to please him who demands my death,
My blood must flow in virgin liberty.
And if my words have the least strength to move you
(Now Priam's daughter speaks, nor captured slave),
Then give my body to my weeping mother,
Who'll pay in tears for it—don't ask for gold,
The usual fee to place it in a tomb;
She has spent gold enough as well as tears"
All those who heard her wept; her eyes were dry.
And as the weeping priest stepped to her side
He drove his knife home to her waiting breast.
Even to the last and as she fell to earth,
Her white face held its look of brave decorum,
And as she fainted into death she swept
Her cloak around her limbs to shield her body.

HECUBA'S GRIEF

   As Trojan women carried her away,
They named all the misfortunes, one by one,
That women of King Priam's household shared.
They wept: "O princess fallen, O queen mother,
Mother of Asia and a queen of sorrows,
Now a poor queen in chains, less than a slave,
Nor would Ulysses care to look at her
If he had not known she was Hector's mother,
Nor does the shade of Hector find her queen."
Then Hecuba embraced her daughter's body,
Gave her the tears that measured, if they could,
The loss of country, husband, sons, and home;
Tears filled her daughter's wounds; she filled
Her lips with kisses, then again, again
Her gestures spoke the grief that bruised her heart.
Her wild white hair stained with her daughter's blood,

She cried aloud, "O my dear child, my darling,
The last of all I had, your wound, my wound—
They murdered all of you, even this last,
Even a woman taken by the sword.
Achilles who made way with all your brothers,
Even his ghost pursues you here—he who damned Troy!
When he was killed by Paris, then I said,
'There's no one now who fears the dread Achilles,'
And yet his ashes rising from his urn
Stir in a fiery wind against our house.
Even his tomb is filled with rage against us,
And all the children of my womb for him!
Troy now lies underground; the city's vanished;
The people's agony has turned to dust.
In me alone the Trojan spirit lives;
The stream of Trojan passion in my veins
Still winds its living waters to the sea—
And only yesterday I stood secure,
As on a mountain higher than the world,
My husband, sons, and daughters there to guard me;
Now homeless, broken—and they had to tear me
Out of the tombs that held the ones I love,
I'm taken as a gift, a freak of nature,
To please the fancy of Penelope.
As I shall sit to spin my task in wool,
She'll call in half the women of Ithaca
To say, 'Here's Hector's mother, Priam's queen.'
And you my daughter, you the last of all,
Are now a wreath to gild Achilles' tomb.
And every child I carried in my body
Was born as victim for my enemy.
I've grown too old for human feeling now;
Why do I live? Or old age makes me wander
Through these long days that have no end but night?
Why do I live to please the heartless gods,
To weep another funeral into earth?
Was Priam glad when Troy fell into ruins?
His happiness is death; his eyes are closed
Even to the body of a murdered daughter;
He left his life behind him with his city.
And O my princess, is your dowry this?

An honoured urn within a Trojan tomb?
Our house no longer has the right to ask it.
Your funeral wreath shall be your mother's tears,
Your tomb the sanded waste of foreign shores.
My life is loss, yet a last hope of life
Still stirs in these last moments I draw breath—
Sight of my last but once my youngest son,
My Polydorus, sent to Thracian shores,
These shores, adopted son of a great king.
First, quickly, I must wash the blood that stains her.
O daughter, there's no time for further tears!"

Then with the trembling walk of one grown old,
Seaward she wandered. "Trojan wives and mothers,
Bring me my urn!" she cried. She had in mind
The thought of drawing water from the sea.
But as she looked she saw dead Polydorus,
His body thick with wounds, washed to the shore.
The Trojan wives screamed at the naked horror,
But she stood silent, all her words past speech,
Her tears drowned in the desert of her grief.
And like a desert rock she stood above him,
Gazing at earth, or lifting eyes to heaven,
As though to outstare heaven and the gods;
With that same face she looked upon her son,
To fix his wounds, to feed her raging mind.
As if she were still queen, rage took her blood,
Possessed her with a fury none could master;
She saw the image her revenge would take.
Then like a lioness whose cub is taken,
Who tracks the invisible thief, so Hecuba
Gathered her strength beyond old age itself
And marched to Polymestor's palace where
She begged to speak to him to show him how
She'd hidden gold to give him for her son.
The king believed her, and his love of gold
Guided his steps to find the place she named.
Then with a few soft words he welcomed her,
"Dear Hecuba, we must have gold at once.
The boy must take his pleasures like a king,
And by the gods—and there are many of them—

I shall make sure that all is his, not mine,
That is, what you have given me before
As well as all you have for me today."
She gazed at him and firmly heard each lie,
Then called the Trojan women to her side,
And at a single leap scratched out his eyes.
Her furies gave her supernatural strength;
Her bloodstained fingers thrust holes in his head
Where once his eyes had been. When they had learned
What had attacked their king, the Thracian guards
Sought out the woman, raining spears and stones
In her direction where she stood to meet them,
Snapping and barking at the stones that fell.
She had no words for speech. Yet where she stood
The spot is called "The Dog" and it is said
(Because of ancient wrongs) her voice still howls
Throughout the wilderness of Thracian shores.
Her fate moved Trojan friends, Greek enemies,
And all the gods—even the wife of Jove,
Who said that Hecuba was pitiful.

MEMNON

Although Aurora favored Trojan armies,
Troy's downfall and the grief of Hecuba
Were overshadowed by her own affairs,
For she, the brilliant mother of bright Memnon,
Had seen him fall on Trojan battlefield
Pierced by Achilles' spear. And now where skies
Once glowed like rose-red wine at early morning,
The air turned grey in cloudy wilderness.
Nor could Aurora face her son's poor body
As it lay smouldering on a funeral pyre.
In her wild grief (with flowing eyes and hair)
She came to Jove and threw herself before him.
"My lord," said she, "in all these golden heavens
I am the least pretentious of your servants,
Of all of us, Earth builds me fewest temples,
Yet as a true Olympian I come.
I do not ask for more or richer temples,

Nor sweeter incense, and replenished altar fires.
Though all my talents are of feminine gifts,
I never fail to turn each night to morning,
I never fail to give each day new colours.
You may feel this deserves some slight reward,
Yet this is not why I am here today,
To tell you that Aurora begs for honours.
I come to you because of Memnon's death,
Because he fought (and fell) for Priam's sake,
Because he was too young to die, because
You willed his murder by the dread Achilles.
And for his loss, dear master of the gods,
Give him some sign of honour, which gives me
Heart's ease at least for my unlucky son."
Jove nodded and the smoke of Memnon's pyre
Shot up to heaven, turning day to night,
As when a mist that floats above a river
Grows to a cloud that shuts away the sun.
Black ashes rose from earth like fluttering wings
That seemed to join, and form the flames beneath them
They gathered strength and seemed to come to life.
They flew like birds, then turned to birds in flight,
Bird-cry and noise of wings through darkening air,
Sisters and brothers circling round the pyre.
Three times they came to vanish in the sky,
Then a fourth time in clouds with noise of battle,
The fiery ravens split their ranks in two,
And in two racing armies fought: beak, claw,
In cutting fury tearing at each heart,
And as they fell they were memorial
Of Memnon's ashes which had given them birth.
For his sake they were named Memnonides,
And even now when the eternal Sun
Runs through twelve blazing cycles of the heavens,
They meet to fight, to die, to fall again
In memory of him who gave them being.
While dog-voiced Hecuba cried through the night,
And sobs of Trojan weeping filled the air,
Aurora's mind and heart spoke her own loss.
Even today her tears foretell the dawn.

AENEAS

    When Troy's walls fell, the fates still gave the Trojans
Some signs of hope, for Cytherea's son,
Hero Aeneas, carried on his shoulders
Her ikon and his aged, pious father.
Of all his riches that he held most dear
He chose his son Ascanius for rescue.
Then with his company of émigrés
He sailed from Antandros and saw the last
Of guilty Thrace, stained red and wet
With blood of Polydorus, while fair winds,
Even shifting with the tides, had served him well,
Took him to Delos, bright Apollo's city.
Anius, Apollo's priest and worthy king
Of the green land where Phoebus' temples are,
Welcomed Aeneas to this peaceful haven.
Anius showed his guests around the city,
The reconstructed altars, sacred trees
Beneath whose magic branches our Latona
Found shelter for the birth of her two children.
And in that place the pious company
Went through the rituals of lighting incense,
Of pouring wine upon the sparkling altars,
Of slaying cattle, and with reverent eyes
Reading burnt entrails in the altar fires.
Then in the recess of Anius' palace,
They fell to rest and ate the gifts of Ceres
And drank the wine that Bacchus had provided.
Then saintly old Anchises said, "O priest
Of Phoebus, am I wrong or right? But when
I visited your city long ago
I think I saw four daughters and a son?"
Anius, with his priestly temples bound
In snow-white halos, shook his head to say,
"No, no, my friend, you happen to be right;
I was the father of five lovely children.
But men must live by chance, or luck or fate,
And now you see me almost left alone.
My son is little comfort to me here;
He's king of Andros, which took on his name,

A country which he rules as my lieutenant;
Phoebus gave him the gift of second sight,
But Bacchus gave my daughters other virtues,
Which at the time seemed more than they could hope for,
An art of touch, a green thumb, you might call it,
Of making all things grow, from wheat to bread,
From grapes to wine, from olive tree to oil,
For which we thank our grey-green-eyed Minerva—
There were great riches in that magic touch.
When Agamemnon (who demolished Troy
And we felt we'd been hurt by that same fury)—
When he heard what my daughters had to give,
He forced them from my arms, to make them work
To feed Greek troops quartered on Trojan soil.
The girls escaped; two ran toward Euboea,
And two found shelter in their brother's Andros.
Greek troops came after them, and warned that war
Would enter Andros if it held my daughters.
Fear shook my son; he was less brotherly
Than eager to appease; he gave his sisters
To dubious mercy of the enemy.
Yet I almost forgive his timid gesture;
He had no brave Aeneas there to help him,
Nor Hector to hold siege for ten long years.

"As soldiers came with chains to weight their arms,
The girls raised white hands up to silent heavens:
'O father Bacchus, save us if you can!'
And so he did, but in an odd, wild fashion;
They lost their girlish looks—how, I don't know,
But suddenly their bodies grew white feathers,
And they were snow-white birds, like doves of Venus."

With stories such as this they passed the time,
Drank deep as night itself, and went to bed.
When morning shone, they waked to take advice
From voices of the Delian Apollo.
These told them to go find their motherland
To take their refuge on her neighbouring shores.
And as they left, Anius gave a sceptre
To elderly Anchises, to his grandson

A box to hold his arrows and a cloak,
And to Aeneas a fine metal cup
Which Therses, who had been an earlier guest,
Brought to Aonian shores to please his host.
Though Therses gave it to the king, this work
Of art had been the masterpiece of one,
Hylean Alcon, whose engraving told a story:
One saw a city of the seven gates,
Which meant, of course, that Thebes was represented.
Beyond the gates were tombs and flaming pyres,
There women with loose hair and naked breasts
Seemed to speak grief to anyone who saw them,
And nymphs wept over dried-up springs and rivers.
Trees were stripped black, and goats found scanty pasture
In fields of stone and clay. And in the streets
Of Thebes itself Orion's daughters:
One tries to tear her throat with her own fingers,
The other wounds herself with a blunt shuttle;
Both fall to death as civic sacrifice,
Then, carried to their pyres, are changed to ashes
From which, white flames of virginal desire,
Came two boys who were known as the Coroni,
Who kept the Theban house from dying out,
And were the priests who blessed their mother's ashes.
So ran the bas-relief in ancient bronze.
And round the top, in gold, acanthus flowered,
Carved like the crest of a Corinthian pillar.
The Trojans gave their host gifts of like virtue,
A silver chest for incense, a gold shell
From which to pour a stream of holy wine,
And a king's crown, all diamonds and gold.
Then, since the Trojans knew their ancient house
Was once named Teucer and its source was Crete,
They sailed to Crete, but there the soil,
The air above it, and uncertain weather
Forced them to leave; all seemed to smell of death.
Then as they left Crete and its hundred cities,
They steered toward Italy, but winter storms
Broke over them, drove them to rock-edged islands,
Those ports of no return where siren Aello
Clapped wings and claws to frighten them away,

Past lesser islands where that great Greek liar,
The shrewd Ulysses, ruled the foaming waves
From Ithaca to Samos. Then they steered
Past Ambracia, once the scene of war
In godlike conflict, recently made famous
Because Apollo has an altar there.
Then past Dodona where the talking oaks
Took on the voice of Jove to those who listened,
And past Chaonia's harbour where the sons
Of King Molossus grew, quick as Jove's lightning,
Swift wings that saved them from unholy fires.

### GALATEA AND POLYPHEMUS

Next stop they tried the country of Phaeacians,
Famous for fruit, and came to shore in harbour
Of Buththotos which on Corcyra island
Was known as "little Troy," ruled by a priest
Who was a Trojan prophet, skilled in visions,
And from him heard the optimistic voice
Of Priam's son Helenus, who, though dead,
Still hoped for better news in days to come,
Which led them to the shores of Sicily.
This land forked out to sea in three directions:
Pachynos to the south in rain and spray,
While Lilybeaon took mild western winds,
And Peloros stretched northward to the Bears,
Who could not dive in any kind of weather
To cool green waves beneath the tempting sea.
Through friendly tides and able oarsmanship,
The Trojan boats sailed to the sands of Zancle
And dropped their anchors as night settled in.
Scylla made mischief to the right of them,
While wet Charybdis cursed them on the left.
One swallowed ships to spit them out again,
The other had her belly wreathed with dogs.
Her face was one of girlish innocence,
And if the poets aren't a crew of liars,
Scylla was once an innocent and pure.
Like girls of her complexion and great beauty,
She had her faithful lovers, yet refused them

To join the mermaids of the friendly sea
Who took her in their arms to show they loved her,
While she complained that men were stupid lovers.
One day young Galatea combed her hair,
And with the comb held high she sighed and said,
"My dear, your lovers were sweet gentlemen;
You turned them down without a thought of danger.
But look at me—I am Nereus' daughter,
My mother, Doris, is of sea-green colours,
My place of shelter is with sea-born sisters,
Yet I could not avoid the wilful Cyclops
Without a loss of ease and dignity."
She sobbed, and white Scylla soothed the goddess
And wiped away her tears and said aloud,
"My darling, tell me everything you know,
For I'm the dearest friend you've ever had,"
And charmed at this, the goddess spoke again:
"Acis the son of Faunus and Symaethis
Was worshipped by his parents, but to me
He was the best, the loveliest of creatures
And, more than that, he gave me all his love;
He was sixteen and was a perfect beauty,
The first silk threads of hair at lips and chin;
To say I loved him is an understatement.
But Cyclops yearned for me both night and day;
I hated one as much I loved the other.

      "But all the world is moved by mother Venus!
Meanwhile the very forest shook its leaves
And turned away when Cyclops showed his face;
It hurt the eyes of enemy or friend.
Cyclops, contemptuous of Olympian powers,
Of goddesses as well as gods in clouds,
Burned like a torch at Venus' inspiration,
Forgot to herd his sheep and guard his caves.
Then Polyphemus tried the arts of pleasing,
Took care of how he looked and raked his hair;
He scythed his beard, and stared at his wild face
That stared back at him from a crystal well.
He lost his flair for murder and destruction,
And learned distaste for drinking bowls of blood.

The ships that had to sail his rocks and sandbars
Slipped by unwrecked; the monster seemed indifferent.
And when Telemus came to Sicily—
No bird in flight was swifter than the glances
From his round eyes which saw things as they were—
He shot a word or two at Polyphemus:
'Some day Ulysses will unhook that eye
Which hangs above your nose and mars your features.'
To which the Cyclops answered, 'You're a fool.
If you're a prophet, I'm a baby rabbit.
You've come too late; it's stolen long ago—
A lovely lady wears it in her heart.'
So he replied to one who hoped to warn him,
And tramped the beach till his great feet grew tired,
Till he at last sank to his empty cave.
Nearby there was a wedged peninsula
That ran into the sea; on either side
The waves foamed up grey rocks or rose above them.
There on a green plateau the burning Cyclops
Sat at his restless ease, his sheep neglected;
And though they followed him, they seemed to drift
          astray.
He dropped his walking stick, a huge pine tree
That should have been a mast for some fair ship,
Then in an absent-minded mood he raised
His home-made pipes, plucked from a hundred reeds.
As he made music, all the mountains trembled;
So did the waves. And even I, concealed
In Acis' arms, a mile away and shadowed
By rocks above our heads, I heard his singing,
And it's not likely I'll forget his song:

     "'O Galatea, white-limbed Galatea,
O whiter than white-flowering evergreen,
More graceful than the April alder tree,
As tall, as slender, and more glittering
Than crystal on an early spring-day morning—
O lively as a young she-goat at weaning,
As smooth as sea shells polished in clear waters,
And more than these: more welcome than the sun
Seen for an hour in December's noon,

More than green shades that fall through summer
       evenings,
Ripe to the taste as apple or globed pear,
And lovelier within that swaying motion
Than is the tall plane tree. O Galatea,
More crystalline than ice, and far, far sweeter
Than grapes that fall in yellow-leaved September,
O softer than the swan, more white than she,
Or milk that curdles in a shepherd's bowl—
If you would come to me, nor run away,
More beautiful than fountain-watered gardens.

   "'Yet the same Galatea is more stubborn
Than a wild cow let loose in a wild pasture,
Hard as a twist of knotted oak, elusive
As streams of swift hill-water, tougher than
The willow wand, the slender white-vined briar,
Firmer than these grey rocks, more violent
Than rivers that tear through them down that hill.
She has more vanity than any petted peacock,
More cruelty than the sharpest lips of fire,
More bitter-pricking than the pointed thorn;
O she's more raging than a raging bear,
Who battles for her young, O she's grown deafer
Than those broad miles of ocean's ceaseless waves,
And no more mercy than a snake that pierces
The foot that trips its tail. If I had wit,
I'd pluck these curses from you clean and swifter
Than the swift deer escapes the yelping hound.
Swifter than wind they'll vanish into air!
(But if you'd get to know me as I am,
How could you run away? You'd kill yourself
For being much too coy and cling to me.)
I own this mountainside with all its caves,
Caves where the sun's midsummer heat turns cool,
And where the winter's cold turns warm in shelter.

   "'Each tree, each branch I own is thick with apples,
The grape bursts from the vine, or blue or gold,
And these are all for you—your hand may wander
Among flushed strawberries in forest green,

Cherries in October, and black-shaded plums,
Or if you will, the waxlike yellow, fresh-as-sunlight
Chestnuts, or for tart taste, arbute berry—
All these, then have me as your loving bridegroom,
Where every tree is yours for your desire.

"'All fine sheep are part of my estate,
Some in the valley, many in the forest,
Others are cared for through my winding caves.
If you would ask how many, I can't say.
Only the poor man counts his, head by head.
Or don't believe me—look, see that fat cow
Who staggers with her milk across the meadow?
And there are more: young lambs, young goats, young
            calves,
Stabled and warm. And snow-white milk to drink,
And some reserved for junkets and white cheeses.

"'As for the pets and creatures that I'll get you,
They'll all be rare: no small deer or tamed rabbits,
Or doves that seem to crowd these cliffs with young.
The other day I met a black she-bear
And took her cubs away, each like the other;
Come, tell me which is which, toys for your pleasure—
I thought, "I'll give these babies to my lady!"

"'Come, Galatea, from these deep blue waters,
White shoulders and that water-glittering hair,
Nor turn your head away—these gifts are yours.
And I've looked at myself, I saw my face
Shine where I saw it floating in a well;
The more I looked at it, the more I liked it.
I'm big as life, bigger than life, perhaps,
Jove in the clouds no bigger than myself—
For you've been saying he commands the heavens.
But me—look at the growth of hair in front,
It hangs before me; down my back it tumbles,
Good, rich, coarse hair all up and down my body.
Don't tell me man-grown hair is out of fashion;
A tree's not beautiful when grey and bare,
A horse without his mane's not fit to look at;

Feathers become a bird as wool does sheep,
So a deep-matted run of hair looks handsome
On any man who has the luck to wear it.
It's true I seem to have a single eye,
One eye that blazes bravely in my forehead,
Big as a shield. Sometimes it rolls. Why not?
The sun looks down from where he rides the heavens,
Sees everything and with a single eye.

"'My father is the king of neighbouring waters,
That much you know. He'll be your father-in-law.
But hear me, hear my pitiful remarks—
Poor words to move you, yet you are my goddess;
I fall to you alone. No Jove, no heaven,
No fiery thunderbolts can make me tremble;
My fear is you and you could kill me straightly
As though your anger were white shafts of lightning.
Cyclops has your contempt, but what of others?
I'd scarcely mind your sending me to hell,
But there is Acis. Why not Cyclops, too?
He likes himself, Jove damn us, you like Acis,
—For what? I'd love to hold him in my hands
To let him know I'd tear him tenderly;
First his sweet members, then an arm or two,
A thigh, perhaps—and drop them in this meadow,
Or toss them to the sea to sleep with you.
Look, I'm alive with fires everywhere,
Aetna's within me as he shakes my breast—
And you, dear Galatea, calm as day.'
He raved (I saw him clamber to his feet),
And, restless as a bull whose favorite cow
Escaped him as he lunged, he tramped through forest,
Then back across his pastures, known too well.
His great eye turned; it glared at me and Acis—
We weren't prepared for anything like that!
'That's where you are,' he said, 'my pretty lovers,
I'll crush your kisses in a last embrace.'
And like a Cyclops' voice it roared aloud
Until it shook Mount Aetna with its echoes.
The sea was near; I leaped, I slipped within it.
As my Symaethian hero rose to run,

He screamed, 'O Galatea, try to save me,
O father, mother, save me; I'm your son,
And since I'm almost dead, open your kingdom.'
Yet as he ran Cyclops was that much swifter;
He tossed a ton of mountain cliff in air,
And though wet clay and sod half missed the target,
A fragment was enough to bury Acis.
Then I—the only favour Fate permitted—
Used magic words to wake the magic arts
That Acis had as family heritage.
Soon blood began to wet the mound above,
Then came a stream that looked like melting snow,
Mixed with spring rains into a little river
That ran away to leave dry clay behind it;
Then the mound cracked and a great reed grew from it
Beneath split rock and clay, spring waters rippled.
And O, this was the miracle that happened:
A boy rose waist-high from the gushing river;
His new horns held a crown of twisted reeds.
Though he was sea-blue color, like a statue,
Larger than life, I knew the boy was Acis—
A river god whose river took his name."

GLAUCUS

When Galatea finished her romance
The sea nymphs floated off on gentle waves.
Since Scylla was afraid of deeper waters,
She turned to shore to walk along the beach,
At ease and naked, lovely as a picture,
To stroll the sands that drank refreshing waves,
Or when she needed rest, to bathe her feet
In little streams behind a moss-grown rock.
But look! She heard the calling of a shell,
A sea horn raised to Glaucus' lips, and he
A new arrival into blue deep seas;
Though once as mortal as most mortals are,
He had been changed into another creature;
The miracle took place at Anthedon.
Though he was in cold water to his waist,
When Glaucus saw the girl, he turned to fire,

And said things—anything—to hold her there.
Yet she escaped; she climbed a sheet of rock;
It was a mountain that looked out to sea
And cast its shadow over trembling waters,
Nor did she stop till she stood high enough
To stand at proper distance from the man.
She gazed at him and saw a blue-green creature,
Longhaired, and where his manly thighs should be
She saw a scaled and twisted fishy member
Was he a god? Or some aquatic devil?
He looked at her and leaned upon a rock.
"Dear girl," he said, "I'm neither fish nor fowl;
But something better; I've been made a sea god.
Nor Proteus, nor Triton, nor Palamon
Has greater prestige in these dangerous waters.
Once I was merely man, but loved the sea;
It was my life: one day, I netted fish,
The next, I used my skill at deft fly-fishing.
From where I fished there was a lovely meadow;
On one side waters formed a little bay,
The other side was hedged by green things growing—
Herbs which the fat horned cattle never touched,
Nor sheep, nor longhaired goats, nor bees for honey.
Nor were they plucked for garlands, summer crowns,
Nor were they trimmed by any hand I saw.
I was the first to sit among those grasses,
To stretch my lines, to dry my nets, to sort
The fish that nets had trapped, that hooks had fooled.
Then suddenly the fish began to swim,
To be as lively as they were at sea,
And as I looked, I saw them leap the meadow
To vanish in the sea. This kept me thinking,
What touch of magic made fish misbehave?
Was there some god at work or these strange herbs?
I stooped to pick the herbs, to see what happened;
I took a leaf to test it with my teeth—
Then my heart churned and all my body thirsted
To leap toward water. I could not resist it;
I cried, 'Good-bye to everything on land,
Tree, field, or flower; I won't be back forever!'
I threw myself to sea, and where I dived

The sea gods welcomed me. They thought me fit
To join their company. Then Oceanus
And Tethys were invoked to wash me clean
Of what I was before; they chanted rhymes,
Nine times around me singing guilt away,
And bathed me in a hundred sheets of water,
Until I felt all rivers pour upon me,
The voice of waters rushing through my head:
So much I knew; so much I can remember—
Beyond this all turned dark. And when I woke
I was another creature: mind, body, spirit
Were of another kind. I saw this beard
Which is as green as greenest green sea waters
And long green hair which always floats behind me,
Broad shoulders and blue arms, and legs that curl
Into a something like a fish's tail.
And yet today—why speak of what I wear,
Even if sea gods dressed me as their own,
Myself a god? I mean if you won't take me,
If you are shy—" but Scylla ran away,
And Glaucus, purple at her rude behaviour,
Swam off to see the golden court of Circe,
Daughter of the sun and queen of her fair island.

# BOOK XIV

*Though Ovid covers much of the same ground travelled by Virgil's* Aeneid, *he avoids comparison by cutting short the scene between Dido and Aeneas. The more colourful scenes in Book XIV are reserved for a purely Ovidian account of how Ulysses' men met the trials of living in Circe's kingdom. Roman distrust of Ulysses' heroism is clearly shown in Ovid's version of his wanderings; his desertion of friends, his faithlessness are stressed; we scarcely recognize the hero of* The Odyssey. *Our compensation for Ulysses' loss of stature is in the nearly baroque splendour of Circe's magic and her love for Picus. It is believed that Ovid invented the Circe-Canens-Picus romance which symbolizes (through Canens' name:* cano, *to sing) the bringing of song to the banks of the Tiber and to Rome. Book XIV also contains the delightful story of Pomona and the Cyprian romance of the boy Iphis and cold Anaxarete. The latter romance has a curiously modern air, particularly in the suicide of Iphis and the ironic bitterness of his dying speech.*

# BOOK XIV

Blue Glaucus, swimmer of the swollen waves
Turned west of Sicily to leave behind him
Great Aetna smoking on a giant's head,
The untilled fields where Cyclops held his acres,
Untouched by plough or sight of work-day cattle.
Back into distance fell the shores of Zancle,
Even Rhegium, city facing those wild shores
Across wild narrows where many ships went down.
Glaucus' huge hands were oars which swept him onward
Where Tyrrhene waters swayed for miles around him.
At last he came upon a green-hilled island
Where Circe lived, and Circe made him welcome.
"Dear Goddess, I have come to ask your favours;
Take pity on a god, if not a man,"
Glaucus cried out. "You, you alone can help me;
I'm in the very worst of love affairs.
Your island's full of magic herbs and flowers,
I know that magic well: it changed my life.
You might have heard some rumours of my case:
On the Italian shores, across the waters
From where Messene stands, I looked at Scylla.
I blush to tell you what I said to her,
How bland I was, the promises I made,
All like a lover's, yet the girl ran from me;
If—if there's magic in your songs, please charm her,
Or better still, if herbs can turn the trick
Of making her less cold, perhaps indifferent,
Try them on her. Don't worry about my heat:
I'd like to see her turn to melting fires,
To burn as I do now. Dear Goddess, help me!"
But Circe said (and no one more than she
Was ready to make love at any hour—

375

Whether she had an innate liking for it,
Or whether Venus, angry at Circe's father
Because he had betrayed her love for Mars,
Gave Circe more than ladylike desires,
We cannot say—except that she replied),
"Go find a girl or woman who's inclined
To be warm-hearted as yourself and eager—
And more than that, you need a full-grown goddess,
Even myself, a daughter of the sun,
Who has all charms to please you, songs and herbs,
And much besides. I'll take you as you are.
As for that girl, treat her as she treats you;
Take me to bed, and in one loving gesture
You'll give two women all that they deserve."
Glaucus in blind reply to her advances
Said, "Lady, trees shall take roots in these waves
And seaweeds grow on highest mountaintops
Before my love for Scylla fades away!"
Circe went white with rage (an understatement)
Yet could not strike at Glaucus (for she loved him)
And turned her violent mind against the girl:
She made a brew of herbs, and as she cooked them
She sang aloud songs learned from Hecate—
Singing that should make any mortal tremble.
Then with a blue stole thrust across her shoulders,
Ran through her palace where pigs, dogs, and lions
Leaped up to kiss her feet as she swept by.
At once she took her way toward Rhegium,
Across the straits from Zancle's rock-ribbed shores,
Then flashed (as though her feet touched solid earth)
Across the dancing waters of the sea.
Beyond the beach there was a small rock pool,
Bow-shaped as though designed for private bathing.
Scylla adored it. When the sun flared high,
Striking his midday heat from sky and water,
And shadows vanished from the face of earth,
Scylla took baths within her rock-cooled shelter.
Before the girl arrived, the goddess came,
And where the pool shone brightest, Circe poured
Her brew of evil roots and herbs, and over it
She said nine times, then three times more again,

The darkest spells that baleful lips could utter.
When Scylla came, she splashed waist-deep in coolness,
Then to her horror found her legs were gone.
And where her thighs should be, she saw a girdle
Of barking dogs' heads round her naked belly.
At first she tried to shake them off, to loose them,
Tear them away, but found
They grew out of the tender flesh below
Her breasts, as though wild Cerberus had twined
Himself a dozen times around her waist.
And there she sat, half naked girl, half monster
With mad dogs barking round her lower regions.

When Glaucus saw her, the unlucky lover
Wept like a child and swam away from Circe
Whose charms were much too violent for him.
Scylla stayed where she was; to match her hatred
With Circe's hatred of her, she destroyed
Ulysses' shipmates as they sailed the narrows.
She would have wrecked the Trojan fleet to splinters
If she had not turned to a grey rock mounting
The rugged shore line where she stands today,
A rock-faced horror that all sailors fear.

AENEAS VISITS CUMAE

When Trojan ships had safely glided by
Man-eating wild Charybdis and mad Scylla,
And sails were set to reach Italian harbours,
Winds drove them south to shores of Africa
Where the Aeneas met his famous Dido
Who gave him all she had of heart and home—
Unlucky queen, damned by her disposition
To take his loss too keenly when he left her!
Then on a pyre (lit as if it were
In praise of gods) she fell to darkest death,
Sword thrust between her breasts. Herself betrayed,
She then betrayed her life, her home, her country.
From his new city, raised on sand, Aeneas
Sailed back to Sicily to pay full homage
To his dear father's spirit, to light an altar

At old Anchises' tomb; then he raised anchor
Of Trojan ships that Iris almost fired,
And sailed away past the Aeolian Isles,
Past shores of sulphur fire smoking high,
Past rocks where sirens sang—and since his ship
Had lost its pilot, the Aeneas drifted
Toward stranger islands off the Cambrian coast,
Toward Ischia and the famous monkey island,
Where on a naked hill its creatures lived.
For Jove, shocked by the lies Cercopians told,
And all their nasty habits and stale crimes,
Changed them to beasts that looked a bit like men:
Legs short and thick, their noses flat and blue,
And each face wrinkled as an old man's or a baby's;
He grew long yellow fur from neck to feet
On all of them, which kept them warm but hideous;
And since their language was not fit for hearing,
He took away their speech, which left them chattering,
Or shrill or hoarse in ancient monkey fashion.

The Aeneas sailed past straight-walled Parthenope,
Where to his left he saw the bell-shaped tomb
Of Aeolus' son who blew a loud bright trumpet;
These were the shores of Cumae, the approach
A stretch of reed-grown waters and a cave
Where he stepped down to hear an aged sibyl.
The hero asked her: could he find his way
Down to Avernus to see his father's spirit?
Then as she lifted eyes from earth-fixed trances,
He saw them fill with frenzies of a god.
"My Lord," said she, "you ask for miracles,
Yet you have earned them by the things you've done,
By hand, by steel, by faith that walked through fire.
And what you ask, great Trojan, shall be yours:
I'll take you there; you'll see Elysium,
That newfoundland within the nether world.
There you shall meet with your dear father's ghost,
Nor any road closed to a man of virtue."
Through green dark aisles of Proserpina's forest
The sibyl pointed where a golden bough
Shone in the wavering shadows of Avernus,

Telling him to break it from the tree, to carry it,
And as Aeneas did so, as in dreams,
Drear Pluto's kingdom waked before his eyes.
And where he looked, he saw his ancestors,
Among them, white-haired and magnificent,
Ancient Anchises. As the shades received him,
Aeneas learned the trials of Death's own kingdom,
And trials he faced on Earth in future wars.
Then on the long climb upward back to Earth,
To pass the time, to make the road less laboured—
And when the way seemed lost in glimmering darkness—
He turned to her who led him up the slope:
"Whether or not you are a Heaven-born goddess,
Or demigoddess in the Heavens' great eye,
To me at least you've been the gift of Heaven
My life's been yours to spare, and by your mercy,
I've walked the ways of Death and been restored
To life again. And when these shadows pass
To scenes on earth, I'll raise an altar to you
With walls around that shrine to guard your honour."

The sibyl glanced at him, then drew her breath:
"No, I'm no goddess, nor should sacred fires
Be lit for you to praise mortality.
There's some mistake, for what you do not know
Is that an immortality came near me—
Or if my innocent chastity had yielded
In early moments of Apollo's favour.
And while his hopes ran high, he tempted me;
He said, 'My dear, my little friend of Cumae,
I'll give you anything your heart desires,
Or anything or all.' I pointed at
A swirling hill of sand (O, I was stupid!).
'Give me as many years as grains of dust
Are there,' but I forgot the best of it:
That I should be as young as I was then.
He promised me the years—and if I'd sleep
With him, I'd be forever then as now,
A girlish goddess resting in his arms.
But I said no, and took the years unmarried;
Summer is gone, and trembling old age follows,

And years to follow these, and more, and more,
Seven centuries gone by, nor sands nor dust
Is counted end of years; yet I must see
Three hundred seasons of the harvest moon,
Three hundred autumns of the purple vine.
So as my years increase, I shall grow less,
Withering beyond old age to small, then smaller,
Limbs, branches in the wind, then twigs, then feathers,
So dry, so small, so next to nothingness
It shall seem strange that I was someone loved,
Loved at first sight and cherished by a god.
Even Phoebus shall glance past me, seeing nothing,
And then say that he never looked at me.
Myself, almost invisible or vanished,
Shall be a voice, the last poor gift of fate."


## ACHAEMENIDES AND POLYPHEMUS

   The sibyl had her say. When she was done,
She and Aeneas finished their steep venture
Up from the underworld back home near Cumae.
Then after sacrificial rites he sailed
To shores still waiting to be named Caieta.
This was the very place where Macareus
(Friend of well-travelled and well-tried Ulysses)
Stepped off the boat after long misadventures.
And there he ran into Achaemenides
Whom they deserted in the wilds of Aetna;
He was surprised to see the man still living—
"What god preserved you? How do barbarous Greeks
Land from a Trojan ship? Have we gone crazy?"
Achaemenides, looking prosperous,
No longer dressed in rags, or less than rags,
Was quite himself again. He answered roundly,
"If I love home more than this Trojan ship,
Ithaca itself more than a Trojan rescue,
If I forget Aeneas or think he's done
Less for me than my father did before him,
Then send me back to Polyphemus Cyclops,
To see him wash his teeth in human blood,
To see him grin at me for his next dinner.

And if I gave Aeneas all I own,
My debt to him would still remain unpaid;
With every word I speak, each breath I take,
With each look upward at the sky, the sun,
Each time I see the wheeling Zodiac,
I bless the stars for which I thank Aeneas!
Remember the Aeneas! But for him
How could I breathe the light of life today,
Or know that Death would lead me to a tomb,
Rather than hell between the Cyclops' jaws?
How did I feel (fear took my senses) when
(Myself deserted) as I saw you sail—
Your ship take wings to steer the open seas?
I yearned to shout, to call you back, to save me,
And yet I feared the blinded Cyclops more.
Ulysses' shouting almost wrecked the ship;
The Cyclops took a mile of mountain-side
And hurled it through the air in your direction;
As though his giant arms were catapults,
He swung huge rocks to sea, and I, forgetting
That I was not on board, sweated in fear
His storm of falling granite, stones, and clay
Would shake the waves until the ship went down.
When you went out of range, he seemed to know it;
Groaning and blind he clambered—on all fours
He searched through Aetna, his great fingers raking
Forest and rock, and, as he lumbered, tearing
Great sides of flesh from naked arm and shoulder.
And then his bleeding arms reached out to sea
To curse the Greeks, to say something like this:
'O give me Greeks, Good Luck, give me Ulysses,
Or one of his Greek breed. I'll take them living
To eat them naked-raw, their lungs, their livers,
To wet my poor dry throat with their sweet blood,
To tear them gently and to taste their gooseflesh,
Still trembling as I close my teeth. O glory!
My loss of sight is nothing to my pleasure—'
I'm happy to forget the rest he said.
And when I saw his bloody face and hands,
His dead eye streaked with blood, his dirty beard,
White horror filled me—but to look at him

Brought lesser fears than what I had in mind.
Death walked before my eyes. 'He'll take me now,'
I thought, 'and my poor bones and skin to feed
That mountain body waiting for its supper';
For I had seen him pick up friends of mine
(Two Greeks in his right hand) and smash them gently
Three times—and then a fourth to make good measure—
Against the rocks, preparing them for dinner.
Then like a rough-haired lion at a feast
He settled down to eat, his head above them;
He sucked the marrow of their bones, their tender vitals,
Warm limbs, fresh blood. And as I saw him eat,
Working his jaws, spitting the bones away,
Or belching out the rest, I took a chill,
Terror in my bones, until I crawled away.
I knew what waited for me if he caught me.
I hid myself as best I could, but trembled
At sound of wind or footfall anywhere;
I caught a fear of death, yet welcomed it,
And at odd hours starved on grass, leaves, acorns,
Until—it seemed forever—I saw a ship,
Far off the coast. I waved, then ran to shore,
And hoped that someone saw my hopeless waving.
I seemed to move them and a Trojan ship
Then took a Greek on board! And now, my friend,
Tell me your story and your captain's trials."

CIRCE

     Then Macareus spoke up in reply,
And told how Aeolus swayed the Tuscan sea,
And how he kept the wildest winds confined,
Captured in bull-skin, handed as a gift—
A special privilege—to shrewd Ulysses
Who came from Dulichium and knew the sea.
For nine days they had luck with good stiff breezes;
They knew where they were going and saw land,
But on the tenth day things went wrong. Ulysses'
Shipmates, convinced the bull-skin held a treasure,
And envious of Ulysses anyway,
Ripped the bag open, and the winds escaped,

Storming the ship back to Aeolian harbours.
"Then," Macareus said, "we went to Lamus
In old Campania; Antiphates is king,
And with two others, I was sent to meet him;
One friend and I contrived to get away
(The old Campanians had a nasty habit
Of eating men alive); the third man perished.
Antiphates, we knew, was after us.
And as we ran, the natives came behind us,
Some throwing rocks, uprooted trees, and stones,
Sinking a few ships, and all men drowned in them;
And yet Ulysses and myself escaped—
Our ship steered free to sail another day!
We wept our losses and the way was long;
At last we reached a place—look over there!
You'll see it fading on the far horizon.
(I much prefer to look at it from here,
And you, true Trojan, since our wars are done,
And you, Aeneas, are a son of Venus,
You'd better keep away from Circe's kingdom.)
We anchored there but we did not forget
The Cyclops and our race from Antiphates.
We drew lots for the men who landed there:
Myself, the loyal Polites, Eurylochus,
And Elpenor who always drank too much,
And twice nine others marched toward Circe's palace.
As we stepped in the courtyard, suddenly
A thousand beasts leaped at us, wolves, she-bears,
And matron lionesses—what a crew
Of nightmares to receive her frightened guests!
Yet they were harmless—look, they wagged their tails
And licked our feet as though they came to kiss us.
Then girls came out to guide us to their queen,
Who sat remote in oriental splendour,
Wearing a golden veil across her shoulders,
Across her lap a glittering tapestry.
Her ladies were sea nymphs and dancing girls—
They weren't the kind who took up household labours
Like spinning wool or knitting comforters;
Their duties were to sort out herbs and flowers,
Group them in baskets, jars, and dainty vases,

While Circe who was skilled in botany,
And knew each leaf and petal like a druggist,
Instructed every move they made. She smiled,
And offered us the pleasures of the house.
The girls prepared a drink, sweet barley water,
Sweet wine (of heavy alcoholic content),
Rich honey topped with curds, to which was added,
By sleight of hand I think—and Circe did it—
A drop or two of drugs. Half dead with thirst
We drank the cup the Circe handed us,
And she, as if to give us further honours—
She lightly touched our hair, she seemed to crown us
With one stroke of her wand. Drunk—was I drunk?
(I hate to say how drunk, but might as well.)
The floor beneath me slipped and there I was
With pigskin growing on me, tough and hairy,
Grunting and snouted, thick-necked and mired;
And hands that held the drink up to my lips
Were trotters that smeared dirt along the floor.
They shut me in a pen; most of the rest
Of us were there, pigs like myself
(For the drink had power enough to pig an army).
Only straight Eurylochus stayed erect
And still a man who had turned down his drink—
If he had not, I'd be a pig today,
For he escaped to fetch Ulysses to us.
From Mercury who rushed down from Cyllene,
Ulysses got a fabulous white plant,
Sprung from black roots; the gods had called it 'moly'—
This with advice that Mercury advanced.
Ulysses stalked his way to Circe's chamber.
She offered him a drink, but when she rose
To crown him with her wand, he thrust the thing
Away and held her off. How the queen trembled
When he drew out his naked shining sword!
They shook hands with the promise of a wedding,
And since he was (although not quite) her husband,
He said he'd take the first advance toward dowry:
The bodies of his shipmates as they were.
Then we were watered by an antidote
Of what we drank before, our heads were tapped

By Circe's wand reversed, and magic songs
(Undoing magic was their purpose) sung aloud.
We raised our heads, then seemed to stand almost
On our hind legs, and as her songs went on,
We found our feet, our shoulders grew, our arms
Reached out to wind themselves around Ulysses.
We spent a year there; I saw everything
And had my fill of stories. I came to know
Four pretty girls of Circe's company,
The ones who helped her mix the drinks and flowers.
One was my favourite and grew confidential,
And on an afternoon (while Circe took
Her private pleasures with our noble captain)
The girl drew me aside and pointed at
A brilliant marble statue of a boy
Who wore a bird (species scansorial,
Genus Picidae) perched upon his head.
It was unusual, and more than that,
It stood in a small chapel and round its shoulders
Hung floral wreaths. It looked mysterious,
Nor could I stop myself from asking questions:
Who was it? And who prayed to it and why?
And why it had a bird above its forehead?
Then she replied 'Listen, dear Macareus;
This shows how Circe's magic works. That woman
Can get away with anything she chooses;
You'd better keep in mind the things I tell you.

## PICUS AND CANENS

"'Picus was known as Saturn's son, a king
Who had great love of horses, fine war horses,
He was as handsome as the statue is,
And when alive, the living image of it.
His soul as beautiful as what you see before you.
He was under twenty and his looks attracted
All dryads from the hills of Latium,
And as for fountain nymphs and river girls,
Whether from Albula or Numicus,
Or Anio, or where the brief Almo runs,
Or violent Nar or Farfar's shaded stream,

Or those who bathed where white Diana stood—
A statue of herself in forest waters—
All loved him to distraction when they saw him.
Yet he took none of these, and fell in love
With one who was conceived (so people say)
On green-hilled Palatine above the rivers.
The double-headed Janus was her father
(So some believed), Venilia, her mother.
When this sweet child was fit to take a man
Picus was chosen as the best of lovers,
And she, though rare enough in girlish beauty,
Had voice that made her singing rare delight:
Her name implied as much—they called her Canens.
When Canens sang, cold rocks were moved to tears,
Or seemed less granite than a rock should be,
The trees were swayed, rough beasts grew sentimental,
And busy rivers winding miles away
Began to rest, to float, to fall asleep,
And birds who heard her half-forgot to fly.
One day, as she amused herself by singing,
Picus like all Laurentians who go hunting
Went out to hunt the wild Laurentian boar.
Erect and gaily mounted on a charger,
He held a pair of spears in his left hand.
A gold brooch held the red cloak at his shoulder
As he came dashing through the field to forest.
Meanwhile that daughter of the Sun, Queen Circe,
Had left her own estate to pick fresh herbs
In hilly forest glades and green-dark places.
As though sun-struck—one look at the young rider
Made her feel faint—she dropped her herbs and flowers;
Heat mounted through her veins. When her mind cleared,
She thought of telling him how much she loved him,
And tried to call him while his horse flashed by,
His servants following in rapid chase.
She cried aloud, "If I know who I am
You won't go far, not if the wind should catch you,
Carry you up, and spirit you away—
Not if there's magic skill in magic flowers
And voice in me to sing my spells and charms."
Then by an effort of imagination

(And not too great, because her heart was in it)
She used telepathy and sent a shadowy boar—
It seemed quite real and Picus could not miss it—
Glancing across the path before his eyes.
It led him through a deeper run of forest,
Thickets and fallen trees, where horses falter,
Then stop. Young Picus straightway leaped to earth
To track the boarlike image that he followed
Deeper and deeper into wildernesses.
Meanwhile Circe repeated all she knew
Of certain charms that hid the moon's white face,
Even her father's face, in fog and mist.
Strange gods had given her unearthly powers,
So as she sang broad daylight disappeared,
As if the grasses grew dark swirling damps
That climbed the forest into farthest skies,
And all King Picus' men were lost within them,
Wandering in ghostly trails beyond the forest,
Far from their king, wherever he had strayed.
Then since he was alone, she came to meet him,
Saying, "O by your eyes that hold my own,
By all that's beautiful in what you are,
As fair, as young, as sweet as you, my lord,
Take me, even me, a goddess as I am,
And for the rest, a father by our marriage,
The Sun himself who sees all things on earth.
Come, neither shy nor cold, but take me now,
Your Circe and your Titaness in one!"
Then he turned savage: "No, I'm not your husband,
No matter who you are or hope to be;
For someone else has taken all my love.
I hope she holds it to the end of time;
She has my faith as long as Fate will keep her
My only Canens and old Janus' daughter."

     "'Since all her arguments to praise herself
Fell to the ground, the goddess lost her temper:
"But shall you walk free of my charms and pleasures?
You'll learn enough, nor shall your lady take you—
She's seen the last of you and what you are,
And then you'll learn how women take their losses,

When they have loved, lost, and been pushed aside,
And knowing that, you'll see what Circe does!"
Twice to west she swayed, twice to the east,
And three times one she stroked her wand across him—
And three times said her charm. He turned to run
Then found he took more speed than he could master;
He saw himself in air, wings at his sides;
And, mad with hate at what he had become,
He tore at heavy oaks with bill and claw,
And in his anger drilled through trunk and branches.
His wings shone red as the red cloak he wore;
His golden brooch ringed round his throat in feathers—
Nothing of Picus but his awkward name.
During this time and through the neighbouring hills,
Friends shouted "Picus, Picus," everywhere.
Since he was gone, and they discovered Circe
(Her clouds dissolved by rising wind and sun),
They said she plotted murder in her charms;
She had a guilty look; where was their king?
Either she'd bring him back—they raised their spears—
But she, too quick for them, thrust like a veil
Of raining mist her magic at their heads,
The distillation of a million herbs,
And called the ancient gods of night to help her,
Gods from Erebus, ever-falling Chaos,
And Hecate who heard her winding cries.
Then (strange to say) the forest seemed to float;
The earth groaned under it and trees, white-haired,
Were like an arbour turned to frost in winter,
And where her raining mist touched plants and grasses
Blood stained the ground and stones began to bark,
And through that midnight crawled snakes, horny lizards,
And souls of those long dead weaved through the air.
The young who witnessed horror in her magic
Shook with their fears and as she touched their faces
They changed from men to beasts who roamed the
            darkness.

    "'And now as falling Phoebus slipped behind
The shores of Spain, receding to the west,
Poor Canens' soul and spirit were in her eyes

That searched the twilight for her missing lover.
She sent her servants through the wandering night,
Lifting their torches high in hope to greet
Their master home to her; the midnight passed.
Nor could she find relief in usual gestures
Of wifely sorrow, though she tore her hair
And beat her naked breasts as women do;
She ran half mad across the countryside,
Six nights, six mornings of returning day,
Up hills, down valleys as the wind might take her,
Nor did she stop to eat or sleep the night.
Old Tiber was the last to look up at her,
To see her falling body sink beside him.
There, as the dying swan tunes her last music
To autumn leaves and winter silences,
So Canens sang her tears among the grasses
Fading in whispers of a funeral song,
Herself a silver veil of glancing water
That trembles into mist and disappears.
The place still holds the memory of her legend,
The very Muses who had heard her singing
Called it Camena to preserve her name.'

"In that long year I heard and saw enough,
Its careless life had dulled our wits and bodies,
And when at last we got our sailing orders,
And Circe told us of the big, wide sea,
Its pits and perils, which made my nerves uneasy,
I dropped my anchor here and stayed ashore."

### THE CONQUESTS OF AENEAS

With these words Macareus closed his lips,
And the Aeneas took himself to duty:
He placed his nurse's ashes in an urn
And on her tomb a two-line epitaph:
I AM CAIETA RESCUED BY MY SON
FROM GREEK TO HOLY FIRES SO LIKE MY OWN.
Then the Aeneas and his men set sail
From this green coast to steer beyond that country
Where evil Circe tempted men to ruin

To reach the forest where the green-hung Tiber
Empties sand-yellowed waters to the sea.
This place was where Aeneas got possession
Of land and daughter of the reigning king,
Latinus, who was known as Faunus' son—
In savage war, for Turnus claimed the girl
As his own bride, the battle thick with fighting,
Etruria closing in on Latium,
Both with their allies ranged against the other,
Rutuli set against the Trojan armies.
Aeneas got help from Euander's house,
But Venulus was far less fortunate
In getting aid from Greek Diomedes,
Who in his exile founded a big town
Within the southern country of King Daunus,
And took the land where he had raised that city
As partial payment of a wedding dowry.
When Venulus who served as Turnus' agent,
Asked for his help, Diomedes said no,
He had a lack of men, and his wife's father
Could not afford the loss of men in war:
"Nor my refusals based upon a lie,
And when I talk of what I cannot do,
I am all bitterness, for grief tears at my heart,
Yet I shall tell all for the sake of your belief.
When half of Ilium went up in smoke,
And Pergama devoured by Greek fires,
After heroic Ajax raped Cassandra
And made us share Minerva's rage against him,
Greek ships were battered by dark winds and waters,
By lightning and by rocky Caphereus—
Nor shall I tell each step of our disaster;
Even old Priam would have wept to see us.
And though Minerva rescued me from shipwreck,
I had offended Venus long ago
And I was forced to leave my fatherland,
Exiled from Argos to take greater hardships
Of rolling seas and hellish wars until I wished
I had been drowned when Caphereus wrecked us.
Then those who fought beside me in the wars,
And shared my misadventures on high seas,

Lost heart; they were dissatisfied and weary,
They would not follow further. There was one
Called Acmon who was fiery-tongued enough,
And our misfortunes made him twice as hot.
He said, 'Look, we've gone through the worst there is;
Suppose that Venus wants to wear us out,
Yet she can do no more. What can she do?
I'd like to see her try it. If we're afraid,
Our fears will leave us open to more trouble;
And if she hears me (and I think she does)
And if she hates the friends of Diomedes,
Bad luck to her, we'll give her our contempt;
We'll tell her that she's greater than a goddess!'
Of course this brought her anger back to life—
We tried to make him eat his words, some tried
To scold him, but his foolish voice grew thin,
Thin as his throat, and little feathers came
All over him; he got enormous wings,
Great flat-toed feet, and a long-scissored bill.
His friends, Nycteus, Abas, Rhexenor,
And Idas too, looked at him as a freak,
And as they gazed, they turned to birds like him,
Fantastic creatures, very much like swans,
Yet not as handsome and a bit unpleasant;
They circled over men who manned the oars,
Flapped wings, and flew away. Now I'm married,
Most of my friends are gone; I plough the desert
Where my wife's father rules a wretched country."

That's what Oeneus' grandson had to say,
And Venulus left the land of Calydon,
Past Peucetia's bay and Messapia.
There in an arbour under shadowy willows
And where tall grasses sprouted from the sea,
He saw a cave, a place that half-goat Pan
Takes for his own, and not so long ago,
A group of nymphs adopted it for shelter.
An Apulian shepherd came that way,
Which made them run for cover till they saw
He was less dangerous than downright foolish—
While they resumed their nymphlike ballet dancing.

But he who had no taste for female graces
Began to shout for partners down the middle;
Then did a barn-dance turn with jigs and reels—
To say the least, his talk was unrefined.
And on he went, until he found himself
Speechless and wooden as an olive tree
Which he became—uncultivated olive,
Whose fruit, quite like the language he used
Was crude and wild, and looked a bit obscene.

When legates had come home with the bad news
Of no help from the hopeless Diomedes,
The Rutuli fought on as best they could—
A bloody war, until (for a surprise)
Turnus threw fiery torches at the ships,
And what survived from shipwreck was endangered
By fire itself: the flames of Mulciber
Raged through dry pitch and pine, climbed up the masts,
As if to eat the topsails and the bridge.
The hulls burst into smoke—then the great mother
Of all the gods remembered that her trees,
The very pines and oaks that grew on Ida,
Had taken fire in the wooden ships;
She burst upon the scene with noise of cymbals
And wild flutes, while through the air
Her leonine chariot swayed above the battle.
"Turnus," she cried, "your filthy, dirty hands
Shall not destroy whatever I call mine,
Nor any ship that grew on sacred Ida."
And as she spoke there was a clap of thunder;
Hail, rain, and those mad children of the wind
Stormed down to lash the waves. Guided by her,
Great mother of all life, they tore the moorings
Of Trojan ships that floundered, headlong, down
Beneath the rolling waves. An instant later
Ships' sides began to yield, to breathe, to swim:
The figureheads changed into nymphlike features,
Oars into thighs and legs, cross-trees to arms,
Keels into spines and ropes to winding hair,
And all blue-green as ships that sail the sea.
And though these very nymphs once feared deep waters,

They dived and rode the waves in girlish rapture;
No longer dreaming of steep cliffs and mountains,
They lost the memory of their native homes,
Yet they remembered their late misadventures,
Their lives as ships at sea, wave-scarred and lost
And showed their feeling for frail yachts in trouble
By buoying them up on gliding hands and shoulders—
But not if ships were Greek; they knew of Troy
And how it fell, and held resentment
'Gainst every Greek who dared to draw his breath.
They smiled to see Ulysses' ship in splinters
And laughed aloud when Alcinoüs' clipper
Turned into stone and scraped the ocean's floor.

Some hoped that when their navy turned to mermaids
The Rutuli would read that sign as warning
To stop the war—but still the war went on,
Gods ranged on either side to help their favourites,
And both sides took their stand, brave as the gods.
They even lost the reason why they fought,
Even forgot the virgin bride-to-be,
Her father's name, and all his wealthy kingdom.
They fought for nothing else but victory
Against the thought of yielding to defeat.
At last the goddess Venus saw her son
Aeneas take the field and win the day:
Turnus defeated, and Ardea fell
(Which in his time became a prosperous city).
Yet after the invader did his worst,
And Ardea's walls were white-ringed hills of ashes,
A strange bird flapped his wings above the ruins
(The like of him was never seen before!).
His wailing cries, his pallor, his starved look—
And quite appropriate to defeated cities,
Even the red stare of a heron in distress—
Were in that bird who took the city's name,
In Latin "Ardea," a fiery touch,
And twice as deadly when he clapped his wings.

Aeneas pleased the gods by his fine spirit.
Even Juno checked her prejudice against him

(The house of Iulus shone in his bright eye,
His son the founder of a brilliant line).
Himself the son of Venus in her glory,
Was well prepared to take his place in Heaven.
Then Venus came to Jove and with both arms
Slipped round his neck began to ask for favours:
"Dear Father, you have never been unkind,
Unthoughtful, mean, ungenerous to me,
But one gift more, my love, for my Aeneas,
Your darling grandson and a perfect heir.
Give him one touch of immortality—
Or large or small, it really doesn't matter.
But one ride over gloomy Stygian waters,
One look at that unhappy place beyond it,
Are trials enough for any son of mine."
The gods agreed; not even the queen-goddess
Stared with a fixed face at the crowd before her,
But with a placid look gave her approval.
Then, fatherly and easy, Jove replied,
"O, both of you have earned a sign from heaven,
Or what you please; take what you wish, my dear,
This with a father's blessings on his daughter!"
Venus was glad enough to thank her father;
Even as he closed his lips she sailed through air,
On light-reined doves to carry her away
Toward the Laurentian shores where Numicus
Winds his pure waves through shadowing reeds and
            grasses
To pour refreshing waters to the sea.
Then she instructed him to wash Aeneas
Clean of mortality, its taint, its sorrows
Down quiet streams to secret ocean wells.
The hornèd god of the river took his orders;
And all the mortal features of Aeneas
Were washed away in silver-flowing waters.
Only the best were left; his mother dressed him,
Handsome as ever, in immortal essence—
A kind of perfume that the gods enjoy—
And after that she touched his lips with nectar
And made him godlike in his taste for drinking,
Which filled his veins and which the Romans call

Indigenous when they drink a local wine
Or raise a temple up to praise the gods.

## LATER KINGS OF ALBA

From that day onward, Alba and its nation
Were ruled by kings who followed in this order:
Ascanius (one whose other name was Iulus),
Then Silvius and then his son Latinus,
Who took that name for patriotic reasons,
Then famous Alba after him; Epytus;
Capys came after him, then Capetus;
Then Tiberinus, since he lost his life
By swimming in that yellow Tuscan river,
Gave it his name—and that's how he's remembered.
His sons were Remulus and brave Acrota;
The elder boy was Remulus, who tried
To outshout thunder, but fierce lightning killed him.
The other, less ambitious than his brother,
Gave up his rights to able Aventinus,
Who ruled the nation from his favourite hill
Which took his name, and now he's buried there.
Proca came next and swayed the Palatine.

## POMONA AND VERTUMNUS

In Proca's reign there lived a nymph, Pomona,
Who literally bloomed at raising flowers;
She had a "green touch" and made fruit trees bear.
That's how she got her name, but was indifferent
To other trees or how bright rivers ran.
Her one delight was tending fields and orchards;
She never went out hunting, but instead
Held a curved knife in hand which trimmed rough hedges,
Rose-bush or cherry—or a clever twist
Would save a fruitless tree and pierce for grafting
An aged trunk to make large apples grow.
Each orchard was her private nursery:
No tree went thirsty, every root was watered;
Each held her love, her care, nor was she tempted
By what sweet Venus prompted for diversion.

To keep crude country lovers out of reach,
She locked her garden gates against mankind.
O how young satyrs danced to catch her eye!
And Panish creatures with their naughty horns
In pine-wreath head-dress, and well-worn Silenus,
Who kept himself alive with young ideas;
Even that nameless god whose single member
Is pointed as a sickle when it rises
And frightens certain people when they see it—
What did these creatures do to tempt Pomona?
They couldn't do enough. Vertumnus tried;
He deeper than all others fell in love,
Yet had the same results: no luck at all.
He came dressed as a harvester and gay
To offer her a basket of sweet barley,
The very image of an Italian farmer!
As if he came from raking fields of hay,
He'd talk to her with hayseed in his hair;
Then he'd come up with iron spur and whip
As though his oxen were turned out to pasture,
Or come as handy man about the farm,
Carrying a ladder and a pruning knife,
As though his whole intent was picking apples;
Then as a soldier in his battle-dress,
Or lazy fisherman with flies and tackle.
Because he came in many ways to greet her,
He saw her often and got her permission
To look his fill at a respectful distance.
One afternoon he came dressed as a woman,
Bright-turbaned and grey-haired, bent on a stick,
Who stumbled as he walked around the garden,
Saying how fine the apples were, and peaches.
"But you, my dear," he said, "are better-looking,"
And kissed her with more fervent admiration
Than any elder woman would admit.
Then, sinking to the grass, he raised his eyes
To stare at branches hung with autumn's wealth,
Particularly at an elm whose boughs
Were intertwined with grapes, so ripe, so round,
So almost perfect that they charmed the spirit,
And for a while they held him hypnotized.

At last he said, "If that tree stood alone,
We'd look at it because its leaves are pretty;
That would be all. And if that clinging vine
Remained unmarried to the helpful tree,
We'd see it fade away in weeds and grasses.
You haven't read the fable of the vine;
You're still unmarried and you hope to stay so.
If you could change your mind! You'd have more lovers
Than Helen or the girl who caused a war
Between Centaurs and the Lapithae,
Or wife of the Ulysses (who was brave
Whenever he crossed swords with timid men).
And though you turn your face away from lovers,
You have a thousand—count them—men and gods,
And demigods—all those who claim the least
Divinity within these Alban hills.
Now if you have a touch of wisdom left,
Select your man today, and hear someone,
An ancient woman like myself who loves you
More than all lovers, more than you can know!
Forget the ordinary run of men,
And take the best. I speak for Vertumnus—
I know him just as well as he knows me.
He's no world traveller, roaming here or there,
But knows the neighbouring hills like his right hand,
And lives not far from here, and far from being
Like your professional lovers (most men are),
Who fall in love with every girl they see,
You will be first and last; his life is yours.
Remember that he's young and fresh and charming,
And that his ways have an Italian air—
That he can fit himself to any mood,
Do what you tell him, and then do it better!
He has a liking for all things that please you;
And he's the first to touch, appreciate
Your lovely harvest gathered in his hands.
But more than to the beauties of your garden,
He turns to you, to take you in his arms.
Be kind to him, be more than kind, have mercy
On him who loves you even as my lips speak,
Asking for love of you his own desire.

Remember Venus, who takes fearful toll
Of those who wear hard hearts in human bodies.
Remember gods in heat and Nemesis
(Who can forget whatever she remembers!).
To warn you of the dangers I have known
(I've known the worst in many years of thinking),
I'll tell a story that's familiar to
My friends on Cyprus, which may make you easy,
More tolerant, perhaps, and less severe.

### IPHIS AND ANAXARETE

"Young Iphis, born of parents no one knew,
Walked out one day and saw Anaxarete,
A careless queen of ancient Teucer's family,
Who if she glanced at you would stare you down.
He gave one look at her and went all fire
In love that burnt his bones and singed his hair.
For many days he fought for self-control,
But learned that hot blood's never cooled by reason,
And like a beggar haunted her back door.
He met the servants, found his lady's nurse
And told how much he loved the child she cherished.
His voice was ardent and he flattered her—
She must be kind!—and then he wrote love letters,
Soft words that servants carried to their queen.
He draped the lintel of her house with flowers
Watered with tears, and threw himself below it,
Weeping to learn that she had locked the door.
Yet she who had less feeling than the tide
That rises as the Goat-Stars seem to fall,
As cold and harder than a shaft of steel
Tempered and hammered in a German fire,
As stubborn as a rock that clings to earth,
She laughed and turned away—and what she said
Had more contempt than anything she did.
This last was far too much for him to bear;
After his torments one sharp word would break him.
Suddenly he shouted through the silent door,
'Anaxarete, you have won the battle!
Hail victory, and think of me no more!

Go kiss yourself to sleep in all your glory
And blaze a golden wreath upon your hair!
Win! Win! And I am happy to be dead,
Cheers and more cheers, iron and steel forever!
There is one way I know you'll love to see me,
Yet I'll remind you life and love are one;
Two lights go out—my love for you and life.
Nor will you hear the story of my death;
I shall be here and the unyielding light
Of your cold eyes will shine against my body.
O gods, if you look down on what I do
(I'm bad at prayers, my tongue is too unsteady),
Try to remember me and give my story
A future that my life shall never know,
A fame at least as long, as many years,
As hours you've stolen from my span of life.'
The boy threw up white arms to toss a rope
High to the lintel where he'd hung his flowers,
And making it secure he paused to say,
'How does my fatal lady like this wreath?'
Then, with his face still turned in her direction,
He dropped to hang; his feet banged at her door—
A knock that seemed to tell unknown disasters.
The servants cut him down, but all too late,
And since his father had been dead for years,
Carried their burden to its mother's house.
She rocked it in her arms, repeating words,
The futile words unhappy parents say,
And did what poor unhappy mothers do,
And walked a weeping mile through city streets
To lay the body on its cleansing fires.
Anaxarete's house stood near the pyre,
And through its walls she heard the sound of tears
—The gods of vengeance hovered over her.
The girl was moved to say, 'We'd love to see
A wild and weeping miserable funeral,'
And ran upstairs to lean from open windows.
When she looked down at Iphis on his pyre
Her eyes grew fixed upon the thing that held them,
And she grew white as white; blood left her body,
Nor could she turn away from what she saw,

Nor leave the window; there she stood and slowly
The chilled dry veins of marble in her heart
Spread to each vein that once had warmed her blood.
She was all statue, motionless in stone.
To prove this story's true, in Salamis
There is a statue that looks like this lady,
And over it they've built a lovely temple,
Raised, as they say, to house The Staring Venus.
Now come, my dear, to find yourself less cold;
This is no season to resist a lover;
Let's hope no April frost stains apple blossoms,
Or rough winds sweep their flowers to decay."

When the young god had finished his brief sermon
And learned that elderly advice was not
The kind of speech that moved the fair Pomona,
He dropped the dress he wore as an old woman,
And stood as naked as the Sun before her,
Himself as Sunlike as the Sun in glory
Breaking through clouds that held his face in darkness.
With or without consent he stood to take her,
But she, so dazzled by his godlike figure,
Took mutual warmth and melted in his arms.

## OTHER KINGS OF ITALIA

Then after Proca came crooked Amulius
Who ruled Italia with storm troops and tyranny;
Then senile Numitor and his young grandson
Took back the throne and city walls rose up
To celebrate the Shepherd's Holiday.
Then Tatius and Sabine ancestors
Went out to war, and faithless Tarpeia
(Since she revealed a secret way to Rome)
Gave up her ghost by calling up the guards
To bury her beneath their shields and spears.
The Sabines like a voiceless gang of wolves
Came down to Rome while Romans were asleep
To smash the gates that Romulus had battled;
Juno herself could not resist the pleasure
Of slipping back one bolt with silent ease,

And one gate swung ajar. Only sweet Venus
Had seen the trick and would have locked the gate,
But changed her mind, for gods cannot undo,
Or good or bad, what other gods have done.
The water-nymphs of Roman Italy
Lived near the place where Janus had a chapel,
And where they lived they had a well to bathe in,
Lovely and cool. When Venus asked their favour
(Not one of them would fail to help the goddess)
They turned the well into a rushing fountain.
Until that day the road that Janus guarded
Was like a public highway, cleared for traffic;
No one had ever seen a flood across it.
Within the rocks beneath their favourite well
The nymphs made fires fed by tar and sulphur
Which made their fountain boil in clouds of steam—
Water as cold as Alpine snows in winter
Smelled like the gates of hell and hot as fire.
As for the Roman gates which now swung open
To let the Sabines in—what good were they?
Even the hinges smoked with hellish tar—
Until the Roman Army dressed for war.
Then Romulus had everything his way;
First in the field, he led the charge to battle,
And soon the field was filled with fallen men,
Sabine and Roman, like a civil war,
For Romans murdered Sabine women's fathers.
They stopped before they wiped each other out;
They thought it best to have a brace of kings—
And Tatius joined his reign with Romulus.

    Soon Tatius fell dead and Romulus
Gave equal justice to both sides at war.
And as Mars put his helmet to one side,
He raised his head to Jove and said, "Our Father,
Since Rome no longer sways this way or that
Toward one man's will or strength or disposition,
But is a state as strong as its foundations,
The time has come to give a sign of merit
Promised to me and to your noble grandson—
I speak of Romulus—to raise him up,

To sweep him off the earth and up to heaven!
One day in open meeting of all gods
(I've memorized the speeches that you've made,
Each word a jewel—I'll cherish them forever),
I heard you say, 'There's one and only one
That Mars will choose to carry in his arms,
To find a place in our bright Heaven for him.'
And now's the time to put your words in action."
The father of all being bowed his head;
The skies grew dark and lightning lashed the earth.
From this Mars knew Jove's promise was secure,
And vaulting with his spear he leaped aboard
His blood-stained chariot and cracked his whip.
Descending through the air he glided near
The green-hilled Palatine where Romulus
Was handing out (with splendid moderation)
New laws to waiting lines of citizens.
Mars took his arm and swept him off the earth.
Then, as a ball of lead shot from a sling
Becomes a nothingness in distant air,
The mortal features of brave Romulus
Vanished before he reached the heights of Heaven.
Quirinus was the heavenly name they gave him,
And beauty fit to rest in godlike ease
And wear the clothes that the immortals wear.

Meanwhile his wife was sure that he had left her.
And when great Juno learned of her distress,
She ordered Iris to inform the lady
Of all the honours of a widowed queen:
"Shine, lovely lady of our Roman glories
(Or Sabine-Roman glories would be better!),
Wife of a man too great for Earth to hold him.
Who is no less than sacred Quirinus.
Come weep no more, be glad you are a widow,
And if you wish to see him, so you may.
Come, walk with me a mile to that green hill—
Quirinus Hill that has those lovely trees
Above the temple of the king of Rome."
Iris slid down to earth in rainbow fashion
And gave Hersilia greetings from Queen Juno,

Repeating every word that Juno uttered.
Hersilia, with a flutter of eyelashes,
A downward glance, and then a lifted face,
Said, "O dear Goddess (I don't know your name,
But your sweet face has a familiar look,
Which makes me sure that you're a goddess too!)
Please let me see my husband as he is.
One look and that will be my look at Heaven!"
They walked together up the shaded hill
That took the name of Romulus forever,
And there a star came down from heights of heaven
To blaze Hersilia's hair in golden fires;
Then with the star she vanished into air.
The god who founded Rome and made her famous
Received his wife as though she were at home,
He called her Hora; she became a goddess,
And made her second marriage in the skies.

# BOOK XV

*Not only did A. E. Housman show his knowledge of Ovid
through his comments on* Ibis, *one of Ovid's last and least
successful poems, but traces of how well he knew him come
to light in poem LXII of* A Shropshire Lad, *starting with the
line, "There was a king reigned in the East." The subject is not
Ovidian, but the manner is; it is light, ironical, and easy. The
King Mithridates of Housman's poem is scarcely mentioned
in Book XV. Ovid's comments on Julius Caesar's death, with
all the portents of disaster preceding it, are reflected in Plu-
tarch's life of Caesar, and in turn are familiar to all readers
of Shakespeare's* Julius Caesar. *At the very least one can say
that Ovid's mythological recital of Roman history in Book
XV caught the spirit of Rome as it entered the Christian era.
The old gods were fading into a maze of superstitions, and,
in that twilight, joining forces with Asiatic and Egyptian dei-
ties. Ovid viewed the scene with well-sustained scepticism,
yet remained confident of his own immortality. He had given
the ancient world an Ovidian mythology.*

# BOOK XV

And after Romulus, there was another choice
Difficult to make—for who could equal him,
Carry the weight he carried like a king?
Yet popular choice had made the best decision
And took the famous Numa as its ruler.
Nor was he satisfied with what he knew
Of Sabine peoples and the Tuscan north,
For his great spirit saw a larger world,
And sought to learn the secrets of all things,
All men and mysteries of metaphysics.
His passion for the truth made him leave home,
So on he went from Cures to the south,
South to Crotona, to that ancient city
That welcomed Hercules. When Numa asked
An old man of that town
Who knew the local gossip all too well,
The how and why Greek culture settled there
And spread its roots within Italian shores,
The town historian replied as follows:
"When Hercules, the blessed son of Jove
Crossed ocean with a wealth of Spanish cattle,
Good luck had brought him to the happy shores
Of old Lacinium with its young grasses.
And while his Spanish creatures ate their fill,
The demigod himself was welcome guest
At Croton's house, which gave him room and board,
The kind of rest he needed from long labours.
And as he left his generous host he said,
'Your great-great-grandchildren far in the future
Will find your house to build a city here.'
All true—that was the very thing that happened.
Alemon in Argos had a son, Myscelos;

Myscelos was a favourite of the gods.
As he lay fast asleep, the great club-swinging,
Tall Hercules leaned over him to speak:
'Wake up, my dear, to leave your bed and home.
Follow the rock-bound courses of the Aesar
Down far away in south-winged Italy.'
He said much more to warn the boy of terror
If he did not leave home—at which sleep vanished
As quickly as the god rose out of view.
Then as Myscelos woke he recollected
The vision he had had, the frightful warning;
Though he said nothing, for his temper was discreet,
His mind was haunted by the god's command.
He lived in doubt: he had been told to go,
Yet could not leave his country for its laws
Said No to everyone who left the place,
And if one tried to leave, the price was death.
One evening when the Sun concealed that glowing
Bright face of his below the Ocean's waves,
And from those waters came the dark of Night
To raise her starlit head against the skies,
Then came a wraith of Hercules before him,
Who spoke again but made each warning seem
A curse that murdered him—if he stayed home.
He was all fear, and rushed to pack his things,
To ship them off to newfoundlands away.
But talk around the city caught him up;
He was arrested as he turned to go.
His trial was called, and 'guilty' was the word,
The guilt so clear no witness spoke for him,
While poor Myscelos threw his hands up, praying,
And raised his face to cry, 'O Hercules,
You went through half a dozen trials, six more,
And your reward was a fine seat in Heaven.
O help me, help me, for you made my crime!'
In ancient times justice was served at trials
By dropping black or white stones in an urn:
The black for 'guilty' and the white 'acquittal.'
The vote for Myscelos was deadly black,
But when the urn was emptied on a table,
The black stones were as white as alabaster—

A very miracle of Hercules
Who turned the vote in favor of Myscelos
To set him free, for which Myscelos thanked him,
And with a friendly wind blown in his favour,
Set sail across the fair Ionian waters:
Past old Calabria, the Salentine,
Neretum, Sybaris, and Tarentum,
Past Siris Bay and the Crimisan port,
Skirting the coast of the Italian heel—
And there he found the mouth of Aesar's river,
And near it, underneath an earthen tomb,
He found the place where Croton's bones were buried.
And as his patron god instructed him
He planted city walls upon the spot
And named the place Crotona for the honour
Of Hercules and his remembered host."
This was the ancient and official story
Of how that city came to Italy.

THE PHILOSOPHER

Because he hated tyrants and their habits
A man of Samos left his island home
And came to Croton for his place of exile.
Although the gods lived many miles above,
Up in the clouds beyond the great blue sky,
He kept them near by grace of heavenly thinking;
Whatever Nature would not let him see
He saw with clarity of mind and heart.
The intellectual vision of his spirit
Showed him the universe, all things in order.
And when he felt that what he saw was true
He entertained the public with his knowledge,
And silent crowds were captured in the spell
Of what he had to say: first came first causes,
How the great world began, what is Divine,
The source of all things, whether of snow or lightning,
Or was Jupiter's fire in the thunderbolt—
Or was that tearing noise and flash of light
The storm of winds within the roaring clouds?
What unknown power shakes and splits the earth?

What law holds stars within their ancient cycles?
These mysteries of all things dark to man—
And he the first of vegetarians,
Dispraising meat as diet, he the first
(Though not accepted in this prejudice)
To speak of such things with authority:

   "Come, all of you who claim mortality
Should look on meats as poison to your bodies—
Unholy fuel to feed unholy fires.
Here are the fruits of life—of field and orchard:
Apples that sway their branches to the ground,
Ripe, ripe are they, as grapes that crowd the vine,
The rich soil yielding tender roots and grasses,
Which, placed above a fire, are yours to taste,
Nor is there lack of milk and flowing honey
To make a feast that smells of flowering thyme.
Yours are the gifts of earth who spends her riches
Without the taint of butchery and blood,
As some wild creatures tear at flesh for dinner—
And yet not all: look at the gentle herds
Who feed on grass, not like Armenian beasts,
Tiger, mad lion, wild wolf, and roving bear,
Whose rapture is a bloody feast at noon.
Unnatural flesh that feeds on flesh, on blood
For its own blood, body in body
So like its own, swells its own fat, its bowels
With living breathing creatures of its kind!
Here where the best of mothers, our dear Earth
Surrounds you with her riches to each taste,
Men eat the sad flesh of the murdered beast
That's tamed for killing, and their mad teeth tearing
At flesh the way a Cyclops has of eating!
Life eating life to feed the devouring belly
That never eats enough of flesh that dies!

   "Yet the first age of man, a golden age
We named it, for that hour brought us wealth,
A golden summer of the trees in fruit,
And where we walked sweet-tasting roots and grasses,
Nor any man pollute his lips with blood.

Birds took to air without a thought of danger,
And where the fields lay open to the plough,
Meandering rabbits had no thought of fear,
Nor did the fishlike innocence of fishes
Hang them on hooks that swung them in midair.
No traps and no betrayals—all was peace,
Nor was there guilt, or anything gone wrong,
Yet someone (who is not to be admired)
Saw what the lions ate and thought it good,
And as he tore raw meat between his teeth
He led the way toward death and infamy.
Though at first, perhaps, in self-defense,
A raging beast was butchered by cold steel,
Stained with hot blood, and turned to furious heat
(For we must save ourselves when life's in danger),
The actual horror was eating what was killed.

     "From this men entered into deeper crimes;
The legend runs as follows: first the pig
(Because her snout had furrowed up young sprouts,
And spoiled a crop of winter wheat in seed)
Was killed, then roasted at the altar's fires.
Next came the goat who tore at sacred vines,
Ruined the grape, and died before he knew it;
His punishment was death at Bacchus' altar—
For these two creatures made their own undoing!
But sheep, poor sheep—why were they fit for slaughter,
The peaceful sheep who yield us milk and wool,
Warm cloaks to wear, and when alive and stirring
Give us far more than when they drop down dead?
Look at the ox, a simple-minded beast,
Loyal, innocent, and kind, and born to labour—
Has he done anything that's counted wrong?
You'd call a man a crazy, thoughtless fool
Who hasn't earned the right to reap his barley,
The gift of earth, or oats or corn or wheat,
Who, as he lifts the burden of the plough
From his companion's back, then murders him,
Raises an axe to strike across his shoulders,
Raw with the labours of the plough and bent
Pulling through roots and earth to sow new harvests.

Beyond this, deeper evil, for men forced
Themselves to think the gods had joined them
In their delight of blood poured from the ox!
Next came the bull for slaughter—handsome creature
Whose own good looks, decked out with golden horns,
Made him a tempting figure at the altar,
Who heard—of course he could not understand—
The words that spoke his doom in the priest's prayer,
Nor know the meaning of the scattered barley
Between his horns—grain he had helped to sow—
Nor of steel knives seen mirrored in a pool,
Wet with hot blood that gushes from his throat.
And as he falls, his very bowels are ripped
From breast and side, gazed at and read
To find the will of heaven (so quick, so eager
Is man's desire to touch corrupting meat).
And this is how the brotherhood of man
Takes courage when it seats itself at dinner;
But as you eat your joints of lamb and beef,
Remember that I've warned you of your pleasures,
Know that your feast was of good friends and neighbours.

   "Now that a god has moved my lips, my spirit,
His voice shall be my voice, my will his will.
Even now the doors of Delphi open wide
And oracles of heaven speak aloud.
The great Unknown that men have never seen
Shall be the things I sing, the first and last.
So let us walk the skies among the stars
To see earth fade in dreary wilderness,
Ride clouds in glory, climb to Atlas' shoulders,
Lean from that pulpit over men below us
Where none among them knows where he is going,
Lost, strayed, and fears the way beyond himself:
And as I speak unwind the chains of fate.

   "Men who seem born to die, and chilled by death,
Why tremble when the river Styx is mentioned,
Or names that foolish poets have in mind,
All nightmares of a world that never was?
The body that you wear—why think of that?

As for these poor disguises of our flesh
Whether they rise in smoke from funeral pyres,
Or, as time wears them, turn to rags and bones,
Once they're consumed, they know no pain nor evil.
Our souls survive this death; as they depart
Their local habitations in the flesh,
They enter new-found bodies that preserve them.
Back in another age (this I remember)
I was Euphorbus of the Trojan war,
Whose brave advancing breast took the great spear
Thrust by the Menelaus through ribs and heart,
And hung there like a lance that pierced a cage.
Not long ago I strolled through Juno's temple
Set up in Argos, which is Abas' city,
And there I saw the shield that once was mine!
Which proves that all things change, yet never die.
Or here or there, the spirit takes its way
To different kinds of being as it chooses,
From beast to man, from man to beast; however,
Or far or near or strange, it travels on.
As wax might take new shapes in many figures,
None quite the same, the same wax lives within it—
So does the soul pass through its transformations.
If an unholy passion takes the soul,
I warn you as your prophet, soul is evil.
Stop these unholy killings day or night,
Of brother souls, perhaps, each murder-tainted,
Each damned by feeding blood with blood forever!

"And so I ride (which is my metaphor)
A full-sailed ship upon an endless sea,
A universe where nothing stays the same,
Sea, sky, wind, earth, and time forever changing—
Time like a river in its ceaseless motion;
On, on, each speeding hour cannot stand still,
But as waves, thrust by waves, drive waves before them,
So time runs first or follows forever new:
The flying moment gone, what once seemed never
Is now, which vanishes before we say it,
Each disappearing moment in a cycle,
Each loss replaced within the living hour.

"Perceive how darkness turns to purest light,
Midnight to morning, then the blazing Sun;
Nor do the heavens keep the same complexion
Beyond the midnight hours of sleep and rest.
When Lucifer rides out on his white stallion
Another colour fills the rising sky,
Or when Aurora comes to wake the morning
In tint of roses to receive the sun.
The great round shield of Phoebus blazes red
From under Earth and glows in scarlet fires
When it declines beneath the Earth again,
Yet when his shield has climbed the highest Heaven
It is all whiteness, for the air around it
Is farthest from the taint of blood-red Earth.
Nor does Diana ever look the same
From night to night; if she is growing toward
The fullness of her time her face is less
Than it shall be the nights beyond tonight,
Or larger now if she is turning thin.

"And more? Of course! Look at the four-spaced year
That imitates four seasons of our lives:
First Spring, that delicate season, bright with flowers,
Quickening, yet shy, and like a milk-fed child,
Its way unsteady while the countryman
Delights in promise of another year.
Green meadows wake to bloom, frail shoots and
          grasses,
And then Spring turns to Summer's hardiness,
The boy to manhood. There's no time of year
Of greater richness, warmth, and love of living,
New strength untried. And after Summer, Autumn,
First flushes gone, the temperate season here
Midway between quick youth and growing age,
And grey hair glinting when the head turns toward us,
Then senile Winter, bald or with white hair,
Terror in palsy as he walks alone.

"One day—and that was very long ago—
We lived within the womb of our first mother,
And we were scarcely more than hopes of men,

Seeds of the first beginning, till Nature's hands
(How artfully she worked to suit her purpose!)
Gave us our destiny to live beyond
Distending walls which held us coiled in darkness,
So from that home we fell to worldly being.
Yet without strength the child first knew the light,
Rearing itself to creep, four-leggèd, slowly,
Like any littered beast, then slower still,
Unsteady at the knees, it stands, falls, rises,
Grasping at anything to step upright.
From there it walks, and with increasing ardour
Runs through boyhood to man to middle age,
To slip, then downward, toward senility.
Time wears away the energy, the vigour
Of earlier years within the wasting body.
Old Milon, sobbing through a flow of tears,
Looks at his biceps which at twenty-one
Had made him seem another Hercules
—The flesh gone slack and sagging from the bone.
And Helen, no less desolate than he,
Weeps at the old bitch staring from her mirror.
And who would rape her once or twice or now?
Time and Old Age eat all the world away—
Black-toothed and slow, they seem to feast forever
As all things disappear in time, in death.

   "Even the so-called elements are shifting.
I know their transformations; here they are:
In this eternal now, their names are four—
Earth, heavy, water, heavy, down they fall;
And air and fire are the other two,
And both (unless held back) fly up to aether.
Though all four are of different place and kind,
Each comes from each, and to each each returns:
Loose earth becomes a fluid, and as it flows
To water, water itself will change to air,
And air to fire which rises over it
To climb the highest reaches of the heavens.
They then return, last first in backward order,
Fire in smoky air, from air to water,
And waves changed into marshes turn to earth.

"Nothing retains the shape of what it was,
And Nature, always making old things new,
Proves nothing dies within the universe,
But takes another being in new forms.
What is called birth is change from what we were,
And death the shape of being left behind.
Though all things melt or grow from here to there,
Yet the same balance of the world remains.

"Nothing, no, nothing keeps its outward show,
For golden ages turn to years of iron;
And Fortune changes many looks of places.
I've seen land turn to miles of flood-tossed waters,
Or land rise up within a restless sea;
Shells have been found upon a sanded plain
With never an ocean or a ship in sight,
Someone has seen an anchor turn to rust,
Caught among brushes on a mountaintop.
Stormed by great cataracts, a wide plateau
Turns to a valley and Spring floods have swept
Far hills into the chambers of the sea.
And where a swamp once flowed beneath the willows,
Is now a strip of sand, and where a desert was,
A little lake sways under growing reeds.
Here Nature touches Earth with sudden fountains
And over there she closes ancient springs;
And when the underbody of Earth is shaken,
The rivers gush, leap, rise, or fade away,
Even as Lycus, swallowed in a canyon,
Drops out of sight to come to life again
Far from his source, and wears another face.
Erasinus is still another changeling,
Hidden among rocks deeper than abyss,
Only to show his sinuous gliding features
In that broad stream that runs through Argolis.
And some say Mysus grew dissatisfied
With all his native springs, and found another,
A better place and took the name Caicus.
Today the Amenanus pours its waters
To flood the sands of sunswept Sicily,
And yet its very sources have run dry.

And Anigrus, once known for drinking-water,
—Unless we do not listen to the poets—
Is not the kind of water you would drink.
The reason why, according to the legends,
Is this: the centaurs washed their wounds in it,
Blood pouring from swift Herculean arrows.
And what of Hypanis, whose waters travelled
From Scythian hills, sweet to the lips, and now
Ruined with salt and mud, or what you will?

"Antissa, Pharos, and Phoenician Tyre
Once saw the seas around them, but today
Not one of them's mistaken for an island.
And men who used to live at Leucas thought
Themselves peninsular and much at ease;
And now, of course, the waters dance around them.
There was a time when Zancle used to be
As much of Italy as any other region—
Until the sea had cut her off from land.
Now if you look for Buris and Helice,
Achaian cities of another day,
You'll find them at the bottom of the sea,
A listing tower or a sunken wall,
Ruins where leaning sailors point the way.
Not far from Troezen, known as Pittheus' city,
There is a hill where never a tree has grown;
The place was once a levelled field of grass,
Yet there's the hill where winds were locked in Hell,
And fought and raged and smoked and raised the earth,
Like someone blowing up a stuck pig's bladder
Or shaggy belly of a two-horned goat—
Earthquake from hell rose up and there it stands,
A freak of nature that outlives the years.

"And there's much more to illustrate my theme.
A few will be enough: And what of water—
The way it changes? Look at River Ammon
At noon deep cold, but warm at dawn and sunset.
And I've been told that Athamanian waters
(One has to wait until the moon's last quarter)
Sets fire to wood and makes the timbers blaze.

And where Cicones live there is a river
Which as one drinks it down turns flesh to stone,
And turns to marble everything you touch.
And not too far from here, in Italy,
Near Sybaris and Crathis, there are waters
That tint the hair in bronze or golden colours.
Perhaps more ominous than change of body
Are streams and waters that affect the mind.
Is anyone so ignorant not to hear
Of this before? Of lakes in Africa,
Of evil Salmacis who make us old?
Who drinks of them runs mad, or if not mad,
Falls half asleep in endless apathy.
While he who takes a drink at Clitor's fountain
Forgets the taste of wine, and only water
Is drink that gives him heavenly delight.
It may be that cold water clears the system;
At least it balances the heat of wine—
Or was it true that Amythaon's son,
As people said, had cured Proetus' daughters?
The girls went cattle-mad; he exorcised them
With songs and herbs that purified the mind,
Then tossed his magic where the Clitor flowed—
An antidote against the curse of liquor.
Meanwhile there is a Macedonian river
That turns the mind another way about;
One drop too much and you'll go reeling home.
In Arcady and many years ago
A place called Pheneus had dubious fame
Where no one dared to drink its changing waters,
A draught of poison when the moon rode high
But always harmless in the light of day.
So lakes and rivers are erratic waters.
Long years ago Ortygia sailed the seas,
But now she's anchored like all other islands.
When Argo tried to pass the Symplegades
She trembled as she sailed to see those rocks
Smash at each other in a storm of spray,
And now one sees them stand against the wind,
As firm as rock itself and motionless.
Today one feels the furnace fires that rage

In Aetna's belly, but another time
That heat will die to ashes in the quiet
Of what it was before, for Earth itself
Is like an animal that breathes and sighs
Fires and flames and as she shakes her sides,
New doors are opened for her sighing breath
While others close again. When storms are locked
Within Earth's deepest caves, rocks tossed on rocks
Turn flint to fire, yet when the storms die down,
The caves grow cold—or if the heat is fired
By running tar, the saffron sulphur burns
In smoke-ringed heat. Then as the Earth grows weary
Of feeding fuel to fire—for Earth is old—
Nature herself will starve, hungry, depleted,
Neglecting fires that eat her nourishment.

"And here's a curious legend that I've heard,
A Macedonian story of strange men
Who, after they had dived nine times or so
Into Minerva's well, were dressed like birds
And grew fantastic feathers. Perhaps it's true.
I've also heard that females of the North
Grow feathers on themselves for decoration
By smearing strange cosmetics on their bodies—
But this I say without authority.

"Yet some things have been proved: or have you seen
The dead? I mean those bodies black with heat
In their decay, fluid in rot and bursting—
And in that place small creatures come to life?
It is well known that many a buried bull,
Tossed in a trench after he's served the altar,
Breeds flower-loving bees from his torn sides—
Who, following ancient habits of their kind
People the meadow with their hours of labour.
And since the best of horses go to war,
Bury them down, they'll breed a crop of hornets.
Strip a crab's claws and bury him in sand,
And from that grave a scorpion advances,
Creeps toward you with his crook'd tail like a threat
And over here the white-spun caterpillar

Cradles himself within a living leaf
(And this familiar to all country people)
To change into a tombstone butterfly.

"From mud and mire the green frog makes his way
Legless at first, but soon has legs to swim,
The rear long-legged leap from here to there.
Even the cub that the she-bruin carries
Is not a bear but something rolled together
Until its mother's tongue strokes it alive
To make it seem a creature like herself.
Look at the hatch of honeybees in cells
Formless until they stir with legs and wings,
Or Juno's peacock with its star-eyed tail,
Jove's eagle carrying thunderbolts and arrows,
Or Cytherea's doves in golden air—
Who'd think that their beginnings were concealed
Within the featureless white wall of egg?
Some say that when man's backbone rots away
In sleep within the tomb, the spine grows wary
And is a snake that crawls through open doors.

"How many creatures walking on this earth
Have their first being in another form?
Yet one exists that is itself forever,
Reborn in ageless likeness through the years.
It is that bird Assyrians call the Phoenix,
Nor does he eat the common seeds and grasses,
But drinks the juice of rare, sweet-burning herbs.
When he has done five hundred years of living
He winds his nest high up a swaying palm—
And delicate dainty claws prepare his bed
Of bark and spices, myrrh and cinnamon—
And dies while incense lifts his soul away.
Then from his breast—or so the legend runs—
A little Phoenix rises over him,
To live, they say, the next five hundred years.
When he is old enough in hardihood,
He lifts his crib (which is his father's tomb)
Midair above the tall palm wavering there

And journeys toward the city of the Sun,
Where in Sun's temple shines the Phoenix' nest.

   "Yet if these miracles seem marvellous,
Think how the wild hyena shifts her sex.
No sooner does she take husband to bed
Than she's hyena of another gender.
And see this little creature on the floor
Which seems to live on air and has the colour
Of any place it chooses to lie flat.
When vine-haired Bacchus took his India
They gave him wildcat chariots to ride,
And when the beasts made water as they ran,
Pink piss turned into amethysts and rubies,
And, like the pliant coral, weak in water,
Yet hard as polished stones in open air.

   "If I would list the many changes seen,
The day would fall behind us in the sea
Where Phoebus dips his fiery-breathing horses
To rest within that deep green hemisphere.
So times and countries change or weaker, stronger,
To rise or fall within the changing years:
Great Troy, the greater for her men and riches,
Poured blood as water in a ten-year war,
Now shows earth-fallen ruins to the sky,
Her riches ancient names in broken tombs;
Time was when Sparta's light shone through the world,
Mycenae bloomed, and places where Cecrops
And Amphion held their highest seats of power.
But what of Oedipus and Thebes today?
Or Pandion's Athens rising to sky?
Names that are heard in halls of memory,
Names, names, and nothing more!
Now there is news that Trojan Rome is here,
That city built on stone where Tiber winds,
Whose sources are the Apenninean snows.
Each day she changes to a greater city
To rule the great unmeasurable world
From oracles that guide us to the future,

From lips that speak our destiny on earth.
And even I remember, when Troy fell,
The words of Priam's son, grave Helenus,
Who spoke to weeping, anxious-eyed Aeneas:
'Listen, dear friend and son of our fair Venus,
Hold to the prophecy my heart revealed:
So long as you are here and walk the earth
Even Troy itself shall not be total ruin;
For you shall still advance through flame and steel,
So you shall carry her, however far,
Until you find a strange yet greener country
More friendly to your will than thoughts of home.
Even as I speak I see our destiny,
The city of our sons and sons of sons,
Greater than any city we have known,
Or has been known or shall be known to men.
Through those far years where future ages climb
She shall have men to give her strength and power;
Yet one who is a lord of Iulus' blood
Shall make her mistress of the turning world,
And after Earth takes pleasure in his arms
The heavens shall take him for their own delight.'
As if these words were spoken yesterday
They sing within my memory of Helenus
And of Aeneas standing there erect,
Carrying the ikons of his native gods.
How good it is to know my family walls
Shall stand to make a Grecian victory
Become an honour to the men of Troy!

  "But I must not digress, nor let my horses
(A metaphor of what I wish to say)
Run wild, forgetting what my speech should be,
To let you know how all things are mutations—
Heaven or Earth and all that grows within it,
And we among the changes in creation.
Beyond the very natures of our bodies,
Our spirits take to wing through other creatures,
Or sheep or wild. But let those creatures live
Where spirits have flown home, or parent, sister,
Or lost brother in a wandering animal,

Nor eat your fill like Savage Thyestes
Who had a feast of horror at his dinner.
Look, here's a man who has a filthy habit
Of drinking human blood. He kills a calf
And is all deafness as he hears it cry;
Deaf to the lamb that whimpers like a baby,
Or to the bird he fed an hour ago.
Come, is this murder? Where does killing end?
Give bulls the right to die as death may call them,
Grazing among the pastures of old age;
Or sheep the right to shield you from the cold,
The North Wind's terror freezing in your hair;
Or let the she-goat yield her flowing udders
To milking time before the day is done.
Then put away your tricks of nets and knives,
Limed twigs for birds and foolish feathers flapping
From trees to harry deer, and deadly hooks
That hide behind the bait. It's open season
To kill the beast that kills, and yet no killing
Should be the feast that tempts you to a dinner."

### THE DEATH OF NUMA

So it was rumoured that our gentle Numa
Took this advice to heart, went home at last
To civilize and rule the Latin people.
He had two gifts: a sweet and lovely wife,
And special dispensation from the Muses,
A gift of sacred art in sacred songs
Which turned the fighting people of his nation
To thoughts of peace and art, and not of war.
Now full of years he dropped his life and sceptre,
While those in the vicinity of Rome,
Matrons and fathers and the common people,
Wept at the thought of losing him forever.
His wife had disappeared, for she had wandered
Deep in the forests of Arician valleys
And there her wails and groans made such sad music
They damped the celebrations to Diana.
I cannot tell how many times the girls
Of lake and forest tried to calm her down,

To make her grief less noisy and heartbreaking!
Even Theseus' son did all he could to soothe her:
"What good are tears?" he said. "For after all,
You're not the only one to find misfortune;
Think of all others who have loved and lost,
To make your own distress less wild and weeping.
I wish the story of my own affairs
Were less appropriate to tears and sorrow,
Yet it is sad enough to lift your heart.

HIPPOLYTUS

   "Perhaps you've heard the name of Hippolytus,
And how through evil of his wild stepmother,
A credulous father who believed her lies,
He went to death. And here's the shock of truth,
And difficult to prove as it may be,
I'm Hippolytus—and a miracle.
That Cretan woman, Pasiphaë's daughter,
Did all she could to lure me to her bed,
My father's bed it was and she his wife—
Then lied, insisting that her wish was mine.
(Was this through fear of being caught or rather
She could not tempt me with her wild advances?)
And though myself was innocent enough,
My father damned me to eternal exile.
Fresh from these curses, I was sent abroad,
On toward Troezen in my chariot,
Racing along the thin Corinthian shores,
When suddenly the sea came like a mountain,
Up and high up and splitting at the top,
Roaring and leaping like a thing gone mad
That tossed a horned bull through midair at me,
Sea pouring from his snout and open jaws.
Those who were with me stood with shaking hearts,
But I, distracted by my thoughts of exile,
Was unafraid of anything I saw.
Then with a leap in air my nervous horses
Took one quick glance toward water and the bull.
I felt them tremble as I saw them rear,
Careening over rock and sand and spray,

I stretched my reins, wet with white foam and spittle,
And with my weight upon them I leaned back.
And yet I could have held their maddening rushes—
They turned, the chariot's tongue snapped through a
        wheel,
Crashed as the wheel went spinning from its axle,
And, tangled in the reins, my legs were bound,
And I was tossed aside, my body pierced
And stretched, torn by the tongue that held me,
Dragged by the reins that held me to the ground;
I felt my bones break with a shattering noise.
You might have seen my soul slip from my body,
But body itself was like a lake of blood.
And now, my lady, what's your loss to mine?
I saw the dayless land of death below me
And sinking down I washed my ragged body
In dark waves of the rippling Phlegethon.
There I would be today, but Phoebus' son
Restored my life with medical attention:
Fine magic weeds and strange life-giving waters
Which were against the power of Death himself.
But Cynthia, who is our pure Diana,
Came down to shield me from Death's envious eyes
And wrapped me in a cloud for my escape
To save me from the envy of the dead,
And living men as well, she gave my face
The grey look of old age—nor any friend
Would know me if they saw me anywhere.
She was of two minds where to set me down,
Delos or Crete, then voted against both,
And after days of thinking sent me here.
She told me that my name would never do,
For 'Hippolytus' called to mind my horses,
'Come, Hippolytus, you are now Virbius,'
She said, and here I live within this forest,
A demigod, a minor god of light
Who lives within the shadow of his goddess,
And is content to rise or fall with her."

     And yet Egeria's tears were not dispelled
By knowing loss that came to other creatures,

But lying weary there at the mountain's foot
She flowed away in tears till Phoebus' sister—
Because Egeria was a pious soul—
Took mercy on her long-sustaining grief,
Changed what she was into a cooling fountain,
Her tear-stained body an eternal river.

CIPUS

This curious transformation of Egeria
Seemed to the girls of that Italian forest
More wonderful than anything they knew,
And Hippolytus was as dazed and shaken
As the Etrurian farmer at his plough
Who saw a mass of clay move with the force
Of fate within it, for no one had touched it—
Yet as it grew, losing its claylike masses,
It took the image of a talking man,
Lips opened wide to tell tomorrow's fate.
They called him Tages; it was he, the first
To give Etruscans knowledge of the future.
Nor was the ancient Romulus less shaken
To see the spear he struck on Palatine
Sprout green with leaves, the iron-headed shaft
Grow roots in earth—the thing was not a spear
But O, a tree! Look at it on that hill,
Leaning green shade on those who wondered at it.
Nor was our praetor Cipus less surprised,
For as he stopped to gaze into a river
He saw horns growing out above his eyes.
Could he believe it? No! Something went wrong;
And then he touched his forehead; horns were there.
He left the line of march that led to Rome
And raised his hands and eyes to helpless Heaven—
"O gods, O triple gods, or half a dozen,
What does this mean? If it is good, let goodness
Fall on the people of our dear Quirinus
But if this decoration brings us evil,
It's my misfortunate honour to be blamed."
At that he made an altar of green sod
And smoked (the smell was sweet) a lamb upon it,

Poured wine, then read the sacrificial entrails,
And called a seer to help him spell them out.
The seer discovered that great things were there,
But dim. And as he raised his piercing eyes
To nail the spot where Cipus' antlers grew
He cried, "O king, God bless the king of men,
God bless the horns you wear in shining glory,
And where you stand even all Rome shall worship
The greatest antlers ever worn by kings!
Yet hurry, for the gates of Rome are open,
For if you step within that city's walls
Rome shall be yours, and yours to rule forever—
This is the law that fate holds in command."
So Cipus went his way, but as he rode
He kept his eyes averted from the city
And said, "May heaven spare me from that fate.
I'd rather be an exiled prince of men
Than ruler of the city where I lived."
He called a gathering of Rome's senators
And all the common people of the place,
But as he did so crowned his head with laurel
To hide his curse, to show his mind at peace.
Then, standing on a hill that soldiers made
For moments when they felt the need of prayer,
He praised the ancient gods in their old fashion,
Then raised his voice to say, "There's someone here
Who shall be king unless you turn him out.
I cannot tell his name, but by a warning
Of who he is, I hope you know him well.
He wears a pair of antlers on his head,
Which is the truth—a seer has told me so,
And said that if he walks into your city
His charms are such that all will be his slaves.
Because your gates are always swaying wide,
He could have entered any time he chose;
Because he's more like me than life itself,
I had the wit to fight him off, to stop him.
Here is my warning, clever sons of Rome:
Don't let him step one foot into the city,
Or chain him like a dog, or if you wish,
Murder him cold, which is a tyrant's death,

For that poor hero has the will of fate."
Then, like the murmurings of waves at sea
Or tossing winds among high-reaching pines,
The voices of the crowd streamed into air
And from that vast confusion one voice shouted,
"Who is he?" and they turned to one another,
Each looking for a guilty, antlered crown.
Then Cipus said, "You have him. Look at me!"
And ripped the laurel from his bended head;
And as he showed his horns, they tried to stop him.
They were afraid to look at him and moaned.
Who could believe that head produced such marvels?
But there they were. They put the gay wreath on them;
They were embarrassed by his honesty.
Nor could the Senate let him enter Rome,
But as reward for all his good intentions,
They gave him as much land as could be ploughed
From dawn to dark upon a summer's day.
And there in bronze over the gates of Rome
The horns of Cipus shall remain forever.


                                             AESCULAPIUS


    And now, dear Muses, show me how to say
(Nor have the years in furthest reach of time
Made things turn dust in your bright memory)
The story of an island in the Tiber
Where Aesculapius joined the gods of Rome.

    Long, long ago a plague walked through the city
And Roman air was death; one saw pale bodies
Sink into wasting sickness everywhere.
Spent with continual round at funerals,
And knowing that physicians could do nothing,
Men looked to heaven for a sign of cure.
They came to Delphi, center of creation,
To pray at Phoebus' altar and to hear
His temple's voice to cure them of despair.
There at the inmost shrine Apollo's arrows,
His laurel tree, even the shrine itself
Began to tremble with Apollo's spirit.

The Roman visitors were moved with awe.
They heard a voice: "O Roman embassy,
All that you hope to find is far away,
Yet near enough from where your journey started;
Look to Apollo's son and not Apollo;
That way is good, and let my son command you."
The worthy senators, and wise they were,
Decided to obey Apollo's orders,
Chartered a ship and in it a committee
To find the town where Aesculapius lived,
Somewhere along the coast of Epidaurus.
When the committee landed on these shores,
It met a Greek committee of old men
And begged it for the loan of Aesculapius
To end the plague that covered Italy.
Yet the old men were not of single mind:
Some said that help would be an act of mercy
But others claimed it was bad luck to lend
A local god who brought prosperity.
They sat in argument till twilight came
And darkness followed to engulf the world.
And then, as if he came within a vision,
The god of health stood at the foot of Roman beds.
As though he were at ease in his own temple,
He held his flowering wand in his left hand,
And with his right he smoothed his length of beard,
The kind physician speaking to a patient:
"Let all your worries lie at rest, my dears,
I'll journey with you as you cross the sea.
Take notice of the serpent on my wand
Who coils it round, and you must know him well,
For he shall be myself tomorrow morning,
Larger than life as heavenly beings are."
Then with these fading words he disappeared;
The voice was gone, sleep gone, and day was up,
Glad of the morning when night's sleep was done.
Though sweet Aurora swept the waking skies,
And all the fiery stars had run away,
Greek elders still disputed right and wrong.
All gathered at the temple of the god
And prayed for signs from heaven for his will

Whether to stay within his glorious temple
Or take his way to Rome and Italy.
No sooner said, they saw a golden serpent
With a gold crown that glittered round his head—
The god himself who hissed his sinuous way
To let them know divinity was there.
The golden ceiling, marble floors, and railings,
Ikon and altar and the great bronze door
Shook with the coming of a god on Earth.
Lifted midair within the crowded temple,
The people saw him rise and shook with awe
Until a priest came up; one saw his vestments
And how white fillets held his floating hair.
The priest knew god within the snake and cried,
"Look, here's the god himself who comes upon us,
The god is here! Nor speak aloud, but stand
In all humility before his eyes—
And O great god, more beautiful than any,
Stay with us like a dream within a dream
To bless these people bowed before the altar."
Then all fell to their prayers to praise the god,
Their hearts reciting priestly incantations.
And of this crowd the Romans led the chorus,
While in his godlike manner the gold serpent
Bowed his acknowledgment; they saw his crown
Glitter in fire with his salutations,
His flickering tongue that hissed a sound of welcome.
Then down the marble stairs before his temple
The serpent turned to look his last farewell
At all the antique glories of his shrine—
Those golden centuries that held him there.
Then where the streets were carpeted with flowers
He wound his way above the multitude,
Arched like a golden bow into the harbour,
To turn again, to smile at all below him,
A final blessing on his worshippers,
At which he boarded the Italian boat.
The ship had nearly floundered with his weight,
Then righted slowly, swaying in the waters.
The Romans, drunk with gladness, made a feast,
And when they'd killed a bull in pious frenzy,

They dressed the ship in garlands of gay flowers,
Tossed off the ropes that held it to the pier.
A blessèd wind came up to bear them westward,
The god at ease, his golden head bent down
Sternward to look at heaven reflected in
Blue waves that rippled toward the fading shores.
Within six days he sighted Italy,
Fair wind and sea behind them all the way,
Past Lacinium, known for Juno's temple,
Then round the Italian heel, and steering through
Wild rocky narrows off the southern shores,
Gliding beyond the waves of Sicily,
Pelorus' finger through the rock-bound narrows,
Beyond the place where Hippotades ruled,
And where Temesa's earth is filled with ore,
Then round and past the island Leucosia,
Where Paestum's roses seem to bloom forever,
Then past Capri, which is Minerva's island,
Palm-hilled Surrentum, where the flowering broom
Reaches its delicate fingers through the vine,
Herculaneum and those little cities,
Where all the joys of idleness began,
Then past the shrine where Cumae's sibyl spoke,
Then hot springs rising through a mile of desert,
Liternum, shaded in gum-wood forest,
And where Volturnus gushes sand and pebbles
Beneath its violent races to the sea,
Beyond dove-circled roofs of Sinuessa,
And Minturnae, where everyone falls ill,
And where Aeneas left his nurse forever
And where bad Antiphates had his home.
Past swampy Trachas and the land of Circe,
To Antium, which has a thick-ribbed coast.
The sailors rode full sail against this shore—
The waves ran high, and brave they were to make it—
While the great snake uncoiled his godlike size
And glided where his father's temple opened
To greet the pilgrims of its yellow sands.
Meanwhile the sea grew quiet and the snake,
Refreshed by blessings at his father's altar,
Swept like a golden plough along the shore,

Leaving a sandy wake from shrine to harbour,
To rest his head where the ship's stern curved high.
At last he came to Castrum, holy city
Where Tiber's lips fall open to the sea.
And all along the river crowds came cheering,
Elders and young, good wives and girls, and O,
The Trojan virgins who keep fires burning.
There as the ship came gliding up the waters,
One saw the altars rise on either side,
Fire through that sweet smoke that charmed the air
(One almost heard quick fires speak their gladness).
Then came the sacrifice in sparkling blood.
Then into Rome itself the good ship sailed
To greet the mistress of the living world;
The serpent, with his head mast-high, rose up
To face or left or right to find his home,
And chose the place that people called an island,
That spot of green with Tiber's arms around it;
And here it was the serpent came ashore
To be the son of Phoebus that he was,
And not a serpent but of godlike features
To clean the city of its deadly fears
And wake good health among the Roman people.


                                                    CAESAR


    The serpent was a god from foreign shores,
But Caesar is our god of native birth.
Nor war nor peace gave him divinity—
A flaming comet lifted to the skies—
But more than these, his children gave him glory,
Greater than battles and their victories,
For he had made our emperor his son.
Though greatness touched him when he fought the British
And made them slaves upon a sea-washed island,
And glory sailed his navy up the Nile
To conquer Africa, and it was great enough
To make the name Mithridates less great,
To pacify, to civilize, to bring
All these wild rebels to the feet of Rome,
To make them subjects of the Roman people—

So many triumphs and so many more—
But none as great as this: the happy father
Of a great, *great* man. O gods of heaven!
You who have made him ruler of this earth
Have given us, poor creatures called mankind,
A greater richness than our souls can carry!
Caesar, of course, must be a god in heaven
To make a son of more than mortal fires.
Now when Aeneas' mother, dressed in gold,
Read this grave truth that flashed across the skies,
She also saw—and this was death itself—
Assassination and a heap of ruins—
A plot against her own high priest, her Caesar,
Till she grew white as terror in her bones.
To every god she met (she met them all)
She cried, "Look at this treachery against me,
And why? Because of my great Trojan family
That has the name of Julius for its own.
My first wound was the spear of Diomede;
Then I was buried under walls of Troy;
Then my dear son Aeneas went to sea,
And wandered half-lost in death's silent kingdom,
And fought a war with Turnus—but the truth is,
The real war that he fought was caused by Juno.
But why do I recite these old disasters,
These persecutions of the Julius line?
Even now the knives are sharpened—look below
And there you'll see my darling priest in danger,
And Vesta's fires put out in streams of blood."

Venus went wild with her anxieties
And shouted warnings to the skies above her;
She moved the gods, but what could godheads do
Against the iron laws that Fates control—
The will of elder sisters in the sky?
Yet even heaven prophesied disaster.
The signs were there; one heard the crash of battle,
The trumpets blaring through the dark at noon,
Black clouds across the very face of heaven,
The sun himself a yellow-greenish light
To spread the sight of terror everywhere.

At night strange torches flashed among the stars,
And clouds wept blood, and fiery Lucifer
Turned grey to darkest blue, a spotted face,
With wounds as red as flames across his features,
And Luna's chariot grew black with blood.
Then through a thousand wilderness of trees
One heard the cry of owls across death's river,
And in a thousand streets of midnight cities
The statues wept, their faces wet with tears,
And even in suburban sacred forests
Cries of despair were heard, and threats of murder.
No single creature killed at sacrifice
Could spell the secret of impending doom;
Only the liver seemed to speak of trouble.
And all night long one heard the dogs complain
Round every house in Rome, or temple, circus,
And silent dead rose up to walk the Forum
While through the streets one felt the earthquake stir.
Yet portents of the gods on Earth or Heaven
Cannot delay the hour of Fate upon us,
Nor yet unwind the subtle schemes of men.
In every corner where the Senate sat
The naked sword flashed through, for in this city
Only the Senate seemed appropriate
For blood, for murder and the threat of death.
Then Julian Cytherea beat her breasts
And tried to shelter Caesar in a cloud
That saved the life of Paris long ago
When Menelaus came at him and missed,
The very cloud that caught up brave Aeneas
When Diomede's sword struck out to kill.
Then Jove the father spoke a word of warning:
"My dear, I know the spell of your enchantments,
But how can you undo the will of Fates?
Three sisters, if you choose to visit them,
Will show you written words on brass and steel,
Neatly engraved and not to be destroyed;
Nor lightning, thunder, or the fall of heaven,
Could make them less or more than what they are.
Here you may trace the legend of your line,
Down to the last, or Caesar's if you will.

I've read them well, and memorized those portions
That should be interesting to both of us.
And for your knowledge you may learn from me
Future appointments of the scene on earth.
Your son, my dearest child of Cytherea,
Has spent his term on earth; he's fit for Heaven.
Though you may grieve for him, his way is clear:
He has a godhead waiting in these regions
And down at Rome his temples shall be known—
His son and you shall order these affairs.
The son, of course, shall take his father's place,
The best of men to right his father's cause,
To speed revenge on murderers and crime,
And his reward shall be our help in war.
Mutina, city of Cisalpine Gaul,
Shall cry for peace and mercy at his feet,
Pharsalus wet with blood and Philippi,
And Pompey—what a famous man he was!—
Shall be undone off shores of Sicily.
And that Egyptian queen who took to bed
A Roman—what an excellent commander!—
Shall find herself in error; she shall die
Even before his death, and her Canopus
Shall never rise above our capitol.
Why should I speak of all these provinces,
Of savages, seaports and little towns,
For all the Earth and all the people in it
Even the sea's unconquered hemisphere
Shall be servants of your Caesar's son.

"Then peace shall fall on every town and nation,
And he who gave them peace shall make its laws,
His own good life, a way for men to follow,
And then, still mindful of the times to come,
He'll name his heir, the very son of virtue,
Son of his empress who was virtue's pride.
But not until old age has settled on him,
His years to match the years that Nestor knew,
Shall he arrive to take his throne in Heaven
And bow his head among familiar stars.
Now turn to earth below; go to that body

That falls beneath its wounds in Caesar's dress,
Gather the spirit from its dying lips,
To make that soul a star that burns forever
Above the Forum and the gates of Rome."

And as he spoke our mother Venus vanished,
Invisible to senators or men,
To pace her way among the senate's chambers
Where Caesar's soul, caught up between her breasts,
Was hers to find its place among the stars.
Then as she mounted toward the midnight heavens,
She felt his fiery soul burn at her heart
And set it free to see it leap the moon,
Rising through night, a comet's tail of fire,
So Caesar burns as an eternal star.
Though here on earth bright Caesar's son denies
A glory that outshines his father's light,
Fame calls him much too modest, and ignores
His will to be far less than she desires:
So Atreus steps behind great Agamemnon,
And Theseus overshadows old Aegeus,
And Peleus takes his place behind Achilles,
So Saturn shines with lesser light than Jove.
Our triple world of heaven, earth, and sea,
Has Jupiter as father of us all,
And earth is ruled by Emperor Augustus,
Both masters of their kind, or earth or Heaven.
And now the poet speaks to all his gods,
First those who fought with glorious Aeneas,
Then all the gods of our Italian earth,
And Romulus, the father of our city,
And his great father, noble Gradivus,
Vesta, the goddess of our threshold fires,
Whom Caesar guarded and the gold Apollo,
And Jupiter who rides above them all,
Whose temple shines where high Tarpeia rises—
To these, all these, the poet sends his prayer:
Long life to our Augustus here on earth,
And may he live beyond my transient hour,
And when at last he takes his throne in heaven,
Then he may hear a Roman poet's song.

    And now the measure of my song is done:
The work has reached its end; the book is mine,
None shall unwrite these words: nor angry Jove,
Nor war, nor fire, nor flood,
Nor venomous time that eats our lives away.
Then let that morning come, as come it will,
When this disguise I carry shall be no more,
And all the treacherous years of life undone,
And yet my name shall rise to heavenly music,
The deathless music of the circling stars.
As long as Rome is the Eternal City
These lines shall echo from the lips of men,
As long as poetry speaks truth on earth,
That immortality is mine to wear.

# AFTERWORD

*The Metamorphoses* or *Transformations* of Ovid was completed at Rome in the year A.D. 8, which also was the year that the Emperor Augustus sent its author into retirement far away from Rome. Lucretius' great work *De Rerum Natura, On the Nature of Things* had ended with the year of his death in 55 B.C., and in 19 B.C., the year of Virgil's death, that poet's epic, the *Aeneid*, celebrating Rome's heritage from Troy, came to its conclusion. It can be said that *The Metamorphoses*, written at the beginning of the Christian era, was the last long-sustained major work of a great age in Latin poetry—and it was also evidence of a peculiarly Italian genius which places it at a middle distance away from the *Aeneid*, since it was not a true and heroic epic, toward the novellas of Bandello and the lyricism of Petrarch. In English literature *The Metamorphoses* (and here Ovid became "the poet's poet") held sustained appeal for Chaucer, Spenser, Shakespeare, Chapman (whose famous version of Homer's epics shows debts to Ovid), Dryden, Swift. Pope knew his Ovid: though his incident in "Eloisa to Abelard" is medieval, his Eloisa is an Ovidian heroine; her confessions of love, her complaints, her raptures are in the Ovidian manner:

> *To sounds of heav'nly harps she dies away,*
> *And melts in visions of eternal day.*
> *Far other dreams my erring soul employ,*
> *Far other raptures of unholy joy.*

In these lines rather than in his translations from the ninth and fourteenth books of *The Metamorphoses*, Pope's readings in Ovid caught fire and showed his debt to Ovid's nearly flawless understanding of women in love.

The nineteenth century, even among its poets, lost contact with *The Metamorphoses*, or rather, *The Metamorphoses*

438

showed aspects of mythology as well as of human conduct
that the age did not care to advertise. An extremely un-Italian
Victorian Olympus came into view. It had been introduced
by Lord Elgin's marbles shipped from Greece to London.
Pictorially and in sculpture the nymphs and goddesses be-
came ideal English girls, represented in dreamy yet modest
poses by Sir Frederic Leighton; they looked freshly bathed,
well-fed, and nearly sexless. If the *Aeneid* did not represent
a Greek Olympian order, its nobility, its pathos showed a
Roman kind of moral order that would not lead the well-
educated Latin schoolboy astray. Meanwhile *The Metamor-
phoses* was not unread, but placed on a high shelf, almost
out of reach, alongside Suetonius' *Lives of the Caesars.* In
schools Suetonius was regarded as a dubious gossip—he did
not speak too well of Julius' nephew, Octavian Augustus.
*The Metamorphoses* was read as the work of a "capricious"
poet, one who was irreverent, decidedly un-Olympian, and
at times immoral. He was no longer "the poet's poet," but
belonged to readers who were looking for a collection of
"naughty" stories. As studies in classical literature declined,
it had become easier to discard Ovid in favor of Horace
and Virgil; Ovid had lost the prestige he had held for so
many hundreds of years.

There is no doubt that the twentieth century has begun
to rediscover *The Metamorphoses*. Something of its origi-
nal importance is beginning to be understood. Its collection
of myths (once called "fables" by Dryden and by Pope) has
taken on fresh colour and richness, for some of the trans-
formations retold by Ovid are pre-Homeric as well as post-
Homeric in their origins, drifting through the memories of
Mediterranean peasants as well as scholars, and contem-
porary anthropologists are finding new meanings in Ovid's
"fables" and miracles. How far anthropologists are willing
to trust a poet, I do not know, but Schliemann's trust in
Homer opened a new chapter in archeological research,
and historians found an actual Troy to burn. The only warn-
ing that an anthropologist needs is never to read too many
literal meanings into an Ovidian story, for the importance
of the poet's truth is almost never factual. In Book XV of
*The Metamorphoses* Ovid telescoped the battlefields of
Philippi and Pharsalus into a single reference, superimpos-

ing one upon the other. Keats' famous error in mistaking
Cortez for Balboa in his sonnet "On First Looking into
Chapman's Homer" does not invalidate the essential truth
of the poem. The very "realms of gold" that Keats wrote
of in the sonnet came as much from Chapman's reading of
Ovid as of Homer, probably more so. These kinds of poetic
truth are fusions of poetic imagination which transcend lit-
eral facts and historical incident.

We may take for granted that readers of Freud, Brill,
and Jung will find much to rediscover in *The Metamor-
phoses*. Their attraction to it is the same that brought it
so forcefully to John Dryden's attention who went to *The
Metamorphoses* to study the "passions," and with an atti-
tude as critical as any living psychiatrist. He asked a ques-
tion: "Would any man, who is ready to die for love, describe
his passion like Narcissus? Would he think of *inopem me
copia fecit*, and a dozen more such expressions . . . signifying
all the same thing?" He concludes that Ovid at times is too
light-hearted, far too witty—but he ignores Ovid's desire
to show the ridiculous futility, the terror of Narcissus' all-
conquering self-love. Able as Dryden was in reproducing
the smoothness of Ovid's lines, there was much in Ovid that
his cold eye rejected. His temperament was ill-suited to the
contradictory display of the "passions" that Ovid gave him.
Therefore he limited his version of *The Metamorphoses* to
a translation of Book I and what he considered choice pas-
sages from others. Yet the attraction of Ovid's emotional
extremes gave him, as it gave others, inspiration—and
Ovid, witty and passionate by rapid turns, walked swiftly,
smoothly where other Augustan poets feared to tread.

It is in the play of emotional extremes, the forces of il-
logical and conflicting impulses that Ovid offers the rich-
ness of psychological detail to the modern reader. His
many heroines (and there are over fifty stories in *The
Metamorphoses*) are set before us in dramatic moments of
their indecision. Actually they do not meditate; they waver
between extremes of right and wrong. They live and act
within a world of irrational desires which are as vivid to
them as things that happen in a dream. They act in heat
and are caught up in disaster. One might complain that
their motives, however complex and contradictory, are not

subtle. The situations which changed tempting, white-skinned Io to a cow, or incestuous Myrrha to a tree are obvious—and Ovid's comments on their fate are those of the half-cynical, half-affectionate observer. His tone is ironic, warm, humourous, mock-moral. We are asked not to forgive them but to see them. It is by their dreams (desires)—and their actions—that we know them.

As he tells a story of a transformation, Ovid frequently remarks, "so it is believed," or presents a story within a story at second-hand; these are his warnings that he regarded his truths as truths of fiction, which are often far more convincing than any document or "case history" can hope to be. What he gives us is miraculous rather than "abnormal" psychology, so in reading his excursions into sexual psychology, we are as far from literal truth as we are from the literal, or even scientific recital of mythology and historical legend. What he suggests or what we may be able to read into what he writes are other matters. In his miracles and because he expresses the extremes of passionate desire, there are truths so obvious we tend to overlook them. Are there better "case histories" than those found in his versions of the plights of Orpheus, Hermaphroditus, and Narcissus? Of course not. Does Spenser in his great allegory of The Faerie Queen actually excel Ovid's portrait of Minerva and his personification of Envy? I doubt it. Ovid lacks "high seriousness," but not perception.

Because he lacked religious and moral purpose, Ovid's vision of the Olympian gods has less depth than Homer's. But Ovid was not only of another age than Homer's but clearly of a different culture, one that had a broader base, one that contained coarse-textured, material Roman "glory" fused with alloys of Persian, Egyptian, Italian origin, and in The Metamorphoses all scenes are coloured by Italian landscape and Ovid's thoroughly Italian imagination. A. E. Housman (that Dr. Jekyll and Mr. Hyde of latter-day English poets, who was both spokesman for a Shropshire lad and a zealous, often angry, Latin scholar) remarked that Ovid, nearing the age of fifty, and completing The Metamorphoses, had transformed himself from a carelessly well-educated man into a learned one. His masterpiece demanded that metamorphosis. Certainly the

work demanded the resources of a well-stocked library and
an active memory. More than that, there was largeness in
Ovid's vision. His epic, made up of many stories, extending
from the creation of the world to his own day, was very
nearly a mock epic; the variety of stories that he chose to
remember, retell, or invent, was in itself a distraction from
depth of purpose. He ignored Greek unities of time and
place. Through his own lack of reverence for their behav-
iour, he reduced the heroic stature of his gods, demigods,
and heroes.

For us as well as for readers of his own day Ovid opened
many strange windows into the past, showing scenes of sav-
age action, grotesque images of giants, or of Scylla, mon-
strously deformed by a girdle of barking dogs around her
waist. If we think of things classical as being noted for re-
straint and in proportion, certain scenes in *The Metamor-
phoses* may be called less classical than violently baroque.
The very theme of metamorphosis depended on violent
and rapid transformations, distortions, if you will, of normal
law and action. Of these deflections from a "golden mean"
surely Ovid's early contemporary Horace would have dis-
approved. Yet these recitals of miraculous events, the quick
changes, the shifts from images of beauty to the grotesque,
from fear and terror to deadly evil, the migration of human
souls to trees and stones, even to pools and springs, to birds,
to wolves, delighted readers who perceived, not without wit,
the psychological significance of these changes. What could
be more appropriate than placid, yielding Io changed to a
cow? Or matronly, slow-thinking Niobe, still weeping, into
monumental stone? Or the charm of frightened Daphne
into a quivering laurel tree, or a shrewd, quick-witted girl
servant into a red-haired weasel? In all these changes one
can almost say that Ovid anticipated the arts of the Ital-
ian baroque, but for the meantime he knew how to gratify
his own fancy and imagination, and with instinctive wit he
placed a heroine in the foreground of more than half his
stories. His concern for the psychology of women was no
less marked than in the poems of his friend Propertius—or
for that matter, than in the novels of such modern writers
as Flaubert and Henry James. At the very least, his concern
was never petty, but the stress that he placed on the play of

feminine emotions in his stories continued the motifs of his earlier books of poems. His *Amores* and his instructions in the art of love brought him into conflict with Augustus, and at this point it is well to go back to the situation Ovid faced in A.D. 8 as he was exiled to the cold shores of what is now Rumania on the Black Sea.

# II

Publius Ovidius Naso (an ancestor was distinguished by his large nose) was born March 20, 43 B.C., in the very small town of Sulmo, ninety miles due east of Rome. Ovid called himself the pride of his people, the ancient Paelignians, and truly enough his was a knighted family, not rich, but secure in its social position and comfortably well off. It could afford to give him a conventional education in rhetoric and law at Rome and send him to be polished by a final "grand tour" at Athens. Ovid was a boyish and brilliant student of rhetoric, good at poetic but illogical argument, and with a decisive distaste for law. Seneca the Elder, later father of the dramatist and philosopher, was a fellow student at Rome, and he reported Ovid's weaknesses and merits with a knowing air. Ovid could not submit to the disciplines of writing briefs without adding to them touches of poetic compassion, nor could he drop irrelevant lines from an exercise in verse.

After his studies at law and through his father's influence, Ovid secured a few minor public offices; he had no skill in politics, but was graceful enough at moving about in Roman society. He soon dropped law and politics in favor of devoting all his time to the writing of verse—and his day was the Golden Age of Latin poetry. He did not attach himself to the circles surrounding Horace and Virgil, the established and official Augustan poets, but turned to the company of Tibullus and Propertius, with Propertius as master—and as a more distant example, since the elder poet died eleven years before Ovid's birth, Catullus. At ease in social gatherings, and ill at ease among politicians, Ovid's temperament (so close to what we now call "romantic") had an enduring affinity with the Catullus legend, which included Catullus' famous love affair with Clodia (who had

plotted against Caesar), his brilliance in Roman society, the
pathos of his early death.

In the writing of his early verse Ovid followed models
provided for him in the love poems of Propertius. Proper-
tius, some five years older than he, was an acknowledged
master of lyric verse; he converted the Latin elegy into
singing measures, and among his contemporaries, to the
chosen few who read poetry with discrimination, he was
the supreme technician. His poems celebrated his attach-
ment to a "Cynthia," a woman who was probably older
than he, and the image we have of her in his poems is not
unlike Terence's *The Woman of Andros*, who is familiar
enough to American readers in Thornton Wilder's novel of
the same title. Propertius' "Cynthia" was both his patron-
ess and mistress, and, as his poems to her show, his relation-
ship to her was complex and "modern," too complex for
the general popularity of his verse. Ovid quickly absorbed
what Propertius had to teach him, and, with a facility far
greater than the elder poet's, created a courtly convention
for writing on the art of making love. On Italian soil Ovid
established a kind of poetry—and this through his *Amores*,
his *Art of Love*, his *Cure for Love*, even in the trifles of
his *Cosmetics*—that was refreshed and revived fourteen
hundred years later in the sonnets of Petrarch. To these he
added his *Heroides*, his *Confessions of Women*, and a play,
now lost, a Latin version of *Medea*. To the Roman public he
became the successor of Euripides, which was no small dis-
tinction, for among legends of Greco-Roman culture there
are stories of how world-weary Roman generals ordered
their Greek slaves to recite long passages from the plays
of Euripides.

Elder critics of Greek tragedy (including Aristotle) were
often enough disturbed by Euripides' concern for feminine
psychology, and by the presence of children in his plays. To
them it had seemed that the "high seriousness" of Sopho-
clean tragedy, its dignity, its profoundly religious passions
had suffered a decadence, a decline through Euripides' in-
terpretation of the Alcestis story and his obvious sympathy
for the plight of Medea, the murderess of her children and
of Jason's bride. Truly enough Euripides' plays pointed a
direction toward serious comedy, away from the religio-

moral forces present in the tragedies of Sophocles, and they also steered in the direction of paying more attention to domestic situations. To the reader of Ovid's *Heroides* a Euripidean heritage was clear, and all the more charming because the situations of women were presented in new dress, in the form of letters written by women to their lovers. Beyond Euripides and for another age, Ovid had become the authority, the teacher, the guide on the behaviour of women, their dilemmas, their weaknesses, their powers of attraction.

The subject of women, however wittily, however seriously Ovid treated it, was not unimportant in the transition from Republican to Imperial Rome. For among the changes that marked the "new" society that Augustus in his later years attempted to reform was the increasing prominence of women in public affairs. The change had begun in Cato's day and with the coming of Hellenic luxury into Rome. Women were given property rights, and Cato remarked that they had begun "to rule the rulers of the world." Within a hundred years following Cato's observation the elder austerities of Roman family life had been swept away. In high circles women were no longer the custodians of domestic sexual morality. They became patronesses of the arts as well as of business and politics. Divorces were readily granted, and rise to power was usually attended by manipulation of marriages and divorces to gain political ends. Catullus' affair with Clodia, a married woman, his revelation of it, and the disillusion that followed his experience were details of a legend that increased the popularity of his poems. Ovid's *Amores* and his *Confessions of Women* had made him both famous and popular.

Lawyers whose clients were women prospered. Poets whose friends and readers were women were rather more than likely to become well known. It was scarcely necessary for Ovid to make a conscious choice of Euripides' example. His choice was in the very atmosphere he breathed. He liked women. His *Confessions of Women* were briefs written in their defense. Whatever arts he possessed were devoted to their cause. His understanding of their misfortunes, his compassion, his wit, the external polish of his verse made him the fashionable poet of the hour, his verses read aloud at theatres and at public festivals. He did not

frequent circles which paid homage to Augustus, but rather
those that received his daughter, Julia, and her daughter,
Julia, the two Julias whose conduct was the scandal of Au-
gustus' household. Augustus' effort to reform the sexual
morality of the Roman matron had its obvious burlesque
in the conduct of his daughter and granddaughter, for the
younger Julia encouraged the attention of her lovers in the
Forum itself in direct answer to her grandfather's disap-
proval of current sexual morality. Augustus, nearing the age
of seventy, began to feel (as his own blood ran cooler) that
the dignity of the Roman state could be preserved only
by a return to ancient austerities. The office that he held
demanded respect as well as lip service to its power. He
himself had mounted to power up stairs that streamed with
blood. Like Ovid, Augustus had had three wives, and had
taken his last, his Livia, while she was pregnant, from an
earlier husband. As if to undo his own past, as if to turn back
the clock in his old age, his announcement of an Augustan
morality showed signs of an approaching senility. He had
carried his love of order one step too far beyond a practi-
cal solution. His idealism was that of a preternaturally sane
yet unimaginative man of action and ruler of his people.
Ideally he was right: something should have been done to
check the excesses of Augustan Rome, but the Punic Wars
(as Toynbee so forcefully reminds us) had already bred the
seeds of internal decay. Practical statesman as Augustus
was, he could not see or did not wish to see that his effort
to enforce the sexual moralities of ancient Rome by law
was nonsense. Effective as he was, he shared the blindness
of all successful first-rate, second-rate men, who are usually
the rulers of things on earth. That ten years after the pub-
lication of Ovid's *Amores* Augustus found such literature
harmful and immoral should cause no surprise. We scarcely
need—nor did Augustus in late middle age—Plato's *Re-
public* to remind us that the ideal tyranny rejects the poet.

Like Helen's beauty—notorious enough to be named
as cause of war—Ovid's popularity had become a curse.
Perhaps Augustus and he were fated to become enemies,
for the world has always been divided between two distinc-
tively opposing types of mankind: the rational and the irra-
tional; men of words (no matter how often they may break

their promises) and men of deeds; the practical man of state or business (who keeps his word because his true faith is in action) and the compassionate, untrustworthy poet. But Ovid and Augustus also represented the two extremes of Italian temperament, both in themselves, and against one another, with Ovid's role a less conscious, helplessly irreverent, almost feminine, passive one. Augustus represented the Italian love of order to the extreme of tyranny, Ovid the Italian love of disrespect for law, even to anarchy. Ovid's tribute to Augustus at the close of *The Metamorphoses* rings false. Ovid's curious shafts of irony are instinctive or subconscious, and without an effort become poisonous arrows of overpraise. With an instinct as sharp as Ovid's and with considerably greater worldly knowledge than Ovid's to support it, Augustus perceived Ovid's lack of reverence for law. In his defense of women Ovid placed "natural" law above decorum, and the incestuous girls of *The Metamorphoses* argue their cases with inspired anarchistic ardour. Augustus did not have to read too far in any book of Ovid's to detect a consistent lack of veneration for everything except the forces of life itself. This unwilled, nearly hidden stream of anarchy was clear in spite of the controlled, rapid, flowing surfaces of his verse.

In the past Augustus had been known as the benevolent friend and protector of Virgil; Virgil's *Aeneid* had reflections of a moral order and touches of a nobility that Augustus would be happy to associate with his own fame. Augustus also recognized the value of Horace's tact, his discriminating praise, both of which were among the signs of his poetic genius. Horace's critical vision saw existing follies (which are always permanent enough) in contrast to an ever-receding hardy Roman past. The poems of Virgil and Horace could be turned (no matter how superficially one read them) into immediate propaganda for the Roman state. In these two instances Augustus could and did step out of the way to show favour to poets and poetry. These were the two exceptions to the Roman state's distrust of poets and poetry in general, and because from Catullus' day to Ovid's the poets represented Hellenistic culture in fashionable Roman society, they were associated with the "softness," the feminine decadence of the age.

The books of Ovid's *Amores* were obvious targets
for state disapproval. To very nearly the same degree so
were his *Confessions of Women,* his *Heroides*, with their
sympathetic understanding of women in love that seemed
to stress the feminine decadence of Augustan Rome. Ov-
id's penetration into the characters of Phaedra, Ariadne,
Helen, and Penelope could be offered as proof that Ovid
was indifferent to the grave and masculine affairs of state.
In actuality he was indifferent; his deepest concern was
to show how the irrational forces of love took possession
of women. His next concern—and here the artist in Ovid
stepped forward—was to revive Greek drama in the form
of an extended, often lyrical, dramatic monologue. The
technic was both new and attractive—and in it one can
see foreshadowings of the melodramatic monologues of
Seneca's tragedies, and, through them, the soliloquies of
Shakespeare. One can almost say that Ovid invented the
passionate "aside," the "internal" monologue of drama and
fiction. Ovid, being the kind of poet he was, and concerned
as he was with contradictory avowals and denials, seldom
employed his "internal" monologues to advance philoso-
phies. His purpose (and for proof of this we need go no
further than the many "internal" monologues of *The Meta-
morphoses*) was to reveal the conflicts of emotional situa-
tions. This was also the secret of his popularity among his
readers, who saw in his characters motives and projections
of their desires, their own moments of weakness, of vio-
lence, of being overpowered by forces greater than their
conscious wills. It was the purpose of the Augustan state to
channel feelings and emotions toward worship of a mono-
lithic institution, the Empire. In this light Ovid's position
was both heretical (or anarchistic) and reactionary. Ovid,
since he came from an equestrian family, was "aristocratic"
enough, far too "aristocratic" to give full respect to the Ju-
lian line and Augustus' "new" order.

Ovid's *Amores* was undoubtedly read by Augustus'
beloved (even by him) and notoriously delinquent grand-
daughter, Julia. Instead of looking to the delinquencies of
his earlier career (of which Suetonius provides illustrations
of high- and bloody-handed ruthlessness) as examples of
misconduct for young Julia, he was convinced that she had

been ruined by a book. From what little we know of Julia she was not the studious type. We may doubt that the reading of the *Amores* taught her more than her own inclination to perfect the art of love whenever the spirit moved her. Today we would probably call her an "exhibitionist" enjoying that act as much as or more than the act of love. Since she was of the Julian line, we can say she inherited the habit honestly. Neither Julius Caesar nor his nephew Octavian, deified as Augustus, lacked the instincts of showmanship. Julia was like many heiresses of large fortunes and of unassailable social position.

The definite charge brought by Augustus against Ovid was one of *lèse-majesté;* irreverence toward the state and its ruler. One of the items of evidence against Ovid was his *Art of Love,* which Augustus read as an incitement for wives to be unfaithful to their husbands. The difficulty that faced Ovid was this: no poet worthy of the name can retract a poem or a book of poems. He may retract political or even religious affiliations, verbal or written statements made in prose, but not a work of art. This is because a work of art involves an act of imagination, the very identity by which a poet lives, and is of higher authority than conscious will. Not even as sceptical a poet as Ovid, who had few convictions, whose manner was capriciously ironic, who readily gave lip-service to Augustus, his instinctive enemy, could unsay a book of poems. To do so would be a denial of his gift from the muses, a denial of his claims to immortality. So far as the notoriously irreverent Ovid could be religious, his piety was reserved for the muses, for the image of Apollo, for the forces of life in the richness of Italian earth. This last belief, a kind of nature-worship, has proof in his recital of Pomona's story in Book XIV of *The Metamorphoses*. So far we may trust his sincerity. As deep in error as he may have felt himself to be (though he was stunned by the news of his banishment from Rome), he could not retract the promptings of the muses' inspiration. And it is probable that Augustus knew he could not. The nature of Augustus' charge, the fact that the case would not be heard in court, that the order of banishment came directly from himself, had Ovid trapped. Appeal would be futile. Even without Ovid's ritual of giving thanks to the gods and to the muses for his gift, poets, artists of all eras, from Ovid's day to ours, are committed to their characteristic works of art. In submitting to orders of the state (or public opinion) by denying the inspired truth of his own art, the poet loses his authority. The totalitarian temper of the twentieth century, particularly in eastern Europe and in Asia, presents the same difficulty to the artist that Ovid faced. Of contemporary poets Robinson Jeffers has stated the situation with greatest clarity. He once wrote, "I can tell lies in prose," which means that he cannot lie in verse, that in the writing of a poem there is nothing to retract, that in a poem he retains the poet's vision and authority.

In Ovid's *Tristia* (which we may translate as *Poems of Misfortune* or *Regret*) which were written after sentence had been passed upon him and he was sent by Augustus's orders to live at Tomis, a settlement on the Black Sea, other aspects of Augustus's case against him come to light. He was not deprived of property rights; he was ordered to live in a barbarous region, far from the friends, the household, the society he loved. There was as much humiliation in this sentence as actual punishment: it was the full measure of disfavor without the romantic glories of martyrdom. In the *Tristia* Ovid confessed that he had seen or learned something "wrong" that concerned the Julian family line—he could not dare say what—but Roman gossips assumed, since Augustus's granddaughter was discovered in adultery with a certain Junius Silanus in A.D. 8 and banished to the island of Trimerus, that Ovid had intimate knowledge of or encouraged the affair. How far—if at all—Ovid was consciously involved in Julia's deliberate misadventures no man can say, but there is no doubt that he moved in circles that surrounded hers. Ovid's plea in self-defense was *simplicitas*, naïveté in becoming involved in Julia's affairs, a foolish error for a man who knew as much as he. Ovid's humiliation was complete. He had no talent for politics; overnight he had suddenly become *déclassé*. He had paid full price for his irreverence; his social position was gone, the preservation of his many books of poems in grave danger.

# III

Augustus's worldliness had proved itself far more effective than Ovid's poetic genius. Ovid, like the mythological Irish hero Sweeney, was doomed to humiliating banishment. Sweeney, because of his unruly temperament, his lack of reverence for other heroes and the gods, was forced to sit among high branches of a tree to learn the language of the birds. Ovid was sent to Tomis, where he, as lonely as Sweeney, was forced to learn the language of a barbarous northern people. Ovid's *Tristia*, filled with self-pity, show how deeply his vanity was wounded. He was caught up in Augustus's net as neatly as Vulcan trapped his adulterous wife Venus with her lover Mars, embraced and naked for the gods to laugh at. The gifted poet's cleverness was futile; he delayed his trip to Tomis, making it a roundabout journey seaward as long as he could. His friends, his affectionate wife, talked him out of committing suicide. Meanwhile, before he had left Rome, he had finished his major work, *The Metamorphoses.*

In his *Tristia* Ovid claimed to have burned his poems, including the recently finished work, *The Metamorphoses*. Perhaps he actually destroyed one set of manuscripts—a symbolic act of suicide. Of course there were other copies. Although by Augustus's order Ovid's books were banned from public libraries (how closely that order resembles twentieth-century banning of books in Hitler's Germany and Soviet Russia!), private collectors treasured them. Forbidden books always acquire an attractive immortality of their own, quite apart from whatever merits they contain.

Among Ovid's friends *The Metamorphoses* was secure enough. And for that matter, so were Ovid's claims to an immortality in the last lines of Book XV of *The Metamorphoses*. These were no boast; he knew that his masterpiece would last as long as men could read a book. Twentieth-century readers of *The Metamorphoses* are likely to regard it as an invaluable book of Myths, "myths" spelled with a capital M. But it is doubtful if Ovid regarded his masterpiece in quite the same way that we are permitted to read it. As precedent Ovid had before him Lucretius's great philosophical treatise in verse, *De Rerum Natura*, a showing forth, an epiphany, in verse, of the teachings of Epicurus. Ovid was not however a philosopher; he was a collector, a reteller of stories, and his stories were collected and retold with the purpose of showing a cycle of miraculous changes. However familiar some of the stories were, Ovid's interpretation of them provided a new look at the world in which the Homeric epics were no more than a part of a large Greco-Roman tradition of being. Nor was Ovid under any obligation to accept the literal truth of any story he retold or invented. It was enough if the stories had imaginative and psychological reality and were true in their celebration of the life force in its many changes. The stories were written to entertain, to charm, to shock their readers; to move them toward further understanding of the condition of man- or womankind, to show the mystery of life, its savagery, its splendour, and at times its violent waste of blood. The Romans loved show of blood, and Ovid gave it to them. Whenever Ovid supplies a moral to his stories, his moralizings have a false ring (like his overpraise of Augustus in Book XV) or an ironic air. The Age of Virtue belonged to the Golden Age of Book I—but that was very, very long ago.

The examples of virtuous conduct in Ovid's collection of stories are few, of misconduct many. Prime virtue is reserved for the elderly Baucis and Philemon, the two Italian peasants who receive Jove and his son with pious and innocent simplicity. Truly enough the ancient husband and wife have grown too old for any temptations of misconduct to stir their blood; they are, therefore, courteous, mild, and good. They are not torn by conflicting impulses toward good and evil. Their setting is vividly Italian. Next to them may be placed the story of Pomona and her lover Vertumnus, the ancient Italian demigod of the changing seasons. Pomona, goddess of Italian orchards and gardens, seems sincerely chaste, a rarity among Ovidian heroines; nor is she cold. If not high-minded, their impulses seem pure. The story of Deucalion and his wife Pyrrha, saved from the great flooding of the earth through the mercy of Jove, is still another example of loyal and virtuous behaviour (and one may read it as a Greco-Roman story of Noah and his wife), but neither Deucalion nor Pyrrha seems very bright; interest in the story shifts to the miracle of their repopulation of the world by means of throwing stones and clods of earth behind them. The eastern tale of Pyramus and Thisbe also has the motifs of human good intentions at the centre of the narrative; the lovers are young, loyal, and extremely innocent—too young, too inexperienced, one supposes, for them to yield to thoughts of unfaithfulness. Aside from Shakespeare's use of the story in *A Midsummer Night's Dream*, the Pyramus-Thisbe story seems very like a pre-Bandello version of *Romeo and Juliet*; it is believed that Shakespeare based his play upon Arthur Brooke's poem *Romeus and Juliet*, but I am inclined to believe that Shakespeare's play had even more complex sources. We know he read Golding's version of *The Metamorphoses*; evidence of this is clear enough in *A Midsummer Night's Dream* and in *Venus and Adonis*. Thisbe's dying speech in Ovid's version runs close in its forced and rapid maturity to Juliet's last words. We should assume that Shakespeare used both Brooke's narrative of the Veronese lovers and Ovid's story of Pyramus and Thisbe in *Romeo and Juliet* as well as in *A Midsummer Night's Dream*. Ovid took his story from eastern sources and rewrote it so well that it remains one of the more memorable stories in his collection. It is also probable that Juliet's nurse has one source in the indulgent, child-spoiling nurses who attend Ovid's erring heroines— but with the story of Thisbe we leave the major scenes of untainted innocence behind us and enter those where erring passions take the center of the stage.

Ovid's re-creation of myths as stories, within a theme of eternal change, liberated him from the necessity of following a Homeric precedent such as Virgil employed in the writing of his great Roman epic. Ovid used his loosely gathered romances and tales to exhibit his imaginative virtuosity. Within his large design, he incorporated stories from all reaches of the Mediterranean world, from Egypt as well as Crete, nor was his interest that of the anthropologist. It was rather that of one who could not resist the retelling of any story, provided it had color and enough action to hold attention. The story of Iphis and Ianthe reflects the worship of Isis in Augustan Rome, the shadow that Cleopatra left behind her—a shadow, by the way, that Augustus did his utmost to dispel. The inclusion of that story would offer further proof of Ovid's *lèse-majesté*, his lack of concern for elder Roman virtues, his irresponsibility. At the very least, Ovid as poet was incorrigible, not to be trusted in choice of worthy subjects and themes—wilful and sometimes at fault in tracing exact mutations of one myth into another. The fifteen books of *The Metamorphoses* contain a number of repetitious details as men and women are turned into trees, birds, or stones. Ovid's battle scenes have an overflow of blood and destruction; his fond listing of names is often tiresome; his flaws of taste are frequent, and his retelling of some Greek stories coarsens the clear lines of the originals. But having said this much in dispraise of Ovid's masterpiece, one feels that one has missed the reasons why it has survived. At his best no writer of this Golden Age in Roman literature has excelled him in the rapid unfolding of a narrative, nor has any surpassed him in the direct revelations of psychological detail. However farfetched, melodramatic, or strained a few of his situations may seem to the twentieth-century reader, they never fail to create the illusion of life—in its mystery and irony, in its splendour or cruelty; in its affectionate humours and warmth of feeling, in its celebration of earthly beauty. His many mistresses of Jove, his demigoddesses are irresistible carriers of the life-force in nature, and that is why complaints of his carelessness in joining one mythological cycle to another seem an effort at pedantry. As he came to the last of his fifteen books, he felt the need of a philosophy to sustain his device of eternal transformations. An Alexandrian Greek philosopher, a certain Sotion, had recently come to Rome. He was a disciple of Pythagoras, a vegetarian, and a popular lecturer. Ovid incorporated the gist of his lectures into Book XV. The Pythagorean doctrine with its protest against the killing of animals made its appeal to the humane warmth of Ovid's character, and it allowed him to give a semblance of Lucretian seriousness to his entire work. Ovid's nature of things was the nature of transformations. He did his best to make Pythagorean theory support the large design of *The Metamorphoses*. He had rounded out his conception of a world he had promised to reveal in Book

I. However shallow many of Ovid's convictions were, he held to his belief that nothing in the world could be destroyed; all things become transformed—and not least, his own poetry into an immortality.

Banished to Tomis, he spent the remaining nine years of his life in discontent. He did not cease writing. His *Tristia* contained his apologies, his defense of errors against Augustus. He began another long work, the *Fasti*, a Roman almanac of myths, celebrating each day in the Roman year. He wrote a melodramatic elegy, *Ibis*, which more than all else reflected his persecution mania and his failing powers. He had lost his wit, his humour, his grace of irony. Yet the people of Tomis grew fond of him, crowned him with laurel, and gave him freedom of the city. He returned their friendship. As he neared his end, he was deprived of the dignity of a tragic martyrdom. He wrote poems in Getic; he seemed gentle and good. At his birthplace in Sulmo, modern Sulmona, two imaginary portraits of Ovid stand in stone. The medieval portrait has great charm; an ironic saintliness seems to surround the full-draped figure, the figure of a clerk—someone might say, with Julian Benda, "a treasonable clerk." The modern statue, more imposing and far less charming, shows Ovid's head bent in restless meditation. One does not quite believe the latter image; the head should not seem to think; it should be raised to face the sun, to gaze toward a distant future and an immortality.

# IV

And last we come to my adaptation of *The Metamorphoses* into contemporary verse. Of all translators of Ovid, Dryden made the greatest claims for verbal accuracy. He argued well and found himself at odds with Ovid. His own gifts for writing verse of the first order rejected the more extreme reaches of Ovid's fancy and imagination, all the more so because Dryden's genius in writing poetry was committed to the cause of placing ideas, emotions, even the English language (both in prose and verse) in neo-classical order. If Ovid lacked Dryden's firmness, Dryden lacked Ovid's warmth. Dryden's Ovid is the civilized Ovid, smooth and polished. Dryden saw clearly the actual distance be-

tween Virgil and Ovid, and he became the supreme transla-
tor of Virgil's *Aeneid*.

One must go behind Dryden to get a more rounded view
of *The Metamorphoses*, and Golding's version (1593) is an
established classic. No one can dispute its archaic charm,
its baroque richness, its colour, yet it is slow in movement,
heavy in language. One needs a glossary to understand it.
Nineteenth-century bowdlerized versions of it did less well;
these were in prose, practical enough for classroom use, but
having no distinction and less wit. Strangely enough sev-
eral twentieth-century versions of *The Metamorphoses*
seemed to have joined the conspiracy of keeping Ovid in
a nineteenth-century classroom. In verse however smooth,
however pretty some have been, they have fallen into sop-
orific dullness. One needs the presence of a witty teacher,
a brilliant commentator, such as L. P. Wilkinson or Dudley
Fitts, to bring the lines to life.

My adaptation of *The Metamorphoses* has taken a dif-
ferent road, from which I hope the wit, the life, the Italian
warmth of Ovid have not been washed away. To make my
start I began my version of the first lines of Book I in a Re-
naissance room in Rome with noises rising from the street,
and, beyond my shaded window, Rome's golden light. This
early setting for my version of *The Metamorphoses* may be
taken for what it is worth, but at the very least it gave me
an immediate appreciation of Ovid's Phoebus Apollo, the
Italian sun. That presence warned me—as well as the rapid
noises of voices in the street—that my version could not af-
ford the luxury of being too sweetly smooth or dull. In mod-
ern Rome itself the most convincing remains of an Ovidian
spirit were in the baroque sculptures of Bernini, in their
images of flight and movement, of transient beauty, even to
the touch of sweetness that is at times too lyrical, too sweet.
The obvious example is Bernini's Daphne changing into a
laurel. Less obvious are the river gods of Roman fountains,
but they grow upon one in Ovidian shades of night. Least
obvious of all is the survival of pagan Eros in the form of
an angel striking his dart into the breast of Saint Teresa, a
blaze of gold behind him, in the church of Santa Maria della
Vittoria. Of course Bernini's art is overlaid with Christian

feeling and Bernini's Rome is of the seventeenth century; there are elements in Ovid's masterpiece of heavier weight and of coarser fibre than what we see in Bernini's gifts to Rome. But in Bernini's Saint Teresa there is a flash of wit in the smiling features of the angel that reflects Ovidian perception of Saint Teresa's love of heaven. We feel assured that an affinity exists between the ancient poet and the relatively modern sculptor. How reverent was Bernini? We shall never know.

In writing my version of *The Metamorphoses*, my effort has been to recreate the rapid flow of Ovid's narrative, to give the reader a sense of contact with a past that lives today. It will be clear to the reader that I have taken certain liberties with the text, for I have removed many of Ovid's uses of the historical present with his apostrophes to his heroes and demigods which are awkward when the main stream of the story is told in the past tense. The English language, unlike others, does not take kindly to shifts in which the historical present tense is most effective. Whatever sacrifices I have made to literal meaning have been in favor of the immediate evocation of a scene, of a lyrical and narrative flow of lines. The body of the narrative is written in unrhymed blank verse; my variations from this convention are breaks in form to reawaken the attention of the reader.

For information in the writing of this afterword my most recent debts are to Hermann Fränkel's *Ovid: A Poet Between Two Worlds* (Berkeley, California: University of California Press, 1945) and L. P. Wilkinson's brilliant commentary in his *Ovid Recalled* (Cambridge: Cambridge University Press, 1955). My thanks are due to the patience and perceptive reading of the manuscript by my editor, Pascal Covici.

—Horace Gregory

*New York, April 1958*

# A SELECTED GLOSSARY
# AND INDEX OF NAMES